K

by

"This book remains ... ... collection of sensational tales ever culled from that preposterous outbreak of hysteria. . . . It demonstrates that history can be interesting."
The Sun, Vancouver

"Mr. Berton has written a fine book. . . . He has chronicled one of the greatest follies of the last century and he has missed none of the drama, misery and pure excitement that surrounded it."
The Hamilton Spectator

"Berton is a master of the art of telling stories . . . his language is evocative, the reader responds with his five senses alert, his emotions stirred, and his imagination stimulated."
The Ottawa Citizen

"A splendid book."
The Lethbridge Herald

"*Klondike* is worth reading and worth remembering."
Leader Post, Regina

"This book has lost none of its impact and is totally fascinating to read."
Financial Post

"Pierre Berton's book is complete, authoritative and eminently entertaining. I nominate it right now for a Governor General's award."
Star Phoenix, Saskatoon

"Mr. Berton's book is a splendid story."
Whig-Standard, Kingston

A Penguin Books Canada/McClelland and Stewart
Book

Klondike

Pierre Berton was born in 1920 and raised in the Yukon. He spent his early newspaper career in Vancouver, where at 21 he was the youngest city editor on any Canadian daily. He moved to Toronto in 1947 and at the age of 31 was named managing editor of *Maclean's* magazine. He was an associate editor and columnist at the *Toronto Star* from 1958 to 1962 and has written and hosted several national television programs. He is the author of thirty-six books and has received three Governor General's Awards for works of non-fiction including *Klondike*. He is a Companion of the Order of Canada and a member of the Canadian News Hall of Fame. Mr. Berton lives in Kleinburg, Ontario.

"All my life," he said, "I have
searched for the treasure. I
have sought it in the high places,
and in the narrow. I have
sought it in deep jungles, and
at the ends of rivers, and in
dark caverns — and yet have
not found it.

"Instead, at the end of every
trail, I have found you
awaiting me. And now you have
become familiar to me, though
I cannot say I know you well.
Who are you?"

And the stranger answered:
"Thyself."
— *From an old tale*

Pierre Berton

Klondike

The
Last Great
Gold Rush
1896-1899

Revised Edition

A Penguin Books Canada/
McClelland and Stewart Book

PENGUIN BOOKS
Published by the Penguin Group
Penguin Books Canada Ltd, 10 Alcorn Avenue, Toronto, Ontario, Canada M4V 3B2
Penguin Books Ltd, 27 Wrights Lane, London W8 5TZ, England
Penguin Books USA Inc., 375 Hudson Street, New York, New York 10014, U.S.A.
Penguin Books Australia Ltd, Ringwood, Victoria, Australia
Penguin Books (NZ) Ltd, 182-190 Wairau Road, Auckland 10, New Zealand

Penguin Books Ltd, Registered Offices: Harmondsworth, Middlesex, England

First published in Canada by McClelland and Stewart, 1958
Published in this revised edition, 1972
Published in paperback by Penguin Books/McClelland and Stewart, 1990

5 7 9 10 8 6 4

Source notes and a bibliography can be found in the hardcover edition of *Klondike*
published by McClelland and Stewart in 1958.

Canadian Cataloguing in Publication Data
Berton, Pierre, 1920-
Klondike: the last great gold rush, 1896-1899

ISBN 0-14-011759-8
1. Klondike River Valley (Yukon) - Gold discoveries.
I. Title.

FC4022.3.B47 1990   971.9'1   C89-093311-1
F1059.K5B47 1990

Books by Pierre Berton

The Royal Family
The Mysterious North
Klondike
Just Add Water and Stir
Adventures of a Columnist
Fast, Fast, Fast Relief
The Big Sell
The Comfortable Pew
The Cool, Crazy, Committed World of the Sixties
The Smug Minority
The National Dream
The Last Spike
Drifting Home
Hollywood's Canada
My Country
The Dionne Years
The Wild Frontier
The Invasion of Canada
Flames Across the Border
Why We Act Like Canadians
The Promised Land
Vimy
Starting Out
The Arctic Grail
The Great Depression, 1929-1939

PICTURE BOOKS
The New City (with Henri Rossier)
Remember Yesterday
The Great Railway
The Klondike Quest

ANTHOLOGIES
Great Canadians
Pierre and Janet Berton's Canadian Food Guide
Historic Headlines

FOR YOUNGER READERS
The Golden Trail
The Secret World of Og

FICTION
Masquerade (pseudonym Lisa Kroniuk)

Contents

Maps

Drawn by Henry Mindak

To my father,
who crossed his Chilkoot in 1898,
and to my sons,
who have yet to cross theirs

Preface to the Revised Edition

When the first through passenger train of the Canadian Pacific Railway set off for the new terminus of Vancouver in June of 1886, Canada ceased to be merely a geographical expression. Bound together at last by John A. Macdonald's "iron link," the country could expect the speedy fulfilment of his national dream — the creation of a populous and prosperous North West from the empty prairie lands that had been given up a generation before by the Hudson's Bay Company.

But in the decade that followed, that vision was scarcely fulfilled. In the heady construction days of the early eighties, a western boom of unprecedented proportions seemed to be in the making; unhappily, over-optimism, wild speculation, drought, crop failure, and depression brought a swift decline in immigration figures. The bubble burst; and though the settlers continued to trickle in, the wave of newcomers that had been expected to follow the driving of the steel did not appear.

Suddenly, in 1897, the news from the Klondike burst upon the continent and everything was changed. The transition was instantaneous — there is no other word for it. The CPR trains were jammed with passengers heading west to invade the North through Prince Albert, Edmonton, Ashcroft, or Vancouver. Within a year, the interior of British Columbia, the Peace River country, and the entire Mackenzie and Yukon watersheds were speckled with thousands of men and pack animals. For the first time, really, the Canadian north was seen to be something more than frozen wasteland: a chain of mineral discoveries, reaching into modern times, was touched off by the Klondike fever. Every western Canadian community from Winnipeg to Victoria was affected permanently by the boom. Vancouver doubled in size almost overnight; Edmonton's population trebled. The depression, whose catalyst had been the silver panic of 1893, came to an end. It was replaced by an ebullient era of optimism and prosperity. New transcontinental railways were mooted and eventually constructed. A CPR contractor's son, Clifford Sifton, who had just been named Minister of Immigration in the Laurier cabinet, launched his historic propaganda campaign to fill up the empty spaces on the plains. In the North West, a new boom was in the making.

The Klondike story, then, forms a gaudy interlude between the two epic tales of post-Confederation western development — the building of the railway and the mass settlement of the plains. Since the author expects to tell the latter story in a subsequent volume, this expanded and revised edition of a fifteen-year-old work has been redesigned to conform to his two histories of the railway construction period, *The National Dream* and *The Last Spike*.

Because the stampede to the Klondike straddled the international border, it provides a unique opportunity to compare the mores and customs of two neighbouring nationalities. Here was the most concentrated mass movement of American citizens onto Canadian soil in all our history. In the space of fewer than eighteen months, some fifty thousand men and women — brought up with the social, legal, and political traditions of the United States — found themselves living temporarily under a foreign flag, obeying, however reluctantly, foreign regulations, and encountering a foreign bureaucracy and officialdom. In Dawson, and indeed almost everywhere save on the all-Canadian trails, the Americans outnumbered the Canadians by at least five to one.

It has often been said (usually by Americans) that there is no great difference between those who live south of the forty-ninth parallel and those of us who live on the Canadian side; but the Klondike experience supplies a good deal of evidence to support the theory that our history and our geography have helped to make us a distinct people — not better and not worse — but different in style, background, attitude, and temperament from our neighbours.

Our national character has not been tempered in the crucible of violence, and our attitudes during the stampede underline this historic truth. In all the Americas ours is the only country that did not separate violently from its European parents. We remained loyal and obedient, safe and relatively dispassionate, and we welcomed to our shores those other loyalists who opted for the status quo. If this lack of revolutionary passion has given us a reasonably tranquil history, it has also, no doubt, contributed to our well-known lack of daring. It is almost a Canadian axiom that we would rather be safe than sorry; alas, we are sometimes sorry that we are so safe.

Happily, we have had very little bloodshed in our history. Our rare insurrections have been fought on tiny stages blown up out of all proportion by the horrifying fact that they have occurred at all. Lynchings are foreign to us and so is gangsterism. The concept of barroom shoot-outs and duels in the sun have no part in our tradition either, possibly because we have had so few barrooms and so little sun. (It is awkward to reach efficiently for a six-gun while wearing a parka and two pairs of mittens.) When sudden, unreasoning violence does occur, as it did when Pierre Laporte was murdered in October, 1970, we tend to over-react. That was, after all, our first political assassination in more than a century and only the second in our history.

If Canadians are a moderate people, as the whiskey advertisements used to say, it is also because of the presence at our back door of a vast and brooding wilderness. The Klondike was and is a part of a wilderness experience that we all share. For the Americans who rushed north in 1897 and 1898, it was a last frontier; for them there were no more wilderness worlds to conquer or even to know. But the frontier is with us still and it shapes us in its own fashion. The experience of naked rock and brooding forest, of slate-coloured lakes and empty valleys, of skeletal birches and gaunt pines, of the wolf's haunting howl and the loon's ghostly call is one that is still shared by a majority of Canadians but only a minority of Americans. There are few of us who do not live within a few hours' drive of nature. It has bestowed upon us what one American observer, William Henry Chamberlain, has called "a sensation of tranquillity." The North, still almost as empty as it was in the days before the great stampede, hangs over the country like an immense backdrop, providing, in the words of André Siegfried, "a window out onto the infinite." A great Canadian editor, Arthur Irwin, once summed it up in a single sentence to a group of Americans. "Nearly every Canadian," he said, "at some time in his life has felt a shiver of awe and loneliness which comes to a man when he stands alone in the face of untamed nature; and that is why we are a sober and essentially religious people."

We have been lucky with our history. The American frontier was wrested violently from the Indians and that violence continued until the frontier was tamed. Our own experience came later. The Hudson's Bay

Company, which held the hinterland in thrall for generations, and the Canadian Shield, which retarded the settlement of the plains in the days before the railroad, have been seen as drawbacks to progress. And yet this tardy exploitation of the North West is one of the reasons why we have no Wild West tradition. There was a time when we might have welcomed a more violent kind of frontier mythology, but that time is past.

Every television addict knows that the two mythologies differ markedly. The Americans elected their lawmen — county sheriffs and town marshals — whose gun-slinging exploits helped forge their western legends. Summary justice by groups of vigilantes or hastily deputized posses was part of that legend. If the American frontier was not as violent as the media suggest, it was certainly violent compared with the Canadian frontier. There were no boot hills or hanging trees in our North West, and the idea that a community could take the law into its own hands or that a policeman might be elected by popular suffrage did not enter the heads of a people whose roots were stubbornly colonial and loyalist and whose heritage did not include anything as inflammatory as a Boston Tea Party. A variety of incidents on the Klondike trails bears this out, but the Klondike stampede was not the first occasion when the two traditions clashed on the soil of British North America.

In 1858, a newspaper report reaching California of the discovery of gold on the Fraser River caused an almost immediate stampede of some thirty thousand Americans to what was then the sparsely populated Hudson's Bay Company domain of New Caledonia. Almost instantly, all the institutions of the American mining camp were established on British soil: the gambling-houses, the sure-thing games, the dance halls and saloons, the crooked trading posts, and, above all, the quasi-legal institution of the "miners' meeting," which, though it embodied all the grassroots democracy of a Swiss canton, had helped to give the California camps their reputation for lawlessness. All the ingredients, then, were present for frontier violence. Indian revolution was not beyond the realm of possibility. And there was the clear danger that the territory itself might come under American sovereignty, as Oregon had when Yankee settlers poured in.

In the face of this threat, the British government moved with commendable celerity. Within a few weeks, New Caledonia had become a crown colony under James Douglas, Governor of Vancouver Island, and a force of soldiers and lawmakers had been dispatched to the Fraser gold-fields. British justice arrived in the person of that bewhiskered giant, Matthew Baillie Begbie, who proceeded to enforce the law toughly but fairly for Canadian and American alike. Judge Begbie, who thought that democracy was akin to anarchy, established a territorial council whose authoritarianism came under bitter criticism, but he undoubtedly prevented bloodshed among both Indians and whites, saved British Columbia for Canada, and established a pattern that was clearly followed by the Canadian government in 1897 and 1898.

Begbie was to the Fraser and Cariboo gold rushes what Sam Steele was to the Klondike, and, indeed, there is a story told of him that is almost identical to one told of Steele during the great stampede.

"Prisoner," Begbie told an American charged with assault, "I understand you come from the other side of the line. We will not put up with your bullying here. The fine is one hundred dollars."

"That's all right, Judge," came the reply. "I've got that right here in my breeches pocket."

"And six months' hard labour. Perhaps you have that in your other pocket!"

The tale has become part of our authentic Canadian mythology, as any reader who compares it with the one on page 408 will realize.

The second clash between the American and British traditions led to the formation of the North West Mounted Police and the founding of a Canadian frontier mythology that contrasted dramatically with the American. In the late 1860's, a veteran Indian fighter and lawman named John J. Healy (whom the reader will encounter throughout this book) moved up from Montana into what is now southern Alberta to build Fort Whoop-Up, the best known of the American "whiskey forts." Healy and his fellows were intent on making their fortunes by selling a hideous concoction of raw whiskey, red pepper, Jamaica ginger, and hot water to the Indians in exchange for furs. Small wonder that the forts — Robbers' Roost, Fort Stand-Off, Whiskey Gap, and others — were built of heavy logs and defended by cannon: under the influence of such a devil's brew, the Indians were perfectly prepared to massacre the men who sold it to them. It was the natives, however, who suffered a massacre. Some thirty-six Assiniboines were cruelly butchered in the Cypress Hills by Yankee frontiersmen who clung to the tradition that the only good redskin was a dead one.

This was not the tradition of the Canadian frontier. Our handling of the Indians was both callous and unthinking, but our philosophy never included purposeful genocide. For one thing, the Indians were far too valuable to the paternalistic Hudson's Bay Company to be slaughtered indiscriminately. The colonial government and its autonomous successors were equally paternalistic — towards whites as well as towards natives —

and when news of the Cypress Hills affair reached Ottawa, the Mounted Police came into being with all the traditions of a colonial constabulary. When the Mounties reached the foothills of the Rockies, the whiskey traders fled. The old whiskey forts vanished to be replaced by neat barracks, scrubbed clean and whitewashed regularly. Discipline was such that, it was said, the constables often had to be carried onto the parade square feet first to avoid creasing their trousers before inspection. This was the legend of the Canadian west; the impeccable Mountie was a far cry from the rumpled town marshal.

From that moment on the prairies were safe from gunmen, vigilantes, whiskey traders, wolf hunters, wild Indians, thieves, and saloon-keepers. When the Canadian Pacific Railway was constructed, droves of American workmen poured across the border from the construction camps of the Northern Pacific. The police kept them in check. When several thousand of them rioted over lack of pay at Beavermouth on the Columbia in 1885, Inspector Sam Steele — the same Sam Steele who is a major figure in this book — rose from what appeared to be his deathbed and cowed them into submissiveness with nothing more than a loaded rifle and a copy of the Riot Act.

Oddly, it was Johnny Healy himself who brought the Mounted Police into the Canadian Yukon. He had been nurtured in an environment where the community made its own laws and he had flourished in it. But in Fortymile, he himself ran afoul of miners'-meeting justice and, remembering the very police who had driven him from the Canadian foothills, sent out a call for help. It was speedily answered.

The Mounties, then, were established in the Yukon well before the stampede burst upon the Klondike Valley, and so there was on hand a Canadian force for law and order to cope with the influx. It must be pointed out, in parenthesis, that there would have been no foreign problem at all if Canadians had not been so lenient about the pillaging of their own resources. Anybody could stake a claim in Canada and, after the payment of a small royalty, could take the gold out to a foreign land. The Americans were not so easy-going; only American citizens were allowed to mine for gold on United States soil or — as William Moore found out — to establish a townsite; Moore's son Bernard had to become an American citizen before he could hold title to the plot that became part of Skagway. If the Klondike's gold had been across the border, no Canadian could have mined it. As it was, much of the wealth taken from the famous creeks ended up in the United States.

The location of the border itself was a matter of dispute, and here the presence of the Canadian constabulary saved a portion of the Yukon for Canada. Because Charles Constantine was on hand at Fortymile to alert the Canadian government to the news of Carmack's strike before the world was aware of it, Ottawa was able to rush a second detachment of police to the North before the gold rush began. Inspector Scarth and nineteen constables reached Fort Constantine on the Yukon on June 12, 1897. By October, another detachment with Major J. M. Walsh, the new commissioner of the Yukon, had reached the territory. This was augmented by further reinforcements during the winter of 1897-98.

Well before the main body of stampeders had launched itself at the passes in the spring of 1898, the police, armed with Winchester rifles and Maxim machine guns, were in possession of both the White Pass and Chilkoot summits and prepared to collect customs duties on all goods shipped across. This led to a tense situation with the American authorities, who believed that, under the terms of the 1867 treaty with Russia, Alaskan territory extended all the way back to Lake Bennett and continued for four miles beyond the lakehead. American argonauts, building boats along its shore and those of Lake Lindemann, were infuriated that they had to pay duty on construction materials while occupying soil they considered to be their own. A nasty border incident was clearly in the making. Judge John U. Smith, the United States commissioner at Skagway, took time off from feathering his own nest (he pocketed official fees and fines with wild abandon) and started to organize a company of volunteers to cross the mountains and establish the Stars and Stripes on Lake Bennett by force.

By this time Washington had dispatched four companies of infantry to Dyea and Skagway with instructions to "show the flag" and maintain order among the increasingly unruly civilian population. The officer in charge, Col. Thomas M. Anderson, sent a note to Inspector Steele demanding to know why the Canadians "found it necessary to exercise civil and military authority over American territory." Steele forwarded the note to the new commissioner. Walsh, a one-time Mountie himself, refused to budge an inch. Indeed, he boldly seized the initiative by insisting that Canadian territory actually extended all the way to Skagway, though the Mounties had decided not to exert their authority over it. Anderson was convinced that the Canadians would not retreat. He forestalled the impetuous Smith, relayed his impressions to his superiors, and set in motion the long train of international arbitration that eventually resolved the dispute. Today the border runs along the summit of the passes, exactly where the Mounties had placed their machine guns.

The differing behaviour of the two military forces during the stampede — the American infantry companies and the Canadian Mounted Police — gives a further insight into Canadian and American attitudes towards law, order, freedom, and anarchy. The American style was to stand aside and let the civilians work out matters for themselves even at the risk of inefficiency, chaos, and bloodshed. The Canadian style was to interfere at every step of the way in the interests of order, harmony, and the protection of life and property.

During the entire stampede winter, with one brief exception, the United States military held themselves aloof from events in Skagway. The commissioner pocketed public funds; the deputy marshal worked hand in glove with gangsters; men were shot, robbed, and cheated; and the town was under the thrall of an engaging but unscrupulous confidence man who was even allowed to raise a personal army. Skagway was permitted to solve its own problems in the approved American frontier style. In the end, a vigilante committee was formed, the traditional shoot-out took place, and the dictator was violently removed from the scene. Only when the mob threatened to lynch one of the gang did the infantry step in to stop further bloodshed. But previous lynchings, hangings, and whippings had taken place on both American trails without interference from the authorities.

On the Canadian side of the passes, conditions were totally different. Here the soldiers were also policemen, appointed from above in the British colonial tradition. Their job was to maintain order, for it has seemed to be a Canadian quality to opt for order before freedom. The Canadians accepted the benevolent dictatorship of the Mounted Police as a later generation accepted the strictures of the War Measures Act in Quebec. Safety and security, order and harmony — these are qualities that Canadians prize more highly than their neighbours, in spite of all the talk of "law and order" south of the border. It is no accident that we have more per capita money safely invested in banks and insurance than any other civilized nation; the influence of the Loyalists and of the Scots (who control so many of our institutions, educational and financial) has made us a prudent race. "Welfare" is a word that has always smacked of authoritarianism to the American individualist; "security" was for years the object of propaganda attacks by American entrepreneurs. There was very little security in Skagway during the stampede winter, but on the Canadian side, packs loaded with nuggets could be left for a fortnight on the trail without being touched and boats could travel for five hundred miles through unknown waters and be reasonably sure of reaching their destinations because the Mounties, like stern fathers, were on hand to protect the boatmen from themselves. The Americans were often irked by this paternalism. At the Whitehorse Rapids, when Steele laid down the law and refused to allow them to take their own boats through, some of them protested aloud. The scene, which is almost Biblical in its intensity, could scarcely have occurred on the American side of the border, where every citizen considered he had the God-given right to drown himself if he wished.

This tension between the two North American styles was even more marked in that strangest of all international communities, Dawson City, where the Calvinist ethic collided with the American frontier tradition. The officials in Dawson were all Canadian; most of the entrepreneurs — the dance-hall owners, gamblers, and saloon-keepers — were American. An uneasy compromise was arrived at in which all sorts of illegal activities

xxiv

were allowed — but never on Sunday; in which prostitution was openly winked at — but risqué stage performances were strictly censored; in which public officials got away with accepting bribes — but men who chopped their own kindling on the Sabbath were hauled into police court and fined.

Some might call this Victorian hypocrisy, others Canadian common sense. Dawson, as Stroller White wrote, was "far from being a model for the Young People's Society of Christian Endeavour but there was a gayety and lightheartedness about its sinning that was absent in Skagway. And while Dawson provided plenty of places and opportunities for the suckers to dispose of their money, the suckers were never steered, dragooned and bootjacketed into these places as they had been in Skagway." For this, the Stroller, himself an American, credited the presence of the Mounted Police.

Dawson was also a gunless town, virtually devoid of violence. This is one of the several points of confusion about the Klondike that has bedevilled the American media. Writers of fact and of fiction and of motion picture and television scripts have never been able to get it into their heads that the right to carry a gun, of which Americans are so proud, has never been recognized on our side of the border. It is hard for Americans to realize that the Klondike strike took place on Canadian soil (letters still arrive, as they did in my day, addressed "Dawson City, Alaska") and, when they do realize it, even harder for them to accept the fact that our customs and our traditions differ markedly from their own.

Shortly after *Klondike* was published in the United States, an American company purchased the television rights and proceeded to launch a series supposedly based on the incidents in the book. The original idea was to have an American frontier marshal play the central figure — until I explained to the production people that Canadians did not elect or even appoint frontier marshals. An alternative suggestion was mooted: the central character would be a "frontier marshal type," elected by the miners of Dawson City to bring law and order to the Klondike. It became necessary then to explain that the Canadian government not only sent about forty Mounted Policemen to patrol the streets of Dawson but also prudently followed this up with a Yukon Field Force of more than two hundred soldiers. The television company finally decided to move the action out of Dawson and into Skagway, Alaska, where the myth of the American frontier could once again be acted out in all its familiar variations. The Canadian aspects of the tale were ignored but perhaps, in retrospect, that was for the best.

Kleinburg, Ontario
March, 1972

Cast of Major Characters

Along the River Settlements: 1896

LeRoy N. "Jack" McQuesten, free trader working with the Alaska Commercial Company. Ran the Circle City post.

Arthur Harper, McQuesten's partner. Ran the Fortymile post.

Joseph Ladue, Harper's partner. Ran the Ogilvie post.

Al Mayo, in partnership with McQuesten, Harper, and Ladue. Ran the Rampart post.

John Jerome Healy, manager of Fort Cudahy, post of the North American Transportation and Trading Company (N.A.T. Company) at Fortymile Creek.

Bishop William Bompas, Church of England missionary at Fortymile.

Father William Judge, Roman Catholic missionary at Circle City. Later opened St. Mary's Hospital at Dawson. "The Saint of Dawson."

William Ogilvie, Canadian government land surveyor.

Inspector Charles Constantine, in charge of first detachment of North West Mounted Police to enter the Yukon. In command at Fort Constantine (Fortymile).

Robert Henderson, Canadian prospector. Explored Indian River, co-discoverer of Klondike gold.

George Carmack. He and Indian relatives (Skookum Jim and Tagish Charley) worked for Ogilvie packing over Chilkoot Pass. Co-discoverer of Klondike gold.

At Dawson City

OFFICIALS

J. M. Walsh, ex-Mounted Policeman, Commissioner of the Yukon, 1897-98; replaced by William Ogilvie.

Samuel B. Steele, Mounted Police superintendent in charge of the force in the Yukon.

Thomas Fawcett, gold commissioner.

PROSPECTORS

Charley Anderson, "the Lucky Swede," owner of *Twenty-Nine* Eldorado.

Clarence Berry, Fresno fruit farmer, owner with Antone Stander of *Four, Five,* and *Six* Eldorado and *Forty Above* Bonanza.

Pat Galvin, former Helena, Montana, town marshal. Purchaser with Alex McDonald and George Byrne of *Forty* and *Forty-One* Eldorado. Founded North British American Trading and Transportation Company.

William F. "Swiftwater Bill" Gates, part owner of *Thirteen* Eldorado and co-owner of Monte Carlo dance hall.

Thomas Lippy, Seattle YMCA worker, owner of *Sixteen* Eldorado.

Dick Lowe, mule-skinner. Staked "Dick Lowe Fraction," richest piece of ground in history.

Alexander "Big Alex" McDonald, "the King of the Klondike," bought half of *Thirty* Eldorado for a song and acquired dozens of mining properties.

Louis Rhodes, staked *Twenty-One Above* Bonanza. First man to reach bed-rock.

SALOON-KEEPERS

Harry Ash, Circle City bartender. Opened the Northern Saloon, first saloon in Dawson.

Silent Sam Bonnifield, legendary gambler. Opened the Bank Saloon.

Tom Chisholm, a Nova Scotian, proprietor of three successive saloons all known as the Aurora.

James "Nigger Jim" Daugherty, wealthy claim owner. Built the Pavilion dance hall. Married Lottie Oatley.

Pete McDonald, "the Prince of Puget Sound," wealthy claim owner, proprietor of the Phoenix.

Bill McPhee, old-time Fortymile saloon-keeper, proprietor of the Pioneer with Harry Spencer and Frank Densmore. Grubstaked Clarence Berry.

Charles "Arizona Charlie" Meadows, western scout, sharpshooter, and showman. Built the Palace Grand.

Belinda Mulroney, coal-miner's daughter from Scranton, Pa. Opened the Magnet at Grand Forks and the Fairview in Dawson. Married the "Comte" de Carbonneau.

Jack Smith, co-owner with Swiftwater Bill Gates of the Monte Carlo.

At Skagway

George Brackett, former mayor of Minneapolis; built wagon road over the White Pass.

Captain William Moore, former Fraser River steamboat man; laid out Skagway townsite.

Frank Reid, surveyor and school-teacher; helped lay out Skagway and shot Soapy Smith.

Jefferson Randolph "Soapy" Smith, confidence man from Creede, Denver, and Leadville. Operated Jeff Smith's Oyster Parlor.

On the Trails

Captain W. R. Abercrombie, Second U.S. Infantry, stationed at Valdez, Alaska.

Tappan Adney, correspondent for *Harper's Illustrated Weekly.*

Gene Allen, itinerant newspaperman who founded the *Klondike Nugget* in Dawson.

Jack Dalton, frontiersman. Opened the Dalton Trail over which cattle could be brought from Haines Mission to Dawson City.

E. A. Hegg, Swedish-born photographer from Bellingham Bay, Washington, who photographed the stampede.

Norman Lee, Chilcoten rancher; drove a herd of cattle north along the Ashcroft Trail.

Addison Mizner, adventurer; laid out part of Dawson City and was later key architect of the Florida real estate boom of the 1920's.

Wilson Mizner, wit and *bon vivant*, later founder of the Hollywood Brown Derby restaurant. Brother of Addison and of Edgar Mizner, manager of Dawson's Alaska Commercial outlet.

Inspector J. D. Moodie, NWMP officer assigned to open a trail from Edmonton to the Yukon via the Peace River country.

Captain Patrick Henry Ray, Eighth U.S. Infantry, sent north to investigate possible relief of starvation along Yukon.

Stroller White, itinerant newspaperman who worked for the Skagway *News,* Bennett *Sun,* and *Klondike Nugget.*

W. D. Wood, former mayor of Seattle. Led expedition up Yukon River to Klondike.

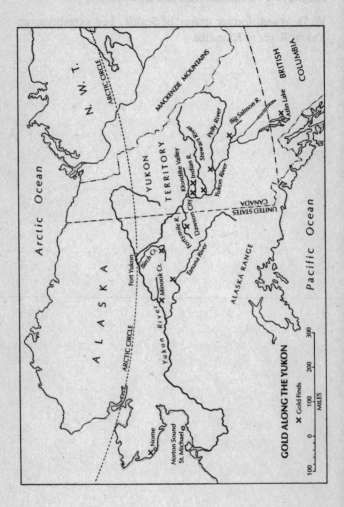

GOLD ALONG THE YUKON

× Gold Finds

MILES
100   0   100   200   300

The Golden Highway

It was the river that fashioned the land, and the river that ground down the gold.

Long before natives or white men saw it, the river was there, flowing for two thousand miles from mountain to seacoast, working its slow sculpture on valley and hillside, nibbling away at the flat tableland heaved up by the earth's inner turmoils before the dawn of history.

The main stream had a thousand tentacles, and these reached back to the very spine of the continent, honing down the mountainsides into gullies and clefts—boulder grating on boulder, gravel grinding against gravel, sand scouring sand, until the river was glutted with silt and the whole Alaska-Yukon peninsula was pitted and grooved by the action of running water.

No mass could withstand this ceaseless abrasion, which lasted for more than five million years. The rocks and metals that had boiled up through fissures in the earth's crust succumbed to it and were shaved and chiselled away. Quartz and feldspar, granite and limestone were reduced to muds and clays to be borne off with the current towards the sea, and even the veins of gold that streaked the mountain cores were sandpapered into dust and flour.

But the gold did not reach the sea, for its specific gravity is nineteen times that of water. The finest gold was carried lightly on the crest of the mountain torrents until it reached the more leisurely river, where it sank and was caught in the sand-bars at the mouths of the tributary streams. The coarser gold moved for lesser distances: as soon as the pace of the current began to slacken, it was trapped in the crevices of bed-rock where nothing could dislodge it. There it remained over the eons, concealed by a deepening blanket of muck, while the centuries rolled on and more gold was ground to dust, while the watercourses shifted and new gorges formed in the flat bottoms of old valleys, while the water gnawed deeper and deeper, and the pathways left by ancient streams turned the hillsides into graceful terraces.

Thus the gold lay scattered for the full length of the great Yukon River, on the hills and in the sand-bars, in steep ravines and broad valleys, in subterranean channels of white gravel and glistening beds of black sand, in clefts thirty feet beneath the mosses and on outcroppings poking from the grasses high up on the benchland.

There was gold on a dozen tributary rivers and a hundred creeks which would remain nameless and unexplored until the gold was found; taken together, they drained three hundred and thiry thousand miles, stretching from British Columbia to the Bering Sea. There was gold on Atlin Lake at the very head of the Yukon River, and there was gold more than two thousand miles to the northwest in the glittering sands of the beach on Norton Sound into which the same river empties. There was gold on the Pelly and the Big Salmon and the Stewart, majestic watercourses that spill down from the Mackenzie Mountains of Canada to the east, and there was gold on the great Tanana, which rises in the Alaska Range on the southwest. There was gold in between these points at Minook and at Birch Creek and on the frothing Fortymile.

Yet, compared with a wretched little salmon stream and its handful of scrawny creeks, these noble rivers meant little. For in the Klondike Valley gold lay more thickly than on any other creek, river, pup, or sand-bar in the whole of the Yukon watershed—so thickly, indeed, that a single shovelful of paydirt could yield eight hundred dollars' worth of dust and nuggets. But white men sought gold along the Yukon for a generation before they found it.

Chapter One

1: *The pilgrims*

We are the Pilgrims, master; we shall go
 Always a little further: it may be
Beyond that last blue mountain barred with snow,
 Across that angry or that glimmering sea.

White on a throne or guarded in a cave
 There lives a prophet who can understand
Why men were born: but surely we are brave
 Who take the Golden Road to Samarkand.

— *James Elroy Flecker: Hassan*

The Russians were the first on the river, in 1834, but they cared not a hoot for gold; no more than the natives who had given the river its name of Yukon, meaning "The Greatest." Even before the river was discovered, whispers of gold in Russian America had reached the ears of Alexander Baranov, the rum-swilling Lord of Alaska, who ruled the peninsula from the island bastion of Sitka. But Baranov, garnering a fortune in furs for his Czarist masters against an incongruous background of fine books, costly paintings, and brilliantly plumaged officers and women, was not anxious for a gold rush. When one of the Russians babbled drunkenly of gold, so legend has it, the Lord of Alaska ordered him shot.

The Hudson's Bay Company traders heard tales of gold, too, when they invaded the Yukon Valley at mid-century, but paid them no heed, for furs to them were richer treasure. They built Fort Yukon at the mouth of the Porcupine, where the great river makes its majestic curve across the Arctic Circle, and they built Fort Selkirk some six hundred miles upstream at the point where it is joined by the sombre Pelly, and they did not know that both forts were on the same watercourse. Nor did they know, at the time, that their Union Jack, flying over Fort Yukon, was deep in foreign territory; the land

2

was remote, the boundaries hazy, and the geography uncertain.

But they knew of the gold and did nothing. Robert Campbell, one of the company's most industrious explorers, found traces of it at Fort Selkirk, but the discovery intrigued him not at all. And sixteen years later another clerk, stationed at Fort Yukon, wrote laconically of gold in a letter home to Toronto: "On one small river not far from here the Rev. McDonald saw so much gold that he could have gathered it with a spoon." But Archdeacon McDonald was intent only on translating prayerbooks for the Crooked-Eye Indians, and as for the Hudson's Bay clerk, he had "often wished to go but can never find the time."

Nor was he ever to find time, for the great company, driven from Fort Yukon by the Americans and from Fort Selkirk by the Chilkoot Indians, packed up and retreated behind the rampart of the Mackenzie Mountains. There were others, nonetheless, who had the time and the burning inclination to look for gold. Alaska was purchased by the United States from Russia in 1867, and there were many who saw the new territory not only as a virgin land to conquer but also as a wilderness to which a man could flee. The newly acquired frontier was shaped like a kitchen pot: a long strip of coastal land, aptly named "the Panhandle," attached to the main body of the peninsula, bordered the Pacific territories of British Columbia. In 1880, at a point midway down this Panhandle, hardrock gold was discovered and the mining town of Juneau sprang up. And to Juneau came the wanderers and the adventurers, the Indian-fighters and the frontiersmen, men from all over the American West who could not sit still. Juneau, in its turn, served as a springboard to Alaska and the Canadian Yukon. Thus was completed a northward osmosis that had been going on since the rush to

3

California, a kind of capillary action that saw restless men with pans and picks slowly inching their way along the mountain backbone of North America from the Sierras to the Stikines, up through Arizona, Colorado, Nevada, and Idaho, leaving behind names like Leadville, Pike's Peak, Virginia City, Cripple Creek, Creede, and Tombstone; up through the wrinkled hide of British Columbia, through the sombre canyons of the Fraser and the rolling grasslands of the Cariboo to the snow-fields of the Cassiars, at the threshold of the sub-Arctic.

The prospectors came first in twos and threes with little more than a rucksack, a gold-pan, a short-stemmed shovel, and a phial of mercury, living on beans and tea and bacon — men fleeing ahead of civilization. Whenever they struck it rich a circus parade of campfollowers crowded in upon them, saloon-keepers and hurdy-gurdy girls, tinhorn gamblers and three-card monte men, road agents, prostitutes, vigilantes, and tenderfeet. Sylvan valleys became industrial bees' nests, meadows were transformed into brawling shack towns; the sighing of the wind and the roaring of the river were drowned by the tuneless scraping of dance-hall violins and the crash of butchered timber, until it came time to move on to the next divide and to seek new valleys beyond unnamed mountains. And so, like the forward patrols of a mighty army, the first prospectors reached the last frontier and began, in the seventies and eighties, to infiltrate the Yukon Valley.

The Yukon is unique among rivers in that it rises fifteen miles from the Pacific Ocean and then meanders for more than two thousand miles across the face of the North, seeking that same salt Pacific water. Starting as a trickle in the mountain snow-fields that feed the green alpine lakes, it pushes insistently through barriers of basalt and conglomerate on its long northwestern quest.

4

On it flows, now confidently, now hesitantly, until it attains the rim of the Arctic. Here it falters, as if unsure of itself, vacillates momentarily on the Circle's edge, changes its mind, turns in its tracks, and, with new-found assurance, plunges southwestward, defying every obstacle until, with the goal in sight, it spreads itself wide in a mighty delta and spends itself at last on the cold waters of Norton Sound across from the easternmost tip of Siberia. It seems an awkward, roundabout way for water to travel, but without the odd tilting of the interior plateau, which produces this phenomenon, without the long and seemingly aimless coil of the great river, there would be no highway into the heart of Alaska.

So with the river, so with the men who sought her gold. They too arrived by circuitous routes, sometimes with faltering pace, sometimes with cocksure step, on a quest that often seemed as fruitless as the river's but which, in the final assessment, was crowned with unexpected fulfilment.

They crept in upon it from three sides, these first gold-seekers:

In 1873 Arthur Harper came in from the interior of northern Canada travelling north and west from the Peace and Mackenzie river valleys in a wide flanking movement.

In 1878 George Holt pushed directly in from the seacoast through the Chilkoot Pass, the only known gap in the armoured underbelly of Alaska.

In 1882 Ed Schieffelin went round to the Bering Sea opposite Siberia and moved up the long water highway of the Yukon River itself.

Harper was the first of this trio, an Irishman with a square face, shrewd eyes, and a great beard that later turned snow-white and gave him the look of a frontier patriarch. Gold had drawn him north on the stampedes

5

to the Fraser and the Cariboo in the fifties and sixties. Here, staring at his Arrowsmith's map of British North America, Harper asked himself why, if the run of gold stretched from Mexico to British Columbia, it should not continue north beyond the horizon. Beyond the horizon he went, with five gallons of strong rum and five cronies, pushing down the Peace River in canoes hacked out of cottonwood poplar trunks following the line of the mountains on their great northward curve across the Arctic Circle and into Alaska. Twenty-five years later thousands would follow in his wake, on the same vain errand.

For two thousand miles Harper and his companions paddled and prospected, tracking their boats across the mountain divides, until at last, in 1873, they reached the Yukon River at its mid-point, where it curves across the Circle. For the next quarter-century the river was Harper's highway; he roamed it, seeking the will-o'-the-wisp in every tributary stream, testing the gravels, panning the sand-bars, always hoping to find the treasure, yet never succeeding. The gold was under his

THE YUKON RIVER
BEFORE THE GOLD RUSH

nose, but he missed it. He explored four rivers that later yielded fortunes — the Stewart, the Fortymile, the Tanana, and the Klondike — but he did not make the longed-for discovery. When he died, in 1897, it was too late. The stampede had started and there was gold to be had by the shovelful, but Arthur Harper was an old man by then, worn out from tuberculosis, slowly expiring in the Arizona sunlight.

Nor did George Holt, the first man through the coastal mountains, find gold on the Yukon, though he sought it as fiercely as Harper. He is a vague and shadowy figure, scarcely more than a name in the early annals of Alaska, but he is remembered for a remarkable feat: he was the first white man to penetrate the massive wall of scalloped peaks that seals off the Yukon Valley from the North Pacific Ocean. These mountains were guarded by three thousand Indian sentinels, and how he got past them no man knows.

In the alpine rampart that Holt conquered, the shrieking winds had chiselled a tiny notch. It could be reached only after a thousand-foot climb up a thirty-five-degree slope strewn with immense boulders and caked, for eight months out of twelve, with solid ice. Glaciers of bottle green overhung it like prodigious icicles ready to burst at summer's end; avalanches thundered from the mountains in the spring; and in the winter the snow fell so thickly that it could reach a depth of seventy feet. This forbidding gap was called the Chilkoot Pass, and Holt was the first white man to set eyes upon it. Because it was the gateway to the Yukon Valley, the Chilkoot Indians guarded it with a jealousy bordering on fanaticism.

They were men of immense cunning and avarice, these Indians — squat and sturdy and heavy-shouldered and able to lug a two-hundred-pound pack across the mountains without rest. They were a crude, cruel race with Mongolian features and drooping Fu Manchu moustaches, who existed on a diet of dried salmon, a pungent concoction that one explorer described as tasting like a cross between Limburger cheese and walrus hide. They reserved for themselves all trade with the "Stick" Indians of the interior, whom they held in virtual bondage; and they had even driven the powerful Hudson's Bay Company from the upper river by burning Robert Campbell's Fort Selkirk in 1852.

Yet Holt somehow ran the gantlet of this tribe, scaled the pass, and penetrated into that dark land where the Yukon had its beginning. In 1878 he emerged with two small nuggets which an Indian from Alaska had given him, and his tales, embroidered by his own imagination, excited the interest of the men at Sitka, the Panhandle capital, which was teeming with the backwash of the Cassiar rush. Twenty prospectors, protected by a U.S. gunboat, debarked at Dyea Inlet not far from the foot of the Chilkoot, and here, after firing a few blank rounds from a Gatling gun, they convinced Chief Hole-in-the-Face that the pass should be opened.

In this summary fashion was the dam broken; each year, from 1880 onward, the trickle of men crossing the divide increased. The Indians did not suffer by this invasion, for they charged a fee to pack the white man's outfits across the mountains, and they always exacted what the traffic would bear, so that by the time of the Klondike stampede the price had reached a dollar a pound. Thus, without ever sinking a pan into the creek-beds of the Yukon, the canny Chilkoots became rich men.

Holt, having breached one barrier, moved west to wilder land and tried to add to his exploits by invading the copper country of the Chettyna. The Indians there had three murders to their credit when Holt tried to slip through. Poor Holt made the fourth.

8

Meanwhile, those who had followed in his wake had begun to find the flour gold that lay in the sand-bars of the Yukon, and rumours of these discoveries filtered down through the Rocky Mountain mining camps of the western United States until in 1882 the stories reached the ears of a gaunt scarecrow of a prospector named Ed Schieffelin.

This was no penniless gold-seeker. In the Apache country of Arizona, Schieffelin had discovered a mountain of silver and founded the town of Tombstone, where Wyatt Earp had already completed his bloody tryst with the Clanton brothers at the O.K. Corral. He was worth one million dollars, but his appearance belied his wealth, for his beard and his glossy black hair hung long and ringleted and his grey ghost-eyes had the faraway look of the longtime prospector. He had panned gold as a toddler in Oregon and had run off at the age of twelve to join a stampede, and in the ensuing generation had been in almost every boom camp in the West. Now he was intent on repeating his Arizona success in Alaska. He, too, had studied the maps and arrived at an enchanting theory: a great mineral belt, he thought, must girdle the world from Cape Horn to Asia and down through the continental divide of North America to the Andes. Somewhere in Alaska this golden highway should cross the Yukon Valley, and Schieffelin meant to find it. The spring of 1883 found him and a small party at St. Michael, the old Russian port on the Bering Sea just north of the Yukon's mouth, aboard a tiny steamboat especially built to penetrate the hinterland.

The expedition puffed slowly around the coast of Norton Sound and into the maze of the great delta, where the channels fanned out for sixty-five miles and the banks were grey with alluvial silt; where long-legged cranes stalked the marshes; where the islands had never been counted; where a man could lose himself forever in half a hundred twisting channels. At this point they were more than two thousand miles from the Chilkoot Pass, which Holt had crossed five years before.

Out into the river proper the little boat chugged — into a land of terraced valleys, sleeping glaciers, and high clay banks pocked by swallows' nests and bright with brier rose and bluebell. Here was an empty domain of legend and mystery. In London, globes of the world were still being issued showing the Yukon River flowing north into the Arctic Ocean instead of west into the Bering Sea. And there were stories told — and believed — of prehistoric mammoths that roamed the hills with jets of live steam issuing from their nostrils, and of immense bears that prowled the mountain peaks in endless circles because their limbs were longer on one side than on the other.

To Schieffelin, the broad Yukon seemed to wind on endlessly, tawny and cold, gnawing through walls of granite and wriggling past mountain ranges, spilling out over miles of flatland at one point, trapped between black pillars of basalt at another. Occasionally a pinpoint of civilization broke the monotony of the greygreen forestland — the old Russian missions at Andreifski, Holy Cross, and Nulato, or the solitary totemic figures on the riverbank that marked the Indian graves. For a thousand miles the steamer struggled against the current, penetrating deeper and deeper into unknown country, past Burning Mountain, a perpetually smoking seam of coal; past the Palisades, fortress-like cliffs of rock that guard the Tanana's mouth: and finally into the brooding hills known as the Lower Ramparts, where the river channels were gathered into a single rustling gorge.

10

Here, poking about among the mosses and the rocks, Schieffelin found some specks of gold and was convinced that he had stumbled upon the mineral belt he believed encircled the earth. But already there was frost in the air, and the prospector, accustomed to the fierce Arizona sun, became discouraged by the bleakness of the Arctic summer. He concluded that mining could never pay along the Yukon, and he retraced his course without exploring the remainder of the long waterway, which drifted back for another thousand miles to the gateway of the Chilkoot. And so, as it had eluded Harper and Holt, the gold of the Yukon eluded the gaunt Schieffelin, who for all the remainder of his life never ceased to prospect and was, indeed, still seeking a new mine when he died of a heart attack in front of his cabin in the forests of Oregon. The year, by then, was 1897, and the world was buzzing with tales of a fortune to be found in that inhospitable land he had dismissed as frozen waste.

2: *"Gold—all same like this!"*

For five years after Schieffelin's departure the Yukon Valley maintained a primaeval silence. Small groups of prospectors continued to dribble over the Chilkoot Pass to test the bars along the headwaters, but the main river was virtually untravelled for eighteen hundred miles. The only boats upon its surface were those of the natives and of the occasional free trader working on a commission for the Alaska Commercial Company, the lineal descendant of the old Russian-American Fur Company.

Arthur Harper was one of these. Frustrated in his attempts to find his fortune in the shifting sands of the tributary creeks, he had taken to bartering tea and flour for furs. Thus his memory endures in the north, for he

11

was one of a trio of traders who helped to open up the Yukon Valley for the prospectors who followed.

The two men who joined forces with Harper had arrived the same year that he did, in 1873, but by a different route. They were a Mutt-and-Jeff combination, one a lean, wiry little thong of a man, the other a six-foot giant with a barrel chest. The little man's name was Al Mayo; he was a one-time circus acrobat driven north by wanderlust, given to practical jokes and blessed with a dry wit. In his later years he used to remark that he had been in the country so long that when he first arrived the Yukon was a small creek and the Chilkoot Pass a hole in the ground.

The big man's name was LeRoy Napoleon McQuesten, but everybody called him Jack. His florid features were marked by a flowing blond moustache and his temperament by that same restlessness which was a quality of almost every man who made his way north in the days before the Klondike strike. He had been a farmer in Maine and an Indian-fighter in the west and a gold-hunter on the Fraser, but, just as Harper was a frustrated prospector, McQuesten was a frustrated voyageur. He had wanted so badly to be one of those strange forest creatures that he gave himself a course in physical training so he might perform the incredible feats of strength and endurance for which the voyageurs were noted. Then he had signed on with the Hudson's Bay Company in the Athabasca country, only to discover, to his chagrin, that he could not sustain the crushing two-hundred-pound loads his French-Canadian companions hoisted so easily on their backs. So he had moved on, drifting across the mountains into the Yukon Valley, where he and Harper and Mayo became partners.

For more than fifteen years these three were alone with the land, the river their private thoroughfare. They could roam for a thousand miles without seeing another white face, and, indeed, McQuesten once recalled that he went for six years without tasting flour. They took Indian wives, but in no sense did they resemble the "squaw men," who were looked down upon by their fellows. The traders did not live like Indians; their wives and families lived like whites in handsome homes of square-cut logs, with neat vegetable gardens at the rear. The wives were partners in the true sense, and the dusky children were sent out to be educated in private schools in the United States. Years later, when McQuesten retired, he took his Indian wife to California, where she became the mistress of a big home in Berkeley; and when he died, she managed his estate and became the head of the family.

The country changed these men. Restless they had been, but over the long decades they developed a serenity of temperament that became the envy of all who encountered them. Frederick Schwatka, a U.S. cavalry officer who was the first man to explore the Yukon River for its full length, came upon McQuesten in 1883 and watched in admiration as the trader bargained for hours with Indians, unruffled through the endless palaver that "would have put Job in a frenzy." McQuesten and his colleagues never presented a bill for an outfit, and they were seldom short-changed. Once when a cargo of goods arrived and a group of miners became impatient for provisions, Harper told them simply to help themselves, keep their own accounts, and hand them in at their leisure. The only discrepancy was six cans of condensed milk.

The trio's first post of Fort Reliance became the focus for future river settlements. Several neighbouring tributaries took their names from the distance that separated them from the post. Thus the Fortymile River and the Twelvemile were named because they joined

13

the Yukon that distance downstream from Fort Reliance, and the Sixtymile was so called because it was sixty miles upstream from the fort. Later on, the towns established at the mouths of these rivers took the same names. It is curious that this first river settlement should have been established a scant six miles from the mouth of that stream which came to be called Klondike, for, although they hunted and prospected along its valley, none of the partners was destined to grow wealthy on Klondike gold. Nor, on the other hand, did they die in poverty as others were to do. When the madness struck they kept their heads, and when they died it was with the respect of every man who had known them. They were, in the words of an Alaska Commercial Company employee, "typically frontiersmen, absolutely honest, without a semblance of fear of anything, and to a great extent childlike in their implicit faith in human nature, looking on their fellow pioneers as being equally as honest as themselves." Few who came after them merited that accolade.

Without these three men and a fourth named Joseph Ladue, who arrived a decade later, the series of events that led to the Klondike discovery would not have been possible. Without the string of posts they set up along the Yukon, the systematic exploration of the river country could not have taken place. They guided the hands of the prospectors, extending almost unlimited credit, sending them off to promising sections of the country, and following up each discovery by laying out a townsite and erecting a general store. Their little steamboat, the *New Racket*, which they had purchased from Schieffelin, was their lifeline to the outside world. Their arrangement with the great Alaska Commercial Company in San Francisco was a casual one. In the early years they were on its payroll, but remained free to

14

prospect if they wished. Later they operated as independent contractors, buying their goods from the company but trading on their own.

Sometimes they worked together, as partners; sometimes separately. There were other traders scattered along the river working under similar arrangements with the A.C. Company — but it was Harper, McQuesten, and Mayo, far more than the others, who were responsible for the mining development of the Yukon.

It is not always realized that a series of smaller gold rushes into the Yukon Valley took place before the Klondike stampede, and that Dawson City was preceded by several mining camps that sprang up along the river in the ten years before the great strike. The gold along the Yukon was placer gold, or "free gold" — gold that had long since been ground into dust and nuggets and so could be mined by any man with a shovel and a pan and a strong back. It is more immediately rewarding than hardrock or vein gold since it requires no large resources of money and machinery to wrest it from the earth.

By 1886 some two hundred miners had crossed over the Chilkoot Pass and gradually worked their way three hundred miles down the Yukon to the mouth of the Stewart River, on whose sand-bars they panned out, in a single year, one hundred thousand dollars' worth of fine placer gold. At once McQuesten and his colleagues built a trading post at the Stewart's mouth, and, sensing that the human flow would increase, McQuesten left for San Francisco to order more supplies from the Alaska Commercial Company.

That winter Harper persuaded two prospectors to try the waters of the Fortymile River, which joined the Yukon another hundred miles farther downstream. Here they found the gold that had eluded Harper, and it was good coarse gold that rattled in the pan, the kind

15

that every miner seeks. With a fickleness that distinguishes the true gold-seeker, the men along the Stewart deserted their diggings and flocked to the new strike. Harper, in a panic, saw what was coming: as soon as the news leaked back up the river and across the mountain barricade to the outside world, men by the hundreds would tumble over the peaks and pour down to the new diggings on the crest of the spring torrents. But there was not food enough in the land to supply this horde; he must get word out to McQuesten to increase his order or there would be starvation along the Yukon.

Harper felt like a man in a sound-proof prison. To all intents, the interior of the northwest was sealed off from the world by winter. The nearest point of civilization was John Healy's trading post on Dyea Inlet on the far side of the Chilkoot. In between lay an untravelled wilderness which few men had negotiated in winter. Who would carry Harper's message?

The volunteer was no hardened musher but a steamboat man named Tom Williams, who, with an Indian companion, set off on a terrifying journey. On the two men plunged for five hundred miles, over the hummocks of river ice and the corpses of fallen trees, through the cold jungles of the Yukon forests and up the

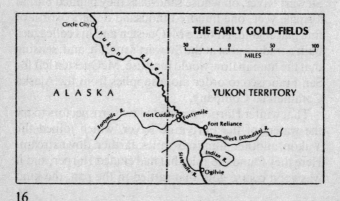

THE EARLY GOLD-FIELDS

slippery flanks of the mountains. By the time they reached the Chilkoot their rations had petered out and their dogs were dead of cold, hunger, and fatigue. At the summit of the pass a blizzard was raging, and travel became impossible. They clawed a cave out of the snow and crouched in it, their faces, fingers, and feet blackened by frostbite, their only sustenance a few mouthfuls of dry flour. When this ran out, the Indian hoisted the exhausted Williams onto his back and stumbled down the slope of the pass until he could carry him no farther. Then he dropped him into the snow and staggered on until he reached Sheep Camp, a long-time halting-point on the edge of the tree line. It was March, 1887, by this time, and a group of prospectors, camped in the lee of the mountains waiting for the storm to abate, watched in astonishment as the figure of the Indian loomed out of the swirling snow. They followed him back up the mountainside and helped bring Williams down and revive him with hot soup. The Indian borrowed a sled and dragged his companion twenty-six miles down the trail to Dyea Inlet. Here the two finally reached the shelter of the trading post run by a one-time Montana sheriff named John J. Healy. Williams lived two days, and the men who crowded around his deathbed had only one question: Why had he made the trip?

The Indian's answer electrified them. He reached into a sack of beans on Healy's counter and flung a handful on the floor.

"Gold," he said. "All same like this!"

3: *The hermits of Fortymile*

Along the high bank at the point where the Fortymile River joins the Yukon, a weird and lonely village straggled into being as a result of Tom Williams's dying message. It was named Fortymile after the river, and its

17

remoteness from the world can scarcely be comprehended today, for it existed eight months out of twelve as if in a vacuum, its residents sealed off from the world. The nearest outfitting port was San Francisco, almost five thousand water miles distant, and the only links with the sea were two cockleshell sternwheelers, the *New Racket* and the Alaska Commercial Company's *Arctic,* built in 1889. These boats seldom had time to make more than one summer trip upstream from the old Russian seaport of St. Michael, near the river's mouth on the Bering Sea. On her maiden voyage the *Arctic* was damaged and unable to bring supplies to Fortymile. The A.C. Company sent Indian runners sixteen hundred miles to the settlement to warn the miners that no supplies would be forthcoming, and that they must escape from the Yukon Valley or starve. As the October snows drifted down from the dark skies, the Fortymilers pressed aboard the *New Racket,* and the little vessel made a brave attempt to reach St. Michael before the river froze. She was caught in the ice floes one hundred and ninety miles short of her goal, and the starving passengers had to continue the journey on foot. Those who remained at the community of Fortymile spent a hungry winter: indeed, one man lived for nine months on a steady diet of flapjacks.

The only winter route to the outside world was the gruelling trek upstream to the Chilkoot, more than six hundred miles distant. After Williams's death it was seldom attempted. Four men who tried it in 1893 were forced to abandon fifteen thousand dollars in gold dust on the mountain slopes and were so badly crippled by the elements that one died and another was incapacitated for life.

Who were these men who had chosen to wall themselves off from the madding crowd in a village of logs deep in the sub-Arctic wilderness? On the face of it, they

18

were men chasing the will-o'-the-wisp of fortune — chasing it with an intensity and a singleness of purpose that had brought them to the ends of the earth. But the evidence suggests the opposite. They seemed more like men pursued than men pursuing, and if they sought anything, it was the right to be left alone.

Father William Judge, a Jesuit missionary in Alaska, described them as "men running away from civilization as it advanced westward — until now they have no farther to go and so have to stop." One of them, he discovered, had been born in the United States, but had never seen a railway: he had kept moving ahead of the rails until he reached the banks of the Yukon. They were Civil War veterans and Indian-fighters, remittance men from England and prospectors from the Far West. Many of them had known each other before in the Black Hills, or the Coeur d'Alene country of Idaho, or in the camps of Colorado. They were nomads all, stirred by an uncontrollable wanderlust, which seized them at the slightest whisper of a new strike, however preposterous. They were men whose natures craved the widest possible freedom of action; yet each was disciplined by a code of comradeship whose unwritten rules were strict as any law.

They were all individuals, as their nicknames (far commoner than formal names) indicated: Salt Water Jack, Big Dick, Squaw Cameron, Jimmy the Pirate, Buckskin Miller, Pete the Pig. Eccentricities of character were the rule rather than the exception. There was one, known as the Old Maiden, who carried fifty pounds of ancient newspapers about with him wherever he went, for, he said, "they're handy to refer to when you get into an argument." There was another called Cannibal Ike because of his habit of hacking off great slabs of moose meat with his knife and stuffing them into his mouth raw. One cabin had walls as thin as

19

matchwood because its owner kept chopping away at the logs to feed his fire; he said he did it to let in the light. Another contained three partners and a tame moose which was treated as a house pet. Out in the river lay Liar's Island, where a group of exiles whiled away the long winters telling tales of great ingenuity and implausibility.

Fortymile, in short, was a community of hermits whose one common bond was their mutual isolation. "I feel so long dead and buried that I cannot think a short visit home, as if from the grave, would be of much use," wrote William Bompas, a Church of England bishop who found himself in Fortymile. A Cambridge graduate who could read his Bible in Greek, Hebrew, and Syriac, he was the fourth son of that same London advocate on whom Dickens had modelled his "Serjeant Buzfuz" in *Pickwick Papers.* His predecessor had been driven to literal madness by the practical jokes of the miners, but Bompas was far too tough for that — a giant of a man with a high dome, a hawk nose, piercing eyes, and the flowing beard of a Moses. He baked his own bread, eschewed all dainties, drank his sugarless coffee from an iron cup, ate from a tin plate with a knife his only utensil, slept in the corner of a boat or a hole in the snow or on the floor of a log hut, and allowed himself no holidays. His only furniture was a box which he used for a seat; he had torn down shelves, cupboard, and table to make a coffin for a dead Indian because lumber was so scarce. And he thought nothing of making a present of his trousers to a pantless native and mushing home in his red flannels.

For almost half a century he lived in isolation, and he was resigned to it. When his wife joined him at Fortymile in 1892, they had not seen each other for five years. She was the daughter of a fashionable London doctor, and had been brought up in Italy. On those dark winter afternoons when she was not on the trail with her husband, she sat quietly in the mission hall with its cotton-drill walls, reading her Dante in the original or — if the keys were not frozen stiff — playing her little harmonium.

This ecclesiastical existence was no more primitive than that of the miners at Fortymile. Each man lived with his partner in a murky, airless cabin whose windowpanes were made from untanned deerhide, white cotton canvas, or a row of empty pickle jars chinked with moss. Cutlery was fashioned from pieces of tin, furniture constructed from the stumps of trees. Four men often lived year in and year out in a space about eighteen feet square. Above the red-hot sheet-iron stove there always hung a tin full of fermented dough, used in place of yeast to make bread, biscuits, and flapjacks rise. This was the origin of the name "sourdough" which was applied to the pioneers of the Yukon to distinguish them from the tenderfeet or *cheechakos,* as the Indians called them.

Men moved from their fetid cabins by night into murky, constricted mine shafts by day. Mining in the sub-Arctic is unique because the permanently frozen ground must be thawed before the bed-rock can be reached; it is this bed-rock, ten, twenty, and even fifty feet below the surface, that contains the gold. At first the miners let the sun do the work. This was a long, laborious process: a few inches of thawed earth were scraped away each day, and an entire summer might pass by before the goal was attained. Soon, however, wood fires replaced the sun. The gold-seekers lit them by night, removed the ashes and the thawed earth in the morning, then lit a new fire, burning their way slowly down to form a shaft whose sides remained frozen as hard as granite. This method allowed miners to work all winter, choking and wheezing in their smoky dungeons far below the snow-covered surface of the ground as they tunnelled this way and that seeking the "pay streak" which marked an erstwhile creek channel. The paydirt thus obtained was hoisted up the shaft and piled in a mound, known as a "dump." In the spring, when the ice broke on the creeks and water gushed down the hillsides, the miners built long spillways or sluiceboxes to counterfeit the ancient action of nature. The gravel was shovelled into these boxes and, as the water rushed through, was swept away. But the heavier gold was caught in the crossbars and in the matting on the bottom, as it had once been caught in the crevices of the streambeds. Every two or three days the water was diverted from the sluicebox as each miner panned the residue at the bottom in what came to be known as a "clean-up." The various stages in this process had been arrived at by trial and error over the years, since the days of '49 in California; in the Yukon Valley they reached their greatest refinement.

The entertainments that lightened this monotony were scanty and primitive. One of the main amusements, apart from the saloons, was a folk-rite known as the "squaw dance." Josiah Edward Spurr, a U.S. government geologist who visited Fortymile in the nineties, has left a description of one of these affairs:

"We were attracted by a row of miners who were lined up in front of the saloon engaged in watching the door of a very large log cabin opposite, rather dilapidated with the windows broken in. . . . They said there was going to be a dance, but when or how they did not seem to know. . . .

"The evening wore on until ten o'clock, when in the dusk a stolid Indian woman with a baby in the blanket on her back, came cautiously around the corner, and with the peculiar long slouchy step of her kind, made for the cabin door, looking neither to the right nor to the left. . . . She was followed by a dozen others, one far behind another, each silent and unconcerned, and each with a baby upon her back. They sidled into the log cabin and sat down on the benches, where they also deposited their babies in a row: the little red people lay there very still, with wide eyes shut or staring, but never crying. . . .

"The mothers sat awhile looking at the ground on some one spot, then slowly lifted their heads to look at the miners who had slouched into the cabin after them — men fresh from the diggings, spoiling for excitement of any kind. Then a man with a dilapidated fiddle struck up a swinging, sawing melody and in the intoxication of the moment some of the most reckless of the miners grabbed an Indian woman and began furiously swinging her around in a sort of waltz while the others crowded and looked on.

"Little by little the dusk grew deeper, but candles were scarce and could not be afforded. The figures of the dancing couples grew more and more indistinct and their faces became lost to view, while the sawing of the fiddle grew more and more rapid, and the dancing more excited. There was no noise, however; scarcely a sound save the fiddle and the shuffling of the feet over the floor of rough hewn logs; for the Indian women were as stolid as ever and the miners could not speak the language of their partners. Even the lookers on said nothing, so that these silent dancing figures in the dusk made an almost weird effect.

"One by one, however, the women dropped out, tired, picked up their babies and slouched off home, and the men slipped over to the saloon to have a drink before going to their cabins. Surely this squaw-dance, as they call it, was one of the most peculiar balls ever seen. . . ."

This aboriginal background appeared all the more bizarre behind the thin varnish of civilization that began to spread over the community as the years passed. There were saloons that contained Chippendale chairs; and stores that, when they sold anything, dispensed such delicacies as *pâté de foie gras* and tinned plum pudding. There were Shakespeare clubs formed to give play-readings, and a library whose shelves contained books on science and philosophy. There was a dress-maker with the latest Paris fashions, and an opera house with a troupe of San Francisco dance-hall girls, and even a cigar factory, all housed in log buildings strewn helter-skelter along the mudbank above the Yukon and surrounded by intervening marshland littered with stumps, wood shavings, and tin cans.

The social life of the camp revolved around ten saloons, which at steamboat time served whiskey at fifty cents a drink (heavily watered to make it last) and the rest of the year peddled hootchinoo, a vile concoction compounded of molasses, sugar, and dried fruit, fermented with sourdough, flavoured with anything handy, distilled in an empty coal-oil can, and served hot at fifty cents a drink. It was sometimes referred to as Forty-Rod Whiskey because it was supposed to kill a man at that distance. By the peculiar etiquette of the mining camp, a man who bought a drink bought for everyone in sight, though such a round might cost a hundred dollars, while a teetotaller who refused a drink offered a deadly insult — unless he accepted a fifty-cent cigar in its place. Hootch, like everything else, was paid for in gold dust, and the prospector who flung his poke upon the bar always performed the elaborate gesture of turning his back while the amount was weighed out, since to watch this ritual was to impugn the honesty of the bartender.

Fortymile thrived on such unwritten laws, its residents enjoying a curious mixture of communism and anarchy. It had no mayor or council, no judges or lawyers, no police or jail or written code. Yet it was a cohesive community. No man went hungry, though many were destitute. Credit at Harper and McQuesten's store was unlimited. If a man had no money, he could still get an outfit without payment. There were few "bad men" in Fortymile; on the contrary, it was a community that hewed surprisingly closely to the Christian ethic. Men shared their good fortune with their comrades, and it was part of the code that he who struck a new creek spread the news to one and all. Each man's cabin was open to any passer-by; such a traveller could enter, eat his fill, sleep in the absent owner's bed, and go on his way, as long as he cleaned up and left a supply of fresh kindling. This was more than mere courtesy in a land where a freezing man's life might depend on the speed with which he could light a fire.

Although Fortymile itself was within the Canadian border, it was really an American town, getting its supplies from the United States without customs payments and sending out mail with U.S. stamps. A number of the mines were on Alaskan soil, and the social characteristics of the district were those of the American Rocky Mountain camps. It was from these parent communities that the legalistic device of the miners' meeting was borrowed.

Canadian and U.S. mining camps grew up with varying legal customs which, to a considerable extent, point up the very real difference between the Canadian and the U.S. character. The American, freed by his own will of what he considered colonial bondage, has always insisted on running his own affairs from the ground up — especially on the frontier. The Canadian, who never knew the blood bath of revolution, has more often preferred to have law and order imposed from above rather than have it spring from the grass roots.

In the three British Columbia gold rushes, constabulary and courts of justice enforced a single set of laws in the British colonial tradition. Mining law was the same everywhere, and the gold commissioner in charge had such absolute power that the lawlessness so familiar to American mining history was unknown in the B.C. camps.

But in the Rocky Mountain camps of the United States, and later in Alaska, each community had its own customs and its own rules made on the spot. The American prospector, with his long tradition of free frontier life, smarted under any restriction imposed from above. Authority was vested in the miners themselves, who held town meetings in the New England manner to redress wrongs or dispense justice. Like the mining process, this institution had its origin in California.

These twin concepts, the one stressing order and often caution, the other freedom and sometimes licence, were to meet head-on during the great international stampede to the Klondike. On Alaskan territory, during the hectic days of 1897-98, there was no organized machinery of government, to speak of; rule was by local committee, sometimes wise, sometimes capricious, always summary. On the Canadian side there was, if anything, too much government, as the graft in Dawson City was to demonstrate; but there were also, at every bend in the river, the uniformed and strangely comforting figures of the Mounted Police.

The American miners' meeting, which operated in the Canadian town of Fortymile, had the power of life and death over the members of the community. It could hang a man, give him a divorce, imprison, banish, or

26

lash him, and in Alaska all these functions were performed in the late eighties and nineties. (The Fortymilers hanged at least two Indians for murder.) Any prospector could call a meeting simply by posting a notice. An elected chairman performed the function of judge, while the entire meeting acted as jury. Both sides could produce witnesses and state their cases, and anybody who wished could ask a question or make a speech. The verdict was decided by a show of hands. Seldom has the democratic process operated at such a grass-roots level.

When the first saloons began to appear in Fortymile, they served as headquarters for the miners' meetings, and it was perhaps as a result of this that the meetings began to degenerate. On several occasions when a man called a meeting to seek redress, he found himself fined twenty dollars by the miners for daring to call one at all, and the sum was spent immediately on drinks. In 1893 the moment came when a man rebelled at the authority of a miners' meeting.

The rebel was as typical a Fortymiler as it was possible to find, a man who for all his life had been seeking out the wild places of the northwest. His name was John Jerome Healy, and he was as tough as hardtack. With his cowlick and his Buffalo Bill goatee and his ramrod figure, he looked the part of the traditional frontiersman. He had been hunter, trapper, soldier, prospector, whiskey-trader, editor, guide, Indian scout, and sheriff. He had run away from home at the age of twelve to joint a band of renegades who made an abortive attempt to seize part of Mexico and establish a Pacific republic. He had been in Salt Lake City in 1857 at the time of the Mormon wars, and he counted himself a crony of Sitting Bull. He had built the most famous of the whiskey forts on Canadian territory, ruled it like a feudal baron, and dubbed it "Whoop-Up," thereby giving a name to the great block of untamed Indian country that straddled the Montana-Canadian border. When the wild wolf-hunters of the prairie formed an armed band known as the Spitzee Cavalry, attacked Fort Whoop-Up, and tried to bargain with him, Healy broke up the confab with a lighted cigar held over a keg of gunpowder — a threat that sent them packing. As the hanging sheriff of Chouteau County, Montana, he pursued rustlers and Indians with a zeal that left some students of the period wondering where crime-control left off and lawlessness began. Then, with the frontier tamed by his own efforts, the restless and aging Healy headed north to virgin country, still hungering for the adventure that had driven him all his life. He followed gold to Juneau on the Alaska Panhandle as he had once followed it through Montana, Idaho, and Athabasca. He pushed on to Dyea Inlet at the foot of the Chilkoot, where he built the trading post into which the dying Tom Williams brought news of the Fortymile strike. Healy quickly saw that there was more than one way to get gold out of the Yukon. Off he went to Chicago and convinced an old Missouri crony, Portus B. Weare, a respected midwestern businessman, that there was profit in the Alaska trade. With the help of the Cudahy meat-packing fortune, these two set up the North American Trading and Transportation Company to break the monopoly of the entrenched Alaska Commercial Company. They laid plans to establish a series of posts along the river, built a fleet of steamboats, and launched a price war on the Yukon. In his post at Fort Cudahy, across the Fortymile River from the main town, the bearded Healy with his fierce Irish face was no man to accept quietly the ruling of a miners' meeting. He had always been a law unto himself, and he did not relish the prospect of knuckling under to the eccentrics of a Yukon mining camp.

He ran afoul of his fellows shortly after his arrival. Although he was successful in bringing down prices in Alaska and the Yukon, Healy was never popular with the Fortymilers, for he was a crusty man who insisted on sending out bills promptly at the end of the month, a presumption to those accustomed to Jack McQuesten's unlimited credit. When his hired girl haled him before the miners' court, his enemies were waiting for him.

The case was an odd one. The girl, whom Healy and his wife had brought in from the Outside as a servant, insisted on staying out late at night and sometimes, indeed, all night. Healy forbade her to go out again to one of the squaw dances being held in the main town. When she disobeyed him and tried to get back into the house, he locked her out. This autocratic attitude in a settlement where freedom of individual action was almost a religion enraged the miners. They decided in favour of the girl and demanded that the trader pay her a year's wages and her full fare back home.

Healy paid under protest, but prepared to deliver a counter-blow. He wrote to his old frontier friend from the Whoop-Up days, Superintendent Samuel B. Steele of the North West Mounted Police, and asked for the protection of the Canadian constabulary.

At almost the same time Bishop Bompas was sending a similar letter to the authorities at Ottawa. The miners, he said, "were teaching the Indians to make whisky with demoralizing effect both to the whites and Indians and with much danger in the use of firearms." The reference was to a shooting affray over a poker hand: Jim Washburn, known as the meanest man in town, had slashed a card-player across the belly and received a bullet through the hips in return.

These submissions to Ottawa ended Fortymile's free-and-easy existence. In 1894 Inspector Charles Constantine of the North West Mounted Police arrived

— thickset, gruff, and incorruptible, the first Mountie to enter the Canadian northland. The following year a detachment of twenty joined him. They had scarcely established their barracks before a meeting was held to take away a claim from a man charged with defaulting on wages. Constantine reversed the verdict and abolished the miners' meetings forever. He had been eight years in the police force, was known for his ability in a rough-and-tumble fight, and never spared himself. He called himself "chief magistrate, commander-in-chief and home and foreign secretary" of the town, and he took his duties so seriously that he had three tables in his cabin, each with a different kind of work on it; he moved continually from one to another, and this brief change of scene was the only respite he permitted himself. His iron hand was quickly felt in various small ways in the community: one of his first acts was to stop the dance-hall girls from wearing bloomers. Another was to collect the excise duty on all locally made hootchinoo. With these edicts, some of the freer spirits decided that the time had come to move again. Once more civilization had caught up to them.

4: *The land of the Golden Rule*

Was it coincidence that in the same year when the first force of constabulary was embarking for the Yukon, an even more unconventional town was springing up farther downstream, to the northwest, on Alaskan soil? Probably. But for anyone chafing under new restraints, Circle City was a welcome haven.

Circle was McQuesten's town. For years he and Harper had been grubstaking men to seek out the legendary "Preacher's Creek," on which a missionary had once seen gold by the spoonful. Two Russian half-breeds outfitted and encouraged by McQuesten finally found it in 1893 on the headwaters of Birch Creek, near the Arctic Circle. Within a year the region was producing an annual four hundred thousand dollars.

McQuesten built his new town in the dreariest section of the Yukon Valley, one hundred and seventy miles downstream from Fortymile, at the point where the river spills over the Yukon Flats. Here the hills suddenly lose their grandeur and seem to sicken and die until they decline into monotonous wastes of sand, while the main stream, broad as a lake and sluggish as a slough, describes its huge arc across the Arctic Circle for one hundred and eighty miles. There is no scenery here in the grand sense; only hundreds of islets and grey sand-bars on which ducks and snow geese and plover nest by the million.

The town was as drab as its surroundings, a hodge-podge of moss-chinked cabins scattered without plan along the curve of the river-bank and stitched together by a network of short streets which were little more than rivers of mud in the springtime. The mines were some eighty miles back from the river, for Birch Creek ran parallel to the Yukon before joining it at the end of its arc. The trail between Circle City and the mines led across a no-man's land of swamp and muskeg and stunted spruce, empty of game but swarming during the summer with mosquitoes so thick that they blotted out the sun, suffocated pack horses by stopping their nostrils, and drove some men insane.

In this lugubrious settlement McQuesten was king. Above his two-storey trading post — the most imposing log structure in town — there rose a flagpole whose cross-arm was handily located in case a hanging should be required. Each year when the squaws, by custom, tossed every white man in a moose-skin blanket, Mc-Questen was honoured by being tossed first. It was traditional to let him escape, then bring him to bay in a mock battle. He invariably landed lightly on his feet, no matter how high he was tossed, and only at the last ceremony, in 1896, having grown old and bulky, toppled onto his back, whereupon the fat Indian women clustered about him, murmuring and patting him as a sign of sympathy.

By 1893 the trader's former partners had scattered: Mayo was farther down the river at the mouth of Minook Creek, in the region where Ed Schieffelin had once poked about for gold; Harper and his partner, Joseph Ladue, had poled their way up the river, deep into Canadian territory. McQuesten staked everything he had on Circle. His credit was so liberal that by 1894 the miners owed him one hundred thousand dollars.

William Ogilvie, the Canadian government surveyor who established the boundary line between Alaska and Canada, once witnessed McQuesten's credit system in operation. A miner came into the store from the creeks and asked McQuesten how much he owed.

"Seven hundred," said the trader.

"Hell, Jack, I've only got five hundred. How'm I going to pay seven hundred with five?"

"Oh, that's all right. Give us your five hundred and we'll credit you and let the rest stand till next clean-up."

"But, Jack, I want more stuff. How'm I going to get it?"

"We'll let you have it, same as we did before."

"But, damn it, Jack, I haven't had a spree yet."

"Well, go and have your little spree; come back with what's left and we'll credit you with it and go on as before."

The miner had his spree; it took everything he had. McQuesten without a word gave him a five-hundred-dollar outfit and carried a debt of twelve hundred dollars against him on the books.

Such sprees were the high points of Circle's social life. There was something almost ceremonial about them. A man on a spree moved from saloon to saloon, swinging a club as a weapon, threatening the bartenders, pouring the liquor himself, treating the house to cigars and hootch, then driving everybody ahead of him to the next saloon, where the performance was repeated. When a spree reached its height, the miners would line up on two sides of the saloon and throw cordwood at each other from the pile that stood beside the stove. Then someone would jump onto the water barrel to make a speech, upset it, and finally roll the stove itself, often red hot, around the floor. When the spree was over, the man who began it would hand his poke of gold dust to the saloon-keeper and ask him to take the damages out of it. A spree could last for several days, and one such bill for damages came to twenty-nine hundred dollars.

For Circle was subject only to the law of the miners' meeting. In its first year it had no jail, no court house, no lawyers, and no sheriff, yet there was neither lock nor key in the community. It had no post office and no mail service, and a letter might take from two months to a year to reach its destination, arriving crumpled and odorous, impregnated with tar and bacon. It had no taxes and no banks except the saloons, where men kept their money; and the smallest coin in use was a silver dollar. It had no priest, doctor, church, or school, but it had the squaw men with Oxford degrees who could recite Greek poetry when they were drunk. It had no thermometers to measure the chilling cold, save for the bottles of quicksilver, whiskey, kerosene, and Perry Davis Painkiller which Jack McQuesten set outside his store and which froze in ascending order.

It was a community divorced from the customs of civilized society. A man might easily rise and eat breakfast at ten in the evening, since the summers were perpetually light and the winters perpetually dark. On cold days, when even the Painkiller froze in the bottles, it became a ghostly and silent settlement, the smoke rising in vertical pillars to form an encompassing shroud that seemed to deaden all sound save for the incessant howling of the ubiquitous sled dogs — the wolf-like huskies and the heavy-shouldered malemutes. These ravenous but indispensable creatures dominated the town. They were always hungry, and they gobbled everything in sight — leather gloves and harnesses, gun straps and snowshoes, pots of paste, miners' boots and brushes, and even powdered resin, which was devoured as swiftly as it was sprinkled on the dance-hall floors. One man watched a dog eat a dish-rag whole for the sake of the grease in it; another stood helpless while a dog rushed into a tent and swallowed a lighted candle, flame and all. To prevent the dogs from eating their precious cakes of soap, the Indians hung them from the branches of trees. Circle's skyline was marked by the silhouettes of log caches built on stilts to keep supplies away from the dogs, whose teeth could tear open a can of salmon as easily as if it were a paper package. There were those, indeed, who swore the dogs could tell a tin of marmalade from one of bully beef by a glance at the label.

Men crowded into Circle City ostensibly to look for gold, but they also came because they were the kind who wished to be left alone. Where else could a man attempt to cut his throat in plain view without anyone interfering? But here one did just that; his name was Johnson, and he made a bad job of it because he was drunk. The onlookers, seeing that he was obviously failing in his plan, patched him up and then told him

34

courteously that he might try again if he wished. (He rejected the idea, grew a villainous black beard to hide his scars, and revelled ever after in the nickname of Cut-throat Johnson.)

Only when a man's freedom of action encroached upon that of his neighbour did the miners' meeting take hold. When a saloon-keeper seduced a half-breed girl, a meeting decreed that he must either marry her or spend a year in jail, even though there was no jail in town. The miners were quite prepared to build one on the spot, but were spared this labour by the accused, who chose a shotgun wedding.

Theft was a more heinous crime, and when one man stole from a cache his comrades sentenced him to hang. This was commuted to banishment when no one could be found to stretch the rope. The culprit was ordered to live by himself twelve miles out of town until the annual steamboat arrived. The miners gravely took up a collection, bought him a tent, stove, and provisions, bade him good-bye, and never saw or spoke to him again.

The U.S. government obviously considered these meetings lawful, for the verdict of one of them was sent to Washington and confirmed. This was a murder case involving a bartender named Jim Chronister and the same Jim Washburn whose shooting affray in Fortymile had so disturbed Bishop Bompas. After killing Washburn in self-defence, Chronister offered himself on trial to a miners' meeting and was acquitted in just twenty minutes.

It was out of these meetings that the Miners' Association, and later the Yukon Order of Pioneers, was formed, a fraternal organization whose emblem was the Golden Rule and whose motto was "Do unto others as you would be done by." It sounds like a curiously saccharine slogan for a group of hard-bitten prospectors, but it was born of experience by men who had learned, over many years, the necessity of dependence upon one another. Each member pledged himself to help every other member should the need arise and always to spread the news of a fresh gold-discovery far and wide.

In the end, Circle City, more than four thousand miles by water from civilization, was not immune to the inevitable corrosion of mining-camp civilization. By 1896 it had a music hall, two theatres, eight dance halls, and twenty-eight saloons. It was known as "the Paris of Alaska," where money was so free that day-labourers were paid five times as much as they were "Outside," as the Alaskans called the rest of the civilized world.

In the big new double-decker Grand Opera House, George Snow, half miner, half entrepreneur, who had once starred with Edwin Booth in California, produced Shakespearean plays and vaudeville turns. Snow's children appeared on the stage and picked up nuggets thrown to them by miners hungry for entertainment. One troupe of vaudevilleans, sealed in for the winter with only a limited repertoire, was forced to enact the same routines nightly for seven months until the audience howled as loudly as the malemutes who bayed to the cold moon.

Circle City grew richer. Into the bars roared the miners, flinging down handfuls of nuggets for drinks and dancing out the change at a dollar a dance. They danced with their hats on, clumping about the floors in their high-top boots; and they danced from midnight until dawn while the violins scraped and the sled dogs howled on.

Circle City grew bigger. A thick porridge of chips and sawdust from newly erected buildings mixed with the mud of the rutted streets. By 1896 it had twelve hundred citizens. John Healy's N.A.T. Company opened up a store in opposition to Jack McQuesten of the A.C. Company. The Episcopal Church bought land for a hospital. The Chicago *Daily Record* sent a foreign correspondent into the settlement, which now boasted that it was "the largest log town in the world."

Circle City accepted culture. Up from the University of Chicago came Miss Anna Fulcomer to open a government school. The miners established a library which contained the complete works of Huxley, Darwin, Carlyle, Macaulay, Ruskin, and Irving. It filed the standard illustrated papers and supplied its members with chess sets, a morocco-bound quarto Bible, an *Encyclopaedia Britannica,* and an *International Dictionary.*

Circle City had its greatest year in 1896. The gold-production that season had exceeded one million dollars, and lots were selling for two thousand dollars apiece. Who would have believed that before the winter was out the Paris of Alaska would be a ghost town, the saloons closed and barred, the caches empty and left to rot, the doors of the worthless cabins hanging open to the winds, and scarcely a dog left to howl in the silent streets?

But, as the winter of '96-'97 wore on, strange rumours began to filter down from the upper-river country about an almost unbelievable event on a little stream whose name nobody could properly pronounce. At Christmastime these rumours were confirmed, and Circle City was never the same again. The first act in the drama of the Klondike was already under way.

Chapter Two

1: *The prospector and the squaw man*

The man in the poling-boat slipped silently down the river, moving swiftly with the stiff current of the grey Yukon, keeping close to the shoreline, where martins darted from the high clay banks and the willows arched low into the water. Beneath him the waters hissed and boiled, as if stirred by some inner fire. Above him thrush and yellow warbler fluttered and carolled. And all around him the blue hills rolled on towards the rim of the world to melt into the haze of the horizon. Between each twin line of hills was a valley, and in the bottom of each valley a little creek gurgled its way down to the river. Below the wet mosses of some of those creeks, the man in the poling-boat knew, there was gold. But in this summer of 1894 he had no more stomach for it. For twenty-three years he had been climbing the hills of the world and trudging down the valleys, picking away at quartz and panning the black sand of a thousand creekbeds. Always the gold had eluded him.

He was a lighthouse-keeper's son from Big Island off the tattered coast of Nova Scotia, and he could scarcely remember the time when he had not thought of gold. As a child he had read Alaskan histories and wandered about Nova Scotia searching for gold but finding only white iron. "Well," he would console himself, "It's a *kind* of gold." As a youth of fourteen he made the deliberate decision to spend his life seeking it. He believed that the southern hemisphere held out the best hope, and so he signed aboard a sailing-ship to search the seven seas, panning and picking to no avail in New Zealand and Australia and other corners of the globe. After five years he tried the northern hemisphere, working his way up through the Rocky Mountain states to the mines of Colorado, and then, after fourteen years, he was borne north with the human tide flowing towards Alaska. It was characteristic of his nature that, while other men rushed to familiar ground on the Fortymile or on Birch Creek, he had chosen to press his search in unknown country on the upper reaches of the Pelly. But he found no gold on the Pelly; and now, out of funds and out of grub, with two equally disconsolate companions he was drifting.

His name was Robert Henderson. He was tall and lean, with a gaunt hawk's face, fiercely knit brows, and piercing eyes. His full moustache, drooping slightly at the edges, accentuated the dour look that betrayed his Scottish ancestry. He wore his broad-brimmed miner's hat proudly, as if it were a kind of badge. All his life he wore it, on city streets and wilderness pathways; it proclaimed to the world that Robbie Henderson was a prospector.

Henderson and his companions had drifted for about one hundred miles when they reached the mouth of the Sixtymile River, whose tributaries curled back towards the headwaters of the Fortymile. Here, on an island, they espied a pinprick of civilization — a few cabins and tents, a sawmill and a big two-storey trading post of square-cut logs operated by the white-bearded Papa Harper and his partner, Joseph Ladue. This little community had been named Ogilvie after William Ogilvie, the Canadian who surveyed the boundary between Alaska and the British Northwest Territories.

Harper was away, but Ladue — a swarthy, stocky figure of French Huguenot background, and a veteran of the river since 1882 — was on the bank to greet Henderson. From delta to headwaters, for two thousand miles, he was known to Indian and white man alike simply as "Joe."

He too had been obsessed with the idea of gold for most of his life. It had a very real meaning for him, because without it he could not marry his sweetheart,

41

Anna Mason, whose wealthy parents continued to spurn him as a penniless drifter. She was waiting faithfully for him three thousand miles away while he sought his fortune here in a starkly furnished log post on the banks of the Yukon.

For twenty years Ladue had pressed the search, ever since heading west from his foster-parents' home in Plattsburgh, New York. In the Black Hills country he took a job operating a steam engine in a mine. He knew nothing about engines, but he could learn, and within eighteen months he was a foreman. He knew nothing about mining either, but he could study at night, and within a few more months he was superintendent. But Ladue did not want to mine other men's gold, and he was off with the herd at the whisper of a new strike — from Wyoming to New Mexico, from New Mexico to Arizona, from Arizona to Alaska. He was one of the first to scale the Chilkoot, and in the next half-dozen years he dipped his pan into scores of gravelly creeks from the Stewart to Nuklayaket, including one gurgling stream whose name would later become world-renowned as "Bonanza." But for Ladue there was no bonanza. When prospecting failed, he tried farming. When the frost ruined his cabbages and his barley, he set up as a trader. When trading was slow, he built a sawmill and sold sluicebox lumber. He did not daunt easily, for he was a confirmed optimist, wiry, keen-eyed, and cheerful to the point of enthusiasm.

Now he expended some of this enthusiasm on the dour, dogged Henderson and his two companions. It pleased Ladue to see prospectors arriving, for, with his promoter's mind, he foresaw that sooner or later one would find what all were seeking, and then each would be rich. If there had been a chamber of commerce in the Yukon, Ladue would have been president, for he was a born booster. The slightest trace of a colour in a pan

prompted him to talk in glowing terms of a new Eldorado. He was the first in a long line of northern
outfitters who realized that a gold strike often brought
more fortune to merchant than to miner — but he was
by no means the last. Within a few years there would be
a thousand Ladues exploiting the wealth of the Yukon
Valley.

Ladue's post lay roughly one hundred miles upstream from Fortymile. Between the two settlements,
two other rivers flowed into the Yukon from the opposite side: the Indian River, about thirty miles downstream from Ladue, and then the Thron-diuck River,
another thirty miles farther down. Ladue had explored
the Thron-diuck in the old days, and had gone so far as
to make out an affidavit swearing that there was no gold
on its streams. In spite of this, he now professed to
believe that the neighbouring Indian River country was
ankle-deep in nuggets, and had been extolling its possibilities to every prospector who stopped at his post.
Indeed, he had so annoyed the prospectors at Fortymile
with his stories of the Indian River that they had all but
driven him from camp. As it turned out, Ladue was
right about the Indian (and wrong about the Thron-
diuck), but he would have been astonished to hear it.

The ragged men, in their thick gum boots and fraying
mackinaws, were welcomed into the trader's spartan
quarters, whose grimy walls were ornamented with yel-
lowing woodcuts torn from old newspapers. They sat
down at a rickety table, and over beans and tea Ladue
talked of the Indian River.

Henderson was ready to try anything.

"Let me prospect for you," he said. "If it's good for
me, it's good for you. I'm a determined man. I won't
starve."

His two companions were less enthusiastic. They
chose to quit the north and return to Colorado. But

Henderson stayed on, lured by Ladue's promise of a grubstake, and for the next two years he stubbornly combed the Indian and its tributaries for gold. He searched with that same inquisitive restlessness that had governed his life, shifting from hill to creekbed to island but never settling for long at any given spot. He found gold, but never enough to satisfy him. On the surface bars of the main river he found gold as fine as sifted flour. On Australia Creek he found gold as delicate as lace. He dragged his sled up Quartz Creek, and here he found gold as coarse as sand. It still was not what he was seeking. It is possible, indeed, that had he found a cache of twenty-dollar goldpieces or a mountain of solid gold, he would have felt a vague chagrin, for with Henderson it was the search itself that counted.

Ill-fortune and misadventure served only to stiffen his resolve. He suffered the agonies of leg cramps from constant immersion in the chilling streams, and of snow-blindness from the ceaseless glare on the white slopes. On Australia Creek he endured a harrowing experience when, falling across the broken branch of a tree, he was impaled through the calf and suspended over the rushing torrent like a slab of beef on a butcher's hook. For fourteen days he lay crippled in his bivouac; then he was away again, living off the land, eating caribou or ptarmigan, limping through the forests or travelling the shallow streams in a crude boat made from the skins of animals.

Occasionally he would raise his eyes northward to examine a curious rounded mountain whose summit rose above the other hills. The creeks of Indian River flowed down the flanks of this dome, and Henderson guessed that on the other side more nameless creeks flowed into another river — probably the Thron-diuck or "Klondike," as the miners mispronounced it. At last his prospector's curiosity got the better of him. He climbed the dome to see what was on the other side.

When he reached the summit a sight of breath-taking majesty met his gaze. To the north a long line of glistening snow-capped peaks marched off like soldiers to vanish beyond the lip of the horizon. In every other direction the violet hills rolled on as far as the eye could see, hill upon hill, valley upon valley, gulch upon gulch — and each hill of almost identical height with its neighbour, so that the whole effect through half-closed eyes was of a great plateau creased and gouged and furrowed by centuries of running water.

From the summit on which Henderson was standing, the creeks radiated out like the spokes of a wheel, with himself at the hub, three falling off towards the Indian River and three more, on the far side, running to some unknown stream. He could not know it, but these were six of the richest gold-bearing creeks in the world. They wound through beds of black muck and thick moss, bordered by rank grasses from which the occasional moose lifted its dripping snout; they twisted in sinuous curves across flat valley floors whose flanks, notched by steep gulches, rose in tiers marking the concourse of once mighty tributaries.

Almost at Henderson's feet a deep cleft dropped off, gorge-like, from the dome. He walked down a little way and dipped his pan into a small creek. When the gravel and sand washed away, there was about eight cents' worth of gold left behind. Eight cents to the pan! This was a good prospect; he felt that he had found what he was looking for. Back he went over the divide to the Indian River, where about twenty men, lured by Ladue's tales, were toiling away on the sand-bars. He persuaded three to return with him to the creek which he named "Gold Bottom" because, as he said wistfully, "I had a daydream that when I got my shaft down to bedrock it might be like the streets of the New Jerusalem."

By midsummer of 1896 the four men had taken out seven hundred and fifty dollars, and it was time for Henderson to head back to Ladue's post for more supplies. To each man he met he told the story of a V-shaped valley back in the hills; for this free interchange of information was part of the prospector's code, to which Henderson fiercely subscribed. He not only told strangers of the gold, but he also urged them to turn back in their tracks and stake claims. In this way he emptied the settlement at the mouth of the Sixtymile. Every man except Ladue headed downstream.

His order filled, Henderson drifted back the way he had come in his skin boat. It was late summer, and the water was low. The Indian River was so shallow that Henderson, fearing he might tear his craft to shreds trying to navigate it, determined to continue on down the Yukon towards the Thron-diuck, guessing correctly that Gold Bottom Creek must flow into it. Thus, on a

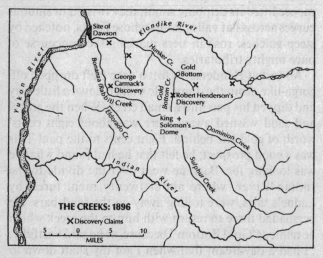

THE CREEKS: 1896

✗ Discovery Claims

5   0   5   10

MILES

46

fateful summer's day he approached his meeting with George Washington Carmack, the squaw man. The memory of that moment, bitter as gall, was to haunt Henderson all the days of his life.

As he brought his boat around a broad curve in the river and past a rocky bluff, he could hear to his right the roar of the Thron-diuck or Klondike as it poured out from between the flat-topped hills to join the Yukon. Directly before him now, just beyond the Klondike's mouth, rose a tapering mountain, its pointed peak naked of timber. Slashed across its flank was an immense and evil scar in the shape of a stretched moose hide, the product of slow erosion by subterranean springs spurting up from within the bowels of the hills. At its base a wedge of flat swampland covered with scrub timber bordered the riverbank for a mile and a half — unprepossessing, fetid, and mosquito-infested. It seemed an almost impossible place for settlement, yet this was to be the site of the gaudiest city in the North.

The Thron-diuck was known as the finest salmon stream in the Yukon — hence its name: an Indian word meaning "Hammer-Water" which, pronounced in the native fashion, sounded like a man in the throes of strangulation. It was so called because the Indians had hammered stakes across the shallow mouth in order to spread their nets. Henderson could smell the stench of the fish drying in the sun, and on the bank just below the river's mouth he could see a white man moving about.

The idea of anyone fishing for a living when there was gold to be had appalled him. He later recalled his first thought: "There's a poor devil who hasn't struck it."

As was his habit, he decided to share his good fortune with the fisherman, and a moment later he was up on the bank talking to George Washington Carmack, or "McCormick," as the men at Fortymile called him.

The two men, who would later be dubbed "co-discoverers of the Klondike" and around whom so much controversy was to swirl, were opposites in almost every way. Henderson, lean and spare, with his keen, chiselled features, serious and intense, bore little resemblance to the easy-going, ever optimistic squaw man with his heavy jowls, his sleepy eyes, and his rather plump features. But they had one trait in common: an incurable restlessness had dominated their lives.

Carmack was the child of an earlier gold rush. His father had crossed the western plains in a covered wagon in '49, heading for California, and Carmack had been born at Port Costa, across the bay from San Francisco. He had gone to work at sixteen aboard the ferryboats, shipped to Alaska as a dishwasher on a man-of-war, jumped ship at Juneau, and pushed steadily north. In 1887 William Ogilvie, the Canadian surveyor, encountered him at Dyea. By that time Carmack could speak both the Chilkoot and the Tagish dialects, and was exerting considerable influence over the Stick Indians from the interior or "Stick" country. At a time and place when every man was a prospector, Carmack appeared to be a misfit. He alone of all men did not want gold. Instead he wanted to be an Indian in a land where the natives were generally scorned by the white man and the word "Siwash" was a term of opprobrium. His wife Kate, a member of the Tagish tribe, was the daughter of a chief, and it was Carmack's ambition to be chief himself. (Among the Tagishes, descent is through the chief's sister.) He worked with the other Indians as a packer on the Chilkoot Pass, and by the time he moved into the interior with his wife and her two brothers he had three or four half-breed children. He had grown an Indian-type moustache that drooped over his lips in Oriental style, and when anybody said to him: "George, you're getting more like a Siwash every

48

day," he took it as a compliment. He did not in the least mind his nicknames "Stick George" and "Siwash George," for he considered himself a true Siwash and he was proud of it.

While other men scrabbled and mucked in the smoky shafts of Fortymile and Birch Creek, Siwash George was slipping up and down the river with his Indian comrades. His temperament, which was indolent and easy-going, matched that of the natives, who were a different breed from the fiercely competitive and ambitious Tlingit tribes of the coast. When it suited Carmack, he bragged of gold discoveries he had made. It was certainly true that he had discovered a seam of coal on the Yukon River, but nobody took him seriously as a prospector, including Carmack himself. In the words of a Mounted Police sergeant at Fortymile, he was a man "who would never allow himself to be beaten and always tried to present his fortunes in the best possible light." The men at Fortymile summed him up more tersely with a new nickname. They called him "Lying George."

Yet he was no wastrel. He had an organ, of all things, in his cabin near Five Finger Rapids on the Yukon, and a library which included such journals as *Scientific American* and *Review of Reviews*. He liked to discourse on scientific topics, and occasionally, as on Christmas Eve in 1888, he wrote sad, sentimental poetry. ("A whisper comes from the tall old spruce, And my soul from pain is free: For I know when they kneel together to-night, They'll all be praying for me.")

He was also something of a mystic. In May of 1896 he was sitting on the bank of the Yukon near the ruins of old Fort Selkirk, and here, if one is to believe his later recollections, he had a premonition. He stared into the blazing sunset and came to the conclusion that something unusual was about to take place in his life. On a

49

whim he took his only coin, a silver dollar, from his pocket and threw it in the air. If it came down heads, he told himself, he would go back up the river; but if it showed tails, he would go downstream to test whatever fate had in store for him. Tails it was, and Carmack loaded his boat and started to drift the two-hundred-odd miles to Fortymile.

That night he had an extravagant and vivid dream in which he saw himself seated on the banks of a stream watching grayling shoot the rapids. Suddenly the fish scattered in fright and two enormous king salmon shot upstream and came to a dead stop in front of him. In place of scales they were armoured in gold nuggets and their eyes were twenty-dollar goldpieces. It reveals a great deal about Carmack that he took this as a sign that he should go fishing; prospecting never entered his head. He determined to catch salmon on the Throndiuck and sell it for dog-feed; and so here he was, with his catch hanging to dry under a small birch lean-to, when Henderson encountered him.

His Tagish friends had joined him at the Klondike's mouth: Skookum Jim, a giant of a man, supremely handsome with his high cheek-bones, his eagle's nose, and his fiery black eyes — straight as a gun-barrel, powerfully built, and known as the best hunter and trapper on the river; Tagish Charley, lean and lithe as a panther and, in Carmack's phrase, "alert as a weasel"; the silent, plump Kate with her straight black hair; and Carmack's daughter, known as Graphie Gracey because no white man could pronounce her real name.* It was this group that Henderson approached with news of the strike at Gold Bottom. Carmack later set down

* Although there is no contemporary record of his presence, a small boy, Patsy Henderson, is said to have been present. Years later, in Whitehorse, his account of the incident was recorded on tape.

his version of the conversation, which does not differ substantially from Henderson's briefer account:

"Hello, Bob! Where in the world did you drop from and where do you think you're going?"

"Just came down from Ogilvie; I'm going up the Klondike."

"What's the idea, Bob?"

"There's been a prospect found in a small creek that heads up against the Dome. I think it empties into the Klondike about fifteen miles up and I'm looking for a better way to get there than going over the mountains from the Indian River."

"Got any kind of a prospect?"

"We don't know yet. We can get a prospect on the surface. When I left, the boys were running up an open cut to get to bedrock."

"What are the chances to locate up there? Everything staked?" Henderson glanced over at the two Indians who were standing near by. Then he uttered the phrase that probably cost him a fortune. "There's a chance for you, George, but I don't want any damn Siwashes staking on that creek."

He pushed his boat into the water and headed up the Klondike. But his final remark rankled.

"What's matter dat white man?" Skookum Jim asked, speaking in Chinook, the pidgin tongue of the traders that prevailed on the river. "Him killet Inchen moose, Inchen caribou, ketchet gold Inchen country, no liket Inchen staket claim, wha for, no good."

"Never mind, Jim," said Carmack lightly. "This is a big country. We'll go and find a creek of our own."

And, as it turned out, it was to be as simple as that.

2: *The exculpation of Lying George*

Carmack did not immediately follow Henderson's suggestion to go upriver and stake at Gold Bottom. He was less interested in gold than he was in logs, which he hoped to chop on Rabbit Creek, a tributary of the Klondike, and float down to the mill at Fortymile for twenty-five dollars a thousand feet. Skookum Jim had already reconnoitred the creek and in passing had panned out some colours, for, just as Carmack wished to be an Indian, Jim longed to be a white man — in other words, a prospector. He differed from the others in his tribe in that he displayed the white man's kind of ambition. He had, in fact, earned his nickname of Skookum (meaning "husky") by his feat of packing the record load of one hundred and fifty-six pounds of bacon across the Chilkoot Pass. In vain he tried to interest Carmack in the prospects along Rabbit Creek; the squaw man was not intrigued.

It was as much Carmack's restless nature as his desire for fortune that took him and the Indians to the site of Henderson's strike some days after the meeting at the Klondike's mouth. They did not follow the river but decided to strike up the valley of Rabbit Creek, which led to the high ridge separating the Klondike and Indian watersheds. The ridge led to the head of Gold Bottom.

They poled up the Klondike for two miles, left their boat in a backwater, shouldered their packs, and began to trudge through the wet mosses and black muck and the great clumps of grass "niggerheads" that marked the mouth of the Rabbit. As they went they prospected, dipping their pans into the clear water which rippled in the sunlight over sands white with quartz. As Carmack sat on his haunches, twirling the gold-pan, he began to recite Hamlet's soliloquy, "To be or not to be," for he felt that all prospecting was a gamble.

52

"Wa for you talket dat cultus wa wa?" Tagish Charley asked him. "I no see um gold."

"That's all right, Charley," Carmack told him."I makum Boston man's medicine."

He raised the pan with its residue of black sand.

"Spit in it, boys, for good luck."

They spat, and then Carmack panned out the sand and raised the pan to show a tiny streak of colour.

On they trudged, stopping occasionally to pan again, finding minute pieces of gold, wondering whether or not to stake. They came to a fork in the frothing creek where another branch bubbled in from the south, and here they paused momentarily. At that instant they were standing, all unknowing, on the richest ground in the world. There was gold all about them, not only beneath their feet but in the very hills and benches that rose on every side. In the space of a few hundred feet there was hidden gold worth several millions of dollars. The south fork of the creek was as yet unnamed, but there could be only one name for it: Eldorado.

But they did not linger here. Instead they hiked on up the narrowing valley, flushing a brown bear from the blueberry bushes, stumbling upon Joe Ladue's eleven-year-old campfires, panning periodically and finding a few colours in every pan, until they reached the dome that looked down over the land of the Klondike. Like Henderson, they were struck by the splendour of the scene that lay spread out before them like an intricate Persian carpet: the little streams tumbling down the flanks of the great mountain, the hills crimson, purple, and emerald-green in the warm August sunlight (for already the early frosts were tinting trees and shrubs), the cranberry and salmonberry bushes forming a foreground fringe to the natural tapestry.

Below, in the narrow gorge of Gold Bottom Creek, a pale pillar of smoke marked Henderson's camp.

"Well, boys," said Carmack, "we've got this far; let's go down and see what they've got."

Skookum Jim demurred; Henderson's remarks about Siwashes still rankled. But in the end the trio clambered down the gorge to the camp where Henderson and his three companions were washing out gold from an open cut.

Exactly what happened between Carmack and Henderson has long been in dispute. Carmack later insisted that he urged Henderson to come over to Rabbit Creek and stake a claim. Henderson always swore that it was he who urged Carmack to prospect Rabbit — and if he found anything to let Henderson know.

Two facts are fairly clear. First, Carmack did promise Henderson that if he found anything worthwhile on Rabbit he would send word back; Henderson offered to compensate him for his trouble if the occasion arose. Second, the Indians tried to purchase some tobacco from Henderson and Henderson refused, possibly because he was short of supplies but more likely because of his attitude towards Indians, since it was against his code to refuse a fellow prospector anything. This action was to cost him dearly.

Carmack tried the prospects at Gold Bottom, but did not stake, and the trio headed back over the mountain almost immediately. The way was hard. They struggled over fallen trees and devil's clubs, a peculiarly offensive thorn, and they forced their way through interlaced underbrush, brier roses, and raspberry bushes. On the far side of the mountain they floundered into a niggerhead swamp that marked the headwaters of Rabbit Creek, and here they had to hop from clump to clump on their slippery moccasins or sink to their thighs in the glacial ooze. Hordes of gnats and mosquitoes rose about them as they stumbled on, unable to swat the insects for fear of losing balance.

Thus they came wearily to the fork of Rabbit Creek once more, and pressed on for about half a mile before making camp for the night. It was August 16, the eve of a memorable day that is still celebrated as a festive holiday in the Yukon Territory.

Who found the nugget that started it all? Again, the record is blurred. Years afterward Carmack insisted it was he who happened upon the protruding rim of bedrock from which he pulled a thumb-sized chunk of gold. But Skookum Jim and Tagish Charley always claimed that Carmack was stretched out asleep under a birch tree when Jim, having shot a moose, was cleaning a dish-pan in the creek and made the find.

At any rate, the gold was there, lying thick between the flaky slabs of rock like cheese in a sandwich. A single panful yielded a quarter of an ounce, or about four dollars' worth. In a country where a ten-cent pan had always meant good prospects, this was an incredible find. Carmack flung down the pan and let out a war-whoop, and the three men began to perform a wild dance around it — a sort of combination Scottish hornpipe, Indian foxtrot, syncopated Irish jig, and Siwash hula, as Carmack later described it. They collapsed, panting, smoked a cigarette apiece, and panned out some more gravel until Carmack had gathered enough coarse gold to fill an empty Winchester shotgun shell. Then they settled down for the night, the Indians chanting a weird song of praise into the embers of the fire while Carmack, staring at the dying flames, conjured up visions of wealth — of a trip around the world, of a suburban mansion rimmed with flower borders, of a suitcase full of gilt-edged securities. In that instant of discovery something fundamental had happened to Siwash George: suddenly he had ceased to be an Indian. And he never thought of himself as an Indian again.

The following morning the trio staked claims on Rabbit Creek. Under Canadian mining law, no more than one claim may be staked in any mining district by any man except the discoverer, who is allowed a double claim. Carmack blazed a small spruce tree with his hand-axe, and on the upstream side wrote with a pencil:

TO WHOM IT MAY CONCERN

I do, this day, locate and claim, by right of discovery, five hundred feet, running up stream from this notice. Located this 17th day of August, 1896.

G. W. Carmack

The claim, also by law, straddled the creek from rim-rock to rim-rock. Carmack then measured off three more claims — one additional for himself, by right of discovery; *One Above* discovery for Jim; and another below for Charley, which, under the claim-numbering system, became *Two Below.* Jim's story, later, was that Carmack took the additional claim for himself, having persuaded Jim that, although he had made the discovery, as an Indian he would not be recognized as discoverer.

This done, and with no further thought to Robert Henderson, waiting for news on the far side of the hills, the three set off through the swamps, to emerge five hours later on the Klondike again, their bodies prickling with thorns.

They had moved only a short distance downriver when they came upon four beaten and discouraged men wading knee-deep in the mud along the shoreline and towing a loaded boat behind them. These were Nova Scotians who had come to the Yukon Valley by way of California and had since tramped all over the territory without success. They were starving when they reached the Klondike looking for salmon, but here they had heard of Henderson's strike, and now, in the intense August heat, their hunger forgotten, they were dragging their outfit upstream, searching once again for gold.

The leader, Dave McKay, asked Carmack if he had heard of Henderson's strike.

"I left there three days ago," Carmack said, holding his boat steady with a pike pole.

"What do you think of it?"

Carmack gave a slow, sly grin. "I don't like to be a knocker, but I don't think much of it."

The faces of the four men fell: all were now at the end of their tether.

"You wouldn't advise us to go up there?" Dan McGillivery, one of the partners, asked.

"No," said Carmack, still grinning, "because I've got something better for you." With that, he pulled out his nugget-filled cartridge case, like a conjurer plucking a rabbit from a hat.

As the Nova Scotians' eyes goggled, Carmack gave them directions to his claim. Without further ado, the four men scrambled upriver, the tow-line on their boat as taut as a violin string. This chance meeting with Carmack made fortunes for all of them.

"I felt as if I had just dealt myself a royal flush in the game of life, and the whole world was a jackpot," Carmack later remarked, when recalling the incident.

He reached the salmon camp at the Klondike's mouth, and here he hailed two more discouraged men — Alphonse Lapierre of Quebec and his partner, another French Canadian. These two had been eleven years in the north, and now, en route downriver to Fortymile, almost starving, out of flour and bacon, their faces blistering in the sun, they had reached the nadir of their careers.

"If I were you boys, I wouldn't go any further," Carmack told them as they beached their boat. "Haven't you heard of the new strike?"

"Oh, yes, we know all about heem. I tink hees wan beeg bluff."

"How's this for bluff?" Carmack shouted, producing the gold. Again the effect was electric. The two men unloaded their boat, filled their packs, and fairly ran across the flat, gesticulating with both hands and chattering in a mixture of French and English. The abandoned boat would have floated off with the current if Carmack had not secured it.

As Carmack made preparations to set off for Fortymile to record his claim, he continued to tell anyone he encountered about the gold on Rabbit Creek. He made a special trip across the river to tell an old friend, then sent Jim back to guard the claims and drifted off with Tagish Charley down the Yukon, still spreading the news. He told everybody, including a man who on hearing the tale called him the biggest liar this side of hell.

Only one man Carmack did not tell. He sent not a whisper back to Robert Henderson.

Late in the afternoon he landed at the mining camp and went straight to Bill McPhee's saloon. It was crowded with men, for autumn was approaching and many had come in from their claims to secure their winter outfits before snowfall — a ragged, tattered group living almost from day to day in a settlement that had become a poor man's camp.

Carmack was no drinking man, but on this occasion he felt the need for two whiskeys, and it was not until he had swallowed these that he was ready to break the news. After more than a decade his moment had come, and he savoured it. He turned his back to the bar and raised his hand.

"Boys, I've got some good news to tell you. There's a big strike up the river."

"Strike, hell!" somebody shouted. "That ain't no news. That's just a scheme of Ladue and Harper to start a stampede up the river."

"That's where you're off, you big rabbit-eating malemute!" Carmack cried. "Neither Ladue nor Harper knows anything about this." He pulled out his cartridge full of gold and poured it on the "blower," upon which gold was weighed. "How does that look to you, eh?"

"Is that some Miller Creek gold that Ladue gave you?" someone asked sardonically.

A wave of suspicion swept the room. Nobody believed that Lying George, the squaw man, had made a strike. Nevertheless, they crowded to the bar and examined the gold curiously. A seasoned prospector could tell from which creek a given amount of gold came simply by looking at it, and this gold was undeniably foreign. It did not come from Miller Creek, nor from Davis, nor from Glacier; it did not come from the bars of the Stewart or the Indian. In texture, shape, and colour it was different from any gold that had been seen before in the Yukon Valley.

The men in Bill McPhee's saloon looked uneasily about them. All of them had been on stampedes before, and almost all of those stampedes had led them up false trails. And yet. . .

One by one, on one excuse or another, they started to slip away. Bewildered, some went to see William Ogilvie, the Canadian government surveyor, to ask his opinion, and Ogilvie pointed out that Carmack must have found the gold *somewhere*. That was enough. Silently, in the twilight hours of the August night, one after another, the boats slid off. By morning Fortymile was a dead mining camp, empty of boats and empty of men. Even the drunks had been dragged from the saloons by their friends and tied down, protesting, in the boats that were heading for the Klondike.

Carmack and Charley crossed the mouth of the Fortymile and went into the police post to record their claims. The recorder took one look at Lying George and laughed at him. Once again Carmack produced his shell full of gold dust. The recorder stopped laughing. From that moment on, few men laughed or called him Lying George again.

3: *Moose pastures*

Up and down the Yukon Valley the news spread like a great stage-whisper. It moved as swiftly as the breeze in the birches, and more mysteriously. Men squatting by nameless creeks heard the tale, dropped their pans, and headed for the Klondike. Men seated by dying campfires heard it and started up in the night, shrugging off sleep to make tracks for the new strike. Men poling up the Yukon towards the mountains or drifting down the Yukon towards the wilderness heard it and did an abrupt about-face in the direction of the salmon stream whose name no one could pronounce properly. Some did not hear the news at all, but, drifting past the Klondike's mouth, saw the boats and the tents and the gesticulating figures, felt the hair rise on their napes, and then, still uncomprehending, still unbelieving, joined the clamouring throng pushing up through the weeds and muck of Rabbit Creek.

Joe Ladue already was on the scene. His quick merchant's mind had swiftly grasped the essence of the situation. Others were scrambling to stake claims, but Ladue was more interested in staking out a townsite on the swamp below the tapering mountain at the Klondike's mouth. It was worth all the gold of Bonanza; within two years, lots sold for as much as five thousand dollars a front foot on the main street.

Ladue headed for Fortymile to register his site, but on the way he met a man who wanted timber to build a house. Ladue's agile imagination saw a thousand houses rising on the swampland. Back in his tracks he turned, sending his application down to the police by runner. At Ogilvie he loaded his raft with all the available dressed lumber, then floated his sawmill to the new townsite. Soon he had a rough warehouse built, and a little cabin for himself which did duty as a saloon. It was the first building in the new mining camp, which Ladue had already named Dawson City after George M. Dawson, a government geologist.

By this time Rabbit Creek had a new name. A miners' meeting hastily convened on a hillside had given it the more romantic title of "Bonanza." Carmack's strike was scarcely five days old, but already the valley was a scene of frenzied confusion. Men were ramming their stakes in anywhere, jumping their neighbours' claims, arguing and scrambling for ground, and convening mass meetings which, in spite of their grass-roots democracy, served only to produce more anarchy. It took six months to straighten out the tangle.

At the Klondike's mouth the boats piled up on the beach, day and night, arriving as if by magic from the silent forests of the Upper Yukon Valley. Many of those who tumbled from them and floundered up the river acted like madmen in their desire to stake, and this was strange, for there were few who really believed that any gold lay in the region of the Klondike. They staked from force of habit, as they had staked so often before, and once this ritual was completed, often enough they forgot about it, or failed to record their ground, or sold it for a trifle. A Klondike claim was considered virtually worthless. If a man had enough food he stayed on, but many returned hungrily to Fortymile thinking they had found nothing.

And some did not bother to stake at all. Two men arrived at the mouth of the Klondike from the Indian River country and debated about going up. "I wouldn't go across the river on that old Siwash's word," said one, recalling Carmack's reputation, and on they went to Fortymile and oblivion without further ceremony. Another party argued for three hours at the river mouth, agreed in the end not to stake, and pushed off for Circle City.

Uly Gaisford, a barber from Tacoma, passed by the Klondike, still sick at heart over the infidelities of his wife, which had driven him to Alaska, and stunned by the boat wreck on the Pelly River that had cost him everything but the clothes on his back. He staked on Bonanza, but thought so little of the claim or of his own personal prospects that he went on to Circle City to take up barbering. To his later astonishment, his property produced for him fifty thousand dollars within a year.

Another trudged up Bonanza as far as *Twenty Above,* then shrugged his shoulders. "I'll leave it to the Swedes," he said, using the classic term of derision, for Scandinavians were alleged to work ground that no other man would touch. A companion drove his stakes into the neighbouring *Twenty-One,* then decided not to record. He wrote a wry comment on the stakes: "This moose pasture reserved for Swedes and Cheechakos." Along came Louis B. Rhodes of Fortymile, put his own name on the stakes, and wondered why he had bothered. For two bits, he told his friends, he'd cut it off again. Nobody had two bits, and so Rhodes stayed on and thanked his stars he had. By spring he was worth more than sixty thousand dollars and had staked all his cronies to mining properties.

It was the old-timers who were sceptical of Bonanza. The valley was too wide, they said, and the willows did not lean the proper way, and the water did not taste right. It was too far upriver. It was on the wrong side of the Yukon. It was moose pasture. Only the cheechakos were too green to realize that it could not contain gold, and this naïveté made some of them rich.

The men who staked were men who saw the Klondike as a last chance, men in poor luck, sick and discouraged, with nothing better to do than follow the siren call of a new stampede. Many of these sold their claims in the first week, believing them worthless, and many more tried vainly to sell, so that in that first winter two thirds of the richest properties in the Klondike watershed could have been purchased for a song. Most men were too poor to work their claims; they went back to Dawson or Fortymile to try to get work to raise funds. Others, infected by the excitement of the moment, simply wandered back and forth aimlessly up and down the valley.

Carmack himself could not start work at once. He was forced to cut logs for Ladue's mill to earn enough to feed himself, and even then was so short of funds that he could build only three lengths of sluicebox; as he had no wheelbarrow, he carried the gravel in a box on his back for one hundred feet to the stream to wash out the gold. In spite of this awkward arrangement, he cleaned up fourteen hundred dollars from surface prospects in less than a month. But even in the face of this evidence there were only a few men who believed religiously that there was actually gold in the valleys of the Klondike.

4: *The kings of Eldorado*

By the end of August all of Bonanza Creek had been staked, and new prospectors, arriving daily, were fanning out across the Klondike watershed looking for more ground. None realized it, but the richest treasure of all still lay undiscovered.

Down Bonanza, in search of unstaked ground, trudged a young Austrian immigrant named Antone Stander. For nine years, ever since he had landed in New York City from his home province of Unterkrien, Stander had been seeking his fortune in the remote corners of the continent, working as a cowboy, as a sheep-herder, as a farmer, as a coal-miner, and now as a prospector. When he arrived in the New World, unable to speak a word of English, he had just one dollar and seventy-five cents to his name, and after mastering the language and walking over most of North America on foot he was no richer. All his funds had been spent on the trip north in the spring of 1896. Now, on this last day of August, he was embarking on a final gamble.

He was a handsome man, just twenty-nine years old, with dark, curly hair and sensitive, romantic-looking features. As he reached the south fork of Bonanza Creek, a few hundred feet above Carmack's claim, he stopped to examine it curiously. Later Stander would look back upon this as the climactic moment of his life, for after this day nothing was ever again the same for him. The narrow wooded ravine, with a trickle of water snaking along its bottom, still had no name. The prospectors referred to it in Yukon parlance as "Bonanza's pup." It was soon to be known as Eldorado.

Stander arrived at the fork with four companions, all of whom had already staked on Bonanza. They had little faith in their property, but on an impulse they walked up the pup in a group and sank their pans into the sand. Like Stander, each had reached the end of the line financially. One, Jay Whipple, was an old prospector who had come down from the Sixtymile country. Another, Frank Keller, had been a railway brakeman in California. A third, J. J. Clements of New York, had almost starved to death the previous winter. The fourth, Frank Phiscator, a Michigan farm boy, had worked his way west, carrying the mail on horseback in order to earn enough money to come north. Now they stared into the first pan and, to their astonishment, saw that there was more than six dollars' worth of gold in the bottom. They had no way of knowing it, but this was the richest creek in the world. Each of the claims staked that day eventually produced one million dollars or more.

As Stander and his companions drove in their stakes, others up and down Bonanza began to sense by some curious kind of telepathy, that something tantalizing was in the wind. Louis Emkins, a leanfaced and rangy prospector from Illinois, was toiling up Bonanza when he saw will-o'-the-wisp campfires flickering among the bushes of the unexplored creek. It was enough to send the blood pulsing through his veins. He and his three companions quickened their pace and burst upon

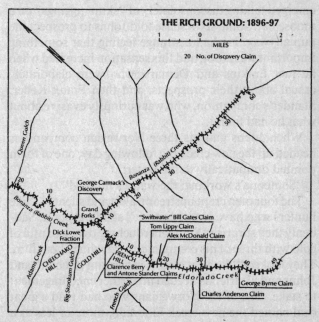

THE RICH GROUND: 1896-97

MILES

20 No. of Discovery Claim

Stander and the others, who tried to discourage the newcomers, saying that the prospects were small and only on the surface. Already the old code of the Pioneers was being thrown into discard.

Two of the men turned back at once, a fortune slipping from their grasp, but Emkins and his partner George Demars stayed on. *Seven* had already been staked illegally for a friend in Fortymile, but Emkins, a resolute figure with a forbidding black moustache, would have none of it. He tore up the stakes and substituted his own and by that single action made himself wealthy. Within a year he was able to sell out for more than one hundred thousand dollars.

William Johns, a black-bearded and rawboned ex-newspaper reporter from Chicago, was at the mouth of Eldorado when Emkins's two discouraged comrades emerged talking disconsolately of "skim diggings" on a moose flat. Some sixth sense told Johns to prospect the pup anyway. He had a strange feeling that something important was afoot, and this sensation increased when he met Emkins and Demars, who were elaborately casual about their prospects, and then Frank Keller, Stander's companion, who was curiously evasive about what he had found.

When Johns and his three Norwegian companions headed up the new creek the following day, one of them pointed dramatically to the water:

"Someone's working; the water's muddy!"

The four men crept upstream, alert and silent — "like hunters who have scented game," as Johns put it. Suddenly they surprised Stander crouching over a panful of gold with three of his companions crowding about him. They looked "like a cat caught in a cream pitcher," and Johns and his friends needed no further encouragement to stake. One of the Norwegians who had read a great deal named the new creek Eldorado, more or less as a joke, but, as it turned out, the title was entirely appropriate.

To the newcomers, however, this narrow cleft in the wooded hills was just another valley with good surface prospects. These really meant very little, for gold lying in the gravels on the creek's edge did not necessarily mean that the valley was rich. Before that could be determined, someone would have to go through the arduous labour of burning one or more shafts down at least fifteen feet to bedrock, searching for the "pay-streak" (which might not exist), hauling the muck up by windlass to the surface, and washing it down to find out how much gold there really was. This back-breaking labour could easily occupy two months. Even then it was pure guesswork to estimate a claim's true worth. Until the spring thaw came and the rushing creek provided enough head of water to wash thoroughly the gravels drawn up the shaft all winter, no one could really say exactly how rich Eldorado was — if, indeed, it was rich at all.

Most of the men who staked claims on the new creek in that first week had already done their share of prospecting. They had sunk shafts and shovelled gravel on creek after creek in the Yukon watershed without success. To them this little pup looked exactly like any other in the territory. If anything, it looked scrawnier and less attractive. To most men, then, Eldorado was as much of a gamble as the Irish sweepstakes. Some, such as Stander, determined to take the gamble and hold their ground and work it to see whether it really did contain gold. Others decided to sell out at once for what they could get. Still others bravely set out to take the risk and then got cold feet and sold before the prize was attained.

Nobody then knew, of course, that this was the richest placer creek in the world, that almost every claim from *One* to *Forty* was worth at least half a million, that some were worth three times that amount, and that a quarter of a century later dredges would still be taking gold from the worked-over gravels.

But in that first winter enormous untapped fortunes changed hands as easily as packages of cigarettes, and poor men became rich and then poor again without realizing it. Jay Whipple, for instance, sold claim *One* almost immediately, for a trifle. The purchaser, a lumberman from Eureka, California, named Skiff Mitchell, lived for half a century on the proceeds.

Frank Phiscator, on *Two,* saw fortune slipping from his grasp on two occasions, but in each instance retrieved it. He had scarcely hammered his stakes into the ground when F. W. "Papa" Cobb, known as one of Harvard's best quarterbacks, tried to seize it from him. Cobb insisted that Phiscator already had a claim on Bonanza, therefore could not legally stake a second one on Eldorado. This was true, but Constantine of the Mounted Police, who always tempered justice with common sense, decided that Cobb was too greedy since he could easily have staked close to Phiscator without causing a fuss. Thus did a fortune elude Cobb. Yet Phiscator thought so little of his claim that he sold half of it for eight hundred dollars, only to buy it back later in the year for fifteen thousand.

Charles Lamb, who had been dismissed from his job as a Los Angeles streetcar conductor and had come north as the result of a swindle, hung on to claim *Eight.* Two years later he and his partner sold it for three hundred and fifty thousand dollars.

George Demars sold half of *Nine* for eight hundred dollars. Within three years it was valued at a million.

William Johns, the newspaperman, immediately sold half his claim, *Twelve,* for five hundred dollars and considered himself lucky to unload it. Three months

68

later he sold the other half for twenty-five hundred. The claim was one of the richest on the creek.

On September 5, a few days after Eldorado was discovered, the Alaska Commercial Company's steamer *Alice* arrived at the Klondike loaded with men from Fortymile, and the rest of the creek was quickly staked.

A group of Scotsmen from the British Columbia coal-mining town of Nanaimo staked *Fourteen, Fifteen, Sixteen,* and *Seventeen.* Rather than keep all their eggs in one basket, they abandoned *Sixteen* and *Seventeen* in order to retain staking rights on another creek. The other creek turned out poorly, but *Sixteen* was the most incredible claim of all Eldorado. It was re-staked by a muscular, God-fearing young man named Thomas Lippy, who had been a YMCA physical instructor in Seattle and had thrown up everything the previous spring because a hunch told him to head north. Lippy had already staked higher up on Eldorado, but, because his wife was with him and wanted to live in a cabin, he decided to move down the creek where the timber was better. It was a providential move. There was little gold in the upper reaches of Eldorado, but *Sixteen* produced $1,530,000 for Lippy.

Two of the Nanaimo boys next door to Lippy got cold feet when their shaft reached the eighteen-foot level. They were unsure of finding gold and were happy to sell out their interests to Bill Scouse and his two brothers for fifty thousand dollars each. A third man hung on. His share of the clean-up that spring came to fifty thousand, and there were hundreds of thousands left in the ground.

On the other side of Lippy's claim was *Seventeen,* also rejected by the Nanaimo group. It was staked by French Joe Cazalais, who sold it almost immediately for six hundred dollars to Arkansas Jim Hall, a veteran of ten years in the Yukon, and to his partner, a French-

Canadian squaw man, N. E. Picotte. The pay-streak on this claim was the widest in the country, extending five hundred feet from rim to rim, and when Picotte and Hall discovered how rich it was, they gave French Joe seventy-five feet of it as a consolation prize.

So the roulette wheel spun around on Eldorado. Al Thayer and Winfield Oler had staked out *Twenty-Nine* and, believing it worthless, returned to Fortymile, looking for a sucker on whom to unload it. They found their quarry in Jimmy Kerry's saloon in the person of Charley Anderson, a thirty-seven-year-old Swede with a pinched face, who had been mining for several years out of Fortymile. Anderson was so doubtful of the Klondike that he had delayed his trip to the new field until all the ground was gone. Now he was drinking heavily, and Oler, a small and slender man from Baltimore, saw his chance. Anderson woke up the next morning to find he had bought an untried claim for eight hundred dollars. He went to the police post to ask Constantine to retrieve his money for him, but the policeman pointed out that his signature was on the title. Anderson glumly headed for Eldorado. He had no way of knowing yet that a million dollars' worth of gold lay in the bedrock under his claim and that for the rest of his life he would bear the tag of "the Lucky Swede." As for Oler, he became the butt of so many jokes that he fled the country in disgust.

Next door to Charley Anderson, on *Thirty,* the groundwork for the most staggering fortune of all was being laid. The claim had been staked by Russian John Zarnowsky, who thought so little of it that he let half of it go for a sack of flour and a side of bacon. The purchaser was an elephantine Nova Scotian known as "Big Alex" McDonald, who until this moment had known neither weal nor leisure. But the pay-streak on *Thirty* was forty feet wide, and a man could, and did, pan five thousand dollars from it in a single day. With this purchase McDonald began his lightning ascent from unlettered day-labourer to Dawson aristocrat. Any ordinary creature would have been content with this single piece of ground which was rich enough to maintain a platoon for a lifetime, but McDonald was not ordinary. This fortuitous acquisition unleashed within him some hitherto inactive demon, which drove him on for the remainder of his days with an intensity of purpose in sharp contrast to his ponderous appearance. Because of his size and his awkward movements McDonald was known as the Big Moose from Antigonish. He spoke slowly and painfully, rubbing his blue jowls in perplexity, his great brow almost hidden by a shock of sable hair, his heavy lips concealed by a moustache of vaudevillean proportions. The effect was primeval, but Big Alex, in spite of his Neanderthal appearance, was one of the shrewdest men in the North. While others sold, he bought — and he continued to buy as long as there was breath in his body. Within a year he was famous, hailed on three continents as "the King of the Klondike," sought out by Pope, prince, and promoter.

And yet, who is to say which were the lucky ones in the Eldorado lottery? Many who sold out and left the country ended their lives in relative comfort. Many who stayed behind to dig out fortunes lost all in the end. William Sloan, a Nanaimo dry-goods merchant who sold his interest in *Fifteen* for fifty thousand dollars and turned his back on the Klondike forever, invested his money wisely and rose to become a cabinet minister in British Columbia's provincial government. His son became Chief Justice of that province. But the King of the Klondike died penniless and alone.

5: *Henderson's luck*

All this while, on the other side of the Bonanza watershed, Robert Henderson continued to toil at his open cut on the creek he had wistfully named Gold Bottom. Boats were arriving daily at Dawson; shacks were being clapped together helter-skelter on valley and mud flat; Bonanza was staked for fourteen miles and Eldorado for three; and men were spraying across the whole of the Klondike country searching for new discoveries. Henderson knew nothing of this: he had seen no one but his partners since that August day when Carmack had gone off, promising to send word back if he found anything on the other side of the blue hills.

Then one day — some three weeks after the strike — Henderson looked up and saw a group of men coming down from the divide. He asked them where they had come from, and they replied: "Bonanza Creek."

The name puzzled Henderson, who prided himself on a knowledge of the country. He did not like to show his ignorance, but finally curiosity overcame pride. Where was Bonanza Creek?

The newcomers pointed back over the hill.

"Rabbit Creek! What have you got there?" Henderson asked, with a sinking feeling.

"We have the biggest thing in the world."

"Who found it?"

"McCormick."

Henderson flung down his shovel, then walked slowly over to the bank of the creek and sat down. It was some time before he could speak. McCormick! Carmack! For the rest of his life the sound of that name would be like a cold knife in his heart. The man was not even a prospector. . .

When he gathered his wits about him, Henderson realized that he must record a claim at once before the

72

human overflow from Bonanza arrived at his creek. He had explored a large fork of Gold Bottom and discovered much better ground yielding thirty-five cents to the pan. Here he had staked a discovery claim, and it was this that he intended to record at Fortymile. He divided up his small gleaning of gold with his partners and set off at once.

But Fate had not yet finished with Robert Henderson. He had moved only a short way down the creek before he encountered two long-time prospectors. He knew them both. One was Charles Johnson, tall, bearded, and tough as a whalebone, a farmer and logger from Ohio; the other was Andrew Hunker, better known as "Old Man Hunker," a native of Wittenberg, Germany, a man with chiselled features and a dogged face who made a practice of reading Gibbon nightly and who carried six volumes of the *Decline and Fall* about with him. Both men were veteran prospectors of the Yukon Valley and of the Cariboo before that.

Hunker now revealed to Henderson that he, too, had staked a discovery claim on the other fork of Gold Bottom Creek. The partners had got as much as two and a half dollars a pan from a reef of high bedrock, and they were carrying twenty-five dollars' worth of coarse gold with them, all of it panned out in a few minutes. Obviously the Hunker claims were far richer than the ones Henderson had staked.

What was Henderson to do? A discovery claim was twice the size of an ordinary claim. He could insist on his own prior discovery and take a thousand feet of relatively poor ground. But it would be a Pyrrhic victory, since the richer ground was obviously in the area of Hunker's find. The only answer was to allow Hunker the discovery claim and for Henderson to stake an ordinary claim of five hundred feet next to it. Thus the entire watershed became known as Hunker Creek, and only the fork which Henderson originally located was called Gold Bottom.

Henderson, having swallowed this second bitter pill, pushed on down the Klondike Valley. Soon a new prize was dangled before him. He ran into a Finn named Solomon Marpak who had just made a discovery on another tributary of the Klondike called Bear Creek. Henderson staked next to Marpak, his spirits rising; Bear Creek looked rich.

He now believed he had three claims to record — on Gold Bottom, on Hunker, and on Bear — but when he reached Fortymile, Fate dealt him a third blow. He was told that the law had been changed: no man was allowed more than one claim in the Klondike mining district, and that claim must be recorded within sixty days of staking. In vain Henderson protested that when he had staked his ground the law had allowed a claim on each creek, with no deadline for recording. The mining recorder did not know him. Henderson swallowed hard and recorded only the Hunker Creek claim.

"I only want my just dues and nothing more, but those discoveries rightly belong to me and I will contest them as a Canadian as long as I live," he said with force and bitterness. And so began the long controversy over which man was the rightful discoverer of the Klondike. It rages still, and almost always along national lines: the English and Canadians say that Henderson should have the credit; the Americans stand by Carmack.

Henderson's troubles were not over. Indeed, it might be said that they never ended. All through the following winter he lay ill from the old injury to his leg. He was unable to work his claim, but he refused to be disheartened, and the following year, when his injury healed, he was off again. A less restless man might have gone to work on the Hunker claim, which was obviously a good one, but it was typical of Henderson that he ignored it in order to continue the search for new gold-fields. He trudged the length of Too Much Gold Creek, which contained no gold at all, and then, still supremely optimistic, headed for the Stewart River country. Here, too, he searched in vain, though he left his name behind on one of the Stewart's smaller tributaries. At last he decided to return to his wife and children in Colorado, whom he had not seen for four years. He boarded a steamboat for St. Michael, anxious to be away, and here, for the fifth time, ill-luck descended upon him. The steamer was frozen in at Circle City, and Henderson, trapped in the country which had brought him nothing but misfortune, fell sick again. In order to pay his medical bills he was forced to sell his claim on Hunker Creek. He received three thousand dollars for it, and that represented the total amount that he took from the Klondike district. Yet each of the claims that he had staked and tried to record was worth a great deal. The Hunker claim eventually paid a royalty on four hundred and fifty thousand dollars, after which it was sold for another two hundred thousand. For decades it continued to be a valuable property, but Henderson got none of it.

He reached St. Michael ultimately, the following spring, and boarded a steamer for Seattle. He had eleven hundred dollars left in Klondike gold, but his troubles were still not over. The years spent in the country of the open cabin door had not equipped him for civilization's wiles. Before he reached Seattle all his gold had been stolen. Disgusted and disconsolate, he tore an emblem from his lapel and handed it to Tappan Adney, the correspondent for *Harper's Illustrated Weekly*.

"Here, you keep this," he cried. "I will lose it, too. I am not fit to live among civilized men."

Adney examined the little badge curiously. It was the

75

familiar insignia of the Yukon Order of Pioneers, with
its golden rule and its motto: "Do unto others as you
would be done by."

Chapter Three

1: *Clarence Berry strikes it rich*

The story of the Klondike is remarkable for the fact that in an extraordinary number of cases the industrious and sober prospector profited little from the goldfields, while the ne'er-do-wells and profligates often amassed great, if temporary, wealth. It was perhaps coincidental that Horatio Alger, Jr., should die when the great stampede reached its climax, but it is certainly true that many Klondike success stories made mincemeat out of his accepted formula. It seemed almost axiomatic that the Harpers and the Hendersons should seek but never find, while the Swiftwater Bills and the Diamond-Tooth Gerties retained the golden touch. There was, however, one shining exception. The tale of Clarence Berry and his gold is unique in the annals of the stampede.

Berry, a one-time fruit farmer from Fresno, California, not only made millions as a result of the strike, but he also died at a ripe age with his millions intact. His history is marked by none of those anecdotes of personal eccentricity that enliven so many Klondike legends. He was sober, honest, hard-working, ambitious, and home-loving, and he stayed that way. Of all the original locaters on Bonanza and Eldorado, there is scarcely one other to whom those statements apply.

Berry owed his fortune to an encounter in Bill McPhee's saloon with Antone Stander, the Austrian who had staked on Eldorado. The handsome Stander was back in Fortymile, without funds, without food, and, to his pain and bewilderment, without credit at the Alaska Commercial Company's store. It had been refused him by the company's newly appointed agent in charge of the entire Yukon Valley, a merchant of aristocratic tendencies whom the company's own history describes as arrogant and dictatorial. His name was

Edgar Mizner, and his two brothers, Addison the architect and Wilson the *bon vivant*, wit, and playwright, were to become engaging if eccentric figures in the folklore of twentieth-century America. Edgar lacked their charm. He did not believe in McQuesten's system of unlimited credit and was heartily disliked by the miners, who called him "the Pope" and dispatched letters of protest about him to the company's office. When Stander arrived back in Fortymile he discovered he would need a guarantor before the A.C. store would advance him provisions. He was desperately seeking a friend when Berry, who had been tending bar in McPhee's saloon, volunteered to help him. The grateful Stander traded Berry half of his Eldorado property for half of a claim that Berry had staked on Upper Bonanza. With this simple gesture Berry laid the foundations for one of the largest personal fortunes to come out of the Klondike.

Berry had gone north in 1894 as a last resort, a victim of the depression of the nineties, purchasing his outfit and passage with money borrowed at exorbitant interest. A giant of a man with the biceps of a blacksmith and the shoulders of a wrestler, his magnificent strength sustained him when his fellows faltered. Of a party of forty that crossed the Chilkoot, only Berry and two others reached Fortymile. All the rest turned back, discouraged, after a storm destroyed their outfits. But Berry would not give up; he pushed ahead relentlessly with little more than the clothes on his back. A year later he trekked out to California, married his childhood sweetheart, a sturdy waitress from Selma named Ethel Bush, again started off for Alaska, his bride strapped to a sleigh which Berry dragged over the mountains and down the river to Fortymile. He found no gold, so he went to work tending bar for Bill McPhee and in this way was on the spot when Carmack entered

79

with his shellful of nuggets. With a grubstake provided by the open-handed McPhee, Berry left at once for Bonanza, where he staked *Forty Above*, and it was this claim that he now divided with Stander in the shrewd belief that Eldorado was a much richer creek.

That fall, while Ladue's sawmill was turning out rough lumber for the first of Dawson's buildings, while Carmack was treating his friends to drinks at fifty dollars a round, while old-timers continued to jeer and newcomers scouted the valleys for new ground, the industrious Berry and one or two others set about the slow work of burning shafts through the permafrost to bedrock to find out just how much gold there was in the Klondike Valley.

On *Twenty-One Above* Bonanza, Louis Rhodes was also reluctantly grubbing his way down through the frozen muck. He felt a bit of a fool, for his neighbours were laughing at him, but when he tried to sell out for two hundred and fifty dollars there were no takers, and so he kept working. On October 3, at a depth of fifteen feet, he reached bedrock.

The results were electrifying. In the soft rock he could spy, by guttering candlelight, broad seams of clay and gravel streaked with gold. This was the pay-streak; he had hit the old creek channel squarely on his first try. It was so rich that he was able to hire workmen on the spot and to pay them nightly by scooping up a few panfuls of dirt from the bottom of the shaft.

Heartened by this news, Berry kept working until early in November he too reached bedrock. From a single pan of paydirt he weighed out fifty-seven dollars in gold and knew at once that his days of penury were over. He and Stander began to hire men to help them haul the dirt up by windlass and pile it on the great "dump" which, when the spring thaw came, would be shovelled into sluiceboxes so that the gold could be washed free of the clay and gravel.

Shortly after Berry reached bedrock on *Six* Eldorado, the three Scotsmen on *Fifteen* made an even more spectacular strike. The actors in this drama were Bill Scouse and his two brothers, who had worked in coal mines from Pennsylvania to Nanaimo. Bill Scouse was on the windlass and his brother Jack down in the shaft hoisting up heavy buckets of gravel, sand, and clay. Suddenly one bucket appeared whose contents were quite different from the others. Nuggets stuck out from the gravel like raisins in a pudding, and fine gold glistened everywhere.

"What in hell do you think you've sent up, the Bank of England?" Scouse is supposed to have called down the shaft.

"What's up — have we struck it?" came the faint reply.

"Come up and have a look; it will do your blooming eyes good." The two joined the third brother in the cabin, first sprinkling sand over the two pans of paydirt to disguise the find. They asked him to pan the gold out, and when he saw the result he thought he had gone mad. In the two pans were more than four hundred dollars.

These first three claims, Rhodes's, Berry's, and Scouse's, proved that the Klondike was one of the world's richest mining areas — not rich in total quantity, as it turned out, but certainly rich in the wealth of some of the individual claims. Until this time, ten-cent pans had been considered rich. Before the season was out, some men would be getting as much as eight hundred dollars from a single pan of selected paydirt.

Berry and Stander were able to pay their workmen with gold dug out on the spot. They bought the two adjoining claims, *Four* and *Five*, from the original stakers of Eldorado, J. J. Clements and Frank Keller, and eventually split this block of claims in half, Stander taking the lower half and Berry the upper. Berry alone took one hundred and forty thousand dollars from his winter dump the following spring.

Now the Klondike was a frenzy of excitement as every claim-owner began to burrow into the frozen earth. Glowing in the long nights with a hundred miners' fires, the valleys looked like the inferno itself. Those who had scoffed at Rhodes and Berry could now peer down their shafts and literally see the nuggets glittering in the candle's rays.

But some sceptics had staked claims and then left the area without bothering to record. Under the new mining law, these were due to fall open again in sixty days, and a wild scramble ensued for ground that had once been shrugged off as moose pasture. The most memorable of such contests took place early in November on Upper Bonanza and provided an incident in one of Jack London's Klondike novels.

It was a garish scene, for more than a dozen prospectors had decided to re-stake the same claim, and these milled about the site waiting for the midnight hour when the ground would fall open. So tense was the situation that Constantine stationed police on the claim to prevent trouble. Then, as the deadline approached, the farcical nature of the situation was perceived by all, and, one by one, the contestants dropped out until only two die-hards were left, a Scotsman and a Swede. Having prepared their stakes in advance, these two moved stubbornly to a starting-line, where, on the stroke of midnight, a policeman called time and the race began. With feverish intensity the two men hammered in their stakes and dashed off down Bonanza neck and neck.

Out onto the frozen Yukon the rivals sped behind fast dog-teams, each realizing that the recorder's office at the Fortymile police post closed at four p.m. and did not reopen until nine the next morning. Over the humpy ice they slid and tumbled, passing and repassing one another until, weary hours later, the blurred outlines of the log town loomed out of the cold fog. At this moment, with the goal in view, the Scotsman's dogs began to flag, and he leaped from his sled, determined to finish on foot, the Swede instantly following suit. The two reached the barrack gate in a dead heat, but, being unfamiliar with the post, the Swede raced for the largest building, which was the officers' quarters, while the Scot, knowing the layout, let him pass, made a sharp turn to the right, and just managed to reach the door of the recording office. Unable to cross the six-inch threshold, he fell prone upon it, crying with his remaining breath: *"Sixty Above* on Bonanza!" An instant later the Swede toppled across him, gasping out the same magic phrase. When Constantine was recruited to play Solomon, he advised the pair to divide the ground, which in the end they did. It was one of the small ironies of the Klondike that the claim turned out to be entirely worthless.

2: *The death of Circle City*

All this time Circle City, two hundred and twenty miles down stream, had remained in ignorance of the Klondike strike. An occasional rumour drifted into town with the thickening ice — and was disbelieved. Sam Bartlett, for instance, floated in one day before freeze-up on a raft of logs, but all he told his friends was that Ladue was trying to hoax the country so that he might profit from his new townsite.

Into Oscar Ashby's smoky saloon, ten days before Christmas, came J. M. Wilson, of the Alaska Commercial Company, and Thomas O'Brien, an independent trader. They brought gold from Eldorado and a bundle of mail. Ashby read one of the letters to a group of

83

seventy-five men who crowded into the bar to hear it, but their reaction was one of scepticism.

" 'This is one of the richest strikes in the world,' " Ashby read. " 'It is a world-beater. I can't tell how much gold we are getting to the pan. I never saw or heard the like of such a thing in my life. I myself saw one hundred and fifty dollars panned out of one pan of dirt and I think they are getting as high as a thousand. . . .' "

The crowd had heard this kind of talk before in other letters from other distant creeks, and they laughed uproariously, ordered drinks all round, and then forgot about it.

But two old-time sourdoughs, Harry Spencer and Frank Densmore, received a second letter from their partner, Bill McPhee, the Fortymile saloon-keeper who had grubstaked Berry; and Densmore, who was nobody's fool, fitted up a dog-team and decided to see what was what. He was a respected man who had been fourteen years in the country and had tramped across most of Alaska. Indeed, long before Mount McKinley, the highest peak on the continent, received its name, it was known as Densmore's Mountain because this two-hundred-pound pioneer was the first white man to see it at close range. Therefore, when Densmore sent back word that the Klondike was really as reported, every man knew that something extraordinary had happened.

By this time, more news had arrived. In January, Arthur Treadwell Walden, a well-known dog-driver, walked into Harry Ash's saloon, threw a bundle of letters on the bar, and asked for a cup of hot beef tea (for dog-drivers did not dare drink whiskey in the winter). Ash paid no attention to the request, but began to riffle feverishly through the mail. He looked the part of the bartender of the nineties, with his round, florid face, his curly moustache, and his slick, centre-parted haircut,

84

but he was as much prospector as saloon-keeper. He had been a stampeder in the Black Hills country of South Dakota, and he had sensed for some time that something unusual was afoot upriver. Finally he found the letter he was looking for, tore it open, and devoured it. It confirmed what he had suspected.

"Boys, help yourself to the whole shooting match," he shouted, leaping over the bar. "I'm off to the Klondike."

An orgy followed. Men smashed the necks off bottles and drained them while others rushed about Circle trying to buy dogs at any price. The normal value of a sled-dog was between twenty-five and fifty dollars, but the price leaped immediately to two hundred and fifty, and then to fifteen hundred. Cabins once valued at five hundred dollars were now worthless, for Circle's gay days were ended. Only Jack McQuesten stayed behind to minister to the handful of miners who continued to work the Birch Creek claims.

All that winter and all that spring the residents of Circle straggled up the frozen Yukon in twos and threes, the affluent racing behind dog-teams over the hummocks of ice, the poor dragging their sleds by hand. All of Alaska, it seemed, was moving towards the Klondike.

The lives of many of these trudging figures were to be changed by the events of the year. One in particular was heading for the traditional fame and fortune. He was a former Texas marshal, just twenty-six years old, with knit brows and a pencil-thin moustache, who had come to Alaska the previous year. His name was George Lewis Rickard, but his friends called him Tex. It took him and his partner twenty days to pull a sled-load of provisions up the river that February, but when they reached the Klondike they were able to buy a half-interest in *Three Below* Bonanza. They sold it almost at once for twenty thousand dollars and bought an interest in *Four Below,* which they sold for thirty thousand dollars. It was the start of the career that led Tex Rickard to Madison Square Gardens in New York as the greatest fight-promoter of his day.

In the procession up the river that spring were two middle-aged women — a Mrs. Adams, who was a dressmaker and would shortly be making thirty dollars a day with her needle, and a Mrs. Wills, a laundress of apparently inexhaustible energy. Mrs. Wills had gone north in 1895 to try to support her invalid husband, vowing she would not return until she had made her fortune. On reaching Dawson she staked a claim and then turned cook to finance her mining project. She bought a stove, baked bread, and sold it for a dollar a loaf until she had cleared the two hundred and fifty dollars she needed to purchase a single box of starch. With this she was able to set up a laundry and pay for the labour of her mine. This determined and enterprising little creature fought off every attempt to jump her claim, held it against all comers, and, when it began to pay off, refused with disdain an offer of a quarter of a million dollars.

Of the seventy-score men and women who made that long trek up to Dawson from Circle City, there was one who had no interest in gold, no desire for material wealth. This was a Jesuit missionary named William Judge, a one-time apprentice in a Baltimore planing mill, who for the last dozen years had been a servant of the Lord in Alaska. His fellow travellers eyed him curiously — an emaciated man with a skull-like face, high cheek-bones, and huge cavernous eyes, accentuated by small gold-rimmed spectacles. He was ill-nourished, for he had loaded his sled with medicine and drugs rather than food; and he trudged along in harness with his single dog in order to preserve the animal's

86

strength. The new camp, he knew, would soon be facing plague, and he was determined to build a hospital with all possible dispatch. They called him "the Saint of Dawson"; death was already written across his face.

All spring, until the ice broke, the ill-assorted procession made its way up the river. In the end McQuesten himself joined it, for there was nothing left for him at Circle. He was too late to stake the rich ground, but he managed to secure a small-paying claim that netted him about ten thousand dollars. It was the largest sum of money he had ever known.

3: *The birth of Dawson*

The new arrivals found a tent town stretched along the margin of the Yukon near the Klondike's mouth. By January there were only four houses in Dawson besides Ladue's, but the tents, like dirty white sails, were scattered in ragged order between the trees on the frozen swampland. It was not an ideal townsite; but it was close to the source of gold.

No one in the outside world yet knew of the existence of the burgeoning camp or of the gold that nourished it. In Fortymile, William Ogilvie, the Canadian government surveyor, was searching about for some means to apprise his government of the situation. Scarcely anyone was attempting the tortuous journey up the river to the Chilkoot Pass, but Captain William Moore, a remarkably tough septuagenarian, offered to take a brief message. Moore was a steamboat man who had been in almost every gold rush from Peru to the Cassiars and who now made his home on Skagway Bay, at the foot of the Coast Mountains. At the age of seventy-three, when most men were over the hill of life, the white-bearded old pioneer was going strong. He had accepted a contract to bring the Canadian mail across the mountains and into the interior of the Yukon, and when his U.S.

counterpart failed to deliver, Moore took on his job too. That fall of 1896 he had already been down the river to Circle City and was now heading back again like a man on a Sunday jaunt when he picked up Ogilvie's message. Moore put all other mushers to shame; three young men, strong and vigorous, had all started from Fortymile the previous week in an attempt to make a record trip to the coastal Panhandle. When the aged mail-carrier overhauled the trio, they were exhausted and starving. Moore popped them onto his dog-sled and whisked them out to Juneau without further mishap. As far as Ogilvie was concerned, the trip, though memorable, was a waste of time. His preliminary report of the Klondike went on to Ottawa, where nobody paid any attention to it.

On January 21, Ogilvie tried again, sending a note by another dog-driver and reporting that the new camp gave promise of being the greatest yet in the Northwest Territories and one that might startle the world. This intelligence did not reach Ottawa until the early spring, when it methodically moved through civil-service channels and was eventually published in an austere little pamphlet which caused not a ripple of interest.

No further news left the Yukon until mid-June, when the conscientious Ogilvie, squatting on the riverbank, scribbled a short report to the Minister of the Interior, estimating the season's output at two and a half million dollars. He gave the note to two men in a canoe who were travelling fast, but by the time the report was digested in Ottawa, others had carried the story to the world in more dramatic circumstances.

If no news was leaking out, neither was any seeping in. The last arrivals in January brought in some two-month-old newspapers which a friend in Seattle had sent to Dick Butler and Charley Myers. Prospectors from all over the valley crowded into their cabin on

Eldorado to read the three-month-old news: Queen Victoria was ill, and so was Pope Leo XIII; war was imminent between England and Russia; and a fight was being promoted between James J. Corbett and Bob Fitzsimmons. There was no further news until May, and so the whole camp devoured the papers again and again, advertisements and all, dropping nuggets into a contribution box until Butler and Myers had four hundred dollars for their Seattle crony.

As the town of Dawson slowly took shape around Ladue's sawmill and saloon, a subtle change began to work among those prospectors who for years had had nothing to call their own except a bill at Jack McQuesten's store. Accepted standards of wealth vanished. There was a desperate shortage of almost everything that a man needed, from nails to women. But there was no shortage of gold. Those who had struck it rich could claw the legal tender from the dumps with their bare hands; and thus, to many, gold became the cheapest commodity in the world.

No other community on the earth had a greater percentage of potential millionaires, yet all its citizens were living under worse conditions of squalor than any sharecropper. Food became so scarce that all but the most expensive dogs had to be killed because the owners did not have enough to feed them. Only the fortuitous arrival of a raftload of beef cattle saved the camp from starvation. Willis Thorpe, a Juneau butcher, sold the meat for sixteen thousand dollars; within a year he was worth two hundred thousand.

The story of the Klondike, at this point, provides a classic example of the workings of the law of supply and demand. Salt was so scarce that it fetched its weight in gold. One man paid two hundred dollars to have the tip of his finger amputated. Charley Anderson, the Lucky Swede, so badly wanted to build a sluicebox that he gave eight hundred dollars for a small keg of bent and blackened nails salvaged from a fire.

There was no writing-paper in Dawson and nothing to read save for Myers's newspapers and the labels on the packing-boxes. The only eggs came from two hens owned by a policeman's wife, and these cost a dollar apiece. Laundry was so expensive that most men wore their shirts until they could no longer stand them and then threw them away. One French Canadian turned a net profit by retrieving these garments, laundering them, and reselling them, often enough to the former owners. The camp's single bathhouse consisted of a small tent with a stove and up-ended log as a stool; for five minutes in a wooden laundry tub the unclean paid a dollar and a half.

The ante at stud poker was one dollar, but it might easily cost five hundred to see the third card. A night on the town — which meant a night in Joe Ladue's bareboarded saloon, drinking watered whiskey — could cost at least fifty dollars. Few minded the expense; it was so easy to pan out a few shovelfuls of dirt from the dump to pay for the fun. One man went to work in the morning and came back to town at night with fourteen hundred dollars in gold. In Ladue's he ordered two whiskeys, toasting his former self in the one and making believe his former self was drinking the other, then stuck two cigars in his mouth and smoked them together. This behaviour was less peculiar than it seemed, since it was undeniable that every man's life had been changed by the strike; on the day he reached the paystreak and realized that he was rich, he became a different person. Some men could no longer eat or sleep at the thought of mining so much gold. One, who had washed out thirty thousand dollars, became so obsessed by the fear of being robbed that he suffered a mental collapse and shot himself.

90

4: *A friend in need*

By midwinter the haphazard staking on the creeks had brought about a state of complete confusion. The original staking of Bonanza had been so frenzied and unorganized that both the ownership and the size of many claims were in dispute. Work stopped; men argued and fought; and by January, when William Ogilvie arrived to survey the Ladue townsite, the miners begged him to re-survey Bonanza and Eldorado. Ogilvie agreed on the condition that his decisions should be accepted as final.

Few men were better fitted for the task of unsnarling the Klondike tangle, where the shifting of stakes by a few feet might mean the loss or gain of thousands of dollars. Ogilvie was as incorruptible as he was scrupulous, and no one would dare attempt to bribe him. He firmly believed that no government servant should enrich himself by virtue of his position, and stubbornly refused to stake an inch of ground or to turn a single cent of profit from the Klondike strike. This sense of propriety had become an act of faith with Ogilvie, and he insisted that his son, Morley, who was with him, hew to the same creed. Only one other man in the Yukon felt the same way, and that was Charles Constantine, the NWMP superintendent, who also left the country poor but respected, though some of his constables staked out fortunes.

With his round, solemn face and his dark beard, Ogilvie had the features that were later to be associated with reigning British monarchs, but this gravity of appearance masked a puckish sense of humour. His whole character, indeed, was an unlikely alloy. The face that he presented to the public was that of the dedicated government official, punctilious and sedate. But in private he was a clever mimic, an unregenerate punster, a practical joker, and an accomplished raconteur known for his dialect recitations and for his ability to play anything on the piano, especially Scottish reels. He went about his tasks on Bonanza and Eldorado with professional seriousness, for his tidy civil-servant's mind was shocked by the raggedness of the original staking. At the same time he carefully filed away in the neat pigeonholes of his memory a small anthology of anecdotes which, embellished and sharpened, served him as after-dinner stories in the years that followed. He was both dismayed and amused, for instance, to discover the way in which one prospector — a Mounted Policeman at that — had located a claim in the twisting section of Lower Bonanza. Instead of measuring off five hundred feet in a straight line, as the law required, he had followed the wriggling line of the creek, which doubled back on itself in such a way that when Ogilvie surveyed it he discovered that the unfortunate policeman had got eight feet *less* than a claim.

As the maximum legal stake was five hundred feet, many oversize claims were chopped down by Ogilvie's survey, leaving thin wedges of land sandwiched in between the new boundaries. These fractional claims could be very valuable: one on Eldorado, for instance, just ten feet wide, was thought to be worth between ten and twenty thousand dollars, and another, a mere five inches wide, was sold to the owner of the adjacent claim for five hundred. Jim White, an Irishman from Circle City, was convinced there was a fraction between *Thirty-Six* and *Thirty-Seven* Eldorado. He staked it and used the ground in an effort to bully the owners on either side to come to terms with him. He waited on tenterhooks for Ogilvie's survey to set the proper dimensions. In order to madden White, whom he considered a scoundrel and a blackmailer, Ogilvie deliberately delayed the work. When the ground was finally surveyed, the fraction turned out to be just three inches wide. For the rest of his days its owner smarted under the nickname of Three-Inch White.

The richest fraction of all lay hidden on Bonanza Creek just above Carmack's discovery. Here, almost at the juncture of Bonanza, Eldorado, and Big Skookum Gulch, one John Jacob Astor Dusel had staked *Two Above*. In order to take in the mouth of the gulch, he had bitten off too much land. When Ogilvie measured the claim, he found left over a pie-shaped piece of ground eighty-six feet at its broadest point.

One of Ogilvie's chainmen, a Circle City prospector named Dick Lowe, gazed meditatively upon this sliver.

"Had you thought of staking it?" he asked Ogilvie.

"I am a government official and not permitted to hold property," the surveyor replied, as he had so often before. "You go down if you like and record."

Lowe felt at a loss. It was really a very small piece of ground, and if he staked it he would lose all rights to a bigger claim. On the other hand, he had reached the Klondike very late: there was not much left to stake.

He was a rugged and wiry ex-mule-skinner who had already made and lost one fortune. Years before, he had struck gold in the Black Hills and invested it all in a transportation outfit, only to have it wiped out by the rampaging Sioux. In the years that followed, he had trekked through Idaho, Montana, and Alaska, trying without success to recoup his losses. Now he was faced with a tricky decision. He told Ogilvie he would look for a larger fraction before staking the little wedge on Bonanza, but the search proved fruitless and he took the fraction. It did not excite him. He vainly tried to sell it for nine hundred dollars and then he tried to lease it, but there were no takers — it was just too small. In the end he decided to work it himself. He sank one shaft and found nothing. He sank another and in eight hours cleaned up forty-six thousand dollars. The claim eventually paid out half a million, and remains for its size the richest single piece of ground ever discovered. It could have been Ogilvie's — but in all the surveyor's letters, articles, pamphlets, and memoirs there is no hint of regret; indeed, it is doubtful if the possibility ever crossed his mind. As far as he was concerned, the gold might have been on the moon.

The fraction that came into Lowe's possession was situated on the most promising spot in the whole district. Two of the richest creeks, Bonanza and Eldorado, met here, pouring down their gold onto his property. A third stream, Big Skookum Gulch, cut directly through another ancient alluvial channel of whose hidden presence nobody was yet aware. Just above stood Gold Hill, still unnamed, still unstaked, but heavy with coarse gold, much of it washing down onto the property below.

Lowe's ground was so rich that a wire had to be strung along the border of his claim to prevent trespassers. Whenever a nugget was found along the boundary line, its ownership was determined by a plumb bob which slid along this invaluable wire. A single pan of paydirt, scooped up from the adjoining claim in August, 1899, a few feet from Lowe's fraction, yielded one thousand dollars in gold, including three large nuggets each worth one hundred dollars. It was said that as much gold was stolen from Lowe's property as he himself recovered from it, for in some places glittering pieces were visible from a distance of twenty feet. And, like all the others, Lowe was never the same man again. Almost from the moment of discovery, he got drunk and stayed that way.

After Lowe's strike, fractional claims assumed a greater importance, and Ogilvie tried to be dispassionately fair about them. When he discovered a fraction over the legal five hundred feet, his only way of making it known was to mark it on the posts bounding the end of the claim for any sharp-eyed stranger to see. Only in one memorable instance did he depart from this procedure.

It was a bitterly cold spring day, about ten below zero, and a biting wind was whistling up the trough of Eldorado when Ogilvie reached the upper limit of Clarence Berry's *Five*. Dusk was falling, and, as his assistants gathered up his instruments, the surveyor stood working out the figures in his notebook to see how long the claim really was. Around him was gathered the usual group of miners, all guessing at the claim's size; for months they had been searching and measuring on their own, hoping without success to discover a fraction on Eldorado. Now Ogilvie whistled in surprise when he discovered that *Five* was forty-one feet six inches too long. It was on this section of his claim, and on this section only — one of the richest locations in the history of placer mining — that Berry had done his winter's work. Hundred-dollar pans were the rule here; five-hundred-dollar pans were not unusual. Now it turned out that Berry did not own this rich sliver of land. Nor could he stake it, for he had used up his staking rights. His dump of paydirt stood on the fraction; it could not be washed out until spring. Ogilvie realized at once that if he announced the fraction Berry would lose everything he had worked for that winter, and also that a riot would probably ensue as dozens fought to stake ground known to be worth hundreds of thousands. And now in that conscientious mind, so used to the rule book, a struggle ensued; should he cling to procedure and take the consequences, or should he depart from the rigid path he had set himself? His solemn, bearded face did not change expression as, turning to Berry, who was standing near by, he said: "Let's go to supper. I'm cold enough and hungry enough to eat nuggets."

95

A ripple of suspicion ran through the throng, and Berry sensed it as Ogilvie hurried towards the cabin.

"Is there anything wrong, Mr. Ogilvie?"

"Come out of hearing," the surveyor whispered. He had made his decision.

"What's wrong?" cried Berry, in an agony of impatience. "My God, what's wrong?"

Ogilvie maintained his cracking pace. "There's a fraction forty-one feet six inches on claim number five, and nearly all your winter's work is on it."

"My God!" Berry almost shouted. "What will I do?"

Ogilvie's civil-servant mask returned. "It is not my place to advise you," he said. And then — another rent in the rule book: "Haven't you a friend you can trust?"

"Trust — how?"

"Why, to stake that fraction tonight and transfer it to yourself and partner."

Berry thought at once of George Byrne, who was at work on a claim five miles up Eldorado. He rushed to the cabin, told his wife to get supper for Ogilvie, then dashed up the creek.

He returned with Byrne about half past nine, and in the presence of a baffled Mrs. Berry a strange charade took place. The two men meticulously questioned Ogilvie about the proper method of legally staking a fraction, and Ogilvie replied courteously and impersonally. There was no suggestion that this was anything but an academic discussion, but the surveyor took the trouble to draw a detailed plan of the method of staking on a sheet of wrapping-paper, which he handed to Byrne. In the small hours of the morning Byrne staked the fraction, which in that single season produced for Berry one hundred and forty thousand dollars; in return Byrne got an equal length off the lower unworked end of the property so that Berry's block of land would remain unbroken. As Ogilvie wrote, "A friend like that, in such a need, is a friend indeed."

Ogilvie himself later that spring washed out a pan of dirt taken at random from Berry's shaft. On it was one hundred and nineteen dollars' worth of gold, or, as he remarked, "about half a year's salary for many a good clerk."

And yet Berry and his wife lived under the most primitive of conditions in a twelve-by-sixteen-foot hovel without floor or windows, whose only furniture was two home-made chairs and two rickety bedsteads built of unplaned lumber and curtained with calico. By the door stood a sheet-iron stove which the Berrys had packed in over the trail. Beside it was the panning-tank of dirty water in which one of Berry's twenty-five work-men periodically tested the paydirt.

A small glass kerosene lamp and a pair of copper gold-scales supplied the only other ornament.

The gold was everywhere. The wages Berry paid to-talled one hundred and fifty dollars a day, which he washed out himself each evening. When Mrs. Berry needed pocket-money, she merely walked to the dump and with a sharp stick smashed apart the frozen clods and pulled out the nuggets. One day she went down to call her husband for supper and, while she was waiting for him to come up the shaft, picked up fifty dollars' worth of coarse gold.

Ethel Berry's only female neighbour was Tom Lippy's wife Salome, a sinewy little woman from Kinsman, Ohio, who lived with her husband in another tiny mud-roofed cabin, about a mile up the valley. Lippy, like Berry, was industrious, sober, level-headed — and lucky. A sudden and inspired hunch had brought him to the Yukon; a blind trade had given him his present claim.

He had started life as an iron-moulder in Pennsylvania, but his almost fanatical belief in physical culture had led him into the YMCA and thence west to Seattle as a physical-training instructor. As a volunteer fireman he had once held the title of world's champion hose-coupler, and, like everybody else who came in over the trail, he was tough: solidly built, dark, good-looking, and clean-shaven, the prototype indeed of the Arrow Collar man. An injury to his knee had forced his retirement from the YMCA, and a strange intuition had sent him north in 1896 on borrowed money. Now he had one of the richest claims in the Klondike. Although this was the most memorable winter of Thomas Lippy's life, it certainly was not the happiest, for the Klondike, which gave him his fortune, took the life of his adopted son, and not all the gold in Eldorado could have saved him.

5: *Big Alex and Swiftwater Bill*

The winter passed slowly, dreamlike in its unreality. It was hard, sometimes, to disentangle tangibility from fantasy. In their dark hovels the miners watched in fascination and disbelief as the small heaps of gold accumulated in jars and bottles on the window-sills. Fortune, chimerical, seemed to be making game of them; and yet the gold was palpably there. It supplied the only ornament on the naked walls, glittering in the flat light of the sunless noons or in the precious luminescence of hoarded candles. In such a setting do myths have their beginning. It was a time for fancies and illusions; it was a time for fables; it was a time for legend.

Now, subtly, two of the most durable legends of the Klondike began to take form. One was the Legend of Big Alex McDonald, the King of the Klondike; the other was the Legend of Swiftwater Bill Gates, the

Knight of the Golden Omelet. Of all the human specimens placed on public exhibit by the great strike, none were destined for greater immortality than these two oddly dissimilar figures, the one a towering and sober Scot, the other a diminutive but flamboyant Yankee.

Both of these men acquired their fortunes because of the "lay" system which the lumbering and taciturn McDonald introduced into the Klondike. He had come to the north after fourteen years in the silver mines of Colorado and a stint at Juneau on the Panhandle. Although he had no money at all, he had developed a shrewd sense of values while working as a buyer of land for the Alaska Commercial Company, and by the time of the strike he had an abiding faith in the value of property that amounted to a religion.

While other men owned a single claim and worked it themselves, McDonald determined to own a great many and let others do the work. He began by acquiring half of *Thirty* Eldorado for a few groceries. He made no move to mine it, but instead let a section of it out on lease or "lay," as it was called, to Charley Myers and Dick Butler, receiving from them a percentage of the take. In the next forty-five days the two lay men took out thirty-three thousand dollars. McDonald got half.

As fast as the lay men gave him his share, McDonald bought more property. His policy was to make a small downpayment and give a note for the balance, payable at the time of the spring clean-up. To raise enough money for these downpayments he borrowed funds at exorbitant interest rates, and in some cases he paid as much as ten per cent for a ten-day loan, which is a rate of 365 per cent per annum.

By late spring McDonald's speculations were the talk of the camp. Clean-up time was approaching, and it was no longer possible to work in the drifts and shafts, which were filling with seepage. The miners were building flumes and log sluiceboxes and paying a higher price for the rough lumber than they would have paid for mahogany in New York. An air of expectancy hung over the camp. Not until the gold was washed out from the gravel of the winter dumps would anyone know exactly how much he was worth; until this process was completed it was mere guesswork.

Bets were laid as to whether Big Alex would be bankrupt or wealthy by summer. His creditors were demanding payment; his notes were falling due; and often enough he fulfilled his obligations at the last moment with gold still wet from the sluiceboxes. On one occasion Fate stepped in to save him from ruin. He owed forty thousand dollars to two brothers, and when the note fell due he still had not washed out enough gold to cover the debt. Then, at the eleventh hour, one of the brothers conveniently died. The ensuing litigation delayed all payments until McDonald was able to meet his obligations.

Before the summer of '97 was out, McDonald had interests in twenty-eight claims and his holdings were reckoned in millions of dollars. "I've invested my whole fortune," he remarked complacently, "I've run into debts of a hundred and fifty thousand dollars besides. But I can dig out a hundred and fifty thousand any time I need it."

The King of the Klondike presented a deceptively simple face to the world, with his painful articulation and his great ham hands and his blank oval visage, which rarely betrayed any animation; but the deals he made were often staggering in their complexity. In June of 1897 he walked into the tent office of Ron Crawford, a former Seattle court clerk who was setting up in business to draw up legal papers for prospectors. McDonald deposited his huge frame upon the three-legged stool in front of Crawford's rough spruce table and announced that he wished to borrow five thousand dollars. Crawford, who had just twenty-five cents to his name, asked him how much interest he was willing to pay.

"I don't want to pay interest," said McDonald in his slow way, rubbing his chin. "Interest is always working against you, and I can't sleep at night when I think of that. But if you let me have the money, I'll give you a lay of a hundred feet on *Six Below* Bonanza at fifty per cent. I'll also give you thirty-five per cent of thirty-five feet of *Twenty-Seven* Eldorado and a mortgage on *Thirty* Eldorado as security."

Considering the value of the three claims involved, this was an enormous sum to pay for the use of five thousand dollars. Crawford, stalling for time, promised to give McDonald an answer by morning. Then he rushed to a neighbouring saloon and raised five thousand dollars from the owner in return for a half-interest in the mortgage on *Thirty*. After the loan was made, Crawford sold part of his share of the section of *Twenty-Seven* for five thousand dollars to a Dawson barber. The barber worked it the following winter and took out forty thousand dollars.

McDonald's example was widely copied, and claims were swiftly carved up like so many apple pies, to be mortgaged, leased, traded, loaned, and lost. Carmack, for instance, sold half of Tagish Charley's claim for five thousand dollars. The purchaser made a five-hundred-dollar downpayment, and from a fourteen-foot tunnel took out eight thousand, from which he paid the balance. Ogilvie, who liked to work with figures, reckoned that on this basis the claim could be worth up to two and a half million.

"My God," cried the new owner aghast, "what will I do with all that money?"

"I wouldn't worry," Ogilvie told him. "It's hardly possible your claim will average anything like that," and he went on to reason that if the only wealth on the claim was on the one fourteen-foot strip, there would still be eighty-three thousand in the ground. "Which," he added dryly, "is enough to kill you."

It was this lay system that catapulted Swiftwater Bill Gates into the notoriety which he craved as fervently as McDonald craved property. Gates was one of a group of seven men who were finally persuaded to take a lay on *Thirteen* Eldorado, which, because of the jinx implied by its number, had been shunned by all. The new lay men sank seven shafts before they hit the paystreak, but when they did they saw at once that it was incredibly rich. To keep the find a secret, they burned in the sides of the shaft and then let it be noised about that they were getting a paltry ten cents to the pan. The owner, J. B. Hollingshead, was delighted that April to part with the property for forty-five thousand dollars, a sum which the new owners were able to dig from his former claim in just six weeks.

Until the moment of this discovery there was little to distinguish William F. Gates from his fellows. He was an unimpressive five foot five in height, and his moon face was ornamented by a straggling black moustache that gave his features a comic cast. Nobody had ever taken him seriously, even when, to attract attention, he boasted of his former prowess as a boatman on the Coeur d'Alene River in the placer district of Idaho. They laughed and dubbed him Swiftwater Bill.

Like most of his companions, Swiftwater Bill Gates was nearly destitute. But all he needed to transform his personality was gold. One season he was a nondescript dishwasher in Circle City, begging jobs from George Snow of the Opera House; the next he was a man in a Prince Albert coat, with a top hat, a white shirt with a

102

diamond stickpin in his tie, and the only starched collar in Dawson. It was said that Swiftwater Bill was so proud of this unique collar that he took to his bed while it was being laundered, rather than be seen without it. He was a small man; all his life he had been inconspicuous. He did not intend to remain inconspicuous any longer, and in this resolve he triumphed.

He could not wait for his share of the gold to be hoisted up the shaft of *Thirteen* Eldorado. He borrowed money at ten per cent a month so that he could play pool at a hundred dollars a frame, or throw his poke on the faro table and cry: "The sky's the limit! Raise 'er up as far as you want to go, boys, and if the roof's in your way, why tear it off!"

William Haskell, an old prospector, watched Swiftwater lose five hundred dollars in a few minutes one evening in '97.

"Things don't seem to be coming my way tonight," he said, rising casually from his seat. "Let's let the house have a drink at my expense."

The round cost him one hundred and twelve dollars. He threw his poke on the bar, lighted a dollar-fifty cigar, and strolled out.

Like Big Alex, he hired others to mine his property, but whereas Big Alex used all this time to acquire more gold, Swiftwater needed every waking moment to get rid of his. Like Big Alex, he paid his workers in land rather than in funds, and he paid them well. One of his helpers was a former milk-wagon driver from Seattle named Harry Winter, who worked one hundred days for Swiftwater and received in return a fifty-foot-square plot. From this ground he took five thousand dollars, and with that sum he bought from his former employer a second plot, thirty feet square. This, in turn, yielded eighty-five thousand, which meant that Swiftwater had, in effect, paid Winter eight hundred and fifty dollars a day for his labour.

Swiftwater Bill allowed no wine to touch his lips (though he occasionally bathed in it), but he indulged in other pleasures of the flesh. It was his habit to escort dance-hall girls in coveys to his claim and let them clamber down the shaft to pan out all the gold they wanted. They turned out to be as expert as seasoned miners.

Bill's favourite was Gussie Lamore, a comely strumpet of nineteen who had come to Dawson from Circle City in the spring rush, and who shared top billing with him in an incident which has become the liveliest of the Klondike's imperishable legends. Gussie, it developed, was inordinately fond of fresh eggs, possibly because they were as scarce as diamonds in the Dawson of 1897. One day, so the tale goes, Swiftwater Bill was seated in a restaurant when, to his surprise and chagrin, he saw Gussie enter on the arm of a well-known gambler. The pair ordered fried eggs, which were the most expensive item on the menu, and it was then that, in a fury of jealousy, Swiftwater achieved a certain immortality by buying up every egg in town in an attempt to frustrate Gussie's cravings.

There are many versions of this tale. Arthur Walden, the dogpuncher, who claimed in his memoirs to have witnessed the incident, wrote that Swiftwater had the eggs fried one at a time and flipped them through the window of the café to a rabble of dogs outside, commenting to the gathering crowd on the cleverness of the animals in catching them. Other versions have it that he presented the entire trove of eggs to Gussie as a token of his true emotions; or that he fed them to other dance-hall girls in order to awaken Gussie's jealousy. Belinda Mulroney, a famous Klondike innkeeper who arrived in Dawson early that spring, recollects that there was about half a case of eggs involved, and that these had been brought over the ice from the Pacific coast and were fast growing mellow. Mrs. Iola Beebe, one of Swiftwater's several future mothers-in-law, wrote that there were two crates of eggs and that Swiftwater paid for them with a brace of coffee tins filled with gold. The details of the story have thus been obscured, for there was no writing-paper in Dawson at the time to set them down, and no scriveners either, since every would-be historian was too busy seeking a fortune to attend to such footnotes. Whatever the details, the fact remains that the incident brought Gussie to heel, at least temporarily. She offered to meet Swiftwater Bill in San Francisco that fall and marry him, failing to mention that she was already wed to one Emile Leglice and had been since 1894.

Swiftwater's journey to San Francisco was ostensibly for business. He had gone into partnership with a shrewd entrepreneur named Jack Smith to establish the most famous of the Klondike's palaces of pleasure, the Monte Carlo Dance Hall and Saloon. Smith was an old showman who had a variety troupe in Fortymile at the time of the strike. He had reached Bonanza with the first wave, staked a claim, sold it for one hundred and fifty-five thousand dollars, opened up a small saloon on the creeks, and turned a handy profit. The transaction convinced him that it was easier to dig gold out of miners' pockets than out of the ground. He quickly saw the potentialities of Dawson's Front Street, and in the spring established the Monte Carlo in a tent. He made only one error of judgement, but it was a whopper. He persuaded Swiftwater Bill to put up some of the funds for a permanent building, and then allowed him to go out to San Francisco to rustle up a cargo of furnishings, liquor, and dance-hall girls. Sending Swiftwater Out-side to bring back girls was like sending a greedy child to a candy shop and hoping to get a full box back. But the awful realization of what he had done did not begin to dawn on Jack Smith until the following summer.

6: *City of gold*

Dawson grew slowly all that winter, as the news spread through Alaska and sifted as far south as Juneau on the Panhandle. By April 1897 there were about fifteen hundred people in the community and the camp had became a carbon copy of Fortymile and Circle City, its customs and traditions as yet untarnished by any large influx of strangers.

All winter long a thin trickle of men — one thousand or more — had been scaling the Chilkoot and hammering boats together along the shores of Lake Bennett on the headwaters of the Yukon. Now they waited on the frozen lake for the spring thaw. Their destination was Circle City; if they had heard of the Klondike at all, it was only in the vaguest terms.

At noon on May 14 the rotten ice in front of Dawson snapped with a mighty rumble and the whole mass began to crack and heave and move slowly off towards the sea. For two days a solid flow of ice cakes, some of them the size of houses, drifted past the town, until by May 16 the ice had thinned to the point where boats could navigate the river. The first small vessels to arrive belonged to men who had wintered somewhere along the river, but the main body of boats was only a few days behind.

The newcomers, sweeping around a bend in the river, came unexpectedly upon two tent cities scattered raggedly along both sides of the Klondike at the point where it joined the Yukon. The first city on the south bank of the Klondike was known officially as Klondike City, but rejoiced in the more common title of "Lousetown," for it was the site of the old Indian salmon camp. On the far side, on the swamp beneath the scarred mountain, was Dawson City proper. The two saloon-keepers in Lousetown had erected a large sign — "Danger Below: Keep to the Right" — to mislead the newcomers and prevent them going on to Dawson, where Joe Ladue was planning to sell them the last of his whiskey. Within twenty-four hours some two hundred boats had landed at Lousetown with the first news from the Outside: "The Pope's alive, the Queen's well, there's no war, and Bob Fitzsimmons knocked hell out of Jim Corbett!" Then William Ogilvie conceived the impish idea of tying down the steam whistle on Ladue's sawmill, and as its piercing shrieks echoed through the Klondike hills the makeshift fleet left Lousetown and moved down to Dawson, which swiftly became the hub of the gold-fields. Soon boats of every size and shape were pouring in day and night.

Harry Ash, the big, florid bartender from Circle City, was one of the first to benefit from the influx. His Northern Saloon was little more than a plank floor with a tent covering, but the very sawdust on the floor glittered with fine gold. On May 23, Monte Snow, a teenage boy from Circle whose father had arrived with a theatrical troupe, walked into the saloon and was greeted by Ash, who pointed to the sawdust-covered space in front of the bar.

"Take that sawdust, go down to Joe Ladue's and get two more sacks. Pan it out, and I'll give you what you get."

Snow did not think this worth while, but when Ash offered him twenty-five dollars for all the gold he could pan from the sawdust he changed his mind. In two hours he took out two hundred and seventy-eight dollars in fine dust which had sifted out of miners' pokes slapped onto the bar above. All business was transacted in gold. Bank-notes, indeed, were so scarce that when the occasional twenty-dollar bill turned up it could be sold for twenty-five dollars.

By June, Ash was taking in three thousand dollars a day. On the night that he opened his saloon in a permanent log building he took in thirty thousand, perhaps because he had the only piano in Dawson. The previous fall he had written to an old friend in Juneau, Billy Huson, to bring a piano in to Circle City, and all that winter Huson and his wife had been lugging the instrument over the Chilkoot in bits and pieces, the sounding-board carefully wrapped in wool yarn for protection. It was a tiny upright, made in Hong Kong for the steamer trade, and within a month every dance-hall girl in town had scratched her name on its surface with hatpins. As for the wool yarn, Mrs. Huson knitted it into sweaters which sold for a handsome profit. Within three months of the opening Ash was able to leave town with one hundred thousand dollars.

Before summer's end there were ten saloons in Dawson, none taking in less than three hundred dollars a night. Some were only tents, like the Blue Elephant and the White Elephant, so named because of the colour of the canvas. Others were substantial log structures like Jimmy Kerry's moved down from Fortymile, or Bill McPhee's new Pioneer with its stuffed mooseheads. In front of one saloon there hung a great ship's bell which rang every time a Klondike king laid down his poke, as a signal for everyone to crowd in for a free drink. Bartenders were paid twenty dollars a day and soon learned to underweigh gold dust, so that a customer could expect to lose a dollar and a half for every ten he laid out.

Once the gold was taken, wet and glistening, from the sluicebox, it seemed to shift from poke to poke as if carried by the winds. Money ceased to have value. Dance-hall girls were paid a hundred dollars a night;

108

town lots were selling for as high as twelve thousand. The Alaska Commercial Company was planning a warehouse that could have been put up for four thousand dollars in any midwestern town but which cost ninety-three thousand to erect in Dawson. Log cabins sold for as much as two hundred dollars per square foot of floor space. Bacon and tea cost seven to eight times their Outside values.

The more enterprising of the new arrivals quickly realized that there were easier ways to garner Klondike gold than to mine it, and that there were business opportunities everywhere for a man of imagination. In six months a Pennsylvania cigar salesman turned his small stock into a hundred-thousand-dollar fortune. He sold his ten-cent cigars for a dollar and a half apiece and used the profits to make downpayments on a dozen city lots. In less than twenty days he had turned over the lots for a net profit of twenty thousand. He reinvested this money in a number of ingenious ventures — hiring Indians, for instance, to peddle fresh water at twenty-five cents a pail, and women to bake bread at a dollar a loaf — so that by fall he was ready to ship two hundred pounds of gold to the coast. In this fashion he grew rich without ever setting foot on a mining claim.

By summer, with the population nearing thirty-five hundred, with the ring of hammer and axe heard all over town, with buildings sprouting up in helter-skelter fashion and the muddy roadways encrusted with chips and sawdust and blocked by newly planed logs, Dawson had lost its original character. The old rules and customs which had made the Alaska-Yukon camps cohesive communities no longer applied. The Golden Rule of the Yukon Order of Pioneers was honoured only in the breach, and the old sourdoughs no longer felt free to leave their cabin doors ajar for all who passed by. Constantine, coming up from Fortymile, looked over

109

the newcomers with contempt and wrote to his superiors that some of them "appeared to be the sweepings of the slums and the result of a general jail delivery." He was closer to the mark than perhaps he knew, for that eddying multitude concealed at least one murderer and, pressing close behind in that same throng, his Nemesis, an indefatigable private detective who had travelled twenty-five thousand miles searching for his man and who now found himself, somewhat to his own amazement, in the midst of a gold rush.

The murderer's name was Frank Novak. His pursuer was Detective C. C. Perrin, an athletic and square-jawed employee of Thiel's Detective Service in Chicago. The chase had been on since February, when Novak, having gambled away his firm's funds on the Chicago grain market, had killed and cremated a farmer in Iowa in the naïve belief that his insurance company would confuse the victim with himself and pay off Novak's family. A coroner's jury easily identified the corpse, and the relentless Perrin was put on the murderer's trail. The chase had zigzagged back and forth across the continent, from Iowa to Maryland, back to Iowa and on to Nebraska, then finally to Vancouver, British Columbia, and north up the Pacific coast to Alaska. When Perrin found that his quarry was heading for Canadian territory, he had to entrain for Ottawa to get extradition papers and then speed back to the coast, five weeks behind his victim. The detective reached Alaska in June, searching for his man in the faces of the crowd that climbed the Chilkoot. At one time pursuer and pursued were only a few miles from each other, respectively building boats on Lake Lindemann and Lake Bennett. Indeed, both started off on the same morning, and at one point Perrin actually passed Novak's scow without knowing it.

In Dawson, while others scrambled for fortune, hunter and hunted moved warily through the throng, oblivious of their strange surroundings. At this point both could have made themselves wealthy, for they had arrived unwittingly in the gold-fields before the Outside world yet knew of the strike. But neither had any interest in gold. From tent to tent the dogged Perrin moved, staring fixedly at face after face without recognition. Then he came upon one tent that excited his suspicions. He noticed that only two of its three occupants moved about by day, while the third emerged stealthily after midnight for a quiet stroll about the unfrequented parts of the camp with his miner's hat low over his eyes. Perrin settled down to a long vigil, seeking to make out the features concealed behind a matted beard. In the end he identified his quarry and, with Constantine's co-operation, made the arrest. He had been six months on the trail and history was being made all around him, but he was a man with a single purpose. Once his job was done, he left town with his handcuffed prisoner without another glance at the bizarre community that gold was building on the banks of the Yukon.

Dawson itself was about to become front-page news, for with the coming of summer its isolation from the world was at an end. The camp waited impatiently for the arrival of the first steamboat in June. The Klondike's *nouveaux riches* were ready to return to a civilization that some had rejected ten years before. There were more than eighty, each possessed of a fortune that ran from twenty-five thousand to half a million dollars. Some were determined to leave the North forever and had already sold their claims, content to live modestly but securely for the rest of their lives. Others were intent on a brief but gaudy celebration in the big cities of the Pacific coast before returning to the Klondike for more treasure. All felt the desperate need to escape from the dark confines of their cabins and tents and from the smoky depths of their mine shafts, just as they had once felt a similar need to escape the smoky, populous cities.

Then early in June a shrill whistle was heard out in the river and the Alaska Commercial Company's tiny stern-wheeler *Alice* rounded the Moosehide bluff and puffed into the shore. The entire town poured down to greet her. She was loaded with equal quantities of liquor and food, and the whole community went on a spree, as every saloon served free drinks across the counter. A couple of days later John J. Healy's boat, *Portus B. Weare,* arrived, and the performance was repeated. When the two boats left for the trip downstream they carried with them the men who would bring the first news of the great strike out to the unsuspecting world.

Chapter Four

1: *The treasure ships*

Down the hissing Yukon puffed the *Portus B. Weare* on her seventeen-hundred-mile voyage to the sea, white wood smoke erupting from her twin black stacks. Two days ahead of her chugged the A.C. Company's ungainly little *Alice,* a tiny smudge on the leaden expanse of the river. The brief sub-Arctic spring had yielded to summer, and the hills along the river were ablaze with crimson drifts of fireweed, accented by the blues of lupins and the yellows of arnicas and daisies. The air was heady with the pungent incense of balm of Gilead. Robins warbled among the birches, woodpeckers drummed against the spruce bark, moosebirds and chicken hawks wheeled and hovered in the sky. But, save for the occasional Indian or stray woodcutter, the two awkward little riverboats represented the only human movement along most of the Yukon, for the river country had long since been sucked dry of men by the news of the strike. In three months all this would change again, for the *Alice* and the *Weare* were heading for civilization each loaded with a single cargo: gold.

There was gold in suitcases and leather grips, gold in boxes and packing-cases, gold in belts and pokes of caribou hide, gold in jam jars, medicine bottles, and tomato cans, and gold in blankets held by straps and cord, so heavy it took two men to hoist each one aboard. Stacked on the decks (its weight made it safe from theft) and in the purser's office and in the dark, uncomfortable, verminous cabins, there was a total of three tons in the form of dust and nuggets. On the three-storied *Weare* the decks had to be shored up with wooden props, so heavy was the treasure, and there would have been more but for the lavishness of the farewell ceremonies. One Dawson saloon took in four hundred ounces of gold on the day the *Weare* left.

Most of the eighty-odd passengers aboard the two vessels had been paupers only a few months before. Some had not seen civilization for years, and none had heard from their families since the previous summer. Now each was worth a fortune. One, imprisoned in the Yukon for two years and reduced to a diet of half-raw salmon, had been planning suicide a few days before the Klondike strike, and now here he was, heading for civilization with thirty-five thousand dollars. Another had left Seattle the previous spring, impoverished and desperate, and was now worth more than one hundred thousand. Joe Ladue, gaunt and drawn after thirteen winters in the north, had become the owner of Dawson City, soon to be the hottest piece of real estate on the continent; he had more than enough money to marry the sweetheart whose family had spurned him for so long. Tom Lippy, the YMCA physical instructor, and Clarence Berry, the Fresno fruit farmer, were both coming out, each secure in the knowledge that he was worth at least a million.

The decks were crowded with Eldorado and Bonanza kings with a variety of backgrounds: a former dry-goods merchant, a former blacksmith, a former laundryman, a former Mounted Policeman, a former busboy. They hailed from every part of the globe: from Norway, Nanaimo, and Nova Scotia; from Stockholm, Sydney, and Seneca Falls. They had two things in common: all had been poor, all were now rich.

Not all were prospectors by choice or background. Many had gone north seeking gold through sheer desperation and had found it through a combination of stubbornness and good luck. J. O. Hestwood, a diminutive, pale-eyed man with a determined chin, leaned across the deck rail of the *Alice* and watched the blue scroll of the low Alaskan hills unwind slowly past. He had been a preacher, teacher, lecturer, and artist, and he

115

had not held a steady job since 1893, when he painted murals at the World's Columbian Exposition in Chicago. But on Bonanza Creek he had been getting sixteen dollars to the pan.

William Stanley, on board the creaking *Weare*, looked less like a prospector than any of his fellows, though he had made and lost three fortunes on previous Rocky Mountain stampedes. He was a Seattle bookseller, grey-haired and lame, and fifteen months earlier he and his wife and seven children had been impoverished. As a last resort Stanley had decided to go to the Yukon and look for gold. He and one son, Sam, headed north on borrowed money. On board ship they fell in with two brothers, Gage and Charlie Worden, from Sackets Harbor, New York. All four decided to pool their resources. Stanley limped over the Chilkoot Pass with the other three, and together they floated downriver. Pickings were slim on the bars of the Stewart, and the quartet was at the end of its tether and ready to give up when an old Indian drifted by in a canoe to say that a white man had found much gold on the Klondike. Now the old man was going home with one hundred and twelve thousand dollars while his partners stayed behind to work a million-dollar claim on Eldorado.

In spite of their riches, the passengers aboard the *Weare* and the *Alice* had yet to taste the sweet fruits of success. They had been living all winter in leaky cabins of green wood on an unvarying diet of beans and hardtack. No wonder, then, that when a crate of onions was discovered aboard the *Weare* there was a near-riot to devour them. To anyone else the wretched little port of St. Michael on the Bering Sea, with its melancholy mud flats, its grey warehouses, its rusty Russian cannon, and its stink of rotting fish, might have seemed to be the end of the earth. But to the prospectors it was Utopia. As

116

each vessel in turn puffed out of the labyrinth of the Yukon delta and headed up the sombre coastline to the volcanic island on which the port was perched, a wave of excitement rippled among the passengers. For there was food at St. Michael, and an orgy followed each landing. It was fruit and vegetables the miners wanted, and they devoured tins of pineapple, apricots, and cherries, swilled cider at a dollar a bottle, and gnawed away on raw turnips.

Anchored in the shallow sea off the mud flats lay two grimy ocean-going vessels, the N.A.T. Company's *Portland* and the A.C.'s *Excelsior,* one destined for Seattle, the other for San Francisco. As the *Portland* was to leave first, the majority boarded her. The trip was tedious, the ship rolled horribly, and most of the passengers took to their beds. One grew so ill that he had to be forcibly restrained from flinging himself overboard. Others, more hardy, drank champagne for most of the voyage or sat out on deck contemplating the future. Clarence Berry and his wife were like two excited children. They talked of the farm that he intended to buy, where he had once worked as a hired hand for starvation wages, and of the diamond wedding ring which she would now be able to afford — poverty had forced them to omit it from the ceremony before they set out on an Alaskan honeymoon. Mrs. Berry, in the rough, mannish costume of a prospector's wife, weather-beaten by the Yukon elements, presented a sharp contrast to her fellow passenger Mrs. Eli Gage, the fashionably attired daughter-in-law of the U.S. Secretary of the Treasury. Mrs. Gage's husband was one of the directors of the N.A.T. Company, and she was a prominent member of Chicago society. But Ethel Berry could have bought her, lock, stock, and bustle, with the gold from *Five* Eldorado.

The *Portland*'s journey took almost a month, and the passengers celebrated Independence Day aboard her. Under her previous name, *Haitian Republic,* she had been known as a hoodoo ship, but she was shortly to become the most famous vessel in America. She steamed into Seattle early on the morning of July 17 to the cheers of five thousand people crammed onto Schwabacher's Dock to greet her. For the *Excelsior* had beaten her, arriving in San Francisco two days earlier, and the word "Klondike" was already on the lips of the nation.

2: *Rich man, poor man*

The Klondike stampede did not start slowly and build up to a climax, as did so many earlier gold rushes. It started instantly with the arrival of the *Excelsior* and *Portland,* reached a fever pitch at once, and remained at fever pitch until the following spring, when, with the coming of the Spanish-American War, the fever died almost as swiftly as it arose. If war had not come, the rush might have continued unabated for at least another half-year, but, even so, the stampede remains unique. It was the last and most frenzied of the great international gold rushes. Other stampedes involved more gold and more men, but there had been nothing like the Klondike before, there has been nothing like it since, and there can never be anything like it again.

The treasure ships from Alaska reached the Pacific coast at the peak of that era known nostalgically as the Gay Nineties. The gaiety is remembered, the misery that accompanied it largely forgotten. It was the era of Buffalo Bill, Mark Twain, Carry Nation, Little Egypt, Lillian Russell, Richard Harding Davis, and the *Floradora* Sextette. The Gibson Girl stared haughtily from the pages of the ten-cent magazines; the Yellow Kid leered gap-toothed from the penny press. Fitzsimmons

118

had just knocked out Corbett, and William Jennings Bryan was on the rise. The world was riding tandem bicycles, singing "Daisy Bell," and reciting Gelett Burgess's mad jingle about a purple cow. It was an era whose various symbols are still remembered as emblems of "the good old days": the leg-o'-mutton sleeve, the cigar-store Indian, the stereopticon, and the moustache cup.

It was also an era in which the rich grew richer and the poor poorer, when the "haves" had almost everything and the "have-nots" almost nothing, when melodramas starring wicked landlords and destitute widows were believable and understandable slices of life, when the word "mortgage" had connotations of terror, when banks foreclosed and men quite literally died of hunger in the street. Next to the headlines in the penny press about the foibles of the wealthy ("RICH GIRL'S SUICIDE A MYSTERY — MONEY HER BANE?") were other headlines about the torments of the poor ("PRIDE MADE HER STARVE IN SILENCE"). If it was the era of Vanderbilt and Rockefeller, of the private yacht and the brownstone mansion, it was also the era of Samuel Gompers and Henry George, of the sweatshop and the tenement house. It was an age of millionaires, but it was also an age of hoboes. In short, it was an era occupied with money or preoccupied with the lack of it. It was an age, in the words of its historian Mark Sullivan, when "moneymaking was the most prized career." No wonder the continent went insane when two ships loaded with gold steamed in from out of the Arctic mists.

For "gold" was the magic word of the nineties. The scarcity of it had conspired to bring the continent to its knees, economically. In 1896, when George Carmack was drying salmon at the Klondike's mouth, the organ voice of Willian Jennings Bryan resounded across the land crying out that "you shall not crucify mankind

119

upon a cross of gold." The production of gold had not kept pace with the soaring population; in some years, indeed, it dropped, and this drop was accentuated by demands from European countries that had adopted a gold standard. As gold dollars grew scarcer they grew more expensive until at one point a gold dollar was worth almost twice as much as a paper dollar. People began to hoard gold, in socks and sugar bowls and under floor boards and in personal safes, so that by the year 1892 there were only one hundred and ninety millions in gold coin and certificates left in the U.S. Treasury out of a total of seven hundred and thirty millions. This drop in the circulation of gold was one of the reasons for the creeping depression that gripped the United States in the thirty years prior to the Klondike strike. It was a depression that favoured the money-lenders and bankers and wreaked hardship on the debtor classes, for those who had borrowed money when it was cheap found that they must repay it when it was expensive. Panic came in 1893 as a result of foreign fears that the government could not maintain payments in gold, and the slump that followed was the blackest the continent had known. Canada suffered just as badly.

It struck the Pacific northwest with particular viciousness, for this was a new land settled by men who had followed Horace Greeley's advice after the California gold rush to go west, and many of those who had done so were now trying to push back the frontier on borrowed funds. Some were reduced to digging clams from the beaches of Puget Sound to keep alive. Indeed, the people of western Washington State were so dependent on clams that, in the words of Frank Cushman, a Tacoma congressman, "their stomachs rose and fell with the tide." For years they had been waiting for a miracle to deliver them. It came, like an electric shock,

120

when the *Portland* docked in Seattle with a ton of gold aboard.

This was perhaps the chief reason for the intensity of the stampede that followed, a stampede out of all proportion to the amount of gold that actually existed on the Klondike watershed. The century had already experienced three other great international rushes, to California, Australia, and South Africa — fields far richer than the Klondike. But, in the phrase of the *British Columbia Yearbook* for 1897, they "did not move the world as the Klondike moved it."

Conditions were almost exactly right for the lunacy that ensued. The world was at peace, and the Klondike had no rivals for public attention for more than six months; another year and the Spanish-American and later the Boer wars would have interfered. Because of the high purchasing power of the dollar, goods and outfits were cheap. Rail and water transportation had reached a state of efficiency which made it possible to move large masses of people swiftly and inexpensively; the Klondike, in fact, started a railway rate war that saw the fare from Chicago to the Pacific coast drop to ten dollars. The Yukon was just far enough away to be romantic and just close enough to be accessible. Rich men could, in theory at least, travel all the way by boat without lifting a finger, while poor men could speedily reach the passes and travel by foot and home-made boat on a fast current to the gold-fields. Moreover, the Pacific-coast ports, hungering for trade, were prepared to use every weapon to promote themselves as outfitting ports for the stampede. Their greatest talking-point was the apparent wealth of the new fields. The area might not be extensive, but some of the claims were proving to be the richest in history.

There was something magical about the era, too. The Victorian Age was drawing to its close, and Eng-

121

lishmen, raised on a diet of adventure in far-off lands, were ripe for a fling. In North America, gullibility and optimism marched side by side and men were ready to believe that anything was possible. The novels of Jules Verne and the mechanical marvels of the Columbian Exposition had given the continent a heady feeling. Thrill-seekers rotated about in Ferris wheels; balloonists dared to mount into the clouds; thousands bought and believed in the Indian herb remedies sold by travelling medicine shows or in the gold bricks dispensed by itinerant confidence men. In some ways the Klondike was itself a giant gold-brick scheme in which an entire continent revelled.

Finally, the era of sensational journalism was in full swing. Outcault's *Kid* had given the name "yellow" to the popular press. Richard Harding Davis's *Soldiers of Fortune* had just been published. Bennett, Dana, Pulitzer, and Hearst were the giants of journalism. Human interest was the order of the day, and the scenes in San Francisco and Seattle in mid-July 1897 were made to order for any newspaperman.

3: *A ton of gold*

The *Excelsior* did not look like a treasure ship. She was short and stubby with a lone black smokestack and two masts. Her superstructure was smudged and grimy and stained with rust marks. Her appearance fitted that of her passengers, who still wore their tattered working-clothes, caked with the mud of Bonanza and Eldorado. Under their broad-brimmed miners' hats their lined faces were burned almost black by the Klondike sun, and their chins grizzled with unshaven whiskers. They were gaunt and they were weary, but their eyes burned with a peculiar fire. To the crowd on the dock they looked exactly like miners out of a picture-book.

122

Down the gangplank they came, Lippy, Hestwood, Joe Ladue, Louis Rhodes, and the others, staggering under their loads of gold. The knot of curious people on the dock at San Francisco parted to let them through. Tom Lippy's square shoulders could be seen on the gangway, his wiry little wife beside him, her face tanned the colour of shoe-leather. Together they grappled with a bulging suitcase. It weighed more than two hundred pounds, and the awed spectators realized it was full of gold. Lippy's neighbours on Eldorado, including some of those who had discovered the creek, accompanied him to the dock. Frank Keller with thirty-five thousand dollars and Jim Clements with fifty thousand hoisted their gold down the gangway. Fred Price, who had been a laundryman in Seattle before going north, was relatively "poor" with only fifteen thousand dollars in gold. But even fifteen thousand was a considerable fortune in 1897, when a four-room apartment could be rented for a dollar and a quarter a week, an all-wool serge suit could be purchased for four dollars, a square meal cost twenty-five cents, a quart of whiskey went for forty cents, coffee was thirteen cents a pound, a smoked tongue was worth twelve cents, and two baskets of fresh tomatoes could be bought for a nickel.

A group of the miners hailed a four-horse truck, hired it on the spot, hoisted their gold aboard it, and drove off towards the Selby Smelting Works on Montgomery Street, the crowd surging behind them. The U.S. mint was closed, because the Democratic director was in the process of being replaced by a Republican, but Selby's was happy to buy the gold. The crowd squeezed into the building and watched goggle-eyed while the buckskin bags, the soiled canvas sacks, the glass fruit jars and jelly tumblers, covered with precious writing-paper and tied with twine, were ripped open on the counter and their yellow contents disgorged. The gold lay on the

123

counter, in the words of an eyewitness, "like a pile of yellow shelled corn" while the poker-faced clerks weighed it, paid for it, and shovelled it with copper scoops into a great melting-pot.

The story of this spectacle buzzed through the streets of San Francisco, and soon the news was afoot that something extraordinary was happening. For some time rumours had been sifting down the coast about a big strike made on an unpronounceable stream deep in the Yukon Valley. Ogilvie's report had been published the previous month in the form of an austere and forbidding pamphlet titled *Information Respecting the Yukon District*, to which few paid attention. William Johns, the ex-newsman who had staked on Eldorado, sent a brief mention of the Klondike to a Chicago paper, which printed a few lines in March, but this attracted little notice. Jack Carr, a veteran Yukon dog-driver, left Dawson on June 5 and reached Juneau on July 11 wearing gold nuggets for buttons and bearing the news of the strike. Nobody believed him until they opened their mail. The Alaska Commercial Company in San Francisco also had word of the strike before the *Excelsior*'s arrival, and the word "Klondike" had started appearing in its advertisements early in July.

These hints caused not a ripple until the *Excelsior* docked. But here at last was dramatic proof of a new Eldorado. Here was one grizzled creature, fresh off the boat with a thirty-pound sack of dust in his hand, ordering poached eggs nine at a time, tipping waitresses with nuggets, engaging a horse cab at twenty dollars a day, and exclaiming that he had pulled a hand sled fourteen hundred miles and now intended to ride in luxury for a fortnight.

The *Call* and *Chronicle* spread the story of the *Excelsior*'s cargo prominently, but William Randolph Hearst's *Examiner* literally and figuratively missed the

124

boat and gave it only a few lines. The *Call*'s story was wired to James Gordon Bennett's New York *Herald*. Hearst's New York *Journal* had no story, and the proprietor was furious. Hearst had invaded the big city only two years before and was locked in a journalistic war the like of which New York had not known before. He had lured away some of his rival's top talent, including the famous comic-strip character, the Yellow Kid; and, as the heir to the famous Homestake mining fortune, he had both the funds and the understanding to exploit a stampede. He ordered all-out coverage of the story and dispatched two expeditions to the Klondike. With that imperial dictum, the Klondike fever began.

In Seattle, excitement was mounting to a white heat, for Tom Lippy, who had lugged the largest personal fortune off the *Excelsior,* was a Seattle boy and the papers were full of his story. Lippy and his wife had a suite in the Palace Hotel in San Francisco, where they were virtual prisoners, the halls outside jammed with people bombarding the doors. Now the word was out that a second treasure ship, far richer than the first, was due in Seattle at any moment. The *Post-Intelligencer* chartered a tug, loaded it with reporters, and sent it off to Cape Flattery to intercept the *Portland* as she entered the sound. The newsmen tumbled over the ship's rails into the arms of the excited miners, who were eager to trade news of the Klondike for news of the Outside. The tug raced back to port, and, as a result, the first of the *P-I*'s three extras hit the Seattle streets at almost the same moment that the *Portland* docked: "GOLD! GOLD! GOLD! GOLD! 68 rich men on the Steamer *Portland; STACKS OF YELLOW METAL!*" and the story, written by an ingenious reporter named Beriah Brown, coined the phrase that flashed round the world: "At 3 o'clock this morning the steamer *Portland* from St.

125

Michael for Seattle, passed up the Sound with more than a ton of solid gold aboard. . . ."

Brown had reckoned that the weight of the gold dust would sound more dramatic than its value. His instinct was right. By evening the phrase "a ton of gold" was being published by newspapers all around the world. The rival Seattle *Times,* with more restraint, gave the weight as half a ton, but for once the newspapers erred on the side of caution. When the results were totted up, it turned out that there were at least two tons of gold aboard the ship.

As the *Portland* nosed into Schwabacher's Dock at six a.m. on July 17, five thousand people poured down to the waterfront to greet her. "Show us the gold!" cried the watchers on the wharf as the vessel approached, and the miners on board obliged by hoisting their sacks. Seattle police and Wells-Fargo guards armed with rifles appeared to clear a way for the miners through the jam of humanity.

Now the scene in San Francisco was repeated. Down the gangplank came the ragged, bearded men, lugging their sacks and their suitcases and their blankets full of gold, as the spectators shouted "Hurrah for the Klondike!" One man had one hundred thousand dollars in dust and nuggets tied up in a blanket and had to hire two others to help him drag it away. John Wilkinson, one of the ex-coal-miners from *Fifteen* Eldorado, had fifty thousand dollars in gold in his leather grip, and, although this was tied tightly with three straps, it was so heavy that the handle snapped off as he staggered along the dock. A miner named Nils Anderson dragged a heavy bag down the gangplank. He had two other sacks full of gold back in his state-room. Two years before, he had borrowed three hundred dollars and left his family to gamble on fortune in the north. His wife, waiting on the dock, did not know he was rich until he told her that he had brought out one hundred and twelve thousand dollars.

Staff Sergeant M. E. Hayne of the North West Mounted, who had staked on Bonanza, came down the gangplank and into the arms of Seattle newspapermen, "who clung to us like limpets."

"Let me at least have a thimbleful of Scotch whisky before I suffer the torment of an interview," Hayne cried. Six men seized him and propelled him to a nearby saloon, and each flung a quarter on the bar to treat him.

The reporters clustered around each prospector in turn as the police fought to hold back the crowds. "We've got millions," Frank Phiscator told them. Dick McNulty, who had twenty thousand, announced that the Klondike placers were ten times as rich as any found in California. William Stanley, the old bookseller, said that "the Klondike is no doubt the best place to make money that there is in the world." Stanley's story was quickly circulated. His wife, in Anacortes, had been living on wild blueberries and taking in laundry to keep her family together. When the news reached her she dropped the wet clothes, told her customers to fish their own out of the tub, and moved with her husband into a downtown hotel, where she threw out her meagre wardrobe and called in a dressmaker to design raiment more appropriate for the wife of a Klondike prince.

From this day on, few prospectors arriving from the north were to know any real peace. The Stanleys and the Berrys were trailed by such throngs in the streets that they had to flee to San Francisco, where an avalanche of letters snowed them under. "The Klondike is the richest goldfield in the world," Berry told the reporters who laid siege to his hotel room. Four sacks of nuggets on the floor and a variety of jars and bottles on the table, all filled with gold, lent credence to his words. Jacob

Wiseman tried to go home to Walla Walla, but the press of the curious was so insistent that he secretly left the town and lived under an assumed name in Tacoma. Mrs. Gage boarded the train for Chicago and locked herself in her drawing-room for the entire journey. Frank Phiscator headed for Chicago, too, flourishing a big red pocketbook in which reposed a certificate of deposit for one hundred and twenty thousand dollars; on arrival he checked in at the Great Northern Hotel, where he told the clerk, in ringing tones, that nothing was too good for him.

One prospector, J. C. Miller of Los Angeles, was reduced to a state of nervous prostration by the swarms of gold-crazy men who visited him. Another, William Hewitt, who came out with a five-gallon can filled with dust and nuggets, received more than a hundred callers a day for weeks, and letters from every state in the union. But Ladue perhaps had the most frantic time of all, for the papers quickly dubbed him Mayor of Dawson City, and he was pursued by such a throng of reporters, well-wishers, fortune-hunters, and cranks that he fled to the East. He stepped off the train in Chicago into the arms of another waiting mob, and even when he reached his farm at Plattsburgh in the Adirondacks there was no surcease. A bushel basket full of mail awaited him. The people crowded into the parlour and began to finger the nuggets that he poured onto a table. Ladue left them to it and went off into a barn to hide. Here he was cornered by Lincoln Steffens, the most persistent reporter of his day. "He was the weariest looking man I ever saw," Steffens wrote in *McClure's*. It was a prophetic remark, for Ladue's days were numbered. His life reached its climax in a Cinderella ending, made to order for the press. At long last he married Anna Mason, his lifelong sweetheart, whose parents were now more than happy to welcome the most renowned figure in America into the family. Ladue's name by this time was a household word. He was worth, on paper, five million dollars and was dubbed "the Barney Barnato of the Klondike"; his picture appeared in advertisements endorsing Dr. Green's Nervura blood and nerve remedy; his name was listed as author of a book about the Klondike; and the financial pages were soon reporting that he had been named president and managing director of the Joseph Ladue Gold Mining and Development Company, whose directors included some of the biggest names in New York finance, headed by Chauncey Depew, president of the New York Central.

Alas for Ladue, the thirteen winters spent along the Yukon had taken their toll. A few months after he came out of the north, his partner, the aging Arthur Harper, who had followed him down the coast on the next boat, died of tuberculosis. The following year Ladue also succumbed to the disease, at the height of the great stampede he helped bring about.

4: *Klondicitis*

"Seattle," a New York *Herald* reporter wrote, "has gone stark, staring mad on gold."

By nine thirty on the morning of the *Portland*'s arrival the city's downtown streets were so jammed with people that some of the streetcars had to stop running, which was perhaps just as well since the streetcar-operators had already started to resign and head for the Klondike. Before the week was out the city had trouble keeping its transportation system in operation at all. This was the first of a series of mass resignations which became a feature of the early stages of the stampede. Only a few hours after the *Portland* docked, a Seattle barber suddenly stopped work, closed his shop, and bought a ticket for Alaska. All over the Pacific northwest similar incidents were taking place. Clerks quit by the dozen the same day; the Seattle *Times* lost most of its reporters; shipping men and policemen left their jobs. Within four days, twelve members of the Seattle force had resigned to go to the Klondike. Salesmen jumped counters, doctors deserted patients, preachers quit their congregations. The Mayor of Seattle, W. D. Wood, happened to be in San Francisco attending a convention when the news broke. He did not bother to return home, but wired his resignation. Before the month was out he had raised one hundred and fifty thousand dollars, bought himself an ocean steamer, the *Humboldt*, and formed the Seattle and Yukon Trading Company, whose subsequent history was a troubled one.

The resignations kept coming. The ferry between Vancouver and Victoria had difficulty loading because most of the crew had left for the Klondike. Ships going north had trouble coming south again because so many seamen deserted. Whaling in the Canadian Arctic came to a standstill because the whalers left in a body for the goldfields. Canneries along the Alaskan coast were forced to close for similar reasons. The price of riverboats tripled, and so many were shipped north for Yukon River service that fruit-picking ceased in the Sacramento Valley because of the absence of transportation. The rush threatened to close down the California gold mines. Within ten days the Oneida and Kennedy mines near Jackson lost most of their men.

Everyone seemed fiercely determined to go. More than three-quarters of the members of the graduating classes of San Francisco and Los Angeles medical schools announced that they would accelerate their studies in order to establish themselves as doctors in the Yukon Valley. In Chicago a group of gamblers, harried by a reform government, held a hurried meet-

130

ing in a downtown saloon and within three hours boarded a train for Seattle, taking no luggage but a set of gold-scales and some heavy underwear. In Tacoma the street-car employees organized a mass meeting and chose nine of their number to go to the Klondike to stake claims for the rest. On Bellingham Bay, in Washington State, Eric A. Hegg, a twenty-nine-year-old Swedish-born photographer, closed both of his thriving studios, bought all the chemicals and photographic plates he could afford, and took immediate passage north on a leaky stern-wheeler, the *Skagit Chief*. It was not gold that lured him but the prospect of photographing the greatest adventure story of the age.

The stampede was swiftly given an air of respectability and authority by the numbers of leading citizens who took part in it. John McGraw, a former governor of Washington, a senatorial candidate, and one-time president of the First National Bank of Seattle, was aboard the *Portland* when she left on her return journey. Fellow passengers included Brigadier General M. E. Carr of the state militia, who had the most lucrative law practice in the state, and Captain A. J. Balliot, once Yale's greatest oarsman and footballer, who also gave up a thriving law practice to seek his fortune in the gold-fields. E. J. "Lucky" Baldwin of San Francisco, a millionaire hotel man, miner, and landowner, who had been one of the argonauts in the '49 rush, at the age of seventy-one announced that he would go to the Klondike to seek the mother lode itself. Winfield Scott Stratton, the eccentric millionaire from Cripple Creek, organized an expedition and bought two riverboats to prospect the Yukon River.

The aristocrats of the underworld were equally alert to the possibilities of the stampede; already boom towns, disorganized and ripe for the plucking, were mushrooming up at the foot of the mountain passes.

Shortly after the news broke, an ex-policeman named Willis Loomis encountered, on the streets of Seattle, Soapy Smith, one of the most famous bunko men on the continent.

"I'm going to be the boss of Skagway," Smith told him casually. "I know exactly how to do it, and if you come along I'll make you chief of police."

Loomis had known Smith in the great silver camp of Leadville, Colorado, when he had sold cakes of shaving-soap for five dollars apiece to suckers who believed there was a twenty-dollar bill hidden under the wrapper. Since then Smith had risen in the world: he was the acknowledged master of the sure-thing game, the king of the confidence men, the emperor of the Denver underworld, and the ex-ruler of Creede, Colorado — a man with the reputation of buying and selling police chiefs as if they were so many cattle. Loomis retorted that a team of mules could not drag him to Alaska, and Smith went on alone, with historic results.

Within ten days of the *Portland*'s arrival, fifteen hundred people had left Seattle and there were nine ships in harbour jammed to the gunwales and ready to sail. The town itself was demented. By August 1 every hotel was bursting with men, restaurants were overtaxed, and lodging-houses were roaring. In the area of the docks, the streets were choked with people and animals moving sluggishly between the ten-foot stacks of supplies. Through the crowd moved steerers hired to lure men to the various outfitting stores. Hundreds sat in the roadways, dressed in gaudy mackinaws, miners' wide-brimmed hats, iron-cleated, high-top boots, and heavy wool socks — waiting for ships, playing at cards, and babbling about gold.

Dogs, goats, sheep, oxen, mules, burros, Shetland ponies, and sway-backed cayuses, all designed for Klondike packing, blocked the streets, tied to hitching-posts and lumber piles. Every dog-owner in town learned to keep his pet securely tethered — otherwise he was stolen for the Klondike. Horses kept pouring in from Montana, many of them bony, spavined, and worn out. They had been worth between three and five dollars the week before, but now they sold for twenty-five and more. Mules arrived from Colorado; reindeer with amputated horns were sold as beasts of burden; Washington elks were brought in by the carload priced at two hundred and fifty dollars apiece.

The continent was Klondike-crazy. Transportation-company offices were in a state of siege. One railway company received twenty-five thousand queries about the Klondike in the first few weeks. In Chicago the N.A.T. Company was bombarded by one thousand people a day. In the first twenty-four hours after the news broke, two thousand New Yorkers tried to buy tickets for the Klondike. A day later a New York paper printed an advertisement asking applicants to invest any sum between five hundred and two thousand dollars in a Klondike expedition. Twelve hundred signed up at once. On August 1 the New York *Herald*'s financial page carried advertisements for eight huge mining and exploration corporations all formed within a few days to exploit the Klondike. Their total authorized capitalization came to more than twenty-five million dollars.

The news of the Klondike quickly released the northwest from the economic strait jacket in which it had been imprisoned. The gold coins that had lain so long in sugar bowls and strong-boxes and under floor boards were now suddenly flung into circulation. Money had been so scarce in the northwest that grocery bills habitually went unpaid, and yet within a week five-hundred-dollar grubstakes were plentiful. The feeling was epitomized by one Seattle man dying of lung trouble who nevertheless decided to make the arduous trek north and, as he boarded the *Portland,* announced that he would rather expire making a fortune than rot in poverty on the shores of Puget Sound.

"Prosperity is here," cried the Seattle *P-I* just four days after the *Portland* docked. "So far as Seattle is concerned the depression is at an end. A period of prosperity, far greater than anything known in the past, is immediately at hand. . . ."

Three days later the financial barometers of the Bradstreet and R. G. Dun companies (then separate firms) endorsed this optimism. Bradstreet's report declared that "the demand for supplies for shipment to the Clondyke gold region has made July the busiest instead of the dullest month in the commercial year in Seattle and has had an influence on sales of staples at Tacoma, Portland and San Francisco."

In the first two weeks of the excitement, telegraph orders on the Puget Sound National Bank increased fivefold over any other period in the bank's history. The sale of bank drafts tripled and express business doubled. In August the city's total business had leaped by fifty per cent.

The midwest felt a similar upsurge. "I have never seen such a change pass over the faces and hopes of people in the last two months," wrote Senator C. K. Davis of Minnesota, in October. "In the streets of. . . [Minneapolis] you will see three people and three teams where you saw one two months ago."

Grocers doubled their help, supply stores ran day and night, woollen mills sold out of blankets and heavy clothing. Towns as far away as Winnipeg, Manitoba, were cleaned out of furs and robes in two weeks. Plants making evaporated food stepped up production: one Washington State plant operated night and day processing seven thousand pounds a week while workmen

134

rushed through an addition to the factory. Everyone wanted evaporated food: evaporated eggs, evaporated onions, and even evaporated split-pea soup, which was sold in the form of a sausage, each one guaranteed to make twenty to thirty platefuls. The stampeders bought milk tablets, peanut meal, saccharine, desiccated olives, coffee lozenges, beef blocks, and pemmican. One entrepreneur claimed he could put enough food into an ordinary valise to last a man a year and give him a menu as varied as that of a good hotel. He sold these valises to the gullible for two hundred and fifty dollars, claiming they would be worth two thousand in the Klondike.

The newspapers were full of advice on suitable outfits for the Klondike, but many of the argonauts, as they were universally called, chose to ignore them and hold to their own ideas of what was proper for sub-Arctic travel. Tappan Adney, the correspondent for *Harper's Illustrated,* came across one man in Victoria, B.C., whose outfit consisted of thirty-two pairs of moccasins, a case of pipes, a case of shoes, two Irish setters, a bull pup, and a lawn-tennis set. He was no trader, he told Adney, but simply a tourist going to the gold-fields for a good time. About the same time a forty-seven-year-old spinster, Miss Blanche King, sailed for St. Michael, taking along a maid, a cook, a horse, a parrot, three canaries, a piano, two Saint Bernard dogs, and a seal-skin suit.

Almost anything was salable if it had the name "Klondike" attached to it. Optometrists sold Klondike glasses, rubber manufacturers hawked Klondike boots, drugstores peddled Klondike medicine chests, restaurants dispensed Klondike soup; everything from stoves to blankets suddenly bore the necromantic name. It had become a magic word, a synonym for sudden and glorious wealth, a universal panacea, a sort of voodoo

135

incantation which, whispered, shouted, chanted, or sung, worked its own subtle witchery. The papers talked of "Klondicitis," and the phrase was apt. A New York printer named William Miller, suffering from Klondicitis in the first week of the stampede, tried to raise five hundred dollars from his friends to make the trip north. When he failed to get enough money he lost his reason and the police had to be called to prevent mayhem.

Another curious example of Klondicitis turned up in the same week. A businessman named W. J. Arkell laid claim to the entire Klondike gold-fields, which he insisted were his by right of discovery. Arkell was secretary of the Sterling Remedy Company and proprietor of *Frank Leslie's Illustrated Weekly* as well as the weekly humour magazine *Judge*. In 1890 he had organized the Frank Leslie expedition and sent it to Alaska by way of Haines Mission and the Chilkat Pass, which lies to the southeast of the Chilkoot. Arkell himself had not gone along, nor did the expedition's members set foot in the Klondike watershed, but this did not deter him from laying claim to the entire gold-bearing region. This attack of Klondicitis spread to Arkell's brother-in-law, who offered to buy up the interests of an officer of the expedition, one A. B. Shanz. He offered Shanz fifty thousand dollars for his share of Arkell's non-existent claims. But Shanz, by this time, had Klondicitis, too, and he turned down the offer as being too niggardly. Nothing more was heard of Arkell's suit.

The Klondike had another curious effect on people: they began seeing gold everywhere. A group of Italian labourers in New York City saw gold in some sand in which they were digging and began to talk to newspapermen of fortune. A visitor to Victoria saw gold in an outcropping in a gutter near that city's post office and tried to stake a claim on the main street. Gold started to turn up in almost every state in the union. Trinity County, California, went wild over the alleged discovery of some old Spanish mines. A farm near Elizabethtown, Kentucky, was said to be lined with gold. A report from Marquette, Michigan, claimed that the town was sitting on top of a vein of gold forty feet wide. Promoters in Columbia, Missouri, professed to find gold in the beds of dry creeks. Gold mines that had long been worked out suddenly took on a new lease of life: Peru tried to revive the gold mines of the Incas; Deadwood announced the discovery of a new gold vein; the old Cariboo and Kootenay districts of British Columbia began to report new gold finds. Mexico claimed there was gold in the Yaqui country, Russia insisted there were fabulous mines just across from Alaska, and even China talked about new discoveries. Thousands subscribed to various promotion dodges, most of which were based on no firmer evidence than the deposits of iron pyrites which caused a brief flurry in Missouri.

The prevailing attitude towards gold, as expressed in the journalism and in the personal correspondence of the day, was an entirely sensual one. The phrase-makers hovered lovingly over their descriptions of the Klondike's mineral wealth, caressing it with adjectives that emphasized its tactile qualities. They wrote, and talked, of "rich, yellow gold," of "hard, solid gold," of "shining gold," as if the metal were to be coveted for its own sake, as a jewel or an ornament is coveted.

So infectious was the Klondike epidemic that the flimsiest rumour served to send hundreds dashing to the farthest corners of the northern hemisphere. Transportation companies were not above making capital of these tales, the most flagrant example being the fruitless chase to Kotzebue Sound, on the northwestern tip of the continent, just off Bering Strait. This abortive race was touched off by an old sea-dog in San Francisco who

137

claimed to have dug fifteen thousand dollars out of the ground in two hours with a jack-knife. Several parties swallowed the fairy tale and paid forty dollars each to learn the exact spot in the Kotzebue area where the gold was hidden. The story spread, the price of the inside tip soared to six hundred dollars, and soon steamship companies were advertising "Nuggets as Big as Hickory Nuts" on Kotzebue's cold shore. More than one thousand persons travelled over three thousand miles, each thinking his party, alone of all the others, knew the secret. And so they were trapped for one long winter above the Arctic Circle, a good five hundred miles, as the crow flies, from the Klondike, which they never saw.

Meanwhile the railway and steamship ads were crying "Ho! For the Klondike!" while the slogan "Klondike or bust!" was on everyone's lips. It had become suddenly very fashionable to be a stampeder, and red-lettered lapel buttons with the phrase "Yes, I'm going this spring" enjoyed a brisk sale. J. E. Fraser, who went north from San Francisco with twenty men on a wild-goose chase to the Tanana River, later recalled the sentiment of the times:

"The man who had a family to support who could not go was looked on with a sort of pity... the man who didn't care to leave his business or for other trivial reasons, was looked on with contempt as a man without ambition who did not know enough to take advantage of a good thing when placed in his reach; but the man who *could* go, and would go, and was going to the Klondike, the man who could not be stopped from going, by any means short of a wire cable anchored to a mountain, was a hero. He was looked up to; he was envied by everybody; he was pointed out in the streets."

Anybody who wished to get free drinks in a Pacific coast saloon had only to dress in the approved costume

138

of the stampeder — the colourful mackinaw, the high boots, and the thick cap. Such a one was automatically treated to the best in the house by his envious fellows.

Men who decried their friends as fools for leaving everything and rushing to the Klondike suddenly found themselves shuttering their shops and following suit, scarcely knowing why.

"Have I also gone daft with this fever, this lust for gold?" wrote Raymond Robins, a rising young San Francisco lawyer, to his sister Elizabeth, a London actress noted for her interpretation of Ibsen's plays. "I leave this city for Ice-bound Alaska in a few days, and then across the snow-covered mountains and glaciers to rushing Clondyke, where the Yellow God has been sporting in the turbid waters and upon the gravelly shores." Two years later almost to the day, he was to write her again from Dawson City: "My two years' race with fortune is over and I have lost. . . . I am about one thousand dollars in debt and have no assets of any immediate value. . . ."

Robert Medill, a young and impoverished school-teacher from La Salle, Illinois, who rushed north in August, wrote to his wife from Seattle decrying the "calamity howlers" in his home state who looked upon the Klondike rush as a will-o'-the-wisp. "Was surprised to see how the Klondike fever has struck different parts of the country," Medill wrote, in his curious shorthand style. "The Illinois people are quite bad — I mean this. You meet a calamity howler at La Salle quite bad. At Chicago he lets loose a little. From Chicago to Washington he is fearful, disgusting. At Seattle he is dead and *all* is *Klondyke.* What a relief!" Medill confidently expected to reach the gold-fields in fifteen days; it took him seventy-one — "an awful trip," as he later described it. A year later, still impoverished but much wiser, he was home again.

It was impossible on the Pacific coast to pick up a newspaper and not find the word Klondike, in its various spellings, on almost every page. The advertising columns bristled with references to it.

"I was a physical wreck three years ago and cured by Dr. Sanden's Electric Belt," one testimonial read. "I am now fifty-two years old, but I am going to the Klondike and expect to hold my own with younger men."

Hundreds of personal stories were compressed into a few lines in the classified columns: "Anyone with $150 can secure legitimate paying business — apply Clondyke, *P-I*". . . *"Wanted* by two experienced miners: stake for the Klondike". . . *"Wanted* $700 to go to the Yukon. Will give value and personal property and if successful will give $1000 additional. Will accept grubstake. Address Success". . . "Restaurant and cafe for sale, including valuable lease, beautiful colonial mansion, grand piazza, shady lawns. . . address Klondike, 708 Columbus Avenue, New York."

Tin Pan Alley, meanwhile, was busy hammering out a saccharine ballad entitled "He's Sleeping in a Klondike Vale Tonight," and the various periodicals were printing odes to the stampede. *Review of Reviews* published this poetic exhortation:

> *All you miners wide awake!*
> *Go to the Klondike, make your stake;*
> *Get out your pick, your pan, your pack,*
> *Go to the Klondike, don't come back*
> *Ho for the Klondike, Ho!*

The London *Daily Chronicle* published its Cockney counterpart:

> *Klondike! Klondike!*
> *Libel yer luggidge "Klondike"!*
> *Theers no chawnce in the street ter-dye*

140

Theers no luck darn Shoreditch wye
Pack yer traps and be orf I sye,
An' orf an' awye ter Klondike!

And in New York, Huber's Fourteenth Street Museum, searching about for a new act to headline its bill of Scottish acrobats, tumblers, black-faced comedians, and the new picture-projecting machine called the Cineograph, came up with a surefire attraction:

Great Big Bill — EVERYTHING NEW!
FIRST APPEARANCE OF THE KLONDIKE
BRIDES
15 brave young ladies with courage enough to
go to the Klondike to become miners' brides.
15 wonderful freaks

In most of the civilized world, indeed, the Klondike had become the chief topic of the day, at lunch counters, in trams, aboard elevated trains and street-cars. In the midwest, farmers deserted their haying to drive into town to hear the latest item from the gold-fields. "Technical mining phrases," one contemporary reporter wrote, "have become the cant of the day."

In those first wild weeks there were few who had any real idea exactly where the enchanted land was to be found. The Memphis *Commercial-Appeal,* for instance, told its readers that the Klondike lay near Chicago. One gold-seeker arrived in Seattle and asked the station master which train he should board for Skagway. In London an enthusiast called upon Harry de Windt, an Alaskan explorer, and wanted to know if he could ride a bicycle over the Chilkoot Pass.

By the late fall of '97, however, a Niagara of books, maps, pamphlets, brochures, advertisements, and newspaper reports had poured from the presses. Many were filled with misinformation of every kind, but they

141

did serve to let the average man know roughly where the Klondike was. William Haskell arrived from Circle City and was astonished to discover that "little school-boys and girls knew the topography of the Yukon and the Klondike better than they knew the States." He tested one Los Angeles ten-year-old by asking him to give the length of the California coastline. The boy did not know the answer, but was able at once to quote correctly the exact length of the Yukon River.

Few men there were who remained unaffected by the excitement of the Klondike, save for the hermits, the recluses, and the occasional hobo, winding his wastrel way down the dusty roads of the nation. One such there was in California who remained entirely untouched by the spreading delirium. He had been successively a potato-digger, a gardener in a rural bordello, a dish-washer, a sandwich man, a sandhog, and an orange-picker. At this point in his speckled career he was a bum, picking up food in gutters, accepting handouts from soup kitchens, begging at back doors for bread, and strumming on his guitar to verses of a sort that he composed and sang himself. As the stampeders raced north he moved indolently south towards Mexico, scarcely aware of the frenzy that surrounded him.

His name was Robert W. Service.

5: *Warnings all unheeded*

In the fevered chorus chanting anthems to the Klondike, a few reed-like voices could be heard faintly coun-selling caution. On July 28 the white-bearded Louis Sloss, one of the founders of the Alaska Commercial Company, said flatly: "I regard it as a crime for any transportation company to encourage men to go to the Yukon this fall. . . . The Seattle people who are booming the steamship lines may be sincere, but a heavy responsibility will rest on their shoulders should starvation and crime prevail in Dawson City next winter. . . . It is a crime to encourage this rush, which can only lead to disaster for three quarters of the new arrivals." This statement, coming from the head of a pioneer company which stood to gain immeasurably from the stampede, could be counted as an honest and reliable appraisal of the situation. Few heeded it, perhaps preferring the advice of the colourful Joaquin Miller, published the same day. The grey-bearded "Poet of the Sierra," a veteran of earlier Rocky Mountain stampedes, was already en route to the Klondike as one of Mr. Hearst's quintet of journalists. He announced that there was "no possible chance of famine" and that "the dangers and hardships and cost of getting through have been greatly exaggerated." Miller, who was almost sixty years old, boasted that he was travelling light, with very little in the way of provisions or equipment — a fact that was to cause him great distress before the year was out.

There were further warnings. The Travellers' Insurance Company announced it would refuse insurance to any stampeder. An Ottawa paper published, in the form of a "Miner's Catechism," a series of questions that every would-be prospector should ask himself before setting out for the Klondike:

"Have I a capital of at least five hundred dollars? Am I subject to any organism or chronic disease, especially rheumatism? Am I physically sound in every way and able to walk thirty miles a day with a fifty pound pack on my back? Am I willing to put up with rough fare, sleep anywhere and anyhow, do my own cooking and washing, mend my own clothes? Can I leave home perfectly free, leaving no one dependent on me in any manner for support? Can I do entirely without spirituous liquors? Can I work like a galley slave for

143

months, if need be, on poor fare and sometimes not enough of that, and still keep up a cheerful and brave spirit? Am I pretty handy with tools and not subject to lazy fits? Can I swim and handle boats and canoes; put up with extremes of heat and cold, and bear incessant tortures from countless swarms of mosquitoes, gnats and sand flies?"

Only a fraction of the tens of thousands who streamed across the passes in the months that followed could say *yes* to these questions. Most of them were sedentary workers, clerks and salesmen and office help, but once they caught the fever they were not to be deterred by mere words, especially when many newspaper writers, egged on by local chambers of commerce, were painting the journey to the gold-fields in the most vivid and enthusiastic terms.

Ambrose Bierce was a rare exception, one of the handful of journalists who took a jaundiced view of the stampede. "The California gold hunter did good by accident and crowed to find it fame," he wrote in the San Francisco *Examiner.* "But the blue-nosed mosquito-slapper of Greater Dawson, what is he for? Is he going to lay broad and deep the foundations of Empire [for Great Britain]? Will he bear the banner of progress into that paleocrystic waste? Will he clear the way for even a dog sled civilization and a reindeer religion? Nothing will come of him. He is a word in the wind, a brother to the fog. At the scene of his activity no memory of him will remain. The gravel that he thawed and sifted will freeze again. In the shanty that he builded, the she-wolf will rear her poddy litter, and from its eaves the moose will crop the esculent icicle unafraid. The snows will close over his trail and all be as before."

By August 10 the U.S. Secretary of the Interior, C. N. Bliss, felt it necessary to issue a state paper warning against anyone attempting to get to the Klondike that

144

season. Clifford Sifton, the Canadian Minister of the Interior, had already published a similar plea, but both warnings fell on deaf ears. The *Excelsior* landed in San Francisco with a second cargo of gold, and this time the newspapers did not underestimate the quantity. There was only about half a million dollars on board, but the press reports made it two and a half millions, exciting such enthusiasm that the publicity-shy William Ogilvie, who was a passenger, had to disguise himself as a crew member to escape the reporters. There was further excitement when it was learned that a U.S. government revenue cutter was escorting the *Portland* down the coast on her second trip to protect her from Chinese pirates said to be lying in wait to capture the two million dollars reported aboard her.

Such tales lent impetus to the rush which was gathering speed, snowball-fashion. When the government warning was issued, three thousand people were already hived in the erupting tent towns of Dyea and Skagway, at the foot of the passes, together with two thousand tons of baggage. Thousands of horses were already struggling, dying, and rotting on the trails. Before the warning was a fortnight old, twenty-one more steamers as well as three sailing-vessels and two scows, all jammed with men and animals and freight, had put out from Pacific coast ports, steaming towards the Lynn Canal. In one single week in mid-August, twenty-eight hundred people left Seattle for the Klondike. By September 1 nine thousand people and thirty-six thousand tons of freight had left the port.

Although few would believe it, there was by this time no chance of any traveller reaching the diggings before the following summer. This fact was conveniently glossed over by the merchants of the various coastal ports who were bidding for the Klondike outfitting trade. Every city was a madhouse. The streets of Victoria bustled with strange men — Scots, Irish, French, German, Australian, American — garbed in outlandish costumes and dragging oxen and horses through roadways piled high with sacks of provisions, knockdown boats, fur robes, and Klondike knickknackery. In Seattle the streets were crowded all night long. Unable to get lodgings, the stampeders slept in stables and washed at fire hydrants. All the coastal ports — San Francisco, Tacoma, Portland, Seattle, and Victoria — were locked in an intense struggle for the lion's share of the booty, each city screaming that it was the only possible outfitting port for the Klondike. The Canadians cried that every would-be miner ought to buy his goods in Canada since the Klondike was on British soil and a stiff duty would be levied on American outfits crossing the line. Victoria merchants went so far as to dispatch agents to Seattle to spread this news among the stampeders who were pouring off the trains. The Americans shouted just as loudly that every miner would have to cross the isthmus of the Alaska Panhandle, where he must pay duty on Canadian goods or else pay U.S. guards a fee to accompany bonded supplies to the Canadian line.

Up and down the coast the arguments reverberated. Seattle papers published bitter editorials attacking the claims of Tacoma and San Francisco, and the rival cities retorted in kind. One San Francisco merchant displayed in his window a poster showing two stampeders. One was depicted tired and beaten at the foot of the Chilkoot, complaining: "I outfitted in Seattle." The other was shown fresh as a daisy atop the pass, crowing triumphantly: "I bought *my* goods in San Francisco."

But it was Seattle in the end that seized the bulk of the gold-rush trade with a campaign planned as carefully as any military exercise. Within a week of the *Portland*'s arrival the Chamber of Commerce had organized a committee to boost Seattle as the only possible outfit-

146

ting port. The city's subsequent paid advertising in the nation's press exceeded that of its competitors fivefold, but it was the superiority of Seattle's free advertising that won the day.

This was largely due to the secretary of the advertising committee, a veteran newspaperman of subtle ingenuity named Erastus Brainerd, a Harvard graduate who had once been an art-gallery curator. The term "public-relations man" had yet to be coined, but Brainerd was a worthy forerunner of the PR breed. In publicizing Seattle he left nothing to chance. He inserted advertisements in small-town newspapers until he calculated he had a total circulation for them of almost ten million. He saw that the Klondike edition of the Seattle *P-I* was sent to seventy thousand U.S. postmasters, six thousand libraries, and four thousand mayors; then, for good measure, he distributed fifteen thousand to the Great Northern and Northern Pacific railroads for prospective stampeders heading for the west coast. Brainerd was a student of psychology, and one of his most successful schemes was to persuade Seattleites of recent origin to send letters back to their home towns, to friends and local editors, exhorting their former neighbours to go to the Klondike via Seattle. Brainerd made it easy to send such letters, for he wrote them himself, leaving blanks for names and signatures, supplied the postage, and even dropped them in the mailbox. Another scheme involved the sending of Klondike views, with Seattle's compliments, as Christmas gifts to the crowned heads of Europe. This worked out satisfactorily in all cases but one: the German Kaiser refused to open his package for fear that it might contain dynamite.

Brainerd had printed a series of circulars of various kinds which he sent to newspapers, diplomats, prospective migrants, governors and mayors, congressmen and

147

senators. These documents looked more like personally dictated letters than advertising throwaways, and received wide attention. In one such circular Brainerd quoted the correspondent of *Harper's Weekly* on the superiority of Seattle for Alaskan trade. He did not mention that the correspondent of *Harper's Weekly* was Erastus Brainerd.

Another circular tried to suggest that the Klondike trip was not much more arduous than a casual stroll after lunch — an idea that was fostered by all the Pacific coast ports. Shooting the Whitehorse Rapids was made to appear mere child's play: "Of those who have gone in. . . not more than half a dozen have lost their lives and these from carelessness in fording." The last phrase was a masterpiece, for it seemed to imply that the crossing of the various Yukon torrents was not much more than a wading expedition. Brainerd persuaded the Secretary of State for Washington to sign this circular, which he sent to foreign diplomats. This gave it the status of an official communication, and it was immediately relayed to overseas capitals, where it was widely published and distributed.

In addition, Brainerd and the Chamber worked out an espionage system which (*a*) quietly gave Seattle merchants the names of potential customers and (*b*) informed the city of its rivals' plans so that steps could be taken to forestall them. All this energy paid big dividends for the city, which by the early spring of 1898 had garnered twenty-five million dollars in Klondike trade as compared with the five million that went through the other ports. As for Brainerd, he became so mesmerized by his own campaign that, when spring came, he started for the Klondike himself.

6: *Balloons, boatsleds, and bicycles*

Gathering momentum swiftly in the late summer months, the great stampede was moving at express-train speed by midwinter, its course illuminated by the various quirks and eccentricities, personal tragedies, follies, fortunes, and excitements which mark any large exodus of people. The Klondike was certainly responsible for one of the strangest mass movements in history. All that winter and through most of the following summer, men and women by the tens of thousands crossed oceans and continents, moving by train, steamship, scow, horseback, oxcart, foot, and raft to reach the magic land. The movement was truly world-wide. A sloop with ninety Norwegians left Christiania in October, sailed around the Horn, and reached San Francisco in April en route to the Klondike. In February the *Cape Otway* left Sydney, Australia, for Alaska with two hundred and twelve passengers crammed aboard her. A Greek in Jerusalem wrote to the Central Pacific Railroad that he and a group of fellow countrymen were heading for Dawson with stores of goods to trade. An expedition of three hundred Scotsmen sailed for Montreal in January on their way to the gold-fields. A steam yacht, complete with orchestra, personal valets, and Parisian chefs, left England in February loaded with young aristocrats. A company of young Italians moved through San Francisco in the spring, announcing that they were an advance guard for an expedition of several hundred. Belted earls and washerwomen, congressmen and card sharps, millionaires and paupers all rubbed shoulders on the trails that led north. Sir Charles Tupper, the ex-Prime Minister of Canada, wrote from England that one hundred thousand stampeders would sail from that country alone. This turned out to be an overestimate, but it has been reckoned that

149

in the winter of 1897-98 one million people laid plans to leave home and family to seek their fortune in the Klondike and that, at the very least, one hundred thousand actually set out.

The transportation companies were as eager for the Klondike business as the coast cities. Every train travelling across the continent had its own "gold-rush car," the walls lined with glass jars full of nuggets and dust and papered with photographs of the mining areas, and the side cabins and tables cluttered with books, maps, and pamphlets, picks, pans, shovels, hammers, quicksilver, fur, parkas, and heavy boots.

In the fall of '97 steamship tickets sold at fantastic prices. Before the *Excelsior* left on her return voyage from San Francisco to St. Michael, the agents had been forced to turn away ten times her passenger list. On July 29 one man who had bought a ticket aboard her was able to sell it for fifteen hundred dollars, which was ten times its value. By midwinter the fare settled down to a straight one thousand. Suddenly money had become very cheap. Stampeders were willing to gamble almost any sum to reach their goal. In March, 1898, the *Review of Reviews* estimated that the argonauts had already spent sixty million dollars in purchasing rail and ocean transport and Klondike outfits. The Klondike had been oversold: its gold-production for the year 1898 did not exceed ten millions.

The stampeders snapped up almost anything that was offered them. They bought sleds powered by gasoline motors and others powered by steam. They bought "automatic" gold-pans set on a spindle and operated by clockwork on the gramophone principle. They bought scurvy cures, portable cabins, food tablets, earmuffs, frost cures, and a variety of useless bric-a-brac that even included "nugget-in-the-slot" machines for dispensing cigars, paper envelopes, scenes of

150

great battles, and similar northern essentials. Bunko men rushed to the Pacific coast to take advantage of the suckers pouring through the various towns. Arthur Dietz, a God-fearing New Yorker who arrived in Seattle in February on his way to Alaska, described it as "more wicked than Sodom." Dietz wrote that "the Devil reigned supreme. It was a gigantic chaos of crime and the city government, as an institution, protected evil." The streets were infested with agents and beggars and confidence men hawking everything from bottled mercury to evaporated beans. Gambling-houses, saloons, and brothels ran wide open. Government stores got rid of army surplus blankets, tents, and knapsacks, many of them worn out and useless. Dietz and his party bought one hundred pounds of evaporated eggs from an agent who poured some of the yellow powder out of the sack and cooked it before their eyes to demonstrate his honesty. It tasted like scrambled eggs, but when the party reached the shores of Alaska and opened the sack they discovered that the salesman, by sleight-of-hand, had substituted yellow cornmeal. Dozens of other parties reported similar experiences.

The so-called "Klondike Bicycle" was a popular item with the stampeders, for the Klondike strike came at the height of the bicycle craze. The velocipede was to the 1890s what the television set came to be to the 1950s. Sunday newspapers actually found their circulation decreasing because everyone spent the Sabbath on wheels. When the New York *Journal* held a contest to name the ten most popular bicyclists and send them on a tour of Europe, it received six and one half million responses. Everybody from princes to policemen pedalled, and the *Herald* reported with approbation that one woman had tracked down her faithless husband on a bicycle and thus secured a divorce. It was freely predicted that the next war would be fought on bicycles,

151

and the Sunday-supplement drawings of what the world would look like a hundred years hence invariably showed the entire populace pedalling determinedly down the streets. Such was the faith in the bicycle that thousands were prepared to believe that this was the ideal way of crossing the mountain passes. Two youths, cycling around the world for a Chicago paper, switched plans and began propelling themselves towards Alaska. On September 20 the Misses Olga McKenna and Nellie Ritchie, described as "two of the best wheel-women in Boston," started pedalling north, announcing that they expected to enlist one thousand women in their move to cycle to Dawson City. Two wheel-men from a Brooklyn club were a day ahead of them, pumping furiously across the continent wearing broad-brimmed slouch hats, blue shirts, knee-trousers, heavy woollen stockings, and bicycle shoes, a costume they described as being halfway between a cyclist's and a miner's garb.

A New York syndicate meanwhile was busily marketing machines designed especially for the stampede to which were attached four-wheeled trailers with a freight capacity of five hundred pounds. There were also "ice bicycles" with a forward ski, and something else called "bicycle skates." Two New Yorkers in the fall of '97 left for the Klondike on a strange contraption consisting of two bicycles joined together with iron bars heavy enough to support a small rowboat containing their outfit. They declared they would reach the Klondike in ninety days by this method, but the ensuing winter found them still at the foot of the White Pass.

Another much-advertised contrivance was the Klondike "boatsled," a sectional steel vessel which was purported to be amphibious. Sails were provided to propel it across northern lakes; on land, a couple of panels at the side were supposed to be let down to form a flat surface under the keel, which was hollow, being fitted with air chambers to ensure buoyancy, and a burglar-proof compartment in which to store the gold dust that everybody expected to dig from the ground as easily as if it were so much sand.

Like so many others, the boatsled scheme flopped miserably. There seemed to be no end to the ingenuity and impracticability of the inventions that sprang up during the stampede. A noted electrical expert of the times, Nikalo Tesla, a one-time associate of Thomas Edison, attempted to market an X-ray machine which he said was essential for prospectors because it could detect the presence of gold hidden in small beds of sand and gravel. Three Washington State men worked out a scheme to suck gold from the riverbeds, using compressed air. Another optimist headed north with diving-equipment, explaining that he planned to walk along the bed of the Yukon River picking up nuggets. The Secretary of the Treasury, Lyman Gage, actually gave his blessing to a snow train, propelled by a giant sprocketed wheel, that bore a remarkable resemblance to the modern snowmobile (but which never worked). An organization called the Trans-Alaskan Gopher Co. offered shares at a dollar apiece and promised returns of ten dollars a minute when it got into operation: it proposed to take contracts for digging tunnels in Klondike claims with trained gophers. A root-beer salesman announced he was leaving for the Chilkoot Pass with a thousand packages of root beer; it was his intention to sell the beverage to thirsty argonauts at an eight-hundred-per-cent profit. A Dr. Armand Ravol, the city bacteriologist of St. Louis, planned to go to the Klondike armed with packages of deadly germs suitable for eliminating mosquitoes. And there was that abortive corporation with the jaw-breaking name known as the Klondike and Cuba Ice Towing and Anti-Yellow Fever Company, which proposed, with a wild disregard for ocean geography, to tow icebergs from the Klondike to the South Seas, where, it was believed, they could be transformed into cold compresses to alleviate the suffering of fever victims.

Portus B. Weare, the balding and distinguished chairman of the board of the North American Trading and Transportation Company in Chicago, was the target of a small platoon of fortune-seekers who wanted financial backing for a variety of wild schemes. A lady clairvoyant cornered him in his office and asked for two thousand dollars. She claimed to be able to find the hiding-places of nuggets, no matter how far they were below the surface. A penny-dreadful writer asked Weare for a few thousands to go to the Klondike, which, he felt, must be swarming with notorious criminals in hiding. It was his plan to use his detective-novel knowledge to capture them and claim the rewards.

There were several projects afoot to invade the goldfields with lighter-than-air craft, for the balloon was the sensation of the age, and just six days before the *Portland*'s arrival in Seattle, Solomon Augustus Andrée, the Swedish polar explorer, had set out to reach the North Pole by balloon. In Dublin an Irish gold-seeker announced the construction of an enormous balloon large enough to take fifty passengers to the Klondike. In New York one Leo Stevens, Jr., adopting the more romantic title of Don Carlos Stevens, raised one hundred and fifty thousand dollars and announced he was building the biggest balloon in the world, which would take off from a point near Juneau and soar over the coastal mountains into the Klondike carrying eight to ten passengers and six or seven tons of freight. In Kalamazoo another entrepreneur declared that he would establish a regular balloon route to the Klondike, each balloon to carry a ton of goods and make a return trip in a fortnight. People all over the country wrote to him offering ridiculous sums for passage or even "a berth in steerage," and one Illinois citizen sent along a bank draft for five hundred dollars. But after Andrée was swallowed by the polar mists, the enthusiasm over balloons began to fade.

One of the periodic features of the stampede was the emergence of the "syndicate of wealthy New Yorkers," a vague and shadowy group of titans who continually popped up, propounding various get-rich-quick schemes. One "syndicate of wealthy New Yorkers" was said to be establishing a reindeer postal service to the Klondike along the lines of the pony express, while another syndicate of wealthy New Yorkers was reported engaged in building a bicycle path to the Klondike to service a chain of trading posts.

A scheme devised by a Milwaukee man involved the use of carrier pigeons to establish communication between the Klondike and the rest of the world. A series of pigeon stations was envisaged, with the birds carrying letters that had been photographically reduced to the size of a needle point. These were to be enlarged at Victoria, B.C., and re-mailed from there. The trouble with this idea was that nobody could work out a fast way of getting the pigeons to the Klondike.

If these schemes were taken seriously, it was because of the peculiar blindness produced by the Klondike fever. One plan actually entertained by responsible businessmen in Canada and the United States called for the construction of a railway from Chesterfield Inlet on Hudson Bay across seven hundred miles of Arctic tundra to Great Slave Lake, a region almost totally unexplored, unmapped, and unknown. This was only part of a grandiose rail-and-water route which was pictured as stretching all the way from Sault Ste Marie to Dawson City, a distance of more than four thousand miles — and thence on to the Bering Strait, where the

155

ferry line would link North America with Russia. A writer in the Toronto *Globe* reckoned that by this route a traveller could reach Dawson in seven days. A group of Canadian businessmen actually secured a charter for it, and the *Financial Times* of London commented favourably on the scheme. Needless to say, no such railway has ever been built, but there is little doubt that the Klondike boom spurred the tremendous railway expansion that marked the development of Canada in the first decade of the twentieth century. By 1910 the Canadians had commenced two more transcontinental railways, in addition to the Canadian Pacific. Both eventually went bankrupt.

But in the fall of 1897 the wildest plans seemed practical, the most impossible ventures attainable. There was the Irishwoman who planned to take a group of children to the Klondike: she would teach them lessons by day, they would dig gold by night. There was the dancing-master who planned to practise his craft in Dawson City: he would teach the two-step to Indians and miners all winter and dig gold all summer. "Dig" was the operative word. To many, it was as simple as that: you stuck your spade into the golden soil and shovelled the results into the bank. There were those who actually took gunny-sacks with them on the trip north to serve as containers for the nuggets.

All across the land, syndicates, co-operatives, investment and colonization companies were being formed to exploit some aspect of the Klondike. On August 1 the New York *World* carried a solid page of advertisements for Klondike organizations of one kind or another. By the end of August there were eighty-five syndicates in operation in twenty-two American cities, with a total capitalization of one hundred and sixty-five million dollars. Dozens more were forming almost hourly.

These syndicates and co-operatives operated with a

board of directors or executive; each member paid a weekly sum to finance a few men to go to the Klondike and strike it rich for the whole. Some of the syndicates were fairly far-fetched: a group of Chicago spiritualists formed a syndicate, gazed into crystal balls, drew maps with the aid of clairvoyance, and sent a representative to the Klondike; a group of barbers met and formed a syndicate to shave the beards off Klondike miners, an enterprise generally considered rewarding in view of the whiskers sported by prospectors debarking from the treasure ships. The Bowery Mission of New York formed a syndicate and sent an expedition of seven men to the Klondike, headed by a reformed gambler who proposed to convert his fellow stampeders en route and dig for gold at the same time. Dozens of Bowery habitués tried to go along, threatening to empty the mission.

In Philadelphia a promoter talked twelve technical-school students into persuading their fathers to buy a schooner and send them around Cape Horn to the Klondike. It was a measure of the madness that the fathers acquiesced. The promoter was supposed to be a navigator, but turned out to be a very poor one. After a series of fits and starts, delays and bunglings, storms and calms, the vessel finally stumbled into Juneau, Alaska, where it foundered. All of the boys went home except one, a particularly determined youth named Frank Neill who was not deterred by shipwrecks or bankruptcy. He continued to press on towards the Klondike and finally reached his goal in the summer of 1900. The gold was all gone, but, as others were to discover, it was not all in the ground. Neill made a small fortune hauling logs, used it to get a start in the construction business in Long Island, and did well enough to marry and make a wedding trip back to the Klondike.

Of the colonization schemes, the most intriguing was

a plan, launched by members of the congregation of the Beecher Memorial Church of Brooklyn, to charter a boat and build a second Brooklyn City on the Yukon River, from which gamblers, drinkers, and other un-Christian citizens would be banned. The group announced that the city would be eventually the largest on the western side of the continent. None of the participants seemed very sure of where it was they were going, but their literature placed the site at the foot of "a mountain which is said to be the fountainhead of the gold field."

The single status of ninety-eight per cent of the Klondike miners was not lost on the entrepreneurs promoting various expeditions to the gold-fields, or upon the hundreds of spinsters who put personal ads in the newspapers offering to accompany men to the Klondike "in any capacity." The movement for emancipation was well under way in the nineties, and the distaff side was beginning to insist with increasing vigour that anything men could do, women could do better. One of these was Charlotte Smith, a well-known sociologist of the era, who talked up a scheme to transport four thousand spinsters from the sweatshops and factories of New England to the Klondike. She received thousands of applications but no financing. There were other ideas along the same lines. A midwife announced that she would guarantee a yearly income of fifty thousand dollars to any partner who would invest five hundred in a hospital she planned to build in Dawson. There were no takers. A man from Pittsburgh laid plans to establish a matrimonial agency in the Klondike: he said he would secure employment in advance for groups of one hundred women, "poor but thoroughly respectable." Their future employers would advance funds for the trip north and "under their influence the camp would take on a homelike appearance and the miners would not feel a sense of isolation which sends so many to their graves."

Another promoter in South Dakota, described as "a strict Presbyterian," proposed to send a consignment of marriageable women north, plus a clergyman to marry them. Each maiden was asked to sign a pledge that she would not get off the steamboat until she and her would-be spouse had taken the vows and paid a commission.

Several women's Klondike expeditions were actually financed and organized. One ambitious group, promoted by a New York newspaper-woman, planned to travel in caravans which could be collapsed and taken on horseback over the passes and then floated down the river on rafts. There were to be five vans for every twenty people, three of them to be fitted with portable sleepers to accommodate seven women in each.

Few of these schemes got under way, but one party of women actually did set out for the Klondike under the aegis of Mrs. Hannah S. Gould, a nurse and businesswoman who booked passage for five hundred passengers, mostly widows, to the gold-fields as part of the Women's Clondyke Expedition. The company chartered the steamship *City of Columbia,* painted a four-leaf clover on the smokestack, and announced that they would sail it on a twenty-thousand-mile voyage around the Horn to Alaska. J. J. Clements, one of the original stakers of Eldorado, broke a bottle of champagne over the ship's bow in New York harbour, while Mrs. Gould, in a natty yachting-cap and pea jacket, toasted the voyage in wine, talking all the while of establishing a library, church, recreation hall, restaurant, and hospital in Dawson. One hundred cases of champagne were stowed away below decks as a cure for seasickness, and the ship got under way. The champagne came in handy in the Strait of Magellan, where the entire expedition was shipwrecked and the luckless women marooned for twenty-four hours on a bleak rock off Tierra del Fuego. Here Mrs. Gould had a brief but unhappy encounter with a Patagonian cannibal who, as far as could be determined, was attempting a proposal of marriage. The doughty widow refused to be swerved from her Klondike objective, which, at this point, was quite literally at the other end of the earth. "Go away, you ugly brute!" she exclaimed and led her flock back aboard the patched-up vessel, which limped on into Valparaiso. By this time the company was on its last legs.

The unhappy women scraped up twenty-eight thousand dollars to repair the ship, and reached Seattle in April, all their savings dissipated. They had paid in advance for outfits which were supposed to be awaiting them in Seattle, and also for their steamer passage north, but there was nothing for them on arrival. The entire party disbanded, their dreams of rich husbands shattered. Only one ever reached the Klondike, a determined little woman with snapping black eyes named Nettie Hoven who simply walked aboard the steamship *Hayden Brown* and worked her way north as a stewardess.

The great majority of the Klondike syndicates met similar fates. Few paid off for the investors who stayed behind. In the spring of 1898 Captain W. B. Richardson of the U.S. Army, who had been sent to Alaska the previous fall, reported from St. Michael that almost all the syndicates had laboured under incapable management and with insufficient means, and that "in nearly all instances" they had come to ultimate grief or abandonment.

7: *Fearful passage*

As the winter progressed, a grotesque flotilla of oddly assorted craft, many of them little more than floating coffins, shuttled up and down the Pacific coast crammed with stampeders bound for Skagway, Dyea, Wrangell, or St. Michael. By February there were forty-one regular ships operating out of San Francisco harbour alone, "greater in point of numbers, efficiency and carrying capacity than any fleet ever collected in any harbor in the world to engage in a specific enterprise," according to the *Examiner* — enough ships, indeed, to transport one hundred thousand people and six million pounds of freight to Alaska.

Ships that had long been condemned were resurrected from boneyards, hastily patched up, and put into use. Yachts, sloops, barques, scows, barges, ancient steamboats, and sailing-schooners — anything that could float was pressed into service. The *Tartar,* a once proud mail boat on the Cape Line which had carried South African millionaires through tropical waters, steamed north from Vancouver past the peaks and glaciers of the Lynn Canal. The *Danube,* which had brought Livingstone's body to Europe from Africa, puffed out of Seattle so crowded that during one storm the captain was forced to lock forty-four men in the hatches among the horses.

The *Rosalie,* a transformed sailing-vessel, the *Cutch,* once the private yacht of an Indian rajah, the *Laurada,* an old blockade-runner from Cuba, and the *Hermosa,* an ancient Catalina Island—San Pedro ferryboat, were all pressed into service. The *North Fork,* which for years had been freighting soap across San Francisco Bay, was headed for the boneyard when the stampede began. Soon she was shuttling passengers to St. Michael at one thousand dollars a head. The *Ning Chow,* a creaky

161

Chinese freighter, was brought across the Pacific for the coastal trade and fitted out with rough lumber bunks four tiers high. So cramped were these quarters — she carried close to one thousand people — and so bad the food, that a Texan, suffering from claustrophobia and indigestion, tried to shoot the dining-room steward. The *Cleveland,* a very old steamer that had barely survived a series of ugly accidents along the South American coast, headed north with two hundred passengers, all of whom had the gravest misgivings, for the vessel was known as an unlucky ship. And indeed, as later events were to prove, bad luck was to be visited upon them.

In the first five weeks of the stampede, twenty steamers left the Pacific coast for Alaska. New ones were being chartered daily. The little *Al-ki* was the first to set off, on July 19. So great was the excitement among the thousand who squeezed onto the dock that scores refused to give up their places to go and eat.

"If the ship doesn't leave soon, my husband will be crazy," one woman was heard to say. "He hasn't closed his eyes for twenty-four hours, he won't eat, and if he fails to find gold in Alaska, well, God pity him and his family."

All day long and into the night the crowd waited patiently. An aged confectioner moved about selling peanut candy cakes called Yukon Nuggets at a quarter apiece (the price of a meal) while small boys dodged in and out hawking copies of the British mining laws. "Hurrah for the Klondike!" cried the crowd, shouting the accepted cliché for all northern good-byes, as members of the ship's crew forced them back and drove a bleating herd of nine hundred sheep aboard. There were, in addition, one hundred and ten passengers, sixty-five cattle, thirty horses, and three hundred and fifty tons of supplies. When the *Al-ki* finally got away, there was not an inch of room left.

Every ship going north was similarly overloaded. When the *Humboldt* after a series of delays finally escaped from San Francisco on August 16, W. D. Wood, the Seattle mayor who had chartered the ship, tried to leave some fifty thousand pounds of his passengers' personal baggage behind. This so enraged them that a group actually attempted to hang the former mayor on the dockside. Cooler heads prevailed, and the ship was reloaded.

Space was at a premium on all Alaska-bound vessels. On the *Islander,* which left for Alaska on July 28 with four hundred passengers, the horses were wedged side by side so tightly that there was no way for them to lie down. Many of these wretched creatures had their heads so close to the engines that they were in a state of continual panic, rearing, biting, kicking, and throwing themselves on their halters at the throb of the machinery and the blast of the whistle.

A passenger aboard the Canadian steamer *Amur* described it as "a floating bedlam, pandemonium let loose, the Black Hole of Calcutta in an Arctic setting." This vessel, which had normal accommodation for one hundred passengers, crammed five hundred aboard, together with almost as many dogs — Danes, mastiffs, collies, Saint Bernards, Newfoundlands, and wolfhounds, all yapping, howling, and struggling, and none of them, as it turned out, of the slightest use under northern conditions. The tickets promised separate berths, but the passengers, who included among their number fifty prostitutes, were stacked ten to a cabin. As there were only three berths to a room, each argonaut had to be prepared to pounce upon a bunk as soon as it was vacated, and to sleep in his clothes for the entire voyage. The ship's dining-room could accommodate

163

twenty-six people comfortably, which meant that every meal took seven hours to serve, and the famished passengers fell into the habit of lying in wait for the stewards as they passed by and ravenously snatching morsels of food from the trays.

Such conditions did not deter thousands from purchasing tickets at premium prices for the voyage north. In Vancouver men tried to bribe ships' officers to let them onto northbound vessels; and some who were known to have tickets were slugged and robbed by others who would take their place on deck. One Tacoma man, unable to buy a ticket aboard the *Willamette*, raised such a furore that the captain was obliged to put him in irons.

When the *Willamette* left Tacoma on August 7 there were seventy-five hundred people pressed together on the dock to wish her Godspeed, an ocean of struggling humanity who waited for hours for the ship to get under way. The voyage that followed was seared into the minds of passengers and crew for the remainder of their lives. The *Willamette* was an old coal-carrier converted into service by the Pacific Coast Steamship Company. Rough berths for the passengers had been thrown together by carpenters and, as in many similar vessels, were designed to be ripped apart at Skagway and sold as dressed lumber for three hundred dollars a thousand feet. As nobody had bothered to sweep the coal dust from the vessel, the passengers were soon grimy with it. The ship carried eight hundred men, women, and children, three hundred horses, and so much hay that the bales had to be stacked on deck, where the piles cut off the forward view from the bridge. Since the company had built eating facilities for only sixty-five, the meals went into nine or ten sittings, with one man sliding in behind another as soon as the first had finished. The food was sickening, the surroundings filthy, and the

164

floor sprinkled with shavings to hide the refuse. Beef was hung on two sides of the dining-room, so that no one could get to one side of the table without rubbing against raw meat. The passengers were quartered under the rough plank decks upon which the horses were tethered, and the excretions of these animals leaked through the cracks in the boards onto the sleeping men. Most of the passengers tried to stay up above decks because of the unbearable stench below. Here for much of the voyage they stood drenched in the driving rain, since there were chairs and shelter for only a third. Second-class passengers were even worse off. The hold where they were quartered was, in the words of one witness, "a veritable beehive [where] the atmosphere resembled that of a dungeon in Afghanistan."

Few of the ships plying the coastal waters bothered with safety precautions. The steamer *Bristol* steamed out of Victoria early in August with six hundred horses jammed in two-foot-wide stalls and rough bunks filling every available cranny. She was so badly and heavily loaded that a few miles out of port she almost turned turtle and was forced to creep back to harbour to readjust her topload. In her wake she towed a frail sternwheeler, but this craft was so unseaworthy that the captain cut her adrift off Vancouver Island — an action that touched off a series of lawsuits and recriminations.

There were many similar mishaps, some ludicrous, some tragic. The *Nancy G.*, billed as "a fine schooner in tow of a powerful ocean tug," started off for Dyea twenty days behind schedule and sank on her return voyage. Neither captain nor pilot aboard the *Whitelaw* had been in Alaskan waters before. This ship foundered in the Lynn Canal, and although her passengers were saved, they lost everything they owned in the fire that followed the wreck. The *Clara Nevada*, ignoring the laws against booking passengers when the cargo

165

contained dynamite, blew sky-high between Skagway and Juneau with the loss of all sixty-five souls, except for the inevitable dog that survived. The *City of Mexico* struck West Devil's Rock off Sitka and was sunk, though her passengers and crew were saved. The *Corona* struck a reef at the Skeena's mouth and sank, a total loss. The *Laurada,* attempting to tow two old river steamers to St. Michael, was driven ashore at Sitka in the teeth of a gale. The barque *Helen W. Almy,* an old South Seas trader, was wrecked on the Alaskan coast. The *Queen* broke her steering gear in Wrangell Narrows and threatened to keel over, causing such a panic that one woman tried to kill the captain with a pistol and had to be handcuffed. The *Pakshan's* decks were piled so high the pilot could not see and smashed the steamer upon a rock. The sailing-schooner *Hera* lay becalmed two months off Vancouver Island, her crew and passengers almost starving to death when food supplies ran low. The barque *Canada,* loaded with lumber, horses, and freight, ran onto the rocks a few miles south of Dyea; all the horses had to be shot, but the passengers were rescued by a passing ship. That same week another barque, *Tidal Wave,* was wrecked, the steamer *Oregon* all but foundered on a sand-bar near Treadwell, while the passengers on the *Cleveland,* having been lost for four days (although within hailing distance of Skagway) and out of water for sixty hours, were reduced to making coffee from brine.

The *Blakely,* a square-rigged brigantine condemned by the U.S. government two years before, was chartered by four Klondike syndicates from Connecticut, New York, Texas, and Minnesota, although she had been rotting on the Tacoma beach for twenty-four months. The trip that followed was a nightmare, the leaky hull groaning and creaking, the pumps working continuously, the captain refusing to take charge until he had

166

consumed the entire supply of whiskey. The ship survived a storm so fierce that one seaman was flung overboard by the wind, and one passenger died of starvation because he was too seasick to eat. The cargo, badly loaded, shifted to one side and threatened to capsize the vessel; the passengers had to fight to get it back into position to restore equilibrium. Conditions were so bad that many of the dogs died in their crates. After more than a month at sea, the old vessel, waterlogged and coated in a thick jacket of ice, was finally beached at Yakutat on the south coast of Alaska, where her rueful passengers found that all of their machinery, equipment, and food had been ruined by sea water. But their subsequent trials on the Malaspina glacier made the trip up the coast seem like a pleasant Sunday outing.

The strangest voyage of all, however, was the one made by the *Eliza Anderson*. Her bizarre odyssey was the epitome of all the crazy peregrinations of that demented winter. The ship herself was the oldest vessel on the coast, an ancient side-wheeler built forty years before and long since consigned to the boneyard. She had once figured prominently in the rush to the Coeur d'Alene, but for years she had been tied up at a bank in Seattle harbour, where she did duty as a road house and gambling-hall. The news of the Klondike was but a few days old when this decrepit craft was plucked from retirement and hastily made fit for a three-thousand-mile ocean voyage to the Bering Sea. So eager were her promoters to squeeze the last ounce of profit from the expedition that duplicate tickets were sold for passage aboard her. This device so enraged her passengers that they tried to hurl her purser into the sea and were only prevented from doing so by the skipper, a redoubtable sea-dog named Tom Powers, who was not in the least fazed by hostile customers, incompetent crew members, or mediaeval equipment.

The *Anderson* seemed to lack every item necessary for a sea voyage. She had no propeller, no up-to-date boilers, no water-condensers, no steam hoisting tackle, no electric power, no refrigeration, and, incredibly, no ship's compass. Her coal-bunkers were makeshift and totally inadequate, a factor that almost proved her undoing.

She was the flagship of a weird flotilla of five vessels that set out from Seattle on August 10 to the cheers of five thousand well-wishers. The limping side-wheeler led off the pack, her decks jammed with the familiar paraphernalia of the stampede: tables and chairs, collapsible silk tents and collapsible canvas beds, sleeping-bags, tin and granite pots, pans, cups, dishes, and stoves, patent gold-rockers, assorted sleds of curious shape and odd construction, and mounds of clothing and provisions. Close behind, puffing furiously, came the tiny ocean-going tug *Richard Holyoke*. She had three queer craft in tow. The first was a coal barge of romantic origin: a former Russian man-o'-war, the *Politofsky*, built in Sitka a year before the Alaskan Purchase, once the flagship and pride of the Russian Pacific fleet but long since shorn of her superstructure and now a hulk — weather-beaten, derelict, and black with coal dust. The second looked at first glance like a replica of Noah's Ark. This was the *W. K. Merwyn*, a seventeen-year-old stern-wheeler which had been used as a hay-and-grain carrier but was now intended for Yukon River traffic. It was planned to abandon the *Anderson* at St. Michael and transfer the passengers to the *Merwyn* for the river trip to the Klondike. Her smokestack and paddle-wheel had been removed for safety and stowed on her main deck, and the entire steamboat was now encased in a wooden jacket from stem to stern. Inside this grotesque craft, boxed like rats in a cage, were sixteen passengers, the overflow from the *Ander-*

168

son. All that kept the *Merwyn* on a steady keel was a cargo of tinned goods and supplies, which, lashed to the main deck, acted as a sort of counterweight. The final craft in the flotilla, also towed behind the tug, and looking oddly out of place among its ungainly neighbours, was a sleek pleasure yacht, the *Bryant.* This was owned by an adventurous Seattle clubman named John Hansen, whose brother was the town's leading jeweller. Hansen had tried to book passage aboard the *Anderson,* but even the duplicate tickets had been sold. He persuaded three business friends to come along with him and hooked his yacht behind the *Holyoke.*

The *Anderson's* first mishap occurred at the coal port of Comox on Vancouver Island where she stopped to take on fuel. The seamen were so inexperienced that they loaded the coal unequally into the bunkers. As a result the ship listed dangerously to starboard and her rudder went out of action, whereupon she drifted broadside into the three-masted clipper *Glory of the Seas,* shattering a large section of her side-wheel paddle-box.

This and other mishaps kept the alarmed passengers in a continual uproar, and there were repeated demands for the vessel to turn back. Captain Powers refused all of them with disdain, roaring that he would sail the *Anderson* to St. Michael "come hell or high water," two eventualities that both seemed imminent. By the time the *Anderson* and her sister vessels had reached Kodiak, the port on Kodiak Island off the south coast of Alaska, five passengers were ready to give up. They fled the ship, and no amount of exhortation could lure them back on board.

The *Anderson* struck out for Dutch Harbor, the bleak port on the island of Unalaska at the very tip of the Alaskan peninsula where the Aleutian Islands have their beginning. Soon she was wallowing in a raging

169

storm, her engines straining to keep her on course. At this crucial moment the ship ran out of coal. The lazier members of the crew had hidden half the coal sacks at Kodiak so that nobody would notice that they had not loaded the full amount. The escorting tug and coal barge had vanished into the driving rain, and the *Anderson* was foundering. The passengers were routed out to tear the wooden bunkers apart and use the heavy planks for fuel. When these had been consumed, the large wooden water tanks were ripped asunder and flung into the furnace. The ship's furniture followed, and finally the stateroom partitions, until the *Anderson* was little more than a hollow shell tossing fitfully in the North Pacific.

The passengers by this time were all writing farewell notes and stuffing them into bottles in the accepted tradition of the romantic novels, and there were plenty of bottles for the purpose, since most of the whiskey on board had been consumed in an attempt to bolster waning spirits. By the time the storm reached its height, the life rafts and boats had been swept overboard, the vessel was out of control, and the captain gave the order to abandon ship. Then fate intervened in an extraordinary fashion.

The rescue was in keeping with the general eccentricity of the expedition. A six-foot stranger with a wild mop of greyish-white hair, a hawk nose, and a flowing white beard, dressed in oilskins and rubber boots, appeared suddenly out of the storm, strode into the pilothouse, seized the wheel, got the vessel under control, and steered her into a quiet cove on Kodiak Island, where she was anchored, protected from the raging winds. This done, the mystery man vanished as suddenly as he had appeared. To the terrified and overwrought passengers he must have seemed to be a god or demon from another world, but actually he was a stow-

170

away, a Norwegian recluse who lived on the island with his brother and was trying to get free passage to Unalaska (a fact which did not emerge until a subsequent investigation by the U.S. Navy).

Safe in harbour, but far from her destination and completely out of fuel, the *Anderson* now experienced a second fantastic piece of luck. The passengers happened upon an abandoned cannery loaded with coal. Refuelled, the ancient side-wheeler staggered along the coast of the peninsula towards the tundra of Unalaska. As she stumbled into Dutch Harbor she swivelled sideways, smashing into the docks with what was by now a familiar splintering of woodwork. The ship and passengers were still shuddering from this blow when a pipe in the boiler room burst, sending great clouds of scalding steam in all directions.

None of this in the least deterred the captain, who roared he would sail on for St. Michael, but the numbed passengers had had quite enough. Twenty-eight of them immediately booked passage for home. The remainder, still intent on getting to the gold-fields, chartered the whaling-schooner *Baranof* to take them the seven hundred and fifty miles across the Bering Sea to their destination. The whaler deposited them on the bare mud shores of the old Russian port, where, to the surprise of all, the rest of the flotilla was awaiting them. Here each man breathed an understandable sigh of relief. Most of them no doubt expected that the worst part of the long journey was over and that the remainder of the trip up the Yukon River to Dawson would be swift and gentle. Few realized that the Klondike was seventeen hundred miles and, for them, ten months away. For these people, as for the tens of thousands struggling at the foot of the Chilkoot and White passes, and across the hummocky glaciers of southern Alaska, and up the soggy, tangled interior of southern British Columbia, and down the long, weary stretches of the Mackenzie, the adventure and the hardships, the triumphs and the heartbreaks of the great stampede had only just begun.

Chapter Five

1
Captain Billy's last stand

2
The swarming sands of Skagway

3
The dead horse trail

4
Hell on earth

5
The human serpent

1: *Captain Billy's last stand*

For threescore years and ten the life of Captain William Moore had been crammed with enough adventure and melodrama to fill a dozen paperbacks. Now, at the age of seventy-four, the white-bearded mail-carrier was enthusiastically contemplating the most exhausting enterprise of his career. He was determined to build a boom town at the head of Skagway Bay.

Long before Carmack's strike, Moore was convinced that there would be a gold rush to the Yukon and that the main body of stampeders would pour through the narrow funnel which he had discovered in the Coast Mountains and named the White Pass. He had staked out a townsite on the edge of the glistening tidal flats, in the shadow of the chalk-white peaks, and now, in the dying days of July 1897, he was waiting.

This was the same old man who, the previous winter, had trotted through seven hundred miles of hitherto impassable wilderness to carry Ogilvie's first report of the Klondike to civilization. Moore's whole career had conditioned him for this kind of trek. He had been born in Germany in 1822 and by the age of seven was sailing aboard schooners in the North Sea. He was hardly out of his teens before he had reached New Orleans and was operating a towboat service on the lower Mississippi. He fought in the Mexican War and then for the next half-century followed gold — to California, Peru, the Queen Charlotte Islands of British Columbia, back to California again, and then on to the Fraser, the Cariboo, and the Cassiars. He was the kind of man who would try anything. He had on one occasion transported camels, of all creatures, up the Fraser River in his steamboat *The Flying Dutchman*, the most colourful of the British Columbia sternwheelers.

174

When he headed for Alaska in 1887, the captain had reached his lowest ebb. His five steamboats had earned him a fortune in the Cassiar stampede, but now, with the rush at an end, he was bankrupt, his fleet and his mansion in Victoria auctioned off to satisfy his creditors. His sons had already left for Alaska, and one had sent back word about a mysterious pass in the mountains, not far from the precipitous Chilkoot, which was said to be low enough to allow pack animals through. The old man's imagination was excited by this tale, and, following the instincts of a lifetime, he once again set his face north.

Under the direction of William Ogilvie, Moore sought out and surveyed the pass with the help of Carmack's Indian friend Skookum Jim, and named it after Sir Thomas White, the Canadian Minister of the Interior. It was forty-five miles long — ten miles longer than the Dyea trail across the Chilkoot but more than six hundred feet lower — a zigzagging, roller-coasting, switchbacking route through hill and canyon, mountain and valley, suitable in good conditions for travel by pack horse, ox, mule, dog, or goat. Moore saw its possibilities at once. As Ogilvie later recalled, "Every night during the two months he remained with us, he would picture the tons of yellow dust yet to be found in the Yukon Valley. He decided then and there that Skagway would be the entry point to the golden fields. . . and the White Pass would reverberate with the rumble of railway trains carrying supplies." He had no doubt about the future of the area. His son Bernard told a pioneer banquet in Skagway in 1904 that from the very outset "my father would tell me and numerous other people in Juneau and elsewhere how he pictured to himself the future of this place. He never tired of predicting how roads would be built through here; of a little city built here; of steamers on the upper Yukon; and of large

175

steamers, loaded with freight and passengers docking at the waterfront." All of this came to pass.

In 1888 Moore built a cabin at the foot of the pass, where the Skagway River rushes eagerly from the mountains to spend itself on the wooded flat at the head of Skagway Bay. The name is derived from an Indian word, "Skagus" — the home of the North Wind — and here at his front door was a setting of unequalled majesty. The bay forms the northern tip of the great Lynn Canal, a limpid fiord which runs for ninety miles, straight as a stiletto, to pierce the throat of the Alaskan peninsula at the point where it joins the body of the continent. In its glassy waters the sharp-peaked mountains with their tumbling cataracts and swirling glaciers are mirrored with perfect fidelity.

In these idyllic surroundings Moore was virtually a monarch, for the only other cabin in the district was the trading post established by John J. Healy on the neighbouring Dyea Inlet, three miles to the west. But on July 26, 1897, when the first gold-rush steamer anchored in the bay and dumped its load of kicking horses, yelping dogs, and scrambling men into the shallow waters, Moore's idyll ended.

They poured ashore like an invading horde, these first arrivals, and they paid as little attention to the protesting old steamboat captain as if he had been one of the trees that were now slashed down to make room for their tents and shacks. They heaped their goods on the beach, tethered their animals in the forest, then burned, hacked, and gouged away at Moore's sylvan sanctum until the rough semblance of a town began to emerge. Ship after ship spewed its human cargo onto the beach, until by early August there were enough newcomers to set up a local government and choose a committee to lay out the town properly with sixty-foot streets and neatly parcelled lots fifty by a hundred feet.

Frank Reid, a gimlet-eyed ex-school-teacher and Indian-fighter, was appointed town surveyor, and a commissioner was assigned to take a five-dollar registry fee from everybody who wished to locate on the land. Rule by committee, as Skagway was to learn, did not always mean rule by justice. In vain Moore protested that the land was his; nobody listened. It was the practice of the hastily assembled "miners' courts" to march upon those buildings that failed to conform to the new street pattern and demolish them out of hand; and though this summary action was often resisted by men with guns and axes, the community invariably got its way.

The crowning ignominy came when it was discovered that Moore's own home lay in the middle of one of the newly surveyed thoroughfares. He was ordered to move. When he angrily refused, another committee was elected to move him anyway, and Moore looked out one day to find it on his threshold with peevees and handspikes. The old man grabbed a crowbar and, while his wife stood sobbing in the doorway, slugged the man nearest to him, ripping off his trousers with the first swing. The crowd dispersed, but Moore knew that the game was up. He moved, but still refused to give in. He applied to the courts for redress and hung on stubbornly while the litigation dragged on for four years. In the meantime he shrewdly realized a fortune from a mile-long wharf which he had built out over the tidal flats so that the boats could dock properly. In the end he won his court action and was awarded twenty-five per cent of the assessed value of all the lots within the original townsite.

Thus did the indestructible Moore end his days in Skagway, a wealthy man long after the great rush abated; few of those who trampled across his front yard during those first wild days met the same reward.

2: *The swarming sands of Skagway*

The town of Skagway was conceived in lawlessness and nurtured in anarchy. The pattern was set early in August when a Frenchman was caught stealing from a cache on the White Pass trail. Again a committee was elected to deal with the offence, and deal with it they did, lashing their prisoner to a pole before his tent and, as he screamed for mercy, pumping him full of bullets. For three days his bloody cadaver hung suspended as an object lesson in summary justice.

As the fresh fall snow powdered the mountains and the winds began to howl down through the pass and across the shining tidal flats, the ships continued to pour in until the long bay was speckled with hundreds of craft, ranging from great, grimy freighters to slim Peterborough canoes. Snub-nosed scows, creaking with excessive loads, shuttled from boat to beach and back again, or from Skagway to Dyea, three miles away, picking their way between the thrashing forms of goats, dogs, mules, and oxen left to fend for themselves in the cold waters. Each incoming cargo ship was forced to anchor a mile offshore and to dump men, outfits, and animals into the shallow sea. Horses were swung from the decks in special boxes whose bottoms opened up, plunging the terrified and kicking creatures into the water. Trunks and packing-cases were dropped unceremoniously into waiting scows (where they were often smashed to kindling) and then cast helter-skelter onto the gravelly beach (where they were often lost or stolen). There were no stevedores; these had all deserted to the gold-fields. Captains struggled to preserve their crews, on the one hand, and to placate their passengers, on the other. The master of the *Bristol* narrowly escaped with his life when he refused to pay the exorbitant lighterage fees to move cargoes to the beach and was brought to heel only when a committee of eighty passengers — the inevitable committee — threatened to chain him hand and foot and heave him overboard.

All the world had suddenly heard of Skagway. A San Francisco newspaper tried to get John Muir to write a series of articles from the new town, but the great naturalist, who had known the land when it was silent and empty, was repelled by the suggestion. He likened the spectacle on Skagway Bay to that of "a nest of ants taken into a strange country and stirred up by a stick."

The beach had truly become a human ant-hill, a confused *mêlée* of swearing men and neighing horses, of rasping saws and sputtering campfires, of creaking wagons and yelping dogs — a jungle of tents and sheet-iron stoves and upturned boats scattered between the mountainous piles of goods and hay.

Atop these sprawling heaps, knee deep in flour sacks, and frying-pans, perspiring men bawled out the names on every outfit and tossed them down to the waiting owners. The most far-sighted of the stampeders had organized themselves into landing committees to rope off areas and to guard their stacks of provisions at gun point, but none was able to cope with the problems posed by international geography. Skagway, being on the narrow neck of the Panhandle, formed an American bridge into Canadian territory which lay on the far slopes of the Coast Mountains. Those outfits that had been purchased in Victoria or Vancouver could not be opened in Skagway, but had to be escorted across the pass in bond, and the escorts fed and paid ten dollars daily by the luckless owners. On the other hand, those outfits purchased in the United States were charged duty by the Canadian customs men on the border. Every man, then, had to pay some sort of tribute to one government or the other.

179

Night and day, the beach was never still, for rubber-booted men in constantly shifting streams were forever dragging their outfits across the tidal ooze in an effort to get above the high-water line. The extreme rise and fall showed a difference of thirty feet, and the onrushing waters advanced at such a speed that many returning to their stacks of provisions found that they had been totally submerged in the salt water.

Above the beach, in the forested flatland, the town of Skagway was still taking shape, a shifting and ever changing *mélange* of shacks and tents, crammed with men frantic to get over the trail and into the Klondike before freeze-up. The main street was nothing more than a single rut of black mud down which a river of men and animals ceaselessly flowed, but it bore the proud name of Broadway, and four makeshift saloons, the Pack Train, Bonanza, Grotto, and Nugget, lent it a tinsel air. Along its ragged route were campsites renting at ten dollars a week; a blacksmith's shop where it cost five dollars to have a single horseshoe hammered on; a doctor's tent serving as a drugstore; and a restaurant which advertised its wares on an old pair of trousers slung from a line with the single word MEALS daubed upon the seat.

"Restaurants" by the score sprang weedlike from the gumbo of the streets, flourished briefly in tattered tents or board shacks, and vanished. Many of these were operated by men with "icicle feet," whose only desire was to flee the enclave of Skagway and whose slender bill of fare consisted entirely of the half-ton of grub they had brought north at such expense and hardship. As soon as they raised the return fare to Seattle they sold out or closed up and were gone. A notable exception was the Pack Train Restaurant, opened in the fall of 1897 by Anton Stanish and Leo Ceovich. It began in a tent, moved to more permanent quarters (which it shared with the Pack Train Saloon, under separate ownership), and in twelve years never once closed its doors, developing an international reputation for prompt service, good food, and an ingenious cuisine. This, in the words of one steady customer, ran the gamut from salmon bellies stewed in champagne to eggs sizzled in beer: "There was no telling what a customer might order after a gruelling pack trip to the Summit, a big winning in one of the gambling houses, or a hard night on the dance floor."

Through this mish-mash of hovels and tree stumps moved a farrago of preposterous contraptions which the owners prayed would lighten the burden of the days to come, but which in most cases only increased it. Two men moved by, pushing pedal-less bicycles on which frames had been mounted suitable for carrying two hundred pounds of goods. A covey of stampeders laboured up the pass dragging little carts mounted on buggy wheels. Another party slushed through the mud striving to maintain the balance of an enormous single wheel around which a platform had been built. And threaded in between these grotesque devices were three thousand pack horses, loaded to the breaking-point. Panic was already mirrored in their eyes, but their agony had only begun.

3: *The dead horse trail*

Of all the routes to the Klondike, the Skagway trail across the White Pass, more than any other, brought out the worst in men. None who survived ever forgot it, and most who remembered it did so with a sense of shame and remorse. It looked so easy: a jaunt through the rolling hills on horseback, not much more. And yet the men who travelled it were seized by a kind of delirium that drove them to the pit of brutality. Like drug addicts, they understood their dementia but could

181

not control it. There was only one comfort — everyone was suffering from the same condition.

Frank Thomas of Plymouth, Indiana, expressed this feeling when he wrote a letter home from Skagway in the early fall of 1897:

"I am a few days older than when I left. . . and a great deal wiser. I have been working like a slave since I came here trying to get over the trail and am not over yet, and furthermore do not think I will be in time to get down the Yukon this winter. Since I came in we have lost our mule and one horse on this accursed trail. . . . This is the most discouraging work I ever did. . . . There are thousands of people here. . . all mad and crazy just like us. . . . I am undoubtedly a crazy fool for being here in this God-forsaken country but I have the consolation of seeing thousands of other men in all stages of life, rich and poor, wise and foolish, here in the same plight as I."

The trail on which Thomas found himself was a forty-five-mile switchback that plunged through bog and mire, over boulder and shale, skirted cliffsides, crossed and recrossed rivers, leap-frogged mountains, and followed canyon, valley, summit, and slope until it ended on the crescent beaches of Lake Bennett, where the Yukon River has its beginning.

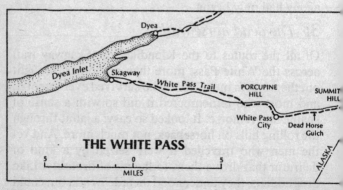

Unlike the Dyea trail that led directly to the base of the Chilkoot and then spanned the mountain barrier in a single leap, the Skagway trail straddled a series of obstacles. Its beginnings were deceptive — an attractive wagon road that led for several miles over flat timber- and swampland. Then began the series of precipitous hills, each hill separated by the almost continuous mire of the soggy riverbed, which had to be zigzagged by the narrow pathway.

First there was Devil's Hill, around whose slippery slate cliffs the path, scarcely two feet wide, wound like a corkscrew and where a single misstep by a badly loaded horse could mean death a sheer five hundred feet below.

Next there was Porcupine Hill, a roller-coaster ride where the wretched animals must pick their way between ten-foot boulders.

Then came Summit Hill, a thousand-foot climb, where liquid mud streamed down in rivulets, where sharp rocks tore at horses' feet and flanks, where slabs of granite barred the way and yawning mudholes swallowed the floundering animals, packs and all.

The summit marked the border between Canada and Alaska, but it was not the end. The slender trail skirted a

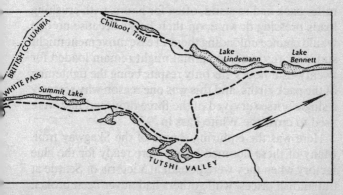

network of tiny lakes and then hurdled Turtle Mountain, another thousand-foot obstacle, before descending into the Tutshi Valley. One more mountain pass blocked the way before Lake Bennett was finally achieved.

Of the five thousand men and women who attempted to cross the White Pass in the fall of '97, only the tiniest handful reached their goal in time to navigate the Yukon River before freeze-up. One man who succeeded compared the slow movement over the pass with that of an army in retreat, those in the forefront struggling on against hopeless odds, followed by a line of stragglers moving forward like a beaten rabble. On the coastal side of the divide an incessant grey drizzle shut out all sunlight, producing streams of gumbo that acted as a sort of mucilage for the hopeless tangle of men and animals, tents, feed, and supplies. As the trail was not wide enough to allow two animals to pass, time and again all movement ground to a stop. Fires sputtered and smouldered in the misty half-light while shivering men, haggard, dazed, and forlorn, hovered over them, waiting for the human chain to resume its slow movement across the dark hills.

During these tedious delays the wretched horses for miles back had to stand, often for hours, with crushing loads pressing down upon their backs because no one would chance unloading them in case movement might suddenly resume. An animal might remain loaded for twenty-four hours, his only respite being the tightening of the pack girths, and this was one reason why scarcely a single horse survived of the three thousand that were used to cross the White Pass in '97.

Here was the enduring shame of the Skagway trail. Many of these doomed beasts were ready for the glue factory when they were bought at Victoria or Seattle at outlandish prices, while others had never been broken

184

or felt the weight of a pack. Few of the men who stampeded to the Klondike had ever handled animals before, hence it was not unusual for two partners to spend an entire day trying to load a single horse. By the time they reached the summit, horses that had fetched two hundred dollars in Skagway were not worth twenty cents, for the Klondikers felt impelled to get across the mountains at any cost — and the cost always included an animal's life.

A quarter of a mile from the Canadian border, each owner performed a grisly rite. He carefully unloaded his pack animal and then smoothed a blanket over its back to conceal the running sores that most horses suffered at the hands of amateurs. The Mounted Police would shoot a sore or injured horse on sight if he was brought across the line into Canada.

The macabre scenes on the trail that autumn and winter were seared into the memories of most of the men who witnessed them, so that fifty years later, when subsequent horrors had been blurred by the fog of time, these ghastly moments were as sharply etched as if they had occurred the week before. Samuel H. Graves, who was to play a leading role in the building of the railway over the White Pass, would never forget the day he passed a horse that had broken its leg a few minutes before at a point where the trail squeezed between two huge boulders. The horse's pack had been removed, and someone had knocked it on the head with an axe; then traffic was resumed directly across the still warm body. When Graves returned that evening there was not a vestige of the carcass left, save for the head on one side of the trail and the tail on the other. The beast had literally been ground into the earth by the human machine.

A veteran horseman, Major J. M. Walsh, one of the most famous officers of the original North West

Mounted Police, now retired and on his way to the Klondike as Commissioner of the Yukon, crossed the trail that fall with a government party and was horrified at the spectacle. To Clifford Sifton, Canadian Minister of the Interior, he wrote that "such a scene of havoc and destruction. . . can scarcely be imagined. Thousands of pack-horses lie dead along the way, sometimes in bunches under the cliffs, with pack-saddles and packs where they have fallen from the rock above, sometimes in tangled masses filling the mudholes and furnishing the only footing for our poor pack animals on the march — often, I regret to say, exhausted but still alive, a fact we are unaware of until after the miserable wretches turn beneath the hoofs of our cavalcade. The eyeless sockets of the pack animals everywhere account for the myriads of ravens along the road. The inhumanity which this trail has been witness to, the heartbreak and suffering which so many have undergone, cannot be imagined. They certainly cannot be described."

T. Dufferin Pattullo, Walsh's secretary, who later became Premier of the province of British Columbia, was one of several stampeders who reported that the tortured animals were actually trying to commit suicide rather than negotiate the trail. To his dying day Pattullo insisted that he saw an ox trying to fling itself over a cliff. Tappan Adney, correspondent for *Harper's Illustrated Weekly,* reported a similar incident: a horse had walked over the edge of Porcupine Hill, and every man who witnessed the incident swore it was suicide.

In the crowd that fall was a sensitive young ex-sailor, his pack crammed with books — Darwin, Marx, Milton — and he, too, was to describe the ordeal of the horses on the White Pass.

"The horses died like mosquitoes in the first frost and from Skagway to Bennett they rotted in heaps," Jack London wrote. "They died at the rocks, they were poisoned at the summit, and they starved at the lakes; they fell off the trail, what there was of it, and they went through it; in the river they drowned under their loads or were smashed to pieces against the boulders; they snapped their legs in the crevices and broke their backs falling backwards with their packs; in the sloughs they sank from fright or smothered in the slime; and they were disembowelled in the bogs where the corduroy logs turned end up in the mud; men shot them, worked them to death and when they were gone, went back to the beach and bought more. Some did not bother to shoot them, stripping the saddles off and the shoes and leaving them where they fell. Their hearts turned to stone — those which did not break — and they became beasts, the men on the Dead Horse Trail."

Within a month the trail was almost impassable, and by September all movement had come to a standstill. Sylvester Scovel of the New York *World*, in a colourful gesture, offered several thousand dollars on behalf of his paper to dynamite the pass so that the stampede could resume. Scovel had come with his bride to Skagway, in a dashing costume complete with guitar — high leather boots, tight corduroys, white sombrero, and fancy buckskin shirt — but this final piece of flamboyance was too much for his paper, which refused to go along with the scheme and recalled him to New York. He had, in the meantime, spent some money widening a section of the trail and hiring a guard of twelve men at fifty dollars a day to barricade it against intruders. "Any man crossing the barrier dies!" the leader would shout, but with the press of three thousand behind it, the barrier did not last long.

By this time it was obvious to all that no one else was going to reach the Klondike until spring. Thousands were already in retreat and vainly trying to sell their outfits, which were to be seen strewn along the right of way for more than forty miles. The tidal flats of Skagway were black with a thousand horses, "For Sale" signs on their backs, blood streaming down their lacerated thighs. And everywhere a pall of despondency hung like a shroud over the multitude. Hal Hoffman of the Chicago *Tribune* happened upon one huge strapping gold-seeker in a red shirt, seated on a rock, a picture of despair; he could not get his goods across the first ridge, his money was gone, his adventure was at an end, and he was sobbing his heart out.

Men had been willing to pay any sum to reach Lake Bennett. Scores had given fifty cents apiece simply to use a log that one enterprising stampeder had flung over a stream. One packer, who landed in Skagway without a dollar, made three hundred thousand in transport fees before he blew out his brains. But, as these argonauts were to learn over and over again, money alone was not enough to take them to the Klondike.

Finally the trail was closed to all, and George Brackett, an ex-mayor of Minneapolis who had lost his fortune in the panic of '93, began to construct a wagon road along the mountainsides. When it was completed, the stampeders who followed in the winter were glad to pay tolls to use it, but each one who passed that way was haunted in some fashion by the ghosts of the pack animals that had died that fall. One winter evening a nineteen-year-old named Stanley Scearce, whose father raised thoroughbreds in the blue grass of Kentucky, was camped on the edge of Porcupine Hill. He had started an evening fire and set a kettle of beans to boil on it, and then, as the snow began to melt, he saw to his horror the outlines of a dead horse emerging beneath the glowing coals.

4: *Hell on earth*

All this while, Skagway was growing, and, strangely, its growth was due in large part to the very impassability of the trail because so many were forced back from the mountains to remain in the town. Dyea, three miles away, remained an impermanent community because the Chilkoot Pass was seldom closed.

By midwinter there were five thousand in Skagway, and many of these were without the means to move forward or back. The town had its first minister, who held services in a bare hall, and its first newspaper, the Skagway *News* ("nearest newspaper to the goldfields"), and its first murder. George Buchanan, an Englishman who had been appointed manager of the Skagway Townsite Company, found himself frustrated in love by a lady restaurant-keeper and so shot her and killed himself, providing the Seattle *Post-Intelligencer*'s correspondent with an opportunity to display his purplest style:

"A man found time amid the hurry and bustle of the mushroom city to become infatuated with a woman. The icy fogs that stole down from the mountains could not chill his heart of fire. He suffered until the flames stole up and touched his brain — made it glow with a dizzying light — and he looked on the taunting woman with a murderer's eyes and strove to kill the scornful spirit he could not break. . . ."

The prose fitted the personality of the town, whose emerging character was distilled in the sign of Keelar, "The Money King," a pawnbroker whose shop was jammed with hundreds of trinkets and valuables sacrificed by desperate men:

Keelar the Money King has Barrels of Money
Buys and Sells Everything

189

Loans Money, sells by Auction.
Is a Public Benefactor.

Such money-lenders were among the town's elite,
together with the packers who were making swift fortunes with their horses and mules. One of them, Charlie
O'Brien, a Nova Scotian, was seen to walk on board a
steamer one day with fifteen thousand dollars in Canadian bills stuffed into his pockets. He was off to the
bank at Victoria, more than a thousand miles away, to
make a deposit. Another, Joe Brooks, kept the side
pockets of his heavy sweater filled with goldpieces so
that, on entering Clancy's bar, he could pour them onto
the counter in a stream and shout: "Everybody drink!"
Brooks, a Vancouver drayman, was a tough, thick-set
extrovert who arrived at Skagway on one of the first
boats in July, pushed his string of seventeen mules into
the water, and swam ashore with them. Soon his team
had grown to three hundred and thirty-five, and he was
garnering as much as five thousand dollars a day. He
became a familiar sight on Skagway's muddy streets,
dashing up and down Broadway on horseback at breakneck speed with his two small boys, one clutched under
each arm.

Even women entered the lucrative packing trade.
The best known was Mrs. Harriet Pullen, a widow with
a brood of little boys, who arrived in the fall with seven
dollars in her pocket and parlayed it into a comfortable
fortune. She drove a four-horse freighting outfit up the
pass by day, and by night made apple pies in dishes
hammered out of old tin cans. She stayed in Skagway all
of her life and became in the end its most distinguished
citizen.

All that winter the carnival roared on until Skagway
took on the trappings of a great freak show. A Negro
performer straight from Huber's Museum in New York
190

lived comfortably from the fees paid him by men who watched while he stuffed an extraordinary number of china eggs into his mouth. A trained bear named Alexis danced down the streets accompanied by his bearded Russian master. An Italian arrived with hundreds of toy balloons and sold them all at high prices. A strange creature known as Peter the Apostle came up from the San Joaquin Valley to render aid to the wayfarers on the trail. On the edge of town William Moore's granddaughter drove about in a cart pulled by a yearling moose, and the old sea captain himself, building a new home with a ship's pilothouse on top, wandered restlessly about the streets, a gaunt and strangely disturbing figure in his thick yellow overcoat.

It was, in the words of Elmer J. "Stroller" White, who was employed at the time by the Skagway *News*, "a free, unfettered and impulsive populace." Ordinary social conventions were not taken as seriously as they were in the outside world. "It was not unusual," White recalled, "for an avowed and sworn celibate to arise in the morning firm and steadfast in his principles, and before repose again overtook him anything might have happened, including marriage."

The Stroller, as he called himself, once entered a Skagway saloon to find the bartender standing drinks in celebration of his marriage the previous evening.

"What was the name of your bride?" White asked, sensing a news item.

The bartender scratched his head, thought for several moments, polished the bar furiously, and thought again. Finally he turned to White: "Here. You tend bar and I'll run over and ask her. I heard it but I forgot what it was. You'll find rye and Scotch on ice under the bar."

Saloons sprang up on every corner, in spite of Alaska's rigid laws which prohibited the importation, manufacture, or sale of spirituous liquors. The respect for this paper statute was indicated in the statistics for 1897, which showed that there were five breweries and one hundred and forty-two bars in the territory — all doing a roaring business. All liquor arriving in Skagway was billed through to Canada in bond, but by the time the barrels reached the border a good deal of whiskey had been mysteriously replaced with water. Few people, apparently, took much heed of the gigantic red lettering painted on a cliff a thousand feet above the town exhorting the populace to DRINK ROCKY MOUNTAIN TEA.

The Blaze of Glory, the Hungry Pup, the Mangy Dog, the Red Onion, the Home of Hooch, and the Palace of Delight — these and other saloons and gambling-houses provided Skagway with the core of its non-transient population: the managers, bartenders, dealers, faro lookouts, dance callers, case keepers, bouncers, blackjack boosters, and saloon swampers. Among these night people, caste was almost as rigid as it was along the Ganges. Faro dealers were at the top of the social scale. Dance callers ("corral your heifer for the next turn") were considerably farther down. Bartenders had their own caste system depending on the social level of their particular saloon. Blackjack boosters were considered the lowest of the low.

The boosters, whose task it was to inveigle newcomers into a game, were almost invariably known as "Kid." Stroller White estimated that there were between five hundred and seven hundred and fifty citizens in Skagway, that first winter, who would respond to the cry of "Hey, Kid!" Of these, some two hundred worked the twenty-five blackjack games in double shifts. They included the Granulated Kid, the Down-and-Out Kid, the Chills and Fever Kid, the Ping Pong Kid, the Skylight Kid, the Nanny Goat Kid, the Burn-'em-up Kid, and the No Shirt Kid. Their nicknames were acquired through a quirk of character or physique or as the result of an incident from the past, often long-forgotten. The Sealskin Kid was named by the passengers on the ship that brought him to Skagway because he sported an expensive sealskin coat. The Wake-up Kid was so called because he could sleep through almost anything and was therefore subject to constant appeals to open his eyes. It was said of the Evaporated Kid, when he was caught in the dressing room of Little Egypt during that dancer's performance in Clancy's Music Hall, that he had entered through the keyhole. And J. H. P. Smythe, an Australian, quickly acquired the title of the "Hot Cake Kid" because that was all he appeared to live on. He worked for the notorious Soapy Smith on a percentage basis but was actually paid off in the form of a chit on the Pack Train Restaurant, signed each week by the confidence man and bearing the simple notation: "Give him all the hot cakes he wants."

In the dance halls that adjoined the saloons, painted women held court in caricatures of Paris fashions, with names like Sweet Marie, Babe Wallace, the Virgin, Mollie Fewclothes, Sitting Maud, Ethel the Moose, and Diamond Lil Davenport. The man who took a box in a concert hall almost had to beat off women with a stick, for they rushed the boxes in relays, forcing the luckless occupants to treat them to champagne. One packer, under these conditions, paid out seven hundred and fifty dollars one night for a box of cigars and another three thousand for wine.

And all the while the pianos tinkled out a tinny melody — tinkled all night long and into the dawn. In Jimmy Ryan's Nugget Saloon the piano never ceased, save for those moments when the player, English Harry Marston, sodden with drink, toppled senseless from the bench.

193

Above the rattle of the dance-hall bands a more discordant sound was heard: the staccato notes of gun-fire in the streets. For Skagway existed in a state of incredible anarchy. Half the population was composed of transients, unswerving in their single-minded resolution to reach the gold-fields. The remainder were opportunists whose sole object was the making of money. Few had time to occupy themselves with civic affairs, and so the community drifted, like a rudderless ship, towards its own Scylla and Charybdis.

Alexander Macdonald, a worldly Englishman who passed through Skagway late in the fall of 1897, described the character of the town in a few pungent sentences:

"I have stumbled upon a few tough corners of the globe during my wanderings beyond the outposts of civilization, but I think the most outrageously lawless quarter I ever struck was Skagway. . . . It seemed as if the scum of the earth had hastened here to fleece and rob, or. . . to murder. . . . There was no law whatsoever; might was right, the dead shot only was immune to danger."

In the unimpassioned words of Superintendent Samuel B. Steele of the NWMP, Skagway was "little better than a hell on earth." Steele, who was the last man to give way to overstatement, described in his memoirs the nights he spent in the town, when the crash of bands in the dance halls and "the cracked voices of the singers" were mingled with shouts of murder, cries for help, and the crackle of gunshot. "Skagway," Steele wrote, "was about the roughest place in the world."

It must have irked this case-hardened policeman, whose character had been forged in the hot flame of prairie revolt, that, as a Canadian, he was powerless to interfere. One Sunday morning he and a fellow officer were aroused from their slumbers on the floor of a

194

Skagway cabin by a pistol fight; bullets ripped through the walls of the building, but the affair was so commonplace that the two men did not bother to rise from their beds.

Captain Henry Toke Munn, an Arctic adventurer, passed through Skagway about the same time, and his experiences were similar to Steele's. "For the six nights I slept in Skagway there was shooting on the streets every night," he reported. "At least one man was killed that I know of and probably others. The shack I slept in had a bullet through it over my head."

A contemporary account of a typical shooting, which occurred in the Klondike saloon in the spring of 1898, gives an insight into social conditions in Skagway during the stampede year. A man named Brannon got into a fight with another man and attempted to bend him back over the bar. In the ensuing struggle, involving four or five saloon habitués, the belligerent Brannon was shot to death. Although there were more than a dozen eyewitnesses to the murder, everyone in the barroom seemed to have been stricken with a sudden case of blindness. In the preliminary hearing that followed, the bartender, who was within two feet of the corpse, denied all knowledge of the incident, and when the judge asked him what he was doing at the time, he replied with some disdain: "I was drawing two beers." A gambler, when called on to testify, was equally unobservant. When asked the same question he told the court: "I was busy grabbing seven dollars and a quarter from the blackjack table." Thirteen witnesses followed and all denied that the accused, one Keifer, had done the shooting. The judge obviously placed little value on their testimony for he bound Keifer over for trial in spite of the lack of evidence.

Proper machinery for law-enforcement being nonexistent, the vacuum thus created was shortly filled in

195

another manner. Slowly and very quietly, almost without realizing it, the community became aware of a man named Jefferson Randolph Smith, the same Soapy Smith who had announced in Seattle that he would be the boss of Skagway. By midwinter he had made good his boast. Over its citizens and transients he held the power of life and death. Before he was through, he had his own army — drilled, disciplined, and armed — his own spy system, and his own secret police. He cowed the militia and bought out the civil law. Merchants, businessmen, and journalists were in his pocket, and his sway extended along both the Dyea and Skagway trails to the very summit of the passes, where the North West Mounted Police installed Maxim guns to keep him at bay.

Any well-heeled stampeder landing in Skagway that winter found it impossible to escape the attentions of Smith's organization. From the moment he stepped aboard ship at Victoria or Seattle until the day he finally crossed the international border at the summit of the pass, he was under almost constant surveillance. Smith's men ranged far and wide, many of them mingling with the crowd on the docks of the Pacific coast ports, travelling on the steamers plying north, pretending to be bona fide stampeders, and befriending likely-looking prospects. They were at the gangways, in the streets, behind the counters, along the trails, and even in the church pews. They were, in fact, everywhere.

They were all consummate actors, and each had a role which he played to the hilt. The "Reverend" Charles Bowers pretended to be a pious and God-fearing Christian, lending a helping hand to newcomers, advising tenderfeet on where to get supplies, and counselling the unwary against evil companions. Indeed, a good opening for any member of the organization was to warn newcomers to stay clear of the Soapy Smith gang. Billie Saportas, a newspaperman in Smith's pay, interviewed all travellers on their arrival and discovered in this way how much money they had. "Slim Jim" Foster, an engaging curly-haired youth, was stationed at the docks, where he cheerfully helped stampeders carry their baggage uptown. Van B. Triplett, known as "Old Man Tripp," an aging creature of great cunning, worked the trails, posing as a returning stampeder full of information about the Klondike. Like so many others in the Smith entourage, he was a man who exuded benevolence from every pore. With his long white hair and patriarchal mien, he might have been a Biblical prophet, but this saintly exterior masked a heart of granite. One of the strong points of Smith's rule of Skagway was that nobody was quite sure who belonged to his gang, because so many, like Tripp, looked so innocent. In their bowler hats, wing collars, diamond stickpins, and polished high button boots, they posed as business leaders, public-spirited citizens, and churchmen. The ordinary man feared to raise his voice against Smith in public or private for fear he might be addressing one of Smith's own men without knowing it. When the Right Reverend Peter Trimble Rowe, the pioneer bishop of Alaska, was robbed by one of the gang, the miscreant, on learning his victim's identity, handed back the pouch of gold.

"Why do you give this back?" Rowe asked in astonishment.

"Hell, Bishop," replied the thief, "I'm a member of your congregation."

Smith, in fact, almost succeeded in getting one of his henchmen elected to the Board of Stewards of the Union Church. The church, which had been erected by public subscription, was the inspiration of the Rev. Robert McCahon Dickey, whose character was later appropriated by Ralph Connor as the model for the

Preacher in his best-selling novel *The Sky Pilot*. Dickey, a Presbyterian, was chairing the meeting when nominations for each of the seven denominations represented were called. Immediately a man leaped to his feet and nominated "the Bishop." Dickey thought at first that he meant Bishop Rowe, but it developed that the nominee was someone else entirely.

"He's a very holy man, so we call him the Bishop," the nominator explained to the crowd. "He wouldn't rob no poor widow."

"What about the rich ones?" came a *sotto voce* query from the rear.

Dickey (as he later confided to his diary) then recognized the nominee as the man "who guided dead brokes from the beach to the church." He asked quietly what his denomination might be.

"He's a *'piscopalian* — in fact he's a church *warner* like what his Holiness spoke about this morning," the Bishop's backer replied.

"And how long has he been a church *warner?*" Dickey asked.

"All his life — he was always holy!"

"Shut up, you damned fool!" whispered a fierce voice, which all present recognized as belonging to Soapy Smith.

Dickey got around the problem by suggesting that Bishop Rowe examine the nominee on his knowledge of the Episcopalian service. When Rowe suggested he recite the Apostles' Creed, the con man responded with the Gettysburg Address, which he claimed to have memorized from the Bible. He was rejected at once, but such was Smith's wrath at the blunder that plans had to be made to smuggle him out of Skagway under cover of darkness. Dickey described him, at this point, as "the most abject and terrified man I ever saw. . . ."

The town was soon dotted with bogus business premises erected by Smith, or by the men under his protection, for the purpose of fleecing the Klondikers. There were a Merchants' Exchange, a Telegraph Office, a Cut Rate Ticket Office, a Reliable Packers, and an Information Bureau — all complete shams — to which the suckers were steered. Each of these establishments was plausibly furnished and fitted out to give an air of solidity and respectability, and peopled with "clerks" and "customers" who had memorized their lines like veteran thespians.

Slim Jim Foster had a disarming quality that made strangers warm to him. "Why not go over to the Reliable Packers?" he would suggest as he seized a stranger's bags and helped lug them uptown. "They're an honest outfit who'll get your gear over the pass without overcharging. I can vouch for them."

Foster would steer the sucker into the fake packing establishment, where another member of the gang, posing as proprietor, would conduct negotiations in a crisp, business-like fashion. When the matter was finally arranged, the negotiator would ask for a small deposit "just to prove the business won't be given elsewhere." This was the key moment in the confidence game as practised by Smith's organization: to make the mark produce his wallet. Once a billfold was brought out into the open in one of Smith's establishments, its owner could kiss it good-bye. The scene that followed was carefully planned: a member of the gang, attired as a ruffian, would leap up and snatch the pocketbook; another would rise at once and cry out in anger that he could not stand idly by and see an honest man robbed in broad daylight. Others would rise, crying out slogans about honesty and deploring crime, jostling and rushing about to create a scene of confusion. In the spurious scuffle the victim himself would often be knocked flat

199

while the man with the wallet escaped. All involved would pretend to be outraged by the event until the sucker departed dazed, baffled, and penniless.

Other stampeders would be met on the street by men pretending to be naïve cheechakos. The "cheechako" would strike up a conversation about the prospects of getting over the pass, leading up to the fact that new maps, complete information, and weather forecasts could be obtained at the Information Bureau. "Let's go along together and see what we can find out," he would say, linking arms with his quarry, and so the two newfound friends would head for another Smith establishment.

At the Information Bureau a man was posted to find out all he could about the newcomer: the size of his outfit, the amount of his ready cash, his friends, his background, his immediate plans.

At this point the luckless innocent was either steered to one of Smith's crooked gambling-games or, if he balked, the details were filed so that others in the gang could shear him when he took to the trail.

Smith's Telegraph Office was a particularly ingenious establishment, and its operation underlined the ignorance and gullibility of many stampeders. There was, of course, no telegraph line to Skagway in 1898, but Smith guaranteed to send a wire anywhere in the world for five dollars. Scores paid their money and sent messages to their families before leaving for the passes, and Smith always saw that they got an answer within two or three hours. It invariably came collect.

On one occasion the gang had pamphlets printed warning against poison water on the White Pass trail. Smith's men steered newcomers to the Merchants' Exchange, where maps of the poisonous springs were supposedly available. In this false-fronted shack, in dim candlelight, men fresh off the boats were speedily relieved of their money.

Often Smith's operatives were the very ones who organized the landing committees which handled the freight. Thus did they worm themselves into the confidence of hundreds who, swindled out of their money and possessions, found themselves caught in Skagway, unable to move forward or back. At this point, on occasion, a kindly philanthropist with a dark, pointed beard and probing grey eyes appeared and advanced them, in the name of Christian charity, just enough cash to take them home again. And so they returned the way they had come without raising any awkward fuss, comforted that the Devil did not rule supreme in Alaska, their hearts warm towards their benefactor, whose name, of course, was Jefferson Randolph Smith.

5: *The human serpent*

When the mud froze hard as granite, and the rivers turned to ice, and the snow swept down from the mountains so thickly that a man could scarcely see his neighbour, the Dead Horse Trail reopened and thousands once more took up the struggle to cross the White Pass.

But this time the Mounted Police at the border were enforcing a new regulation. No one could enter the Yukon Territory of Canada without a year's supply of food, roughly eleven hundred and fifty pounds. Together with tents, cooking-utensils, and tools, this made about a ton of goods in all — lime juice and lard, black tea and chocolate, salt, candles, rubber boots and mincemeat, dried potatoes and sauerkraut, string beans and cornmeal, cakes of toilet soap and baking-powder, coal oil and lamp chimneys, rope, saws, files, mukluks, overshoes — in short, everything needed to keep going for a year in a northern climate without outside aid.

All of these goods had to be packed on the backs of animals or of men, or dragged on sleds and parcelled up into manageable loads. The average man carried about sixty-five pounds, moved it about five miles, cached it, and returned for another load, continuing this laborious process until the entire ton of supplies was shuttled across the pass. Thus, a man who depended on his own back for transportation might have to make up to thirty round trips to move his outfit, and his total mileage before he reached Lake Bennett could exceed twenty-five hundred miles. Most contrived to pull sleds with larger loads, but even these found they were covering more than one thousand miles, which explains why even a hard-working man took ninety days to move through the White Pass.

All along the trail, often buried in twelve or more feet of snow, lay the packs and equipment of those who were backtracking in this onerous manner. After days and days of painfully slow forward movement, men were ready to fling themselves down by the side of the trail and sob their hearts out in frustration. Others spent their passions on their animals. One who finally completed the journey across the pass uncoiled like a steel spring, and in his rage beat his dogs so unmercifully that they could go no farther. Beginning with the lead dog, he pushed the animals one by one into a waterhole under the ice and only then, coming to his senses and realizing the enormity of his conduct, collapsed in the snow in tears. Henry Toke Munn watched one man deal with a pair of oxen that were so exhausted they could not continue on. He built a fire under them and then began to poke at them with burning brands, but they still could not move the load and so were slowly roasted alive before his eyes. Those who passed such scenes rarely paid them heed, for all were too much occupied with their own misfortunes to mind anybody else's business on the Dead Horse Trail. A dead man sat beside the right of way for hours with a hole in his back staring glassily out at the passers-by, who trudged on past with scarcely a second glance.

As the winter wore on and the snow continued to fall, the trail changed its physical shape, literally rising above the surrounding countryside. The soft snow on either side was blown off down the valley by the screaming gusts, but the trail itself was kept so hard-packed by the trampling of thousands that no wind could budge it. And when more snow fell, it too was packed down, hard as cement, until in certain places the pathway was ten feet high. Bert Parker, a teen-ager from Ontario who crossed the pass that winter and who set down his memories of it years later when he was dying of cancer, likened the trail to a huge pipeline, six to eight feet in diameter, and the men who moved along it to a chain gang. The wind-blown snow on either side was so loose that if a man toppled off the trail he had difficulty clambering back up again.

"If a man forgets for a moment what he is doing, his sled is liable to get off the trail and upset in the snow," Parker wrote. "The minute this happens the man behind him steps up and takes his place and he stays there till the whole cavalcade passes by. Sometimes you would think that a man had gone crazy when his sled had upset off the trail. They would throw their caps in the snow, shake their fists, throw their heads back and ask Jesus Christ to come down there on the trail so that they could tell Him what they thought of Him for playing a trick like that on them."

The solid line was so closely packed with men that it could take four or five hours to pass a given point without a gap appearing. From Porcupine Hill to the summit the movement was unceasing, for there was no level place to sit down. Here each man's individuality seemed to be smothered in the impersonal and all-encompassing human serpent that wound slowly through the mountains. On it moved, with its thousand identical vertebrae, each figure bent forward in its jack-knife attitude of strain, each face purple with the stress of hauling a heavy sled, a rope over every shoulder, a gee-pole for steering purposes gripped in every right hand.

Down the mountain corridor a bitter north wind whistled incessantly. The ranges that guard the coastal strip block off an immense ocean of frigid air which is thirty degrees colder than the sea-tempered air of the coast — and the pass that winter was like a waterfall over which this air tumbled. On the far side of the divide, as if to match the temperament of the men who managed to cross, all was tranquillity. To arrive in the interior, beyond the mountains, was like passing onto the calm body of a lake after breasting a turbulent stream.

The summit of the pass was a symphony of white, although few of the stampeders who reached it had time or inclination for the aesthetics of mountain scenery. Here the sun glittered on the dazzling peaks, and the flanks of the mountains, blue-white in the shadows, merged with the feathery white fog that rose from the sea coast. In the intense cold, men walked in an aura of vapour compounded of the lazy white steam that rose from the campfires and the white jets that burst from the snouts of the animals and the nostrils of the struggling climbers.

Through this eerie world moved the shadowy, frost-encrusted forms of the stampeders, men of every kind and description, made brothers for this brief moment by the common travail of the trail: a man with a string of reindeer pulling a sled, for instance; a group of Scots in furs and tam-o'-shanters led by a bagpiper; a woman with bread dough strapped to her back so that it rose with the heat of her body — every kind of human animal, each struggling forward with a single purpose.

A steamboat man and his wife moved two entire stern-wheel vessels in bits and pieces across the mountains that winter. He was A. J. Goddard, a wiry engine-designer from Iowa, and he was determined to get the first cargo down the river that spring.

A photographer was in the crowd as well. E. A. Hegg, who had closed his two studios on Bellingham Bay, had arrived with a darkroom fastened to a sled drawn by a herd of long-haired goats. He was obliged to heat his developer to keep it from freezing, to filter his water through charcoal, to coat his wet plates with a mixture improvised from herbs and egg albumen, and to work his bulky camera in forty-below weather; but the pictures he made of that strange mountain migration were so effective that when some of them went on exhibit in New York, crowds fought to get a glimpse of them and police had to be called to restore order.

There was a boxing champion among the climbers, too. His name was Jim Carroll, and his fighter's physique was not equal to the journey. But when he dropped exhausted on the trail and called out to his young wife that he was turning back, she put her hands on her hips and turned on him savagely: "All right, Jim, we'll split the outfit right here on the trail. I'm going on to Dawson." The threat spurred him forward, and the following summer found him giving boxing lessons in Dawson while she opened a road house that earned three hundred dollars a day.

For every man who found the strength to press on, there was at least one who turned back. Some grew deathly ill on rotten horseflesh fed to them in the little cafés that sprang up along the way; others suffered the agonies of pneumonia or grippe or spinal meningitis.

On one black night there were seventeen deaths from meningitis, and Goddard, the steamboat man, recalled hearing victims in neighbouring tents screaming with the pain in the nape of the neck that is a characteristic of the disease. Their cries would last for three or four hours, and then, suddenly, they would cry no more.

So the leaderless rabble swarmed forward — leaderless except for the small band of North West Mounted Police who officially took possession of the summit in February, 1898, on orders from the Canadian government. Nobody had paid much attention to the boundary until 1897, but now it was in dispute, the Canadians insisting that it lay close to the seashore, the Americans attempting to push it back to the headwaters of the Yukon. But the Mounties, using an old international principle that possession is nine points of the law, established a custom-house on the razor's edge of the divide. Here, where firewood and cabin logs had to be hauled uphill for twelve miles, where winds howled ceaselessly and the snow seemed to fall day and night, the twenty policemen endured conditions so terrible that no stampeder lingered longer than necessary. The Mounties suffered privations that damaged their health; Strickland, the inspector in charge, worked through a long siege of bronchitis until his superior, the legendary Sam Steele, heard about it. Steele, too, was racked by the same disease as a result of wading waist-deep in icy water and then working in his wet clothes, but he defied his doctor, scaled the pass, ordered Strickland off duty, and carried on himself.

Here, from his perch on the very summit of the mountain wall, high above forest and river, far from the tinny cacophony of Skagway, Steele, the iron man, could gaze down, godlike, on the insect figures striving to reach his eyrie — on the whimpering horses and the cursing men, and on the women bent double beneath
206

man-sized loads. It was a scene that was almost mediaeval in its fervour and in its allegory, and it was enacted against a massive backdrop: the cloud-plumed
mountains in the foreground, the rolling hills in the
middle distance, and far below — as if in another world
— the bright sheen of the ocean and the tiny outlines of
shuttling boats disgorging, endlessly, more human
cargo, and, glittering wetly in the pale sun, the flats of
Skagway, where William Moore had once reigned as a
lonely monarch.

And hanging over the whole, like an encompassing
pall, the sickly-sweet stench of carrion, drifting with the
wind.

Chapter Six

1
Starvation winter

2
Revolt on the Yukon

3
A dollar a waltz

4
Only a coal miner's daughter . . .

5
Greenhorns triumphant

6
The Saint of Dawson

1: *Starvation winter*

Those few hundred souls who slipped through the passes in the fall of 1897 and reached the Yukon River were borne swiftly on the crest of the current towards the Klondike, secure in the knowledge that they had won the race for the gold-fields. They had held the lead while others faltered, because they travelled light, ignoring all advice to encumber themselves with a year's provisions. They had money; they were prepared to make more money; with money you could buy anything.

But as their boats slid past the fog-shrouded banks amid the cakes of floating ice, faint but disquieting cries reached their ears:

"There's no grub in Dawson. If you haven't an outfit, for God's sake turn back!"

The caribou were fleeing the country in thundering herds, swimming the rivers in clusters so close to the drifting boats that the newcomers could almost reach out and touch their horns. In the skies the geese in ragged V's were winging south. Only men, it seemed, were moving north into a dying land.

They stopped for supplies at Fort Selkirk, Arthur Harper's old post, and were baffled to find that the morose and silent trader, J. J. Pitts, had nothing to sell them except condensed milk at a dollar a tin. In vain they proffered bank-notes; no steamer had touched this point since 1895, and their money was useless. It was a tiny intimation of what was to come.

Joaquin Miller, the grey-bearded "Poet of the Sierras," had made a fetish of travelling light. When he stepped off his barge at Dawson's waterfront he happened to pull a lone onion from his pocket. To his astonishment, an onlooker instantly offered him a dollar for it. When Miller refused, the offer was increased at once to five. The significance of this incident escaped the poet, who had eyes only for the gold that was pouring from the creeks, for, like the other stampeders, he confused it with wealth.

"No," he wrote firmly, "there will be no starvation. The men who doubt supplies will get here, where gold is waiting by the ton, miscalculate American energy. As for the gold here, I can only say, as the Queen of Sheba said to Solomon: 'Behold, the half was not told to me!' "

Constantine of the Mounted Police viewed the situation with foreboding. As early as August 11 he had written bluntly to Ottawa that "the outlook for grub is not assuring for the number of people here — about four thousand crazy or lazy men, chiefly American miners and toughs from the coast towns."

The trading companies, too, began to measure the shortage of food against the new glut of people with growing dismay. Both the A.C. and the N.A.T. proceeded to dole out supplies in small amounts as men in queues fifty deep lined up in front of the warehouses pleading for a chance to buy. The company clerks admitted one man at a time, locked the door behind him as they would the door of a vault, sold him a few days' supplies, and sent him on his way. A man could have half a million dollars in gold — as many did — and still be able to purchase only a few pounds of beans, but it was some time before the newcomers could understand this. They found it hard to comprehend a situation in which gold by itself was worthless.

As more and more boats drifted in with the ice, an air of panic began to settle over the Yukon Valley, like the cold fog that rose from the Klondike's mouth. Somewhere downriver there were five steamboats bound for Dawson with cargoes of food, but there was no sign of them. What had happened? In September, Captain J. E. Hansen, the Alaska Commercial Company's assistant superintendent, decided to head downstream to find out.

Some three hundred and fifty miles below Dawson, near the old Hudson's Bay post of Fort Yukon, in the shallow and desolate maze of the Yukon flats, he found the lost steamers marooned in the low water. He knew now, for certain, that Dawson faced famine, and so started back up the river at breakneck speed to warn the town of its danger.

This trip was almost the end of Hansen. His Indian companions deserted him, and for four days and five nights he was isolated on an island in mid-river with neither axe nor bedding. Picked up at last by a passing boat, he commandeered a birchbark canoe and pushed on through the ice as fast as he could force his boatmen, poling and tracking along the banks and changing Indians every few dozen miles as they dropped from fatigue.

He set a record for speed. On September 26 two natives on the hills above Dawson spotted his canoe, and a cry rippled across the town:

"A boat! A boat from the north!"

Four thousand men and women, aflame with excitement and hope, streamed down upon the waterfront in the belief that a steamer laden with provisions had arrived, and then, when the little birchbark canoe rounded the bluff, drew in their collective breath in bitter disappointment, "like the sighing of the wind," as one later recorded.

A deadly calm settled on the crowd. The canoe touched shore and Hansen's tall figure leaped from it, his blond hair tangled by the wind, his aquiline face haggard and blue with cold. He raised his hand for silence and in a loud, nervous voice cried out:

"Men of Dawson! There will be no riverboats here until spring. My Indians and I have poled three hundred and fifty miles up the river to tell you this. I advise

212

all of you who are out of provisions or who haven't enough to carry you through the winter to make a dash for the Outside. There is no time to lose! There are some supplies at Fort Yukon that the *Hamilton* brought. Whichever way you go, up the river or down the river, it's hazardous — but you must make the try."

A silence, pregnant with horror, greeted these words. Most of Hansen's listeners had risked everything to reach the Klondike in the first wave, and now it seemed that they had won the race only to lose the prize. As they stood, wordless, on the riverbank, a variety of sub-human sounds seeped into their consciousness and accentuated the general mood of gloom and despair: the hoarse screaming of the ravens wheeling above in the dismal skies, the grinding and snapping of the ice cakes that poured past in a relentless stream, the mournful howling of the husky dogs tethered to cabins all across the town.

The mood changed. A murmur rippled through the crowd; there were screams of consternation, and one or two people actually fainted. Then the mob broke up into smaller mobs of gesticulating men and women, who gathered on street corners and in saloons, threatening to seize the warehouses, fighting occasionally with their fists, shouting, bartering, trading, pleading. The restaurants closed as the news spread to the gulches and the miners poured in from Eldorado and Bonanza. For hundreds there was no sleep that night as partners pooled what they owned and drew lots to decide who would stay and who would flee. Within a few hours fifty open boats had pushed off for Fort Yukon, three hundred and fifty miles down the river, and another hundred were preparing to go.

And those who had been frantic to reach the Klondike were just as frantic to leave it now. Stampeders who had used their wits and their physical resources to hurdle the mountains and breast the river expended the same energies in a scramble to retreat the way they had come.

The most desperate expedition was that headed by Thomas McGee of San Francisco, who commandeered the rickety steamboat *Kieukik,* intending to sail it as far up the river as Fort Selkirk and then make his way overland to the Lynn Canal. So often did the machinery break down on the shuddering little craft that after a week the fifteen freezing passengers aboard the vessel found they had moved only thirty-five miles. The boat, its hull ripped open, was abandoned and a fresh start made in Indian canoes. So nerve-racking was this trip that the native guide succumbed to a weakness rare among his kind: he broke down and wept. But the party did reach the Lynn Canal, after forty days, and stumbled into Skagway, half-starved and frostbitten. The *City of Seattle* was in port at the time, and as her gold-hungry passengers disembarked and began their headlong race for the passes, they noted, momentarily and without comprehension, the odd spectacle of McGee and his fellows clambering gratefully aboard to book passage for home.

While this exodus up the Yukon was under way, the *Portus B. Weare* and the *Bella* from St. Michael were gingerly navigating the Yukon flats. Stripped of their barges and half their cargo, they inched their way across the shoals and steamed triumphantly into the deeper waters of the main river, only to face a human hazard a few miles farther on: at Circle City each in turn was subjected to one of the most decorous armed hold-ups in the history of piracy.

Some hundred and eighty miners had returned to the old camp when the first flush of the Klondike receded, and these had watched in growing frustration as boat after boat passed them by on the way up to Dawson.

214

When the *Weare* arrived on September 20, they decided to take the law into their own hands. A committee of six climbed aboard and offered to pay the company's price for enough provisions to last the winter. When Ely Weare, the president, refused, fifty men with rifles and shotguns emerged from the bushes and drew a bead on the boat. With the ship's crew at bay, the miners quietly began to unload the cargo, checking it carefully and paying for it as it was removed. When the *Weare* left the following morning, she was thirty tons lighter.

A similar scene was enacted on September 25 when the *Bella* arrived. Her portly and peppery captain, E. D. Dixon, an old Mississippi hand, grew almost apoplectic with rage as the insurgents swarmed aboard. Captain Patrick Henry Ray of the Eighth Infantry, U.S. Army, a passenger aboard the steamboat, shouldered his way to the forefront and tried to reason with the miners, who were already unloading the cargo while the fuming captain shouted and cursed and spat tobacco juice upon the deck. Ray had been sent north by the U.S. government to investigate the possibilities of relieving destitute miners; but now he was forced to tell the very men he had come to succour that their action was unlawful.

"There's no law or any person in authority to whom we can appeal," the chairman of the miners' committee retorted, and since this was only too true, Ray yielded. The government had failed to place any officials in Circle City, whose only law was the law of the miners' meeting. Although Dixon continued to roar that he would not leave a single pound of supplies at Circle, the *Bella* left the town twenty-five tons lighter. Save for the unregenerate Dixon, it was difficult to tell the victims from the hold-up men. As Ray later wrote in his report to Washington, "The feature that was most prominent when the *Bella* was held up was the cheerfulness and

215

alacrity with which all the employees of the company, from the agent down, facilitated the work of the miners — and their expressions of approval."

There was a sequel of sorts to this incident. The following spring, when the steamer *Rideout* docked at Fortymile with two hundred dance-hall queens aboard, the miners, emboldened by the example of Circle City, quietly stole one of the girls for their private use.

2: *Revolt on the Yukon*

The Yukon Valley was aflame with colour that September. The birches and the aspens turned to fiery yellow-orange, while the buck-brush on the hilltops changed to deep crimson-purple. Then, as the month reached its end, the world went grey as the leaves fell away and the ashen trunks stood naked to the autumn winds. In the mornings the hillsides were powdered with a talcum coating of frost, and the pale sun, rising only briefly, seemed to have lost its warmth.

In the lifeless forests the scuttling hare shed its protective brown and turned as white as the first fresh snow; the ptarmigan followed suit, and the darting weasel. Here and there a nodding grizzly, bloated by feasts of blueberry and salmon, sought out the darkness of a mountain cave and relapsed into his long coma. The songbirds were long since gone; only the plump chickadees remained, and the grey juncos, and the white little snow buntings.

As the sun vanished, and the surface soil froze solid, holding its moisture locked within it, the mountain streams dropped to thin trickles and ceased to feed the mother river. Along the margin of the Yukon, shore ice formed, extending for thirty feet out into the stream; and as the river, starved of nourishment, began to drop, this ice was left to project unsupported from the high banks. Chunk by chunk it broke off and toppled into the current until the waters were thick with it.

In Dawson, men took to the hills to search for Arctic hare, while others, sitting on the banks, tried to catch grayling through holes chopped in the shore ice. A few men even ventured towards the distant mountains in an attempt to capture big game.

In front of the town the rustling mass of ice slipped by like an endless chain. Then, on the night of September 28, to the surprise of all, the *Weare,* her twin black smoke-stacks puffing furiously, steamed into Dawson through the floating ice mass. The effect was shattering. Guns were fired and bonfires lit, while cheers resounded from the thousands who greeted her.

As the *Weare*'s whistle pierced the gloom and her gangplank was lowered onto the frozen and crowded bank, John J. Healy shouldered his way through the impatient throng and fairly raced aboard his company's ship. Ely Weare, the son of his old Mississippi crony and now the president of the N.A.T., greeted him with enthusiasm. Healy, in his crusty way, brushed this welcome aside and demanded to know how much cargo was on board. Weare answered, not without a certain pride, that the ship was loaded with all the whiskey and hardware that could be floated across the Yukon flats.

These words drove Healy into a fury, for he had given direct orders, as general manager, to load the boats with food and clothing only. Blinded by rage and frustration, he seized Weare by the throat and might have choked him to death had not his assistant, an amateur boxer, separated the two men.

Two days later the *Bella* arrived with an equally limited and disappointing cargo, and Constantine, who came up from the Fortymile headquarters aboard her, realized that one thousand persons would have to be evacuated from Dawson. They could not get far, as the river would shortly be frozen solid and all water travel come to an end for the season, but with luck they might reach Fort Yukon, Alaska, some three hundred and fifty miles downriver from Dawson — eighty-six miles past Circle City. It was near this old Hudson's Bay post on the Yukon flats that the steamboats loaded with provisions were stranded. Accordingly, Constantine posted a notice on Front Street:

> ... For those who have not laid in a winter's supply to remain longer is to court death from starvation, or at least the certainty of sickness from scurvy and other troubles. Starvation now stares everyone in the face who is hoping and waiting for outside relief. ...

The Collector of Customs and the Gold Commissioner addressed street-corner meetings, urging people to escape, while Hansen of the A.C. Company, nervous and alarmed, ran up and down Front Street from group to group, calling out: "Go! Go! Flee for your lives!"

Only John J. Healy remained calm in the face of the panic. The tough old frontiersman refused to be panicked. Hansen, he said contemptuously, was a hysterical cheechako. There was food enough for all in Dawson, he insisted, and he urged all to stay.

"There will be no starvation," Healy kept saying, to Hansen's annoyance. "Some may go hungry, but no one will starve. If there *is* starvation, it will not be until spring."

In spite of this, Healy permitted those who wished to leave aboard the *Weare* to take passage to Fort Yukon for a nominal fifty dollars. ("There's nothing at Fort Yukon," he warned them.) Constantine, meanwhile, determined to speed the departure of scores more by allowing them free passage on the *Bella* and five days'

218

allowance of food. One hundred and sixty took advantage of this offer; but when the steamboat was ready to leave at four p.m. on October 1, it was found that forty had taken the food and vanished. Many of those who did go on board did so under fictitious names. They did not wish the ignominy of this retreat to reach the ears of their friends Outside.

They crowded up the gangplank like defeated soldiers, the raw north wind plucking at their greatcoats, the leaden and wintry sky hanging over them like a pall. Here was a doctor who had abandoned a growing practice in Chicago to seek greener fields in the north; he was one of three skilled physicians forced out of town. Here was a watchmaker who had arrived with three thousand dollars' worth of jewellery but with no provisions, and was leaving with his wares unsold. Here was a feeble creature of seventy who had scraped five hundred dollars together from his friends and relatives to invest in this last great adventure. "I'd rather starve or freeze to death among strangers than die of humiliation and a broken heart at home," he had cried when the first epidemic of Klondicitis spread across the country. Now he was among strangers, starving and freezing. Here was a bank clerk from Boston who had left for the Klondike to begin a career as a businessman — his career at an end before it had truly begun. Here were half a dozen midwestern farmers who had hoped to garner enough gold from the Klondike to pay the interest on the mortgages that they had been forced to increase in order to secure the means to go north. Sitting morosely on their blankets on the deck or in the messrooms or on top of the cordwood stacked in the hold, they listened to the ice blocks grinding against the hull, which had been sheathed in an eighteen-inch strip of steel for protection.

219

Out into the channel the little *Bella* chugged, leaving behind a forlorn huddle of townspeople who watched this last link with civilization drift stern first in the direction of Fortymile, her rudder jammed in the ice so that the pilot could not correctly head her downstream. Slowly, like a cork in a bathtub, she rotated until the rudder was repaired.

For forty miles she kept her course until the suction pipe feeding the boiler became clogged with ice. Then, out of steam, she was driven ashore and tied up. The passengers cramming every corner slept uneasily in their light blankets or munched on their scanty supplies of hardtack and bacon while her captain and crew fought to get her under way once more.

For another forty miles the resolute Dixon forced his vessel downriver in an unequal battle with the ice. Again she ran out of steam, and again he got her under way. The ice jammed her rudder and she floated broadside towards the mouth of the Fortymile. He forced her into the shore, where the ice formed a solid prison around her. But now a rare and almost miraculous natural phenomenon came to his aid: a warm chinook wind, blowing through the mountains from the distant coast, melted the ice in the main stream. Dixon was able to clear a channel out to the river and continue on his way. The thaw lasted for twelve hours, and then the ice returned with new fury, driving the little steamboat before it into a bank. But Dixon repaired her and chugged on. A few hours later the ice drove the ship onto a sand-bar. She clung to it for two days and nights while the ice poured down at five miles an hour, pounding with terrifying force against her hull, until one enormous block, striking the paddlewheel, smashed a blade and jarred the vessel from stem to stern. But Dixon spat tobacco, dislodged his ship, and finally brought her limping into Circle City. He bore the river no grudge,

220

for he loved her almost as if she were a woman, and would brook no criticism of her. To him she was "one of the prettiest rivers under the sun," and when he died five years later it was at the helm of his steamboat, as she unloaded cargo at Circle City, with the tawny Yukon hissing around him.

While Dixon was battling the river, the *Weare,* having reached Circle, was facing a second bout of armed violence. Her captain had refused to proceed farther, and the passengers, many of them drunk, were talking of seizing the boat by force. Ray, the infantry officer, who was still in town, quietly went about securing arms and ammunition to defend the ship's stores, if necessary with his life. On October 10 the captain of the *Weare,* whose own state of intoxication now matched that of the passengers, announced that if the boat could be cut free of the ice he would continue for eighty-six miles farther to Fort Yukon, where supplies could be had for the winter. At this news, one hundred men set to work hacking away at the ice that fettered the vessel, working themselves into a state of fury because the captain, in spite of his promises, gave no further sign of connecting up the engines. Only the armed presence of Ray prevented a mutiny.

It was at this point that the chinook wind cleared the river of ice. The N.A.T. Company supplied three boats with a capacity of sixty men and provisions for four days, and at eight a.m. on October 12 this small flotilla sailed off and was soon joined by more and more boats fleeing from Dawson. Indeed, the channel, miraculously clear for the moment, was alive with craft of every description, each straining to reach the source of supplies as they had once strained to reach the source of riches. They could not know — and had they known, would not have believed — that at this same moment other boats, farther down the river, were fighting against time and weather, trying to reach the Klondike before freeze-up. In the same week in which one set of passengers fought with the captain of the *Weare* at Circle City to take them away from the Klondike, another set of passengers battled with the captain of the tiny *St. Michael,* also at Circle City, trying to force him to take them on to the Klondike.

Ray's boat was at the centre of the scattered fleet attempting to reach Fort Yukon from Circle. The captain was certain there would be violence when hundreds of hungry men landed, and he was determined to prevent bloodshed if he could.

For twelve hours the river remained clear, and then, as the swift dusk of evening descended and the aurora glowed greenly in the sky, the men in the boats could hear once more the distant roar of ice in motion. An Indian in Ray's boat called out that the river was freezing, and the men steeled themselves for the onslaught, as an army, listening to the rumble of cannon in the distance, waits for an enemy attack.

In inky blackness there followed a macabre scene. The water rose, the current seemed to increase in speed, the boats strove vainly to reach the shore until — roaring and crashing, rending and tearing — the ice descended upon them. Ray and his companions, fighting the current in their whirling craft, found themselves caught in a gorge formed by masses of ice piling high on either side of them as the river froze inward from both shores. Each member of Ray's crew battled desperately to keep the boat on an even keel, their oars and rudder smashed by the repeated blows of the blocks that bore down upon them. Then, almost in an instant, the frothing waters seemed to solidify above them, around them, and beneath them, until Ray's boat was borne upward by the freezing action, as if by unseen hands.

222

Thus they remained, locked in the ice, until morning. In the dawn's pale light Ray spotted five other boats caught in the pack, some of them smashed to kindling. From shore to shore the river now presented an appalling sight: the entire channel as far as the eye could see was clogged with enormous up-ended cakes jammed and frozen together in a solid, unmoving mass.

Across these misshapen hummocks the shipwrecked men made their way until they reached an island in mid-river. Here some hundred and fifty people were gathered. Fort Yukon lay sixty-five miles away, and Ray, taking command, led the party in a weary and exhausting trek through the snow, with only meagre rations and scant bedding.

He arrived on October 25 to find an armed revolution in the making. There was really little he could do about it. To his dismay, he now learned there were far fewer supplies at Fort Yukon than had been made out. Alone in Alaska — save for his subordinate, Richardson — with no legal machinery of any kind and no constabulary, the officer had only his own powers of persuasion to use against the desperate and hungry men who were already arming and planning to seize the two trading companies' caches.

Ray had never felt himself so impotent. All his life he had been an Army man, used to taking and giving orders, a commanding figure with his fierce black Irish brows, his great beak of a nose, and his formidable waxed mustachios. He had served in the ranks throughout the Civil War and then, commissioned, had been placed in charge of the International Polar Expedition to Point Barrow on Alaska's northern tip. In his late fifties and approaching retirement age (he would rise to brigadier general), he felt that he knew the Army and that he knew the North. But never in his career was

223

he to come up against as frustrating a situation as the one in which he now found himself.

On October 29, four days after arriving at Fort Yukon, he was ambushed by a party of twenty-two armed men who planned to hold up the N.A.T. cache. Ray could only bargain, as he had at Circle City. He promised to feed all destitute men at government expense if they would work cutting wood at five dollars a cord in payment; those who had money he would allow to purchase minimum outfits. This offer prevented bloodshed, but Ray realized it was a bad bargain, and the sense of frustration that marked these days in Fort Yukon can be seen in the reports he prepared for Washington. He knew quite well that at least thirty who proclaimed themselves destitute were lying. In the end, they even refused to cut wood for him, and again there was nothing he could do. It was, as he later reported, a straight case of premeditated robbery. On November 19 the N.A.T. store, which he had saved from a sacking, was looted anyway, and six thousand dollars in gold dust stolen. "The tide of lawlessness is rising rapidly all along the river," Ray wrote. Yet he was powerless to deal with the lawbreakers; there was not a single U.S. official qualified to administer an oath within one thousand miles. Ray discovered that one of the "destitute" men had taken his government relief and left for Circle City. This was too much. He ordered the man's arrest on a charge of obtaining supplies under false pretenses, but once again he was frustrated. The miners at Circle broke open the temporary jail in which the prisoner was held and released him. He sold his outfit at public auction, gambled away the proceeds at a faro game, and headed back upstream for Dawson, figuratively thumbing his nose at Patrick Henry Ray, the officer without a command, the leader without authority.

3: *A dollar a waltz*

Some of those who fled the Klondike did not reach Fort Yukon, and these were obliged to trudge back to Dawson along the unkempt surface of the frozen river. One such was Joaquin Miller, who less than three months before had left San Francisco so proudly and so optimistically. He and his party chopped their way through mountains of ice, flinging their supplies away to lighten their loads, and with the aid of Indians along the way reached the Klondike on December 5. The poet was in a sorry state. Both cheeks were frozen, his left ear was sloughed off, part of his big toe had to be removed, one finger was missing, and he was suffering the tortures of snowblindness. He remained in Dawson for the rest of the winter, dependent on the charity of others, a curious gaunt figure in his reindeer parka, his grey beard, stained with food, flowing from his thin, ascetic face.

All that fall the exodus from Dawson continued. In mid-October one thousand men, women, and children were shivering in tents on the banks of the Klondike, but by December 1 some nine hundred had retraced their steps.

Scores attempted to return up the frozen river to the passes, rending their clothes, shredding their moccasins, and shattering their sleighs on the sharp blocks of ice that were sometimes heaped as high as twenty feet. As they stumbled on, they jettisoned their sleds, their food, their clothes, even their shoes, keeping only a single blanket apiece and a meagre amount of provisions, with no shelter but a campfire to keep them from death by freezing.

All of this time the temperature hung at fifty below zero, so cold that any man moving faster than a tortoise pace felt the chill air sear his lungs. On November 29 the temperature dipped again to sixty-seven below, so that the trees cracked like pistol shots with the freezing and expanding sap, and cooked beans turned hard as pebbles, and the touch of metal tore the skin from naked fingers.

Half a dozen died on this fearful journey and many were incapacitated, such as William Byrne, a seventeen-year-old from Chicago who was abandoned at Five Finger Rapids by his half-crazed uncle. The elder man had worked the youth to exhaustion at pistol point until one night Byrne was too tired to remove his soaking moccasins. He awoke next morning to find both feet frozen. A doctor amputated his legs at the knee while the uncle rushed on. Byrne eked out the winter in a shack by the river, more dead than alive. The following spring he managed to make his way Outside, whereupon he announced that he would return at once to the Klondike on artificial limbs to dig for gold.

Dawson, meanwhile, settled down to a second winter in which poverty, famine, and sickness were fortune's bedfellows. In Bill McPhee's Pioneer Saloon homeless men slept fitfully on benches and tables, but across the road, in Harry Ash's Northern, there stood a row of old-fashioned mixing-glasses, each filled with a thousand dollars' worth of dust. Down the street at the Yukon Hotel the buckskin sacks were stacked like cordwood — two hundred thousand dollars alone from the Eldorado claim of the Lucky Swede. Directly above this Croesus hoard, the guests were herded into double-decked bunks beneath bare rafters, to sleep in their work clothes, with only verminous blankets over them and a nail for a coat-hanger. A crack in the wall served as ventilation, a bit of candle stuck into the logs as light; a red-hot sheet-iron stove supplied an uneven heat.

Gold, which would buy so little, slipped easily from hand to hand at the gambling-tables. A man could lose

226

eighteen thousand dollars in a day and a half without giving it a thought, as one man did that winter. A man could lose a thousand dollars in five minutes and cheerfully buy liquor and cigars for all, as another did. Or a man could throw his sack of dust on the high card, collect his winnings, and blow them all on two hundred glasses of whiskey, in the manner of Joe Brand, a dog-puncher.

What would gold buy in Dawson that winter? It would buy a meal of beans, stewed apples, bread, and coffee for five dollars in a restaurant before the restaurants closed. It would buy desiccated potatoes at a dollar a pound or rancid flour at three. It would buy a one-minute waltz with a girl in a silk dress at a dollar a waltz; and it would, under certain conditions, buy the girl in the silk dress too. It was in the Monte Carlo that winter that a twenty-two-year-old French-Canadian girl named Mable LaRose auctioned herself off to the highest bidder; she offered to live with him all winter as his wife and do his housekeeping — the money to be held by neutral parties and paid over when the bargain was completed. Up she stood on the bar, a wistful and diminutive figure with plaited auburn hair, and was promptly purchased for five thousand dollars.

Within the smoke-filled, kerosene-lit interior of the M & M Saloon and Dancehall, Pete McDonald, the one-time "Prince of Puget Sound," was raking in thirty-seven hundred dollars a day. He looked the perfect bartender, with his round head, his bulldog expression, his carefully oiled and parted hair, and his dark, curled moustache, but this man had already made and lost three fortunes in the timber camps of Michigan, Wisconsin, and Washington. When he reached Dawson in March, 1897, he had only ten dollars left, the residue of his enormous take from the Silver Dollar Saloon in Snohomish, Washington's great boom town. He built

227

his Dawson bar on borrowed money, and by midwinter he was in the chips again. Around and around his sawdust floor the silk-clad girls went whirling, so swiftly and so expertly that McDonald was able to crowd as many as one hundred and twenty-five dances into a single evening's entertainment. For each dance his girls received an ivory chip worth twenty-five cents and McDonald got the remainder of the dollar fee. One man so badly wanted to dance that he bought seven hundred dollars' worth of dance tickets in advance and danced like a dervish for a week while the violins scraped and the piano rattled out its tinny waltzes and polkas. Then, on Thanksgiving Night, with the temperature at fifty-eight below, a dance-hall girl threw a flaming lamp at a rival and most of Front Street went up in smoke. McDonald's saloon burned to the ground; his loss was reckoned at a hundred thousand dollars; but he had a new building erected within a week (named the Phoenix because it rose from the ashes). He had no glassware left, for every whiskey glass in town had been cornered by speculators who were charging five to ten dollars each for the hoard, so he made his own drinking-cups of copper and tin, and thus the dance whirled on.

4: *Only a coal miner's daughter . . .*

The fog of winter, thickened by the smoke that poured from the mine shafts, clung like a shroud to Bonanza and Eldorado, but the miners toiled doggedly on. The high dumps formed odd blurred shapes in the mist, and the men who worked upon them loomed out of the haze like ghosts. In midwinter, dusk fell at three p.m., and in the thickening twilight the mouth of each shaft glowed pinkly from the fires within. Down the valleys a weird sound came sighing, like a hundred rusty gates swinging in the wind; it was the cry of the windlasses creaking while miners deep within the earth struggled with the

228

heavy buckets of paydirt. But it was the only sound, for the snow and the moss and the fog muffled the valleys until men themselves fell silent and worked on word-lessly in the numbing cold of their self-dug warrens. They worked like animals, creeping about on all fours among the ashes of their fires, scraping away at the immemorial muck, peering squint-eyed into the chiaroscuro of their deepening pits, seeking always the twinkling motes of gold.

At the junction of the two creeks, a new town, called Grand Forks, had sprung up: twenty cabins and a cou-ple of hotels and saloons. And here a plain-faced young Irishwoman of rigid morals and canny disposition, Be-linda Mulroney by name, was establishing herself as one of the legendary figures of the stampede.

She was a coal-miner's daughter from Scranton, Pennsylvania, who had gone off to the Columbian Ex-position in Chicago at the age of eighteen to open a restaurant and to make her fortune. She earned eight thousand dollars but lost it all in California. Un-daunted, she shipped aboard the *City of Topeka* as a stewardess, where she quickly gained a reputation for her business acumen, her cool resource, and her sharp tongue. When a passenger asked her to black his boots, she retorted that if he so much as put them outside his door she would pour a pitcher of water on them. When, on her first voyage, a baby had to be delivered, she did the job herself, while the captain stood discreetly out-side the cabin door and read the instructions from a medical text. He put her in charge of purchasing all ship's supplies, and she bought everything from ma-chinery to canary birds, charging him a stiff ten-per-cent commission and selling picture hats and satin dresses on the side to the squaws in the coastal towns.

By the spring of '97, when the news of the Klondike reached the Alaskan Panhandle, Belinda had amassed

229

five thousand dollars. She invested it all in cotton goods and hot-water bottles, floated down the river on a raft with two Indians, and on reaching Dawson flung her last fifty-cent piece contemptuously into the river, swearing that she would never again need such small change.

She sold her merchandise on Dawson's Front Street at a profit of six hundred per cent, opened up a lunch counter, and hired a group of young men to build cabins for her, which she sold as fast as the roofs went on.

But she wanted to be nearer the mines. With the aid of a broken-down mule named Gerry, she began to haul lumber to the creeks; and here, as the town jeered at her, she built her road house. In vain her friends told her that Dawson was the place to open a hotel and saloon. By fall her hostelry was open and Belinda herself stood behind the bar, a stern and strangely incongruous figure in her white shirtwaist and long black skirt, dispensing eggs at a dollar apiece, and wine, cigars, and whiskey at the highest prices in the Klondike, always keeping her ears open to the mining gossip and shrewdly noting it all down for future action. Before the winter was out she had half a dozen valuable mining properties in her name.

The Eldorado kings flocked to her road house. Sam Stanley, the wild young son of William Stanley, the lame old Seattle bookseller, leaned on the counter with his partner, Charlie Worden, and laid plans to open a hotel in Dawson. Clarence Berry's partner, Antone Stander, drank crazily, his eyes fixed on Violet Raymond, who was the personal property of Max Endleman, the grizzled proprietor of the nearby Gold Hill Hotel. Endleman had brought Violet and her sister in from the Juneau Opera House that spring, but Stander, with his Austrian good looks and his vast supplies of gold, soon won her away. He bought her every diamond
230

in the area and gave her a necklace that reached almost to her knees. He gave her twenty thousand dollars in gold dust and a lard pail full of nuggets. He gave her a thousand dollars a month to keep her happy. In the end he married her, and she ruined him.

Arkansas Jim Hall and his French-Canadian partner, Picotte, rubbed shoulders at the bar with Dick Lowe, of the famous fraction. All three could now afford to indulge their fancies. Hall had fancied a woman and purchased her for twenty thousand dollars in gold dust. Picotte, who was married to a squaw, fancied a white wife. Off he went to Montreal, and back he came to Eldorado with a bride broadminded enough to help him buy clothes for his three half-breed children. Dick Lowe's fraction had already yielded twenty-five thousand dollars, and he was spending it freely on wine and women, but the ex-mule-skinner seemed to get as much satisfaction out of practising with his long whip outside his cabin door, a rite that consumed a full hour of every day.

Skookum Jim and Tagish Charley clomped into Belinda's in loud plaid shirts and gaudy ties, with scarlet bands on their black miners' hats and heavy watch-chains with double rows of nuggets draped across their paunches. They were treated as white men now, allowed to consume alcohol, and so they bought drinks for the crowd while everybody sang the "George Carmack Song":

> George Carmack on Bonanza Creek went
> out to look for gold,
> I wonder why, I wonder why.
> Old-timers said it was no use, the water was
> too cold.
> I wonder why, I wonder why.
> They said that he might search that creek

> *until the world did end*
> *And not enough of gold he'd find a postage*
>   *stamp to send.*
> *They said the willows on that creek the other*
>   *way would bend.*
> *I wonder why, I wonder why. . . .*

But the most frequent visitor of all to Belinda's road house did not drink at all, or sing. Whiskey could not intoxicate Big Alex McDonald: he was already drunk with the idea of land. By the winter's end he had acquired interests in ten claims on Eldorado, seven on Bonanza, nineteen on Dominion, fifteen on Sulphur, eight on Hunker, three on Gold Bottom, one on Bear, two on Skookum Gulch, and several on the benchland above the fork. In short, he had claims on every one of the Klondike's richest creeks. And he had land in Dawson, too.

None knew how much he was worth, least of all Big Alex himself. It was said that if he so much as stopped to look at a piece of property its value increased at once. He was involved in so many complicated business deals that every time he was introduced to a newcomer he would start the conversation by asking: "Are you a partner of mine?" Wherever he went, a swarm of gesticulating hangers-on followed him, plucking at his sleeve, waving papers, offering business propositions, asking for money. To each, McDonald replied with an immediate "No!" but this meant only that he wanted time to mull over the idea. As often as not he ended by accepting, for he had reached the point where he found it hard to resist any offer. Each man, that winter, seemed to require an outlet for his new-found wealth. For some it was supplied by women, for others by incessant dancing in Pete McDonald's saloon, for many more by faro bank or blackjack. Alex McDonald's outlet was business and property; they consumed his interests and satisfied his appetites, and in the end they ruined him too.

5: *Greenhorns triumphant*

All winter long, sourdoughs and cheechakos alike were haunted by the idea that all the gold had not yet been uncovered in the Klondike area. Scarcely a month passed without a stampede into the hills as whispers of secret finds filtered across the camp.

An old man in a cabin on the Yukon reported gold on Rosebud Creek, fifty miles above Dawson, and every man who could make the journey rushed to it in the dark of the night to stake claims by candle and match-light. But there was no gold on Rosebud Creek.

In February there came a tale of gold on Swede Creek, a few miles above the town, and in the bitter cold and bright moonlight three hundred people streamed up the frozen river, suffering terrible privations in an attempt to secure claims. Two men had their feet amputated as a result, but there was no gold on Swede Creek.

In April there was a third stampede to an island in mid-river which was quickly named Monte Cristo Island. Soon every sand-bar was solidly staked, but there was no gold on the islands of the Yukon.

By spring the gold fever had become endemic and men were hammering stakes and sinking shafts on the townsite of Dawson City itself until the Mounties put an end to it. There was no gold in Dawson anyway.

Yet a few miles away, closer than Rosebud Creek, closer than Swede Creek, closer than Monte Cristo Island, gold, still undiscovered, lay almost as thickly as sand. It was hidden in the bowels of the hills and benches above the creeks. There was a mountain streaked with it above Dick Lowe's fraction and an-other mountain of it above Tom Lippy's Eldorado

233

claim. There was a highway of it running a serpentine course along the western rim of Eldorado Creek and down Bonanza and across the main valley of the Klondike.

It was the greenhorns who found it. They searched the benches while the old-timers jeered, for no seasoned Yukon prospector could conceive of placer gold lying high above the creekbeds. Gold was heavy, was it not? It had to sink into the bedrock; how could it rise? Yet anybody gazing at those terraced hills might have realized that high above the present streams older watercourses had once flowed, and in these former streambeds would be gold. Indeed, as was later realized, it was from one of these ancient channels, cropping from the brow of a hill, that Carmack's original nuggets had come: the flaky gold had simply washed down to be discovered by an accident.

In the fall of 1897 the old-timers in Grand Forks, gazing up at the western rim of Eldorado above the Lowe fraction, were astonished to see some men working away. On one side of the hill was a Californian named Albert Lancaster. On the other side, on the bench above Big Skookum Gulch, were Nathan Kresge and his partner, Nels Peterson. These two had arrived in the summer of 1897, and both noticed a queer thing about the benchland above Bonanza: the miners had been dragging their winter wood down the slopes, and in the furrows left behind, the spring freshets had exposed a peculiar white gravel. This excited the suspicions of Kresge, a born prospector and a geology student who had been seeking gold ever since he had dug in the sand as a child in Pennsylvania. The two men began to look for exposed bedrock on the hills and to sink shallow shafts until, suddenly, from an eighteen-inch hole they pulled a ten-dollar nugget. This discovery sent them tumbling pell-mell down the hill to Grand Forks.

Here they borrowed the traditional miner's "rocker" — a box-shaped sieve, built on the principle of a baby's cradle, to separate the fine sand from the coarse gravel. Dick Lowe's foreman watched them lugging this awkward contrivance up to the ridge, and swore and laughed at them for wasting their time. But in the next ten days they washed out six thousand dollars' worth of gold from a piece of ground no larger than a cabin floor.

Yet, in spite of the stampede that followed, in spite of the fact that both flanks of Big Skookum Gulch were quickly staked, the significance of Kresge's discovery was lost on the prospectors. The hills remained empty because men still did not understand that the white gravel above Big Skookum was part of an old riverbed. On the opposite side of Gold Hill, as it was now called, Lancaster, the Californian, continued to work in plain sight, and to endure for the duration of the winter the laughter of the Eldorado kings and their employees. His little hundred-foot claim — actually the first bench claim staked in the Klondike — was eventually to produce two hundred thousand dollars for him.

It is odd that out of all the hundreds and thousands who roamed the creeks that winter and dashed off on abortive stampedes to nowhere, only two others besides Kresge and Lancaster unravelled the riddle of the Klondike hills. Both were newcomers to the country, and each worked out his theory quite independently of the other.

The first was William Dietering, a round-faced German immigrant from Evanston, Illinois, better known as Cariboo Billy. The other was Oliver B. Millett, who had quit his job in a sawmill the day the *Portland* arrived in Seattle with her ton of gold, and, lightly equipped, had managed to reach Dawson on October 9.

Cariboo Billy knew something about bench diggings, for he had seen them years before in the Cariboo gold rush of British Columbia. He was convinced that a lost channel ran through the Klondike hills, and so, with his partner, Joe Staley, he began a systematic exploration of both sides of Eldorado. The two men worked their way up slowly from the mouth of the creek until they reached French Hill, directly above Tom Lippy's claim, a mile and a half upstream. They began to dig into the very brow of the hill, and here they hit the same white gravel that had marked Kresge's find. At a depth of four feet there was gold. They sank a second test shaft, and this was far richer: three pans of dirt yielded one hundred and ninety dollars. Boiling with excitement, they filled the holes so that the Eldorado miners, hauling wood along a path just twenty feet away, would suspect nothing. But when on March 19 they recorded their claim, the secret was out and another stampede took place. Still the old-timers refused to believe there was gold on French Hill. They said that Cariboo Billy must have salted his claim; and they let the cheechakos do the staking.

Meanwhile, Oliver Millett was developing his own theories. He had gone to work as a layman on *Forty-One* Eldorado, and it puzzled him that Eldorado gold should be so different in texture from that found on the parent Bonanza. What happened to the Eldorado gold after the creek joined Bonanza? Could it be that the old channel, after reaching the Bonanza valley, moved on through the hills on the left bank of the creek?

All his life Millett had been an adventurer. He came from the old German-Canadian town of Lunenburg, Nova Scotia, and, like so many of his townspeople, he had left home at fourteen to follow the sea before seeking his fortune in the West. Here he was venturing again, a lanky, pale-faced would-be prospector of thirty-three, ambitious, intense, and stubborn. His lay on Eldorado produced no gold — indeed, there was no
236

gold on Eldorado above *Forty* — and so Millett set out to test his theories in the hills of Bonanza just below the point where Eldorado flows in.

He climbed the steep hillside above George Carmack's claim, through two feet of snow, scrub timber, and thick frozen moss, and then worked his way along the ridge until he found the hard rim of the hillside at the point where an ancient creek had started to cut its way downward. He burned a shaft nine feet before he gave up: but not before he found what he was seeking — a single nugget. He sank a second shaft, toiling alone day after day while the labourers below him on Tagish Charley's claim looked up occasionally and thought him mad. He bored twenty-six feet and found nothing, but still would not give up. He set to work at once on a third shaft; and here, suddenly, he came upon the telltale gravel — gravel so white that it might have been bleached — and in the gravel there was gold. Millett had struck the White Channel (as it has since been called), the track of a bygone stream that runs along the rim of Eldorado and lower Bonanza and then crosses Bonanza to vanish into the main Klondike Valley, which was barren of gold.

Now the discoverer worked like a man possessed. He was already suffering from scurvy brought on by meagre rations and overstrain, but he had no time to consider treatment. He rushed down to Pete McDonald's cabin on *Two Below,* asked for lumber, and was told not to waste his time; but he could not be dissuaded. He built himself a rocker, laboured up the hill with it, and in his first day took out more than eight hundred dollars. On he worked, his legs turning black and scabrous, until he had twenty thousand in gold. Then, almost dead from scurvy, his claim still unsurveyed and unregistered, he headed downhill for Grand Forks to get some raw potatoes to arrest his disease. In his absence

237

somebody suggested they call his hill Cheechako Hill because only a newcomer would be silly enough to look for gold there — and Cheechako Hill it became.

Millett was now too ill to work. He got Captain Billy Norwood, a Nova Scotia friend, to certify his discovery as required by the mining law, and then went into hospital. Within a few days Cheechako Hill was swarming with stakers who hammered in their location posts so quickly that Norwood himself was able to secure only a wedge-shaped fraction. Millett, unable to work his claim, sold out for sixty thousand dollars. The new owners took half a million from it.

By summer, every hill in the Klondike watershed was scarred by shovel, axe, and fire, and the Reverend John Pringle, the Presbyterian minister at Gold Bottom, was able to remark dryly that "the only benches not staked are those in my log church." But the new claim-owners were mostly newcomers. The sourdoughs, stubborn to the end, continued to shake their heads and explain why there never could be gold high in the hills of the Klondike.

6: *The Saint of Dawson*

The starvation that Hansen and Constantine had predicted loomed closer. By Christmas 1897 the stock of supplies in the town was running low and the last restaurant had closed its doors. The police were on reduced rations and would arrest no one unless he had his own provisions. There was no escape from Dawson anyway, for once again the town was isolated from the world. An occasional dog-driver could be found who would attempt the trip to Skagway, but the fee for passage was one thousand dollars and the passengers were forced to run behind the sleigh rather than ride upon it.

238

As the cold came down and the food diminished and the days shortened and the sun vanished entirely, the community slowed almost to a standstill, like a man in a state of catalepsy. Back in the hills the bears were in hibernation; so, too, was Dawson. Men lay in their bunks until noon, half suffocated by the glowing oil-drum stoves, then ventured forth into the searing cold, their nostrils sheathed by heavy scarves, to hack a six-foot hole in the river for fresh water, or to haggle with the listless clerks in the stores for a handful of beans or flour. They wolfed their food, half-cooked and cold, and often they rotted from the resultant scurvy.

It cost as much to die as to live. Two men died on Clarence Berry's claim that winter, and the price of their funeral was astronomical. It cost two thousand dollars to hire a team of six malemutes to take the bodies into town. The nails for the coffins cost eight dollars and fifty cents a pound and the lumber forty cents a foot. Two workmen took six days to hack the graves out of the frozen ground and were paid two hundred dollars in wages.

By mid-January, flour was so scarce that hunters had to trade an entire mountain sheep to get a sack of it. Speculators had cornered the market and were doling it out a few pounds at a time to keep the price up. But as spring approached, the price began to drop; and one man who had hoarded one hundred and eighty sacks was ruefully left holding the bags.

The previous fall a small boat loaded with supplies had been wrecked on a sand-bar, and Belinda Mulroney went into partnership with Big Alex McDonald to buy and salvage the cargo. McDonald moved quickly, collaring all the food and leaving her with nothing but several cases of gum boots and whiskey.

"You'll pay through the nose for this," Belinda vowed, and she meant it. That spring at clean-up time

239

when Big Alex arrived at her road house post-haste looking for rubber boots for his workers, she forced him to pay one hundred dollars a pair.

In April a few hardy souls took advantage of the improving weather to mush in from Dyea and Skagway with articles for sale. They did not bring staples such as flour, meat, or butter (which was selling for five dollars a can), but with a rare understanding of human nature brought luxuries. One man arrived with a lady's hat made of black ostrich feathers which was snapped up at once for two hundred and eighty dollars. Another brought in several tins of oysters and a turkey, ready cooked and dressed. Oyster stew went on sale at fifteen dollars a bowl. The turkey was put on display at the Pioneer Saloon, where men gloated over it and licked their lips. It was raffled off for one hundred and seventy-four dollars.

As Healy had predicted, no man starved in Dawson that winter, perhaps because so many had fled the town in the late fall. The real victims were the Indians in the hinterland. On the Porcupine River, north of Fort Yukon, the native women and children were dying on the trail. Once they had been the best customers of the trading companies. Now they were forgotten.

Hunger's companion was scurvy, and the need for Father Judge's new hospital became apparent as miner after miner dragged himself to its open door. The cadaverous priest, who was already earning his name as "the Saint of Dawson," had never ceased working since he had arrived the previous spring. The task of building hospital, church, and staff residences was enough to tax the energies of a much more powerful man, and yet the priest, in spite of his thin and wasted body, seemed able to perform superhuman tasks. He was his own architect, his own contractor, and his own workman. He did every job, including cooking for those who helped him.

He roamed the hills collecting dried grasses to fill his mattresses, and herbs to amplify his small medical stock. He invented a mixture of muslin and sizing, coated with white lead, which took the place of plaster. He made the furniture himself, using rough boards placed on stumps for pews in his church, and tacking heavy white muslin onto frames in place of stained-glass windows.

And he suffered bitter disappointments. His church was scarcely completed, after months of careful work, before fire destroyed it utterly — on the morning of Trinity Sunday. Everything was reduced to ashes: the altar which he had carved so painstakingly himself with a common penknife, and the hand-hewn furniture — even the vestments for the choir. Without complaint, the priest began once again the herculean task of re-building from the ground up. In this he was aided by an immediate collection taken up by the Protestants and Catholics alike and by a substantial donation from Big Alex McDonald, a devout Scots Catholic, who volunteered to pay for the chapel. One of the features of the church, when it was rebuilt, was that the priest refused to collect a penny of pew rent, or to take up collections at any of his services — a sobering decision in a community where on every other occasion gold was tossed to the winds.

The townspeople helped him to raise the thirty-five thousand dollars needed to complete the hospital. Women roamed through the mining areas, passing the hat; others held bazaars and dances night after night. And, in return, Judge took into his hospital all who required aid. By March there were forty-five scurvy cases alone, jamming the wards and even the hallways.

By this time, tales of Dawson's famine had seeped to the Outside. Captain Ray, indeed, had sent a special messenger out by dog-team to tell the world about the

Klondike's plight, and various chambers of commerce in the Pacific coast cities, fearful that the bad news would ruin the spring trade, bombarded Congress with petitions for Yukon relief. Congress responded in December, 1897, by voting an appropriation of two hundred thousand dollars for the purchase of a reindeer herd, which Washington naïvely believed could be shipped north in time, as meat to assuage Dawson City's hunger. Thus was unfolded another tortured chapter in the odyssey of the gold rush.

The reindeer herd, five hundred and thirty-nine strong, was purchased in Norway, shipped to New York, shuttled across the continent by train to Seattle, and then taken north by steamer to Haines Mission, at the end of the Dalton Trail on the Lynn Canal. The herdsmen, specially trained for the job, included forty-three Laplanders, ten Finns, and fifteen Norwegians. They were a hardy lot. One had crossed Greenland with Nansen a dozen years before and had been awarded a medal by King Oscar for the exploit. Another bore the proud title of world's most northerly mail-carrier. But none had experienced anything like the trek upon which they now embarked.

It was May, 1898, before the reindeer reached Haines. Nine months later they were still struggling along the trail towards Dawson, and by this time a series of mishaps had decimated the herd. The swamps, the mountains, the snowfields and glaciers, the canyons and fallen trees which they had to traverse caused them to die by the scores, like the horses on the Skagway trail. Wolves killed several; the Indians shot more; some strangled themselves on their harness. But these were minor mishaps. Most of the animals succumbed to a more ironic fate. In the early stages of the trek, dozens collapsed from lack of reindeer moss, their staple diet, and from then on there was never really enough to eat.

As the months wore on and the very dogs dropped in their tracks from hunger, the herders were reduced to picking up raw beans spilled on the trail by the gold-seekers ahead of them and stuffing them, filthy and frozen, into their mouths.

"Do you think there is any hell worse than this one?" one of the Lapp drivers asked Hedley E. Redmyer, the Norwegian-American in charge of the expedition.

"No," replied Redmyer, "I think this is all the hell I want."

And so, after a trek of seven hundred and fifty miles, the expedition staggered into Dawson City — to the amusement of the townspeople. The date was January 27, 1899, and the herd, which had been a year in transit, was now reduced to one hundred and fourteen animals, about one fifth of its original size. In that Starvation Winter the real victims of starvation had been the wretched reindeer themselves, and the greatest paradox, in that season of paradoxes, was that in the end it was the Klondike Relief Expedition itself that required relief.

Chapter Seven

1: *The trails of Ninety-eight*

On New Year's Eve 1897, six young Englishmen sat at midnight supper in the moss-chinked cabin on the shores of Great Slave Lake in the Northwest Territories of Canada. They had hoarded three quarters of a bottle of whiskey to see the old year out, enough to allow each of them a single swallow; and now, as the unaccustomed liquor burned their throats, they slowly became aware of the incongruity of their position. If anyone had told them six months before that the New Year would find them imprisoned by winter on the shores of a frozen inland sea as big as Belgium, nine hundred miles north of the nearest town, with the grey-green conifer forest stretching endlessly around them, they would have thought him mad. Yet here they were, unable to advance or retreat until spring, with another two thousand miles of hard travel facing them.

The whiskey gone and the New Year properly launched, each man returned to his separate shack and to bed; but one of them, a Cambridge University law graduate named William Ford Langworthy, paused long enough to scribble some reflective notes in his diary.

"I wonder whether Dolly and the others are at St. Moritz dancing the old year out as we did in 1897?" he wrote. "This world is a farce — what a difference between this New Year and my last. At St. Moritz last year and now *here,* — of all places in the world this is the last I thought I'd be in on New Year's Day. I wonder where I shall be this time next year — and in what condition — shall we have found gold? or blank? . . . I did not imagine how lonely one can feel until today, when about six thousand miles from home and friends. I hope to goodness we 'strike it rich' within a couple of years. . . ."

All over the northwest corner of the continent, in an unexplored wilderness area almost a million and a half

246

square miles in size — half as big again as the subcontinent of India — thousands of others were thinking similar thoughts. A scenic artist from Boston, for example, found himself trapped for nine months in an Eskimo village of beehive huts on the upper delta of the Yukon River. A policeman from New York City found himself dragging a sled-load of provisions and machinery across the creaking surface of the terrible Malaspina glacier on the southern underbelly of Alaska. A schoolmaster from Edinburgh found himself living on wild berries on the banks of the frozen Nisutlin River in the southwest corner of the Yukon Territory. A Methodist preacher from Farnellville, Ohio, found himself with his wife and daughter and a scarecrow of a horse on the summit of Laurier Pass in the heart of the northern Rockies. A ventriloquist from Chicago found himself in a huddle of tents on the banks of the Rat River in the tundra country north of the Arctic Circle.

The complete implausibility of each man's situation made the most absurd incidents, the most unexpected scenes, appear commonplace. The gold-rush trails were marked by various episodes which have a tinge of madness to them. There was, for instance, the little circus that wended its way north towards the Klondike along the Ashcroft trail through the wild interior of British Columbia — a circus complete with tightrope dancer, music box, striped marquee, performing dogs, and a beautiful black horse with a white star on its forehead which was lost in the olive-green flood of the cold Skeena. And there were the four young English aristocrats who built a log cabin on the Kowak River along the Arctic Circle five hundred miles northeast of Dawson, named it Quality Hill, and trained an Eskimo as a valet to black their mukluks and serve them coffee and cigars while they lay abed till noon, amusing themselves by shooting at stray mice and at knotholes in the log walls until their castle in the wilderness resembled a Swiss cheese.

As the white fog of winter settled over the north, the stampede ground to a halt. From the Cariboo to the Arctic, from the Mackenzie to the Bering Sea, from the Rockies to the Pacific, thousands of William Langworthys sat huddled in lonely cabins awaiting spring. Major J. M. Walsh, the ex-Mountie appointed Commissioner of the newly created Yukon Territory, could not reach Dawson and fidgeted the winter out at the mouth of the Big Salmon River. Jack London could not reach it either, and wintered on the Stewart River, where his cabin became a mecca for miners, who listened open-mouthed as he told stories memorized from the classics. Nor could Rex Beach reach Dawson; he wintered at Minook Creek several hundred miles downriver from the town. Here he encountered a pessimistic newspaperman who told him: "There's no drama up here, no comedy, no warmth. Life is as pale and as cold as the snow. Back in '49 there was something to write about, but we'll never read any great stories about Alaska and the Klondike. This country is too drab and dreary." Most men in that winter would have agreed; there seemed to be little drama in that chilly vigil. Only when they talked or wrote about it years later did it begin to take on a romantic aura. Then they told each other over glasses of beer or snifters of brandy or at meetings of sourdoughs organized to recall old times that it was an experience they would not have forfeited for all the world's lost gold.

There was no single trail of '98; there were dozens. The stampeders advanced on the Klondike like a great army executing a giant pincer movement, and those who took part in it poured in from every point of the compass.

The main force, planning a frontal assault, was concentrated in the teeming ant-hills of the White and Chilkoot passes. Far to the west, small platoons and companies were making minor flanking movements over the pitted glaciers that sprawl across the mountainous southern coastline of Alaska. But the great left arm of the pincer, several battalions strong, was advancing up the Yukon from the Bering Sea by steamboat.

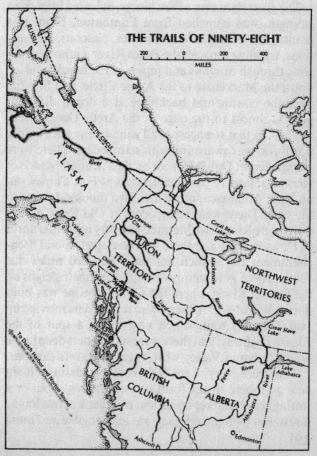

THE TRAILS OF NINETY-EIGHT

A central column was forcing its way northward through the heart of British Columbia, following the route of a forgotten trail cut out by the Western Union Telegraph Company many decades before in an attempt to link Siberia with the United States by cable. This column was joined by a second, moving by steamboat, dog-team, and foot up the Stikine River from the Pacific coast and heading for Teslin Lake on the headwaters of the Yukon.

The great right arm of the pincer, at least a brigade in strength, was launched from Edmonton. From this point it fanned out into companies, platoons, and sections, trickling through the Peace River country, struggling through canyons and rapids of the Liard, pouring down the Mackenzie to the Arctic Circle, and filtering over the continental backbone at a dozen different points, almost to the edge of the Arctic Ocean itself.

Thus, in that strangest of all winters, the once empty northwest was swarming with stampeders. There were stampeders at Dutch Harbor on the Aleutian Islands of Alaska, and there were stampeders at Fort Chipewyan on Lake Athabasca, more than two thousand miles to the east. There were stampeders at Old Crow on the Porcupine River, two hundred and fifty miles due north of Dawson City, and there were stampeders on Disenchantment Bay, which lies three hundred miles due south. There were stampeders dragging their sleighs up the Gravel River, where the Canol pipeline was built during World War II; there were stampeders moving up Jack Dalton's trail, which now forms a spur of the Alaska Highway; and there were stampeders deep in the South Nahanni Valley with its caves and its canyons.

They were everywhere. Relics of their passing remain here and there in the form of a crumbling cabin or a rotting grave-marker on a silent riverbank or in a lonely forest. But their great legacy was less tangible and more enduring. In a very real sense they broke down the barrier of the frontier and opened up the northwest.

2: *Rich man's route*

The rich man's route was the all-water route, and to anyone with money it seemed the easiest route of all. It was a long way round: three thousand miles from Seattle to St. Michael, and seventeen hundred more upstream to Dawson City; but in theory no one needed to walk a foot of the distance: it was a boat ride all the way.

Yet those who chose to buy their way around the left flank forgot or never understood the brevity of the navigation season on the Yukon River. Eighteen hundred stampeders took the all-water route in the fall of 1897, but only forty-three reached the Klondike before winter and, of these, thirty-five had to turn back because in the last frantic moments they had flung their outfits aside and could not replace them in Dawson.

No one who left the United States after August 1 reached the Klondike by the all-water route that season. One of the first ships to leave, after the news was out, was the *Excelsior*, but only ten of her passengers attained their goal. Most of these were newspapermen. John D. McGilvray of the New York *Herald* and his staff artist Max Newberry, for instance, managed to arrive in Dawson, but only by changing steamers four times on the river and hiring Indians to pole them upstream for sixty miles.

When freeze-up came, some twenty-five hundred persons (including several hundred old-timers) were stranded along the seventeen hundred miles of river between Norton Sound and Dawson City. At least one quarter of these were at the end of their financial resources. None would reach Dawson until the following July; some would never reach it at all.

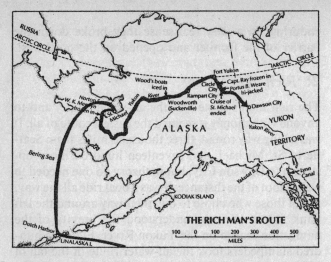

RUSSIA
ARCTIC CIRCLE
Fort Yukon
Wood's boats iced in
Circle City
Capt. Ray frozen in
Portus B. Weare hi-jacked
Norton S.
W. K. Merwyn frozen in
St. Michael
Rampart City
Woodworth (Suckerville)
Cruise of St. Michael ended
Dawson City
YUKON
Yukon River
ALASKA
Yukon River
TERRITORY
Bering Sea
Lynn Canal
Yakutat B.
KODIAK ISLAND
Dutch Harbor
THE RICH MAN'S ROUTE
UNALASKA I.
100   0   100   200   300   400   500
MILES

The embattled mayor of Seattle, W. D. Wood, who had narrowly escaped lynching on the docks at San Francisco, reached St. Michael with his boat-load of stampeders on August 29. Here, on the bleak volcanic beach, the passengers realized for the first time that a steamboat would have to be built before they could embark for the Klondike. A hundred tents were pitched and a mess set up to feed the horde in a style which one described as "worse than a cheap Japanese restaurant." It now became clear to all that the voyage was no luxury cruise. If the passengers wanted to reach the gold-fields they would have to work like Trojans, unloading the cargo and pitching the tents and even helping to construct the river steamer on which they had so trustingly bought passage.

And so there was chaos, confusion, distrust, and discontent. Wood tried to abandon the party but was held almost by physical violence and made to stay as a sort of hostage. It took three weeks to build the steamboat, which was christened *Seattle No. 1* but unofficially dubbed *The Mukluk* because of her uncanny

252

resemblance to that piece of Eskimo footwear. A smaller vessel, the *May West*, was under construction at the same time, and there was considerable rivalry to see which expedition would start off first. The *May West* won by a day, but it really made no difference. The two boats were not able to navigate more than half the distance to the Klondike before they were frozen fast. Dawson City was eight hundred miles and nine months away.

Around these two steamers a jerry-built cluster of cabins and shacks sprang up. Officially titled Woodworth in honour of Mayor Wood and Captain Worth of the *May West*, it was generally referred to as Suckerville by the disgruntled inhabitants. Indignation meetings had already become a regular feature of the Wood expedition; and now more were called to force the mayor to sell, at Seattle prices, supplies which he had hoped to retail in Dawson at a handsome profit. Wood, who by now must have been heartily sick of the word "Klondike," was obliged to agree to these terms. As he pointed out mildly, most of his passengers had been helping themselves anyway. There were undoubtedly many moments when he wished he had never relinquished his post as Seattle's chief magistrate for so-called adventure in the North.

As soon as opportunity afforded, the ex-mayor escaped from Suckerville and made his way on foot back to St. Michael. It was an arduous trip, but anything was better than the ceaseless recriminations that dinned into his ears day and night. His passengers were forced to stay on the riverbank until spring, by which time two of the ladies had married two of the gentlemen. These were the only members of the expedition who gained any reward from the venture. At three a.m. on June 25, 1898, embittered and discouraged, they all finally trudged down the gangplank at Dawson City, exciting considerable comment by their tattered clothing patched with old flour sacks. It had taken them three hundred and fourteen days to reach the Klondike by the all-water route, and those who had any funds instantly booked return passage for home.

While Wood's "Suckerville" was being established, the new boom town of Rampart City was taking form about one hundred miles farther up the river at the mouth of Minook Creek. Had it not been for the Klondike, Minook would itself have caused a stampede from the United States. Here in August, 1896, while Carmack was on Bonanza, a Russian half-breed named Minook was scooping three thousand dollars from a hole eight feet square and fifteen feet deep. In 1897, with steamboats frozen in all along the river, Rampart was expanding. Its population was approaching one thousand, its poorest cabins were selling for eight hundred dollars, and its lots were fetching twelve hundred. Its "mayor" was the same Al Mayo who had been McQuesten's partner on the Yukon for so many years. He presided at the miners' meetings and settled their disputes, including one memorable argument between Sidney Cohen and his partner, Rex Beach. The latter had been dumped at Rampart that fall with a fur-lined sleeping-bag, a rifle, a dogskin suit, and a mandolin. He and Cohen got on each other's nerves so badly that a meeting had to be called to straighten the matter out. Mayo, who had a dramatic flair for old-time justice, decided that they should settle the issue by personal combat. The two men accordingly stripped to their underwear and exchanged a few misplaced haymakers. Then, their sensitivities assuaged, they shook hands and called it a day.

Early in September a curious craft with an equally curious crew chugged into Rampart. This was the tiny stern-wheeler *St. Michael.*She was manned entirely by

254

amateurs who knew nothing about steamboating — a lawyer, a doctor, several clerks, some salesmen, and one lone tramp printer. These people had been passengers on the ocean steamer *Cleveland,* known on the coast as a ship of ill-fortune. The *Cleveland* lived up to her reputation. On reaching Alaska, her passengers were dismayed to learn that the transportation company would not allow them to take more than one hundred and fifty pounds of luggage up the river to Dawson. This left them in a perplexing quandary, since each had, at great expense and trouble, brought along a full ton of appurtenances, ranging from gold-pans and pickaxes to the ubiquitous soup cubes, and none wished to surrender so much as an ounce. Accordingly, sixty of them formed a limited stock company and purchased the *St. Michael* from a nearby Jesuit mission, solely for the purpose of moving their personal freight to Dawson. They elected a crew from among themselves to take the little craft up the river, while the remainder boarded the N.A.T. Company's *John J. Healy.*

By the time the *St. Michael* reached Rampart, fourteen of the stockholders had had enough. The little freighter had been in difficulties ever since Norton Sound, where the ocean swell lifted her stern so far out of the water that the paddle-wheel whirled helplessly in the air. The decampers removed their share of the cargo and went prospecting on Minook Creek, where one immediately froze to death. The remainder insisted on steaming ahead. They had no fuel because the transportation companies had tied up all the cordwood on the river; but by one of those pieces of incredible happenstance which marked so many Klondike expeditions, they discovered a seam of coal in the banks of the river, and this kept them going — even in the face of two boiler explosions and one fire.

On September 19 the unhappy little boat met the *Healy* coming back downstream, having failed to cross the Yukon flats. Six of the stockholders of the *St. Michael* were on board, and they insisted on rejoining their comrades and heading back up the river again in the teeth of the oncoming winter. Twelve more had been set ashore by the *Healy* at Fort Yukon, and when the *St. Michael* reached this river port these twelve climbed on as well. Now, jammed with passengers, crew, and freight, the little craft pushed on to Circle City. By the time the settlement was reached it was almost October and most of those aboard had lost their enthusiasm, yet nineteen die-hards still persisted in pressing forward. As one later wrote, "we were all monomaniacs on the subject of getting to Dawson."

At this point the situation on the river was completely confused. Half the population of Dawson was trying desperately to get away, so that the ice-choked waters were thick with boats fleeing from the Klondike. These boats met other boats jammed with men and women equally desperate to reach the gold-fields at any cost, many of them so heavily laden with shovels, gold-scales, food and clothing, bedding, whiskey, and other paraphernalia that they could make little headway against the current.

The men who remained aboard the *St. Michael* had purchased the outfits of all who had disembarked, and now nothing would do but they take every last scrap of freight with them. The boat was thus so badly overloaded that when she backed out into the river she could not move an inch against the flow, but stood motionless, her ancient engines throbbing and shuddering with futile effort. The captain refused to go farther unless half the passengers got off, but this suggestion was of little use since "each man wished his neighbour to remain but wanted to go himself." When the captain quit in disgust, the passengers elected a new one. It took him four hours to move the vessel one mile. The engineer resigned, too, and again a new one was elected. He placed the safety valve on the boiler twenty pounds higher than his more cautious predecessor, who had survived two explosions. A steam connection began to leak, and a panicky amateur fireman cried out: "Save yourselves! The boiler's bursting!" All hands clambered for the rails, while the new captain, trying to reach shore, rammed the boat into a sand-bar. And that was the end of the cruise of the *St. Michael*.

All this while, some hundreds of miles downriver, the members of the ill-fated *Eliza Anderson* expedition were having their own trials. At St. Michael they had rejoined the other vessels of their odd convoy — the yacht and the steamboat — only to discover that the river steamer *W. K. Merwyn*, scheduled to take them to Dawson, was not large enough to accommodate them all. A makeshift scow with a bunkhouse built on top had to be pushed ahead of the vessel.

On the morning of October 10 the *Merwyn's* voyage began, but she was hardly into the web of the delta when the river froze around her. The steamboat went into the winter quarters of the Alaska Commercial Company, while the scow was tied up at an Eskimo village. It slowly dawned on the passengers that this would be their home for the eight months of the sub-Arctic winter. They reacted in various ways to this dismal news. One of them, an artist, became so morbid that he wandered aimlessly about in the snow until he died. Another, a dog-driver named Jack Carr, simply traded his outfit for a team of huskies and mushed off through sixteen hundred miles of wilderness to Dawson, thereby setting a new long-distance record for Alaska.

The remainder of the *Eliza Anderson* party, being made of sterner stuff than the artist but possessing less

257

stamina than the dog-driver, simply sat and rotted until spring. Most of them had been so numbed by the vagaries of the journey up the coast that this latest episode in the expedition's chequered career only served to desensitize them further. They hibernated on the fog-shrouded banks of the river, and when the ice broke they set off again, mechanically, for the goldfields. The urge to reach the Klondike had become a habit more than an obsession, and when at last on June 30 they walked glumly down the gangplank at Dawson most of them turned right-about-face and went home again. By fall only three members of this expedition were left in the gold-fields. Several had died of scurvy, one had hanged himself, dysentery claimed another. The rest had worked their way or paid their way to the Outside. Only two actually dug for gold. One of these, oddly enough, had started out with less than any of the others — had, indeed, thrown his last ten cents into Elliott Bay out of Seattle, leaving for the north with only the clothing he wore. His name was Thomas Wiedemann, and he returned eventually to Seattle with five thousand dollars.

3: *Frozen highways*

While steamboats loaded with gold-seekers sought vainly to reach the Klondike by the all-water route, thousands more stampeders attacked Alaska from the south, using the so-called all-American route to the mines. An outpouring of guidebooks, none of them reliable, had already trumpeted the advantages of this route, which was supposed to lead the prospector into the heart of golden Alaska without the financial discomforts of dealing with Canadian customs officers. Rumours flew down the coast about a Russian trail supposed to lead into the interior of Alaska from Port Valdez on the sea, while pamphlets put out by various
258

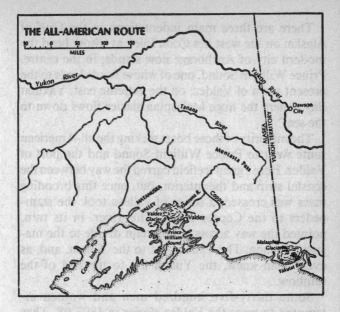

THE ALL-AMERICAN ROUTE

MILES

50 0 50 100 150

Yukon River

Tanana River

Yukon River

DAWSON CITY

ALASKA — YUKON TERRITORY

Mentasta Pass

MATANUSKA VALLEY

Valdez Glacier

Valdez

Copper R.

Tazlina R.

Prince William Sound

Cook Inlet

Malaspina Glaciers

Yakutat Bay

transportation companies to lure prospectors north gave detailed information on what to do and where to go. "Secret" expeditions were launched, companies and syndicates formed, and soon chartered vessels were dumping their human cargoes all along the shores of the Gulf of Alaska.

This great gulf, almost one thousand miles wide, bordered on the west by the thin finger of the Aleutian island chain and on the east by the island-studded coast of North America, is encircled by some of the finest scenery on the continent. Here are massive alpine battlements topped by sprawling glaciers; canyons and valleys glutted by moving rivers of rumpled ice; and peaks that belittle all others on the continent. But, as the stampeders were to discover, the very nature of this scenery, awesome in its beauty, made entry into the interior almost impossible.

259

There are three main indentations in the Gulf of Alaska: on the west lies Cook Inlet, at whose head the modern city of Anchorage now stands; in the centre, Prince William Sound, one of whose fiords leads to the present town of Valdez; on the extreme east, Yakutat Bay, where the huge Malaspina glacier flows down to the sea.

The majority of those boats seeking the all-American route went to Prince William Sound and the port of Valdez. Here a great icefield barred the way between the coastal strip and the interior, but, once this brooding mass was crossed, a series of valleys took the stampeders to the Copper River. This river, in its turn, pointed the way across a mountain divide to the majestic Tanana. The Tanana led to the Yukon, and, as every man knew, the Yukon led to the end of the rainbow.

Some thirty-five hundred men and women attempted to cross the Valdez glacier in 1897-98. They began to arrive early in the fall, but the wet snow, six feet deep, made travel impossible. The real movement began in February when the Pacific Steam Whaling Company entered the passenger trade and the first of its steamers headed for Valdez with six hundred passengers lured on by tales of "nuggets big as birds' eggs" in the land beyond the glacier — and with the usual agglomeration of horses, mules, burros, and dogs. The weather was so wicked in the gulf that most of these animals had to be shot before the ship landed. The mules were useless anyway, because their small feet broke through the crust of snow on the trail. But range horses from Montana and Wyoming which had sold for fifteen dollars in Seattle now brought as much as five hundred.

The new arrivals saw that they must drag their sleds and supplies across three hundred yards of coarse sand

and six miles of snow-covered flatland before the lip of the glacier was reached. The ice then rose in a series of benches so steep that a block-and-tackle was required to hoist goods over them. The glacier itself, glittering and flashing like a sapphire in the sunlight, rose upward towards the mountain parapet until it reached one mile into the sky. To the men from the industrial cities it must have seemed like a nightmare. The slope to the summit was twenty miles in length. A nine-mile descent led to the interior lakes and streams and then to the Copper River.

Except for a group of U.S. Army explorers, the men who faced this monstrous glacial cone were novices. They wandered out onto the chill white breast of the ice sheet with a dauntlessness born of ignorance, and the rabble followed sheeplike in their wake. The wavering trail they established led over the most difficult section of all.

Once caught on the glistening expanse of creaking ice, the stampeders began to suffer the tortures of snow-blindness. Their eyes seemed filled with red-hot sand, and the white world around them changed to quivering crimson. The ailment struck when they least expected it, for it was not commonly known that when the sun was behind the fleecy clouds the resulting diffusion of its rays could do more harm than any direct glare.

There were other torments, mental as well as physical: the eternal strain of crawling across the slippery ice on steel creepers, the loss of sleep brought on by the need to move only at night when the crust was firm enough to bear a man's weight, the constant nausea at having to eat raw or half-cooked food, the fierce glacial reflection that turned faces lobster-red. Quarrels sprang up as swiftly as the squalls that whirled about the summit. Men who found themselves burdened by a snow-blind partner often dissolved the union in the middle of

261

the trail. An old glacier expert, Captain W. R. Abercrombie of the 2nd U.S. Infantry, wryly watched hundreds of co-operative companies break up and wrote to the War Department that "friends of long years' standing became the most bitter of enemies."

Here, as elsewhere, outfits were divided with an eye to meticulous exactitude that often bordered on the farcical. There were the three partners, for instance, who broke a small grindstone into three equal pieces, and there was another trio who, in order to split up two pairs of oars, each took one oar and then destroyed the fourth so that none should have it.

The great body of argonauts crossed the ice between March and June of 1898. Few had progressed beyond the summit by mid-April, and fewer knew where to go when they reached it. At the end of April a four-day blizzard blanketed the ice with five feet of snow. On May 1 the snow turned to rain, and avalanches began to hurtle down the sides of the ice sheet, burying men and equipment. One heavy slide buried more than two dozen persons; they were located by their muffled cries under twenty-five feet of snow, and all but two were saved. Their goods were never recovered.

By this time the constant thawing and freezing had rendered the glacier impassable in the daylight hours. By nine p.m. it was just stiff enough to bear a man's weight, and by one a.m. it would take a horse. All the dark night the eighteen-inch trail was thick with people — those on foot arguing and quarrelling constantly with those on horseback, for each interfered with the movement of the other.

By June's end, water was pouring from the face of the glacier in a steady cascade. Men were trapped for days on the ice, unable to advance or retreat, and forced to abandon all they owned. Warm moist air pouring in through the funnel of Port Valdez from the Sound

262

struck air blowing through the pass and, rising rapidly, fell to the ground as snow, sleet, and rain. A dense white fog steamed from the surface, turning bacon and ham into masses of mould and sacks of sugar into sticky tubes of syrup. The effect was indescribably weird and, to the newcomers, terrifying. The ghostly, fog-shrouded ice sheet, sprawling down from the hidden mountains, would crack like a pistol shot as it settled. The vibrations rumbling down through the valley caused men to halt in their tracks and horses to wheel and snort in terror. After the tremors, and with a deafening roar, thousands of tons of ice torn from one of the hundreds of smaller glaciers fringing the mountains would crash down onto the main body, while bits and pieces would bound off the canyon walls in a series of overlapping echoes that took minutes to die to a whisper in the valleys far below.

In the final ascent to the peak of the glacier, the slope was one in five, so that after twenty yards of movement the energy of even the strongest was taxed. The wind whistled down upon them with hurricane force through the pass, bringing with it gusts of swirling sleet and snow which froze on man and beast as fast as it struck them, coating all in spectral armour.

By August the glacier was impassable. Only one man dared to traverse its slushy, steaming face: Abercrombie, the Army captain, managed to cross it once more after twenty-nine hours of continuous toil without rest or shelter. On the far side, in the valley of the Kluteena, he found the remnants of the mob building their boats and pushing off down the river, still intent on reaching the Klondike.

The first three miles of the Kluteena were deceptively gentle, but the rest was horror. The unsuspecting boatmen rounded a bend and came face to face with chaos. Roaring like a wounded animal, the river

263

plunged down in leaps and bounds over sand-bar and boulder for twenty-five miles, taking the luckless stampeders with it. Drift piles blocked the main channel, and snags like skeleton fingers reached out from bank and river bottom to pluck at the whirling craft. The entire strip of rapids was strewn with wrecked boats, provisions, clothing, and equipment. On June 1 one observer counted thirty-six rafts wrecked and abandoned in the first few miles of the fast water. One man in four was wrecked and ruined on the Kluteena and left to wander aimlessly along its banks without food, spare clothes, or shelter. Some made one or two trips successfully, shuttling their goods downstream, then were wrecked on the next attempt. On seeing the rapids, hundreds lost all stomach for the Klondike. They turned back forever, using any excuse that came to mind: a sick wife, urgent business at home, a suddenly developing illness.

J. J. Rafferty, a government guide who explored the interior routes from Valdez, summed up the situation in May of 1898 when he wrote: "Men who had faced the storms of the glaciers for weeks, living on cold victuals, overcoming obstacles that would discourage any but the most determined, men who would never have thought of turning back, weakened at the rapids."

Of more than three thousand who had landed at Valdez, only two hundred successfully defied the Kluteena. By October these had reached the Copper River and were engaged in an upstream struggle with poling-boat and tow-line. The route, long and weary, led to the Mentasta Pass, the high point of land, which overlooked a wilderness empire of scraggly spruce and birch. Standing on this height of land, a man could see the great blue valley of the Tanana in the distance. Beyond that, somewhere, lay the headwaters of the Fortymile. Beyond the Fortymile lay the Klondike. But it is doubtful if one half of one per cent of all who crossed the Valdez glacier that year ever achieved this final objective.

The great majority turned back before another winter set in, fearful that their retreat across the ice might be cut off by melting snow. Thoroughly demoralized, they blundered back in squads of ten or twenty, cursing transportation companies and government alike. Each had arrived firm in the faith that he could pan a fortune and be home in time to eat Christmas dinner with his family: each tasted the bitterness of disappointment. In this ragtag-and-bobtail crew were two strapping young Virginians, weak from illness brought on by gorging themselves on uncooked beans. They still clung to a bundle of heavy canvas grain sacks, each of several bushels' capacity, which they had brought north with them. The sacks had been intended as containers for the nuggets they expected to find, lying like apples in an orchard, on the shores of Alaska's rivers.

At Valdez the mail was piling up, for there was nowhere farther for it to go. The newly appointed postmaster, inundated by floods of letters and parcels, deserted his post and fled back to civilization. In August the government began to issue rations to more than three hundred who had expected to find gold by the bushel but had lost everything in the Kluteena rapids. The whaling company that had incited them on was compelled now to carry fivescore home again free of charge; another one hundred and eighty-five paid second-class fares to Seattle or Juneau. The Christian Endeavour Society built a relief station on the glacier to pick up those men who were too exhausted to return safely, for by this time some were tumbling into open crevasses and being rescued only at great risk. (It took five hours of unceasing work to pull one from a forty-foot fissure.) Snowslides and high winds often rendered

265

the trail impassable. On November 7 a guide was lifted clear of the ice and carried several yards by the gale. A week later a party on the summit was forced by the storm to claw a cave in the snow with their snowshoes, where they crouched for four days and nights, living on meat capsules.

As the winter of 1898-99 progressed, men began to go mad on the ice. All seemed obsessed by a singular hallucination — a glacial demon who haunted the crevasses. One rawboned Swede related to Captain Abercrombie in detail how this monster had strangled his son. He described a small, heavily built, active-looking creature who sprang from a crevasse and onto the boy's shoulders with such a grasp that he killed him.

"During the recital of this tale," Abercrombie reported, "the old man's eyes would glaze and he would go through all the actions to illustrate how he fought off the imaginary demon. When I heard this story there were some ten or twelve other men in the cabin and at the time it would not have been safe to dispute the demon on the Valdez Glacier, as every man in there firmly believed it to be reality."

By the spring of 1899 the community at Port Valdez presented a pitiful sight. All winter long, men had died one by one of scurvy — often wrongly diagnosed as gangrene and therefore wrongly treated. It was, and is, a hideous disease, confused in the Middle Ages with leprosy, which it resembles. The blood turns thin, so that the whole body appears bruised, and lassitude creeps through the system. The heart beats swiftly and erratically, and the breath comes in gasps. The legs go lame, the joints ache, the face becomes puffy, the flesh turns soft and pliable as dough, the skin becomes dry and harsh and mottled red, blue, and black. The gums swell and bleed, the teeth rattle in the head and eventually drop out. The breath becomes a stench, the face turns yellow or leaden, and the eyes sink into the skull until the victim, a living skeleton, expires. No wonder that when Abercrombie returned to Valdez in April, 1899, the quartermaster's agent ran towards him sobbing: "My God, captain, it has been clear hell! I tell you the early days in Montana were not a marker to what I've gone through this winter! It was awful!"

The Army man could not recognize the people he had known the year before; they looked like scarecrow figures from a Bosch painting, with hair hanging like string to the shoulders, faces masked in matted beards, each man scabrous and frostbitten. Demoralized and wasted, they staggered about in fading mackinaw suits stripped to rags, their footwear fashioned from the tops of rubber boots attached to strips of gunny-sacking. All winter long they had existed sardine-fashion, jammed twenty to a cabin in a twelve-by-fifteen space where wet and steaming clothing hung from the rafters emitting a poisonous stench that sickened even the healthiest.

These were the dregs of the proud expeditions that almost two years before had arrived to conquer the glacier and dig the Klondike's gold. In Valdez alone the taxpayers of the United States had spent three million, seven hundred thousand dollars vainly trying to establish an all-American route to the interior of Alaska.

Two similar all-American trails proved equally abortive. One led inland from Cook Inlet, some distance west of the Valdez area. Lieutenant J. C. Castner of the 4th Infantry had the ill-luck to lead a military expedition through this so-called trail up the valley of the Matanuska and over the divide to the Tanana. By the time they reached the Tanana Valley, Castner and his men were near starvation, their clothing in tatters, their feet torn and bleeding. Castner wrote that "my men often said it would be impossible to make others understand what we suffered those days. No tongue or pen

267

could do the case justice." At this point the party was spending its days hip-deep in freezing water trying to navigate the rapids, and its nights lying so close to the campfire that the clothing was scorched from the men's backs. Running sores covered every man's feet by the time they achieved their objective.

Yet this seems like a pleasant Sunday outing compared with the hardships endured by those who crossed the great Malaspina glacier at the head of Yakutat Bay near the southern border of the Yukon Territory. Into this tortured land of enormous ice masses, treacherous canyons and crevasses, unexplored precipices, and mountains four miles high, a few parties dared to trespass.

Here was an unreal world of shimmering ice, a veritable meeting-place of glaciers, which hung by the dozens from the breastwork of the mountains. They dropped to the sea in crystalline scarps three hundred feet high, from whose coruscating faces great bergs broke off and toppled into the creamy waters. At one point on Disenchantment Bay, which forms a finger of Yakutat, these shining ice cliffs ran for seven miles. And there were other glaciers, of every variety and conformation: some like white ribbons coiling between thousand-foot crags; some like hidden tongues, concealed behind tusks of rock; some like earrings, pendant one thousand feet above the surface of the ocean; some like marble waterfalls dropping from ledge to ledge; some, grey and lifeless, retreating towards the mountain balustrade; some, active and greenly alive, advancing upon the sea.

But all these variant creatures of a dying ice age were dwarfed by the mighty Malaspina, the father of glaciers, whose children, in fact, they were. Down from the mountains it poured in an immense fan shape, an icy desert fifteen hundred square miles in size — the largest piedmont glacier on the continent, its six tentacles squeezing back into the black valleys that lay between the crags of the St. Elias Mountains.

It is not known how many crossed the glacier in the stampede winter, but there are records of four parties, about one hundred men in all, who were landed at its edge by the ill-fated and condemned brigantine *Blakely* in the spring of 1898. Forty-one of these died trying to reach the Klondike, and many more were incapacitated for life. They came from Connecticut, Texas, Minnesota, and New York, and they took various routes across the ice, some heading for the Tanana, others striking directly north into the area now crossed by the Alaska Highway, towards Dawson City. All who survived rued the day they had ever heard the word "Klondike."

The worst experience of which there is a record was that of the party of Arthur Arnold Dietz, a God-fearing young man who advertised in the New York *Herald* in January, 1898, for a partner or two to form a mining company. By February he had recruited eighteen from the scores who replied, and the full group met faithfully each Sunday to plan the trip and familiarize themselves with Arctic conditions. They were a fair cross-section of Klondike stampeders, moderately well educated, middle-class white-collar workers, mainly: a doctor, a policeman, a mineralogist, a tinsmith, an engineer, a clerk, and so on. In April they found themselves dumped on the shores of Yakutat Bay, their machinery and equipment coated with rust, and all their food, except for their flour and meat, spoiled by salt water.

Nevertheless, they ventured off across the glacier on a trip that few men had dared to make before — nineteen sedentary citizens from New York City whose main exercise, until this moment, had been a stroll in the country or a Sunday jaunt on a bicycle.

The setting was unearthly. The ice itself was clear as crystal, slippery as glass, and lovely to gaze upon, being navy blue in colour. But it was treacherous to traverse, its surface washboard-rough and rent by blue-black crevasses, some of them easily seen, others clogged with snow that was sometimes hard-packed and able to bear weight, but otherwise soft as feather down. Off to the distant mountains this monotonous and seemingly limitless expanse faded away, its surface broken only by colossal piles of stones deposited thousands of years before, or by stark ridges of ebony rock that rose island-fashion from the angry ocean of turbulent ice.

Rarely could the Dietz party pitch a tent because of the storms that whirled across the glacier's face. They slept, instead, in the lee of their supplies, waking each morning beneath a two-foot blanket of snow. Fissures barred their passage, forcing them to detour for miles; and snow-blindness plagued them into rubbing their eyes so fiercely that the lashes were worn away. Even the dogs went half blind from the fearful glare.

After the first week no man could speak to his neighbour. They travelled for hours without a word, and when they stopped to rest were too weary to utter a groan, so that the only sound was the gurgling of the subterranean waters and the high whine of the gales above. In the words of Dietz himself, they very much "resembled a party of deaf mutes."

It took them almost three months to cross the Malaspina, and in all that time they were never free of the sight of the hummocky ice stretching in endless expanse into the storm. On those days when the sun's pale halo pierced the haze, they could see in the distance the sharp peaks of the St. Elias Range, the tallest mountains on the continent. Between these massive pinnacles the glacier squeezed like toothpaste, the ice crushed together to form hillocks between which ran deep and

270

jagged fissures. These thin canyons in the ice claimed three of the party before the mountains were reached. Dietz's brother-in-law was the first to go: he, his four dogs, and his sled containing the party's most valuable provisions simply vanished into the pit. A second man, who went insane from snow-blindness and dropped far behind, was also lost with his team and his provisions. By the time the third man fell out of sight the party was reduced to subsisting on bacon, beans, and coffee: there was nothing else left.

After three months the men who had started out were unrecognizable. Some had lost twenty-five pounds, and their sunken faces were matted by unkempt beards. They left the ice-field behind and plunged into a different world, struggling through a precipitous mountain terrain as wild as a jungle, where dense groves of alders forced them to hack a trail out of the forest, where the brambles were almost impenetrable and the ground so thick with decayed vegetation that it made passage as difficult as wading through deep snow. Incredibly, they had managed to drag across the glacier an eight-hundred-pound motor, but they were forced to abandon it in the forests.

Before they reached the headwaters of the Tanana, another man had died of fever. In September, with winter coming on, they were obliged to halt. Now they knew that they were trapped in unknown country until spring. Hastily they built themselves a hovel of logs.

They were all partially insane by this time, acting "like a pack of animals." The boredom was so maddening that three of the party, casting aside all caution, insisted on attempting to reach Dawson overland. They took some provisions, pushed off into the wilderness, and were never seen again. The remainder sat in the makeshift cabin, huddled together for warmth. They had nothing to do but wait, and read, over and over

271

again by the firelight, the single Bible that was their only book. They read it so assiduously that their eyes became affected as badly as if by snow-blindness.

Although the fire was never allowed to die out, the interior of the shack was so cold that ice formed within two feet of the fireplace. They lay in their sleeping-bags, like grubs in cocoons, for twenty hours at a time, emerging only once a day to cook an inadequate meal, often eating their meat raw to save fire, and letting the hours and the days and the months slip by, so that no man knew the date; repeating poems and songs and hymns over and over again to relieve the boredom; and confessing, each one, details of his past life merely to make conversation — details "that could not have been wrung from him by the most severe third-degree methods under ordinary conditions." They lay so long on their backs that they became sore and rheumatic, while their beards ran a foot in length; and still the winter dragged on while they recited their family genealogies, committed tables of weights and measures to memory, and carved up the cabin walls into grotesque shapes to allay the monotony.

Yet none of these privations was enough to destroy their urge to look for gold. On the contrary, the need to find it became an obsession, for without it the whole ghastly nightmare lost its meaning. In vain the mineralogist in the party explained that it was useless to seek fortune in this frozen jungle; when spring came they must needs sink a shaft, and with their ebbing strength construct a windlass and go through the pantomime of mining. They found nothing but sterile gravel, but even this did not entirely deter them. Three of the party set off on an expedition to the base of the distant mountains, still seeking the will-o'-the-wisp of gold. And here an avalanche buried them forever.

272

Now they were nine. Their only desire was escape, but no man wished to recross the fearful glacier. When the warm weather arrived they decided to follow instead the pathway of the Tanana River. Before they could set out, another man died — of scurvy — and they were eight. On through the forests they stumbled, the spring blizzards numbing them until they had to club each other with their fists to restore circulation. Their clothes were in tatters, their socks reduced to masses of filthy wool, their moccasins worn to shreds, and their feet swathed in rags. In this condition they were discovered by a group of Indians, who sold them hair-seal coats and fur mukluks. Thus newly attired, but still half insensible, they plunged on.

And then, to their horror, they found themselves once again face to face with the Malaspina glacier. Try as they would, they had not been able to evade it. It lurked at the forest's rim, a malevolent monster, waiting for them.

The second trek across the ice sheet was far worse than the first. With the coming of spring, the interminable expanse seemed even more of a contorted mass, splintered by the spiders' webs of crevasses. The snow was frozen so hard that it cut like sharp sand, and one man's feet swelled to twice their normal size before he died. The storms were so fierce that nothing could be seen farther than ten feet away, nor could any fire be built or any food cooked. The flour supply vanished after six weeks, and the men existed on raw beans and smoked fish given them by the natives they had met. When these were gone, the dogs were slaughtered and devoured. Only then did the storm clear and, in the distance, a quivering line of blue appear. It was the Pacific.

Now completely demented, the seven survivors reached the beach. They killed and ate the last of the dogs, and collapsed on the cold sands, where the U.S. revenue cutter *Wolcott* found them. Four were alive but uncomprehending; three others were dead in their sleeping-bags.

There was an ironic coda to this tale. When the four survivors were brought to civilization, the Seattle *Times* reported that they had arrived with half a million dollars in gold dust. In fact, Alaska's only legacy was a physical incapacity that plagued them all their lives. Two were rendered near-sighted by the glare on the ice; the other two were totally blind.

4: *"Bury me here, where I failed"*

The Americans who shunned the Canadian routes did so, it was said, for reasons of patriotism; but national pride, real or assumed, was not their prerogative alone. The Canadians and the British had their own sense of public spirit which dovetailed neatly with their desires to avoid the American customs officers at Dyea and Skagway. Boards of Trade in Canadian cities played upon this attitude, and the Dominion rang with chauvinistic slogans about the wisdom and economy of staying on British soil for the entire journey. Indeed, the pamphlets issued in favour of these trails were so alluring that many Americans chose them in preference to those that led through Alaska.

One such route, known as the Ashcroft Trail (and sometimes called "the Spectral Trail"), ran north for one thousand miles through the tangled interior of British Columbia. It began at the town of Ashcroft, which was reached from Vancouver, one hundred and twenty-five miles to the southwest, and then worked its way through the Fraser River country and the old Cariboo mining district. From here it followed the route of the

274

Collins Overland Telegraph towards Teslin Lake at the headwaters of the Yukon River. There were still some faint remnants of the ancient swath cut in the black pines in 1865 by the men of Western Union, who had hoped to link Europe and America with a cable that would run across Alaska and into Russia. This astonishing project had been abandoned when the *Great Eastern* laid the Atlantic cable, but the stampeders could still see the rusting and twisted wire lying along the route. Rotting telegraph poles complete with insulators poked incongruously from the forests, and one native-built suspension bridge was made from bits of wire.

At least fifteen hundred men and some three thousand horses attempted this route, although only a handful reached the final goal. Before the summer of '98 arrived, the trail was a thousand-mile rut, bare of all fodder save for poisonous weeds. Clouds of venomous flies and mosquitoes harried the pack animals as they stumbled through the black bogs, and many stampeders gave up the attempt before the Skeena River was reached. The rest pushed stubbornly northward, swimming their horses over the great olive-green river to enter a dark and desolate land where the moss dripped wraith-like from the firs, where fallen logs and slippery roots blocked the trail, where greasy slate slopes must

THE ASHCROFT AND STIKINE TRAILS

be scaled, where the lifeless forests were empty of grass, where horses sank belly-deep in mudholes, where the rain fell ceaselessly, churning the soil into a deep jelly, and where the only vegetation seemed to be the prickly and evil devil's clubs.

Hamlin Garland, the American novelist and short-story writer, travelled the Ashcroft Trail in '98. Having reached the Skeena country, he reread with astonishment the literature about the route put out by the Victoria Board of Trade, and "perceived how skillfully every detail with regard to the last half of the trail had been slurred over." Garland wrote wryly that "we had been led into a sort of sack, and the string was tied behind us."

The route grew more eerie. Along its length, dead horses lay putrescent beneath the clumps of northern spruce from whose branches the pale moss hung in ghostly green cascades. From the hilltops the men who trudged northward could see endless waves of conifers rolling off to the horizon under the grey, drizzling skies. The forests were so dense that only an occasional patch of pale light penetrated them — on those rare days when the sun shone at all. And there was still no grass for the horses — only leaves and fireweed, skunk cabbages and Indian rhubarb, nettles and poisonweed. The names along the way told their own story: Poison Mountain, Reduction Camp, Starvation Camp and Groundhog Mountain. "As most travellers had only laid in grub for two hundred miles, many of them were glad to eat groundhog," Norman Lee, a Chilcoten rancher, wrote in his diary in August.

Lee was one of several men who attempted to drive cattle north to the Klondike along the Ashcroft Trail. He described it as "a sea of mud — such as I have never seen before." Whenever he tried to move the animals down a slope the mud followed "after the manner of a river, a thick, pasty mud about the consistency of porridge." By the time he reached Groundhog Mountain, Lee and his party — all of them seasoned outdoorsmen — had discarded every pound of unnecessary equipment. Shotguns, shovels, picks, tents, and even gold-pans were tossed aside to join the hedgerow of expensive litter heaped along the entire length of the trail. Lee noticed first-rate riding and stock saddles lying amid the coils of rope, the boxes of candles and matches, and the rusting mining equipment aginst which the limping pack animals stumbled. Three of his own saddles were added to the heap. As for his cattle, some were lame, some were dead from eating poisonous weeds, and all were reduced to bone and gristle from lack of feed. Lee confided to his diary that he could scarcely have imagined a country with no pickings at all until he travelled the Ashcroft Trail. Horses and pack animals were expiring daily from hunger, overwork, and lameness apparently caused by the mud. "It was scarcely possible to travel a hundred yards without finding dead or abandoned horses," Lee noted. Burros, accustomed to dry, rocky country, were especially vulnerable. Lee saw one septuagenarian pack-train owner driven to the point of near madness by his donkeys' inability to move through a swamp. He seized a heavy club and began whacking at the beasts, crying: "You appear to like it, take lots of it!" The animals stood like innocent rabbits, meekly accepting the fusillade of blows, unable to move a foot. Of that pack train of some fifty or sixty, scarcely one got through.

All along this sinister and ill-marked pathway, mingling with the Indian carvings on the trees and the alien telegraph wire and insulators, were notes of despair and defiance left by those who had gone before: rancorous attacks on the road gang that was supposed to be clearing the trail but was never seen; warnings about the

277

conditions ahead; puzzled queries ("Where the hell are we?"); facetious replies — all scribbled onto blazes hacked in the sides of fir and spruce, birch and poplar. One recurring sign, left by men who had abandoned their lame horses without a bite of feed, read: "If my horse is fit to travel, bring him along."

On Groundhog Mountain, Hulet Wells, a farmer's son from Washington State, standing in the rain and mud, scribbled an acridly optimistic piece of doggerel on the side of a spruce tree:

> *There is a land of pure delight*
> *Where grass grows belly-high;*
> *Where horses don't sink out of sight;*
> *We'll reach it by and by.*

Another blazed a hemlock, and with a knife and indelible pencil produced an eight-verse poem illustrated by cartoons and entitled "The Poor Man's Trail," vigorously attacking newspaper editors, swindlers, steamboat-owners, and others who had advertised this all-Canadian route to the Klondike. It followed the style of "The House That Jack Built":

> *This is the grave the poor man fills,*
> *After he died from fever and chills,*
> *Caught while tramping the Stikine Hills,*
> *Leaving his wife to pay the bills. . . .*

One man tried to cross the Skeena in an Indian dugout canoe with a collie dog and five pack horses swimming beside him. He lost them all in the torrent, blazed a tree with his axe, and lamented his ill-luck in a pencilled message. Then he tied what was left of his outfit in a kerchief, slung it over his shoulder, and continued on.

Another pegged a wallet to a tree with the words: "A thousand miles to nowhere." Inside were money and a

278

letter of farewell to a relative in Ohio. The wallet passed through many hands and was finally delivered intact.

And still, in the midst of all this suffering and frustration, these men too could not get the idea of gold out of their minds. It was the Grail that drew them on, deeper and deeper into the labyrinth of the north. Of all the sardonic little stories told of the Ashcroft Trail, none is more plaintive than that of the old man trudging along, all by himself, with a pack on his back, and asking querulously: "Where is the gold?" A group of Indians encountered him at Blackwater Lake, which lies between the Cariboo and the Skeena country. "Where is the gold?" he asked them, and they could not tell him. He grew angry when they inquired, instead, if he wished for food. "I'm not a bit worried," he told them, "but I wonder how far I am from the gold diggings." On he trudged, still asking: "Where is the gold?" When he reached the Stikine River and they told him the Klondike was another thousand miles away, he blew out his brains.

By the time they reached the Stikine, the hundreds who had managed to traverse the Ashcroft Trail were in a similar slough of despond. A few, like the old man, committed suicide. One German hanged himself from the cross-tree of his tent on the riverbank and left behind a hastily scribbled note: "Bury me here, where I failed." Others, swallowing defeat, headed down the river to the coast and booked steamship passage home. Some there were, however, who refused to be beaten and who continued to push north. These were joined by a second force of stampeders working their way inland from the Pacific coast.

For, while one contingent was forcing a passage through the dripping forests of interior British Columbia, another was making its way along the slushy ice of the Stikine River, another of the "all-Canadian" routes.

The two trails came together at the river town of Glenora, which in March of '98 was swollen with five thousand persons.

The Stikine Trail had been heavily advertised by the merchants of Victoria and Vancouver as the only practical route to the Klondike. According to one pamphlet published by the British Columbia Board of Trade, the trail "avoids the danger and hardships on the passes and the Whitehorse and other rapids." Another advantage was that "the prospector on leaving the steamer finds himself in the heart of a gold country practically unexplored." The Canadian Minister of the Interior, Clifford Sifton, investigated the route in the autumn of 1897 and personally put his stamp of approval on it, for he believed that the Stikine, which leads through the narrow isthmus of the Alaskan Panhandle, could be used to circumnavigate the U.S. customs. Sifton had already been deluged by the merchants of the Canadian coastal towns locked in a desperate tug of war with their Seattle rivals for the Klondike trade, and so he determined upon a wagon road, railway, and steamboat line along the Stikine route. On January 26, 1898, he signed a tentative contract with the two famous railway-building partners Sir William Mackenzie and Sir Donald Mann, who promised to construct a railroad from Telegraph Creek at the head of navigation on the Stikine to Teslin Lake, about one hundred and fifty miles distant, and to put a fleet of steamboats on the river itself. In return, the company would enjoy a five-year monopoly in the area and receive almost four million acres of land in alternate lots along the right of way. Surveys were made, material delivered, twelve miles of grade actually built, and thousands of tickets sold on the route, but the Teslin railway remained a dream. The Canadian Senate could not stomach the land grant and refused to pass the appropriation. Thousands ascended the river to find no railroad, and a trail so rutted and lacking in forage that few horses could negotiate it.

All winter and all spring they dragged their sleds up the frozen Stikine. Near the mouth, like a bright, festering sore, was the Alaskan city of Wrangell, whose lurid history went back to the days of the Cassiar rush and the German hurdy-gurdy girls. After a lull of a generation, it was reviving.

Woe to the stampeder who paused at Wrangell! Soapy Smith's confidence men, the overflow from Skagway, were waiting for him with their fake information offices and their phony poker games. Robberies were frequent, and guns popped in the streets at night. Women cavorted nude for high fees in the dance halls, and even the sanctity of the courtroom was not immune from gunplay. In February a whiskey dealer on trial for illicit sales took umbrage at the evidence of a prosecution witness, drew his revolver, and shot him as he testified.

Those scenes of chaos which marked all the jumping-off spots for the Klondike — the tents springing up in clusters, the snow-covered mountains of goods, the swirling, yapping sled-dogs, the brawling and shouting men — were repeated all along the broad mouth of the Stikine. The wet slush that coated the river like soft plaster made travel impossible until about two a.m., when men took advantage of the crust that formed in the cool of the night. As spring advanced and the slush increased, goods began to be discarded, so that this trail, like all the others, was soon littered with the paraphernalia of the stampede. The going became so difficult that it sometimes took a week to move nine miles. It was backbreaking work. "Imagine pulling a hand sleigh loaded with grub through a foot or more of slush, temperature of said slush being at freezing point, often up to the middle in ice water, and a keen Northeast wind rushing down the river to meet you," one man wrote. By April the surface was so treacherous that men began to break through the ice and drown in the freezing waters. "A man would be driving his team with all his worldly possessions on a sleigh. Without any warning, team, sleigh and load would drop through the rotten ice, and the man would be left. Sometimes the man dropped through and the team stayed behind." When the river opened, seventeen steamboats went into service, but the shallow water kept many of these stuck fast on the shoals and sand-bars.

At Glenora the mail was piling up, as it was at Valdez and Edmonton and Dawson City. The postmaster, almost driven out of his mind by the unaccustomed flood, attempted to solve the situation by burning several sacks of letters and parcels, and, as a result, had to be spirited out of town in a native dugout before the infuriated stampeders could lynch him.

For a good many men, Glenora marked the end of the trail. One ambitiously equipped party had set out from Fargo, North Dakota, with the idea of establishing a combined freighting, mining, and merchandising business in the Klondike. To this end they purchased a thirty-by-sixty-foot tent, enough supplies to provision a general store, and a sizable herd of horses. The expedition split into two parties, one group taking the tent and provisions by boat to Wrangell and then up the Stikine to Glenora and the remainder going overland from Ashcroft with the horses. But the animals were all lost in the swamps of the Spectral Trail, and when the overlanders arrived in Glenora they found the rest of the expedition trapped there by winter. With no hope of reaching the gold-fields, they had set up the big tent, whipsawed some lumber for shelves, used the sawdust as floor covering, and were busily selling off the stock to hungry stampeders. No doubt they prospered, for prices were prohibitively high at Glenora, though not as high as they were farther along the trail where salt, which sold in Victoria for half a cent a pound, actually went as high as sixty cents.

It was here that the Reverend John Pringle began to build a notable reputation as a two-fisted mining camp missionary. Pringle had been sent north by the Presbyterian Church of Canada to minister to the Klondike area. He came up the Stikine Trail and as soon as he reached Glenora began to make plans to hold a Sunday service. The only suitable place turned out to be a local saloon; that did not bother Pringle, who set off at once down Glenora's muddy streets, inviting everyone he met to attend the service. His attention, however, was soon distracted by the sight of a man kicking a dog.

"Don't kick that dog," said Pringle.

"I'll kick you," the dog's owner replied. He was a newcomer who had arrived by riverboat and immediately bought himself a dog, a sled, and a harness with the idea of mushing north, though he clearly knew nothing about handling animals.

"Kick me if you dare," replied Pringle, "but don't kick the dog." Then, as his adversary backed off, he patted the dog on the head and gave the newcomer a lesson in training a sled dog to harness. As a result of this incident Pringle's barroom chapel was jammed the following Sunday. He went on to the Klondike to become one of the best-loved missionaries in the Yukon.

A few miles farther up the Stikine was a second frenzied community — the one-time trading post of Telegraph Creek, a former way-point on the abortive line to Russia. From here a wagon road was supposed to lead overland to Teslin Lake, one hundred and fifty-six miles distant, but the road was largely non-existent. By spring the whole country was a great marsh, and half of

283

those who had come this far began to turn back. The rest pushed on, and the route to Teslin became black with people and animals of all descriptions: goats, harnessed like dogs, which munched on the bushes as they went by and thus saved their owners the trouble of feeding them . . . dogs with haversacks strapped to their backs like pack animals . . . weird conveyances based on the wheel-and-axle principle that jerked over rut and hillock before collapsing . . . a cow hitched to a sled by a man who milked it every night . . . a cow and Jersey bull yoked together as a team . . . a man from Los Angeles hauling in the traces like an animal, with his fourteen-year-old son straining barefoot beside him and a boy of ten pushing behind . . . a Mountie's widow with a loaded derringer seeking, not gold, but the man who slew her husband . . . an Idaho lumberman and his wife, wearing a short skirt and high rubber boots and singing in a clear soprano as she trudged along . . . a double murder on the trail — one man axed to death, another shot, a third in full flight northward behind a pure-white horse with the police in hot pursuit . . . a veteran of the D'Oyly Carte Opera Company singing Gilbert and Sullivan in a high tenor . . . piles of useless equipment strewn along the wayside — sacks of sugar, discarded clothing, the wreckage of broken sleds . . . and, at one spot, a heap of dogfood five feet high, piled like cordwood and abandoned . . .

. . . And in the midst of all this hurly-burly, the most outlandish sight of all: two hundred and three uniformed soldiers in scarlet jackets and white helmets marching as best they could in close order, with the help of Hudson's Bay packers and mules, trudging in step through mudholes and over rocks and stumps, performing barrack-square evolutions, spearing fish with their bayonets, and dragging their Maxim guns along with them. This was the Yukon Field Force, made up of officers and men from the Royal Canadian Rifles, the Royal Canadian Dragoons, and the Royal Canadian Artillery, and sent north to reinforce the Mounted Police by a government which feared that the influx of foreigners might cause an insurrection that could wrench the North from Canada.

5: *Overland from Edmonton*

While thousands were trying to reach the Klondike over glaciers, mountain passes, river routes, and swamps, the merchants of Edmonton were doing their utmost to convince the world that their city was the gateway to the only practicable trails of '98. In point of fact, as hundreds were to discover, some of these trails were among the most impracticable. Sam Steele of the Mounted Police thought it "incomprehensible that sane men" would attempt any of the overland routes from Edmonton, and fifty-seven years later one of those who tried it echoed his words. E. L. Cole, a bank cashier from Pelican Rapids, Minnesota, wrote in 1955: ". . . as I think of it now, I can't imagine how sane men could have chosen the Edmonton route to the goldfields."

But at the time, to hundreds of Canadians and Britons and to many Americans as well this appeared to be the sensible way to go. Edmonton advertised that it was "the back door to the Yukon," and the maps and pamphlets its merchants distributed made the trip sound like child's play, for they proclaimed that there was a good trail all the way, no matter which of several alternative routes was chosen. To all inquiries, the Board of Trade replied that "the trail was good all winter" and that "the Klondike could be reached with horses in ninety days."

285

There was, in fact, scarcely a trail at all, but, as Winnipeg's great editor, John W. Dafoe, was to write some time later, to doubt the practicability of the Edmonton trail "was regarded as a species of treason." Patriotism and good business made Canadians believe in it, and they had the word of Arthur Heming, a noted woodsman and outdoor illustrator, who called it "the inside track" and said that the Klondike could be reached from Edmonton in six weeks by canoe or dogteam.

"All you need is a good constitution, some experience in boating and camping and one hundred and fifty dollars," Heming wrote, adding that if the stampeders "are lucky enough to make their pile in the Klondike, they can come back by dog-sled in the winter."

These hasty words were published in the Hamilton *Spectator* and widely reprinted. Because of them, dozens were to lose their lives, including a former mayor of Hamilton, who set out with a party Heming organized (but did not accompany) and died slowly of scurvy in March, 1899, in a hastily built cabin on the Peel River far above the Arctic Circle.

Heming himself had never been over the track he extolled. He knew of it only through the reports of the Hudson's Bay Company, which had used the various overland routes to the Yukon for decades. But Heming neglected to consider that the traders travelled light in canoes and with dog-teams piloted by relays of Indians and voyageurs, that they carried little equipment but used letters of credit on various Hudson's Bay posts to keep them supplied. Between these hardy woodsmen and the amateurs, dragging their sleds and their tons of goods, there was little parallel.

A good deal of confusion about the back-door route sprang from the fact that there was no single trail leading from Edmonton to the gold-fields. The all-inclusive

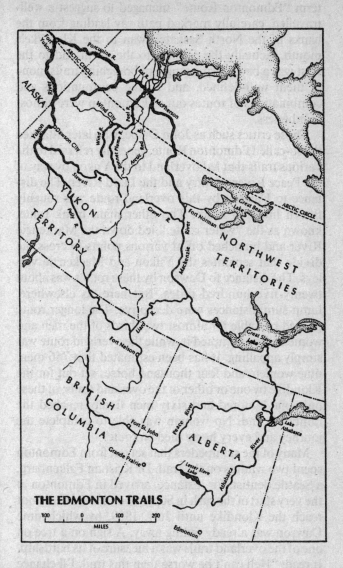

THE EDMONTON TRAILS

100   0   100   200

MILES

term "Edmonton Route" managed to suggest a well-travelled, carefully marked pathway leading from the banks of the North Saskatchewan to the Klondike's mouth. Actually the country to the north and to the west was a bewildering tangle of branching trails, none of them well-defined, and so the permutations and combinations of routes out of Edmonton were almost numberless.

Those critics such as John Dafoe, who later attacked the so-called Edmonton Route, generally referred to the various trails that led overland to the Yukon by way of the Peace River country and the Liard River. The distance to Dawson by this overland route was roughly fifteen hundred miles. The other main trunk route, known as the "water route," led down the Mackenzie River and branched off at various points to cross the divide that separates the Yukon and Mackenzie valleys. The distance to Dawson by these routes was about twenty-five hundred miles. But here, as elsewhere, lump-sum distances were deceptive. The longer route proved passable for almost two thirds of the men and women who attempted it, while the overland route was simply appalling. It has been estimated that 766 men, nine women, and four thousand horses set out for the Klondike by one or other of the overland trails; of these only one hundred and sixty men finally reached the rainbow's end. No woman was able to complete the journey and every horse died en route.

Many of the stampeders that set out from Edmonton spent two winters on the trail. Dr Kristian Falkenburg, a Seattle dentist, for instance, arrived in Edmonton at the very start of the rush in September, 1897. He did not reach the Klondike until July, 1899, by which time Dawson was already fading away. A sign on a tree on one of the overland trails was a measure of its hardship. It read: "Hell can't be worse than this trail. I'll chance it." The man who scribbled those words killed himself in despair.

In 1897 Edmonton was a small agricultural village of about twelve hundred persons. It consisted of a steamboat dock, some log booms, two sawmills, a brick plant, the remains of the Hudson's Bay Company fort, and a five-block business section straggling along Jasper Avenue with a hotel at one end and a trading post at the other. Upon this backwater the gold rush burst like a cyclone. Suddenly thousands of men appeared, jamming the streets. The flats along the North Saskatchewan blossomed with tents. Sleds loaded with provisions clogged the thoroughfares. And the zaniest pieces of equipment since the days of the Ark were trundled through town. Indeed, there actually was an ark, a curious boat of galvanized iron intended for use in all seasons, with a keel for river travel and runners for snow. And there was a forty-foot-long cigar-shaped "boatsled" with a wheel beneath it which did duty as a rudder in the water, since the contrivance was supposed to be amphibious. And there was a contraption built like a lawn-mower, with a sixteen-foot axle projecting from either side, the interior loaded with supplies, the exterior covered in sheet steel.

A man known as Texas Smith arrived with a device designed to cross muskeg, snow, mud, and mountain; its wheels were wooden wine barrels, and it was topped off with a sleeping platform. Smith called it "The Duck" and set off resolutely across the rolling prairie, but after the first mile the hoops came loose from the barrels, and after three or four miles the entire contrivance collapsed.

George Glover of Chicago arrived with an ambitious steam sleigh, complete with locomotive and cars loaded with freight, which was supposed to go through mountain passes and traverse gorges and canyons by

289

means of its huge driving-wheel — a four-hundred-pound steel drum with projecting spikes for traction. Glover christened it *I Will,* and a crowd gathered to watch it set off for the Klondike. Black smoke belched from its funnels and steam hissed from its boiler, but as the wheels started to turn, the whole machine began to shudder and groan. With each turn of the driving-wheel the device clawed itself deeper and deeper into the earth, hurling up clouds of snow and flinging pieces of frozen mud into the faces of the panicky spectators. Thus, firmly embedded in the soil, the *I Will* just wouldn't. Manpower, it turned out, was the only successful means of locomotion on the Edmonton trails.

The stampeders were as picturesque as the machines they brought with them. They ranged all the way from "Steamboat" Wilson, the much-travelled former mayor of Kalgoorlie, Australia, to an Irish peer, Viscount Avonmore, swiftly dubbed Lord "Have One More" by the natives. He arrived with a group of compatriots, most of them old British army cronies, a gaggle of servants and grooms, a hundred horses, and ten thousand pounds of supplies ranging from tinned turkey to folding tables. Legend has it that the outfit also included a hundredweight of toilet tissue and seventy-five cases of vintage champagne. The wine, it is said, was allowed to freeze and so had to be auctioned off on the main street at twenty-five cents a case. Successful bidders took the good bottles, knocked off their heads, and drank them dry on the spot.

The Avonmore expedition died an early death owing to a series of varying mishaps. One of the party, a Captain Alleyne, died of pneumonia contracted in twenty-two-below weather and was buried with full military honours. Another, a Dr. Hoops, sprained an ankle and had scarcely recovered when he stumbled across a sleigh and cracked his ribs. Colonel Le Quesne fell off a sled and broke his arm while another colonel, Jeffreys, was kicked by a horse and suffered a fractured shoulder blade. A Captain Powell, who froze his feet, went out to Vancouver and died there. Captain O'Brien, who assumed command of the group, tried to arrest a colleague on charges of embezzlement but was himself haled into court for common assault. Like so many other parties that took the overland route from Edmonton to the Yukon, this one was riven by squabbles and dissension and finally split up. None of its members reached the gold-fields.

The general direction of the pack-horse trails led northwest to the Rockies where the Peace River rises, then north to the foaming Liard and across the continental divide to the headwaters of the muddy Pelly, one of the Yukon's largest tributaries. Most of those travelling these routes took two years' supplies with them, carried on the backs of eight to ten animals.

There were several ways of reaching the Peace River country from Edmonton. The most southerly route, which several parties attempted in 1897, led directly across bush and muskeg, through swamps and over deadfalls, by way of Lac Ste Anne, modern Whitecourt, and Grande Prairie to Fort St. John, one of several jumping-off points for the North. Its most significant section was called "Dog Eating Prairie" because for decades starving Indians had been forced to eat their animals there.

By late fall, however, most stampeders leaving Edmonton by the overland route headed for Peace River Crossing, 320 miles away. The best route took them by boat down the Athabasca and up the Lesser Slave rivers, then across the seventy-five-mile expanse of Lesser Slave Lake, and finally overland via a last seventy-five-mile portage that led them to the banks of the Peace.

When the lakes and rivers froze, most parties were forced to cross the Swan Hills by way of the so-called Chalmers Trail. The government of the North West Territories, under pressure from the merchants of Edmonton, assigned a party under T. W. Chalmers, a road engineer, to hack out a 120-mile trail between Fort Assiniboine and Lesser Slave Lake. By the time the route was finished in July, 1898, the main body of stampeders had moved ahead of the trail blazers and the "trail" itself was an almost impassable pathway "landmarked with carcasses" and littered with broken boxes, smashed sleighs, and discarded harnesses. Tree after tree had been blazed so that disappointed gold-seekers might scrawl out their feelings about the Edmonton route in poetry and invective. "Due north to Dawson: starvation and death; due south, home sweet home and a warm bed," one such inscription read.

Here the familiar stench of rotting horseflesh, the telltale perfume of the Klondike stampede, began to permeate the route to the Peace. Of the four thousand horses that expired or were shot on the overland routes, two thousand died of starvation in the Swan Hills. The

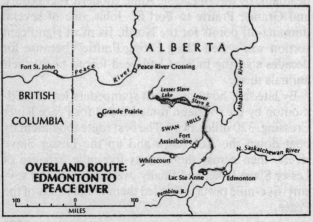

OVERLAND ROUTE:
EDMONTON TO
PEACE RIVER

country was devoid of feed. At some points the maddened animals gnawed the bark from the trees or staggered on, sustained only by scraps of frozen moss, until they dropped in their tracks. With the trail blocked by stranded parties, those who followed were forced to detour, hacking new trails out of the forests as they pressed on towards the Swan River. By spring, the Chalmers Trail had become a two-way route, with those in the rear crying "Forward!" and those in front shouting "Back!" as in the days of Horatius. Close to one hundred men gave up before reaching Peace River Crossing and trudged disconsolately back to Edmonton, where the *Bulletin* was still trumpeting the advantages of the back-door route to the gold-fields.

For the hardy few who pressed stubbornly onward after the Peace was reached, there was virtually no trail at all. Four main routes led out of either Fort St. John or Peace River Crossing to the Liard country, each of them about four hundred miles long. A Canadian guidebook told of a road all the way north to Fort Selkirk, where the Pelly flows into the Yukon, but this was fiction. The Edmonton town council had hired W. P. Taylor for $950 to open a trail from Peace River Crossing by way of Fort Nelson to the Pelly Banks, but his occasional slashes on trees were the only sign of the roadway that some promoters insisted ran clear to the Klondike. Taylor remained loyal to his backers. When, on his return trip, he met a party moving north, he urged them on.

"They're taking lots of gold out of the Nelson," he said cheerfully, "and on the Liard they're making thirty dollars a day."

It was one thousand miles from Peace River Crossing to the junction of the Pelly and the Yukon. Few made this full journey. Some set their faces homeward; others chose the alternative route down the Peace and the

293

Slave to Great Slave Lake and thence down the great Mackenzie to the Arctic. Those who continued onward found themselves in a savage land of muskeg, bogs, and deadfalls, where acre upon acre of dead spruce lay fallen crosswise, the trunks so close together that it was impossible for the horses to avoid scraping their legs to shreds on the rough bark. The animals, clambering and leaping constantly over these miles of obstacles, died as easily as the mosquitoes of summer, and it was said that one could trace their trail over the deadfalls by blood alone.

At the very top of British Columbia the Liard was reached, and up this wild watercourse with its hot springs, its canyons, its whirlpools, and its rapids the remaining stampeders now forced their way in home-made boats. Up they went through Hell's Gate and the Grand Canyon by means of boathooks and pike poles and even their own fingers thrust bleeding into the rock crevices. Up they went through the Rapids of the Drowned, where boats capsized and men vanished into the foam. On they went past banks so precipitous that

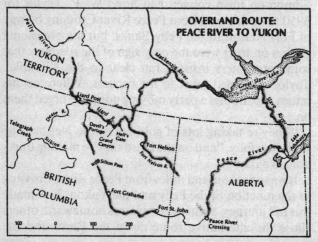

294

there was no footing at water level and they could only pull their craft from the clifftops by means of hundred-foot towlines. On they went across Devil's Portage, where the river, twisting through a horseshoe gorge, became unnavigable and everything had to be dragged for eight miles over an intervening mountain.

By the time the boatmen reached Liard Post on the Yukon border, they were at the end of their tether. The route now led up the Liard's tributaries towards the mountain divide that blocks it off from the Pelly, but only the hardiest dared face it. Dozens began to head back to civilization, striking south through British Columbia to Glenora and the sea coast. In the spring of 1899 men were still faltering through the forests, trying to escape from the trap; some, disabled by sickness, frostbite, and hunger, were imprisoned in little cabins along the banks of the Liard and its tributary, the Dease, emaciated, scabrous, and foul with scurvy. When a local trading company outfitted a relief expedition to succour this human wreckage, about sixty suffering stampeders were gathered up and taken to Telegraph Creek. Some were so ill or so lame that they had to be lifted on and off the pack horses and scows. Of the thirty-five deaths on the overland trails out of Edmonton in the stampede years, twenty-six occurred in the Liard-Cassiar area and most of these were from scurvy.

Of every five men who set out for the Klondike by the overland routes, only one reached his destination. One party that did get through, for which there is a complete record, was not composed of gold-seekers at all but of North West Mounted Policemen. The patrol, headed by Inspector J. D. Moodie, was under orders to compile a gazetteer of information on the best routes to follow across the Rockies and through northern British Columbia to the gold-fields and to supply the government with all the reliable information that anybody leaving

Edmonton would need. The inference was that the stampede would go on for years, but by the time Moodie reached his objective it was all over. Nor was the route he chose, by way of Fort St. John, Fort Grahame, Sifton Pass, and the Dease River, one which the Edmonton merchants believed in or which many stampeders followed.

Moodie started out in September, 1897. It took him almost fourteen months to cover the sixteen hundred miles to Fort Selkirk on the Yukon. He and his men chopped their way through the wilderness, paddled, climbed, waded, and trudged, their clothes in tatters, their horses half dead, their packers constantly deserting them, and their constitutions weakened by illness. In one instance Moodie and his men had to hack their way through three hundred miles of fallen timber. At another point a forest fire almost wiped them out, and only an eleventh-hour change of wind saved them from roasting to death. Their ponies devoured poisonous weeds and expired on the spot. One of their guides went mad and vanished into the forest. Snow threatened to halt them for a full winter, but Moodie fought on through the drifted mountain passes, killing his pack horses to feed his sled dogs and hiring more teams and sleighs to keep going. His superiors thought him lost, for he was out of touch with the world for months, but in the end he crossed the mountains alone and reached the Pelly. Down the great turbulent river he raced in a canvas canoe until the sharp-edged floes tore into the sides and rendered it useless. He built himself a raft and kept on going, but it was too bulky and the ice in the channel blocked its passage. He spent four hundred and fifty dollars to buy a Peterborough canoe from another stampeder and plunged on, half starved, half frozen, his underclothing caked to his body and his uniform in rags. The current grew fiercer, and the ice began to suck him under. He flung the canoe aside, donned his snow-shoes, and plodded onward over the ice-sheathed boulders and through the fast-forming drifts. He would not stop for sleep, and when at last he arrived at Fort Selkirk, dazed with fatigue, Inspector Moodie had been on the move without respite for forty-eight hours. The date was October 24, 1898.

6: *The road to Destruction City*

The alternative route from Edmonton led straight down the Mackenzie river system towards the Arctic Circle. The trails fanned off towards the west and over the mountain divides like the branches of a tree, with the Mackenzie as its trunk. Though all these water routes were far longer than the trails through the Peace River country — longer by as much as one thousand miles — a larger contingent reached the Klondike this way. Many a stampeder learned to his regret that the shortest path to the gold-fields was not necessarily the easiest and that simple routes in the end turned out to be more complicated than those that seemed tortuous on paper. Of an estimated 885 who took the water route to the gold country, it is said that 565 actually reached their destination, although some were eighteen months and more in transit. One couple actually conceived and gave birth to a child somewhere between Edmonton and Dawson City.

Those who chose this circuitous passage first moved overland from Edmonton one hundred miles towards Athabasca Landing. Along that trammelled pathway, where the tall pines often shut out the sun, a river of humanity flowed in two directions, shuttling freight, machinery, animals, trail outfits, and even steamboats from the rail-head across benchland and sloughs to the banks of the Athabasca. Here, as elsewhere, the cosmopolitan character of the stampede could be glimpsed. A. D. Stewart, the former mayor of Hamilton who had become a public figure as a result of laying the formal charges against Louis Riel after the Saskatchewan Rebellion of 1885, was leading the Mackenzie River—Klondike Expedition (Arthur Heming's original party) and planning to build a steamboat on the Athabasca to bear the wistful name of *Golden Hope*. Jim Wallwork, a cowboy from the foothills, actually hauled his steamboat with him; she was the *Daisy Belle*, a North Saskatchewan stern-wheeler, which he and his partner had bought in Edmonton and which they confidently expected would take them to Dawson. For Otto Sommer, of Chicago, this was a honeymoon trip, albeit an arduous one. It had been forced upon him when his girl friend refused to let him depart alone for the flesh-palaces of the Klondike; he solved the problem by marrying her and taking her with him. For Frank Hoffman, a recent immigrant from Germany, the pitfalls of the trail held no terrors — he was a veteran of both the Sedan and the Metz engagements, and even the fact that his wife was pregnant did not deter him.

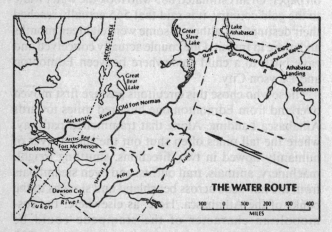

THE WATER ROUTE

298

There were embezzlers on the Athabasca Trail and there were paupers, and these fared no better and no worse than the wealthy boat owners or honest trail-breakers. Somewhere in the crowd was the Edmonton agent of a New York insurance company who had decamped with his clients' funds. And moving along the same route was a Massachusetts carpenter named Frank Nash who had arrived in Edmonton with less than five dollars in his pocket and was working his way north in stages by plying his trade. There was a Dutchman who stood six foot seven in his stocking feet and a French Canadian who was only four foot six (and who was presented on Good Friday with a hot cross bun for being the smallest stampeder on record); and there was one black man on the trail, very much in demand because he entertained his companions with Negro melodies.

By the spring of 1898, the Hudson's Bay settlement of Athabasca Landing had swollen to ten times its original size. Tents bleached the river banks for two miles, and between the tents half-formed pathways had been chopped out of the timber bearing crude signs labelling them "The Strand," "Piccadilly," and "The Bowery." On either side of the settlement were camp grounds known as East and West Chicago, so named because men from that city outnumbered their fellows four to one. On the north side of the river, along a winding trail (identified by a scrawl of red paint on a spruce tree as "Fifth Avenue"), were camped several parties of boat builders from Ontario. Southeast of the Hudson's Bay post lay a line of shacks known as Bohemian Row, "the first thing in the village to resemble a street." Here — where, it was said, ten languages were spoken — the tenants included an artist, two miners, three carpenters, two ex-tramps, an actor, a Boston policeman, a one-time temperance lecturer, a banjo-playing Englishman, a butcher, and "seventeen dogs of every species known to science."

At its peak Athabasca Landing boasted two hotels, a restaurant, four general stores, a butcher shop (which did duty as a concert and dance hall), a barber shop, two bakeries, and half a dozen thriving boat yards where every type of craft was under construction, from ungainly scows to sixty-foot steamboats capable of carrying fifty passengers. "I confess I think no part of the world, Liverpool included, can boast so many different models," one correspondent reported to Edmonton. "It looks as though every man who ever had an idea that he was a boat engineer was here and had tried his hand and the result is boats — beautiful, practical, pathetic, ludicrous. . . ." There were more than one hundred craft, and by late May, the entire flotilla was drifting down north. Within two months it had lost its bunched-up character and was scattered for thirteen hundred miles along the Mackenzie River system.

One hundred and ten miles of rapids faced the boatmen on the Athabasca River before Lake Athabasca was reached. The boats churned around the great boulders of Pelican Rapids, where the spray was flung twenty feet into the air, and then forced their way through Boiler Rapids, Strong Rapids, Crooked Rapids, and Grand Rapids until they reached the Big Cascade, where the current raced over a ledge of rock at twenty-five miles an hour. Boats were mired, crushed, abandoned on sand-bars, and wrecked on rocks. One man was drowned; many turned back. The rest surged on down the broadening river, past the oozing and mysterious tar sands that hung from the banks like treacle, then over the hard portages of the Slave River, whose rapids were so fierce that white pelicans bred in masses on an island in the centre where neither man nor beast could reach them, and finally out onto the leaden

300

expanse of Great Slave Lake, where the storms were as fierce as those on the ocean and the tossing waters vanished over the rim of the horizon.

Once they had crossed this dismaying inland sea, the stampeders found themselves swept into the Mackenzie proper, the great waterway that would lead them to the Arctic. Out of the mountains, from the west, into the mile-wide river poured the turbulent Liard. About eighty men turned up this stream, to fight their way through canyon and rapids in the hope of joining those who had come overland from the Peace (and who were in many cases fleeing the Liard country in favour of the Mackenzie). The remainder continued on down the main river, where hidden seams of coal smoked and smouldered perpetually, where great blue ice-lenses lay exposed on the tottering clay banks, where ghost-like thickets of scorched aspens and "drunken" forests of spindly spruce reeled at awkward angles in the permanently frozen soil, where Indian children ran naked and babbling along the sandy shoreline, and squaws like Oriental idols squatted unsmiling on high green cliffs.

Halfway down the Mackenzie, not far from the site of Old Fort Norman, a second contingent peeled off the main body and turned west to assault the continental divide by way of the Gravel River (later renamed the Keele). Through this gaunt mountain country no white man had yet penetrated, but now a thin human seepage was trickling in. Some ninety-five men assaulted the divide, and of these perhaps seventy or seventy-five eventually got through. But for many the Klondike was another year away.

The hardships, both psychological and physical, were so great that no man could say he remained unaffected. Since no one could haul more than a hundred and fifty pounds at a time over that seven-thousand-foot barrier, the trip had to be divided into ten-mile stages, each man doubling and re-doubling in his tracks between camps so that, in many cases, men trudged a total of twenty-seven hundred miles in order to move their outfits three hundred. It was bitterly cold in the mountains — so cold, indeed, that during one noon-hour break, Ernest Corp of Hamilton watched an inch-long icicle form on the spout of a coffee pot from which steam was also issuing. It is small wonder that almost every party that attempted to cross the divide by way of the Gravel River split up before the gold-fields were reached, and the divisions were often so bitter that equipment was sometimes chopped in half and boats sawn in two.

On the far side of the divide lay the rock-strewn Stewart, and when spring came, those who had managed to cross the mountains plunged down its unknown canyons and rapids aboard home-made scows caulked with spruce gum and winter underwear. They travelled blindly down the boiling stream, never knowing what the next bend would reveal, their numbers diminishing as they whirled on, until the remainder reached the Yukon River and thence, in August and September of 1899, managed to arrive in Dawson City.

This was an eddy in the main current of the stampede down the Mackenzie. The majority kept drifting deeper and deeper into the North, borne along without effort on the tawny breast of the mother stream. On they floated, into the land of the Dogrib Indians, who pitched their ragged tents on islands for fear of an invisible enemy stalking the forest glades; on past the yawning mouth of the Great Bear River, pouring its cobalt waters out of another fresh-water ocean athwart the Circle; on past blue-green forests and rust-red ponds, salt sinkholes, dried-up channels yellow with weeds, and ribbed cliffs jutting blackly a quarter mile above the water's crest; on down the widening river

302

with nothing to do but loll against the rudder bar until the silt-laden waters suddenly splayed out into the skein of the delta within hailing distance of the Arctic Ocean, and the long eleven-hundred-mile slide from Great Slave Lake was at an end.

The boats quit the Mackenzie here to turn up its two northernmost tributaries, the Arctic Red River and the Peel, whose headwaters stretched back like slender blood vessels into the labyrinth of the Mackenzie and Richardson mountains. This was sullen country: the bald, wind-swept land of the Crooked-Eye Indians, who lived in hide tepees and believed in a ghostly cannibal, black-faced and yellow-eyed, who gobbled women and children. Across this dun terrain, with its lifeless plains of muskeg broken only by the occasional stunted spruce and a few thin groves of skeletal willows, the winter snows shifted ceaselessly. Long before the main body of the stampeders reached the divide, the snow was upon them. Some turned off the Peel and headed west up its tributary, the Rat, hoping to cross the mountains and drift down the Bell and the Porcupine into Alaska to reach the Yukon River. Others pushed farther up the Peel, heading for other tributaries, the Wind or the Bonnet Plume, which led to passes in the mountains directly north and east of Dawson City.

Sooner or later the mountains had to be faced, and in the late fall of 1898, as the land congealed under the white hand of winter, the men from the cities and the farms and the offices and the factories began to attack the barrier, dragging scows and boats up and over the divides by the process called "tracking," which is the crudest and most exhausting form of towing. Each man, with a canvas sling over his shoulder, helped haul the boat behind him, trudging thigh-deep through the

303

freezing waters, leaping from rock to rock in the shallow, frothing streams, or struggling along the edges through tangled willows and over shale cliffs, or crawling on hands and knees along the slimy banks. As winter set in and the snow fell and the winds shrieked down the canyons that marked the entrances to the passes, the argonauts began to wheeze and cough with bronchitis. They were seldom dry. Their legs were masses of boils because of constant immersion in the cold water. Their flesh was rubbery from incipient scurvy, for it was six months since they had enjoyed a balanced diet. Beset by shoals and savage currents, by jagged rocks and ferocious boulders, by gloomy caverns and dizzy banks, they numbly forced their way on until the ice shackled the river and all movement ceased.

It was winter. All over the Canadian northwest, along the Edmonton trails, little settlements sprang up, from Great Slave Lake to the Arctic Circle, from the Peace River to the mountains above the Pelly. Some were mere huddles of shacks, like those that lay scattered along the approaches to the McDougall and Stony Creek passes. Some had names like Wind City, on the Wind River, a tributary of the Peel, or Shacktown and Destruction City, on the Rat. In addition there was the established trading post of Fort McPherson on the Peel, in whose vicinity scores of stampeders settled down for the long wait.

Some seventy men were camped at Wind City and many of these suffered horribly from scurvy. When gangrene set in, as it did in one or two cases, their toes were cut off with hacksaws; and when men died — as two or three did — their bodies were stuffed down empty mine shafts, which some of them had dug in the wistful hope that there might be gold here in the land of little sticks. The others whiled away the winter's night with chess, checkers, and euchre, with dances and with lectures on scientific and literary subjects. Wind City's residents even enacted a code of municipal laws so that the winter might pass "pleasantly and profitably away."

Destruction City was situated at the start of a fierce series of rapids on the Rat which marked the ascent to McDougall Pass. Here the river bed rose so steeply — twelve hundred feet in thirty-five miles — that it was impossible to take large craft further. Men were forced to chop their boats down to manageable size and so the banks were marked by a confusion of wreckage that gave the settlement its name.

The only way to cross the pass that fall was to travel as lightly and as swiftly as possible. A French Canadian

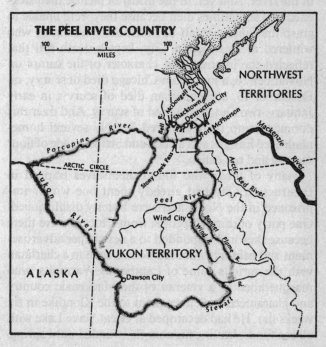

from Ottawa, J. E. des Lauriers, was one of those who threw away almost everything he owned in order to reach the Klondike. He left his entire outfit on the banks of the Rat at Destruction City, taking only a sack of flour, a side of bacon, a rifle, and a small boat. Thus unencumbered he attained his goal. Others found it impossible to get through. Between fifty and a hundred wintered in the immediate area of Destruction City, crouching in tents or cabins or huddled in caves scooped out of the banks, surrounded by piles of goods tossed aside by those who, like des Lauriers, had abandoned the bulk of their outfits in order to get across the divide. Here was everything a man needed, except for footwear — that had all been torn to shreds on the rocks of the river. And yet, in the midst of plenty, men sickened and sometimes died because they were unable to grasp the fundamentals of nutrition. Elsie Craig, who wintered at Destruction City, kept a death roll that reflected the international character of the camp: on November 20, a man from Chicago died of scurvy; on December 13, a Frenchman died of scurvy; in early January, two Dutchmen died of scurvy. And over this doomed camp there fluttered bravely several homemade Red Ensigns and a Stars and Stripes made of flour sacking and red calico.

Many of those who found themselves trapped in Destruction City had already spent one winter imprisoned in the North and were bitterly disillusioned. One party of thirteen people from Chicago were there because they had responded to a newspaper advertisement and paid five hundred dollars each to a charlatan with the curious name of Lambertus Warmolts, who masqueraded as a veteran of the Mackenzie country and guaranteed to deliver them to the Klondike in six weeks flat. He had decamped at Great Slave Lake with all the funds, leaving his charges stranded until spring.

Rather than turn back they pushed on, so great was their desire to reach the gold-fields, and here they were rotting from scurvy on the banks of the Rat, with another winter facing them. A few of them did manage to reach Dawson in August of 1899.

Of all those who left Edmonton in 1897 and 1898 and pursued the various routes to the Klondike, only three, as far as can be determined, found any gold at all. Indeed, many of those who trickled into Dawson, ragged and destitute, did not even bother to go out to the gold-fields but headed back to civilization a few days after arriving. William Ford Langworthy, the Cambridge law graduate who celebrated New Year's Eve, 1897, so nostalgically on the shores of Great Slave Lake, was one of these. His diary scarcely mentions Dawson, and its later entries never refer to gold but reflect the strange lassitude that fell over those who finally succeeded in reaching the end of the Edmonton trails. To these, gold no longer meant very much; survival had taken its place. Otto Sommer, who had turned his Klondike expedition into a honeymoon trip, got no farther than Grand Rapids on the Athabasca before turning back in despair. Frank Hoffman, the veteran of Sedan and Metz, was drowned in Great Slave Lake; his wife went on without him, lost her new-born baby somewhere en route, and wintered at Shacktown. A. D. Stewart, the former Hamilton mayor who had come down the river in the *Golden Hope,* died by inches on the Peel, "teeth all loose and gums very sore. In pitiable condition," as his last diary entry reads.

Some beat the odds. Jim Wallwork, the cowboy, actually dragged his steamboat *Daisy Belle* over the summit from Shacktown to the Bell River, aided by thirty Indian sled dogs. The little craft finally reached the Yukon and there, unable to face the swift current, gave up the ghost. Wallwork transferred the eight-horsepower engine and the boiler to a York boat and continued upstream to Dawson. No doubt it was enough for him that he had made it, for those who set out from Edmonton to seek their fortunes counted themselves truly fortunate if they reached their goal. Others there were who never found what they were seeking — such as the two partners who were discovered in a cabin on the Porcupine River. They had come almost three thousand miles, buffeting the rapids and scaling the mountains and hacking their way through the forest; but when they were found, they were frozen rock-solid beside a stew kettle hanging over a long-dead fire. The pot contained a pair of partly cooked moccasins embedded in a cake of ice. The rest was ashes.

Chapter Eight

1
The Chilkoot

2
Up the Golden Stairs

3
One of everybody

4
Death beneath the snows

1: *The Chilkoot*

For many people today the entire story of the Klondike gold rush is evoked by a single scene. It shows a solid line of men, forming a human chain, hanging across the white face of a mountain rampart. Caught in the instant of a lens opening, each man, bent almost double under the weight of his burden, yet still straining upward towards the skies, seems to be frozen in an attitude of supplication. It is a spectacle that at one glance mirrors all the terror, all the hardships, and all the yearning of '98. The Chilkoot Pass has come to be a symbol of the stampede.

The routes to the Klondike were all deceptive. Who would have thought that this wall of glittering white, with a final slope so precipitous that no animal could cross it, would turn out to be the most effective way to reach the gold-fields? Who would have thought that, in spite of its steps of solid ice, its banshee winds, its crushing fall of snow, and its thundering avalanches, the Chilkoot was to be the funnel through which the majority of men would attain their goal? Yet that was the way it turned out. The trail through the Chilkoot was higher than the White Pass by more than six hundred feet, and only man could defy successfully its dizzy grade. But twenty-two thousand of the men who assaulted it, each burdened by his ton of supplies, eventually found themselves on the other side.

The gateway to the Chilkoot was another feverish little town almost identical with Skagway: a jungle of frame saloons, false-fronted hotels, log cafés, gambling-houses, stores, and real estate offices bound together by a stiff mortar of flapping tents and named Dyea after the inlet on which it rested. For all of its brief existence it was locked in a bitter struggle with its rival, Skagway, which its two newspapers, the *Trail* and the *Press*, depicted, not inaccurately, as a lawless and terrifying

310

hellhole. Dyea, on the other hand (in the hyperbole of the *Press),* was "not a wild and woolly frontier town but a civilized community."

"We desire," the newspaper wrote, "to call the attention of the reading public to the fact that no more orderly or peaceable city of 3,000 in population can be found in the United States. . . . The population of Dyea is composed of the better class and no one need feel alarmed. Property is exposed on all sides — hardly a case of theft occurring — and what few crimes that are committed are confined to a class few in number. There is less public exhibition of vice here than in the cities of the States."

That was not strictly true; Soapy Smith's men operated out of Dyea as they did out of Skagway though Smith himself did not control the town. Skagway was a dead end where vice flourished because men sat in enforced idleness until the pass reopened. But Dyea, during that gold-rush year, was only a way-point; the Chilkoot was open almost continually and so the stampede flowed through the town and on. Dyea existed for little more than a year. The building of the railway through the White Pass in 1898 rendered it obsolete. Until the summer of 1897 it had consisted of a single building — John J. Healy's trading post. By midwinter, with barques, such as the *Colorado,* dumping as much as eight million board feet of lumber on the beach in a single day, with hotels rising almost hourly (not to mention a three-storey opera house), with men and teams working all night by moonlight and lamp, the newly established Dyea *Trail* was able to report that "as we go to press with our second edition, the buzz of the carpenter's saw, the clink of the hammer, the whizz and bustle of the lumber-laden wagons, the tooting of the crowded steamers all tend to prove the healthy condition of Dyea." And yet before another year had passed,

311

the town lay deserted, its buildings reverting to the weeds and undergrowth that sprang up rankly along the braided mouth of the Dyea River.

The setting in summertime was Elysian. The river wound down to the shallow inlet from the chiselled mountains through emerald clumps of grass and darker copses of evergreens, edged by tangled masses of berry bushes reflected in limpid pools. During the stampede this was quickly reduced to mush by the trampling feet of men and animals.

As at Skagway and at Ashcroft, at Edmonton and Valdez, a liquid stream of humanity gushed through Dyea's narrow streets day and night, so that the air was never still from animal cries and human curses. Only the natives remained silent, and, of all the thousands who attacked the Chilkoot that winter, none profited more than they. The Tlingit tribes were quickly put to work as packers: the Chilkoots, who guarded the pass; their brother Chilkats from the western arm of Lynn Canal; and the Stikines from Wrangell. Over the mountains they stolidly trudged, squat and swarthy and taciturn, a tumpline taut around their flat foreheads, a stout stick in one hand, a pack balanced upon their massive shoulders. Constant communion with the whites had made them shrewd bargainers. They worked for the highest bidder, ran their own informal union, refused to labour on Sundays (for all were strict Presbyterians), and continued to raise their fees as the fervour of the rush increased. Sometimes they would fling the pack of an employer into the snow and go to work for another who offered more money. Sometimes they would stop in the middle of the trail and strike for higher wages. They would not accept folding money, for an early prospector had cheated one of them by paying him in Confederate bills; as a result, they quickly took the gold and silver coinage out of circulation. They

312

treated all stampeders with contempt. At a native church service which some cheechakos attended as spectators, the Tlingit minister read them a stern lecture from the pulpit for not removing their hats. "You white men should be ashamed!" he cried.

The first arrivals at Dyea found that, as at Skagway, their outfits must be lightered from steamer to shore, where they were dumped helter-skelter on the tidal beach. When the tide rose, the scenes that followed were chaotic and often tragic. It was absolutely necessary for each man to move his gear above the high-tide mark before the salt water ruined everything. Monty Atwell, who landed at Dyea on February 22, 1898 — Washington's birthday — wrote: "We saw grown men sit down and cry when they failed to beat the tide. Their limited amount of money had been spent to buy their stuff and get it this far. With their flour, sugar, oatmeal, baking powder, soda, salt, yeast cakes, dried potatoes and dried fruits under salt water, and without time or money to replace them, their chances of getting to the goldfields were gone. A terrible blow to the strongest of men." The new arrivals used dogs, horses, and even oxen to push or pull their outfits across the glistening sands. Atwell watched one old man who was unable to pack his boxed outfit on his shoulders rolling the boxes as best he could, barely keeping ahead of the oncoming waves.

When the wharves were built, they were so icy that a man stepping from ship to dockside often slid back into the sea and had to be fished out with his clothes frozen solid. When warehouses went up, they were jammed from dawn to dusk with crowds of gesticulating men, all demanding their goods, so that the owners had sometimes to brandish six-shooters to avert a riot.

Here, too, for a few brief months, the horse was king. Pack animals were so scarce that even the poor ones sold for six or seven hundred dollars. And although the cost of their feed ran as high as one hundred and fifty dollars a ton, each animal could earn forty dollars daily in packing fees before he collapsed. "Every horse that lands at Dyea may be considered as dead," Robert Medill wrote home to friends in Illinois. "If one man is fortunate enough to get all his packing done another man takes the horse, and it rarely passes from his possession until death. They mostly die of starvation, as no one brings enough feed, not anticipating so much packing."

Sturdier animals fared better. Monty Atwell and his two partners purchased a wild Oregon ox, which had been brought to Dyea to be butchered. They named him Marc Hanna, after the notorious Republican Party boss, and employed him pulling their 5,400-pound outfit between Dyea and the foot of the pass. Marc Hanna could pull five hundred pounds easily, and though horses hauling three-hundred-pound loads often passed him on the trail, they tired more easily and the ox invariably beat them into camp. When the job was done his owners did not have the heart to butcher him but sold him for a low price to another party that promised to care for him.

Like so many routes to the Klondike, the first few miles of the Dyea Trail were deceptively easy. A pleasant wagon road rambled along through meadow and forest, crossing and recrossing the gravelly river that meandered through copses of cottonwood, spruce, birch, and willow.

Then, piece by piece, the telltale symbols of the stampede appeared — a litter of expendable goods thrown aside by men who had already begun to lighten their burdens. Here were trunks of every description, many of them filled with jewellery and trinkets and framed pictures that had ceased to have value for men seeking

314

gold. Trunks were the most useless and awkward articles of all, and each stampeder soon learned that the only possible containers for his outfit were stout canvas bags fifty inches long. After every conceivable weight had been discarded, the weary Klondikers, on leaving the river, kicked off their heavy rubber boots and left them behind, as well. Two enterprising Alaskans retrieved this mountain of footwear and took it back to Juneau for resale to newer arrivals, so that hundreds of pairs came back over the passes time after time.

Five miles from Dyea the trail reached Finnegan's Point, a huddle of tents surrounding a hard core of blacksmith shop, saloon, and restaurant. Here Pat Finnegan and his two husky sons tried to charge a toll of two dollars per horse for the use of their corduroy bridge, until the mounting tide of stampeders brushed them aside. From the Point the trail led directly towards the canyon of the Dyea River, a slender crevice two miles long and fifty feet wide, cluttered with boulders, torn-up trees, and masses of tangled roots. Through the slushy thoroughfare of Canyon City the steady stream of panting men trudged on. At the far end of the canyon, in a strip of woods, a third wayside settlement sprang up, called Pleasant Camp because it came as such a relief after the gloom of the gorge. Now each man felt the tug of gravity as the grade began to rise slowly until Sheep Camp was reached at the base of the mountains. This was the last point on the trail where it was possible to cut timber or firewood; everything beyond was naked rock and boulder, sheathed during the winter in a coating of ice and smothered in a blanket of snow.

The camp lay in a deep basin which seemed to have been scooped by a giant paw out of the encircling mountains. In one of these a small notch could be glimpsed; this was the Chilkoot. Sheep Camp was so named

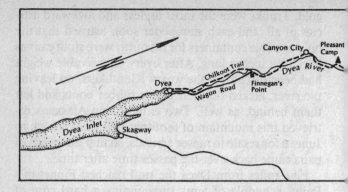

because it had once served as headquarters for hunters seeking mountain sheep, and the stampeders, gazing up at the barrier of encircling white, might well feel that these were the only creatures who could cling to the slippery precipice. On most days the peaks were shrouded in a gloomy fog, but when the sun was out and the sky clear, the pale light glinted on the evil masses of glaciers which hung from the rim of the mountain wall. The summit was only four miles distant, but it was a long way up — thirty-five hundred feet above the town of Dyea.

From the vantage point of Sheep the new arrival could see, spread in front of him and above him, a vast human panorama framed by the snow-grimed hovels of the camp and set against the alabaster backdrop of the sharp-edged peaks. The once-immaculate slopes were spattered by the flyspeck figures of men, and the newcomer, already smarting under the tug of his pack, could view the dimensions of the task that faced him. Within a few days he would be another midge on the mountain inclines, reduced to a cipher by the despotism of the crags above.

There were seldom fewer than fifteen hundred people in Sheep Camp, whose contours shifted daily with the

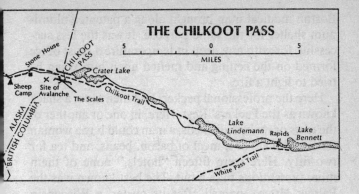

ebb and flow of the human tide. The tents and shacks were wedged so closely together that it was difficult to squeeze between them, the only open space being the semblance of a street, about sixteen feet wide, which curled haphazardly along the bank of the narrowing river. At times the camp seemed like a giant dry-goods repository. Outside of the log and tarpaper cabin occupied by the Red Front Sheep Camp Supply Company hung a ragged curtain of pots and pails and tall rubber boots, while heaped against the front and almost obscuring the doorway were stacks of kitchenware, stoves, barrels, and coils of rope, along with the inevitable piles of firewood. Private post offices, situated in tents, offered to carry mail to Dyea or the lakes for ten cents a letter. Canvas emporiums offered groceries, hay, rifles, and laundry service. The biggest store of all, a log building with a slat and tarpaper roof run by T. Lubeski, offered everything from drugs, medicines, cigars, tobacco, candy, nuts, and stationery to "first class beds."

A potpourri of curious shelters sprang up at Sheep. A group of Maoris, fresh from New Zealand, put up strange huts of wattles to keep out the winds, and a

317

Boston medical man brought along a patented aluminum shelter for the same purpose. It was the less successful, for with any drop in temperature a crust of ice formed on the ceiling and melted upon him when he tried to light a fire.

Here the professional packers had their club, a shack known as the Packers' Rest. Here, in one or another of the tents or makeshift sheds, a man could buy a woman for five dollars or a meal of bacon, beans, and tea for two-fifty. Here were fifteen "hotels," none of them more pretentious than a hut. The best known was the Palmer House, named after its owner, a Wisconsin farmer who had been driven north by hard times just before the stampede began. He had come so far, with his wife and seven children, and, having only eight dollars left, had gone no farther; now, in a shapeless one-room dwelling, he was reaping a fortune. He and his family fed five hundred people a day and slept forty of them each night, jamming them so tightly together on the plank floor that it was impossible to walk through the building after nine in the evening. But, until freeze-up, the Palmer House did boast running water: a brook rippled through one corner of the building.

By the time the snow began to fall, early in the autumn of '97, Sheep Camp had become a bedlam of sweating men, howling dogs, and abandoned horses. Cut adrift by their masters, who could not get them over the pass, these starving creatures hobbled about the camp, their backs raw from wet blankets, their legs lacerated by the rocks, stumbling into tents, tripping on guy ropes, seeking food, shelter, and companionship. In the end they were rounded up and shot and their bodies hidden under the swiftly falling snow. All that winter the snow continued to fall. It fell day and night and sometimes for weeks on end, and was packed down, hard as concrete, by the trampling men, so that the valley floor rose slowly and no man knew how far the ground lay beneath him. In midwinter one party punched a hole in the snow with a pole to test the depth, forcing it down for seven feet before it hit bottom. The pole squinched into something yielding. "Bottom" was a dead horse.

2: *Up the Golden Stairs*

From Sheep Camp the trail rose sharply until in the last assault on the pass it reached more than thirty-five degrees and a man could drop to his hands and knees and still seem partially upright. There were only two points on this four-mile stretch where a climber could properly rest. The first lay beneath a huge overhanging boulder which, because it afforded some shelter, was known as the Stone House. The second was a flat ledge only a few city blocks square at the very base of the ascent, known as the Scales because everything was reweighed here and the packers' rates increased to a dollar a pound. Loaded animals could go no farther, though one or two horses did make the climb; even sleds and dogs had to be packed over on men's backs. Thousands of tons of outfits, half hidden by the ceaselessly falling snow, were piled here, waiting for their owners to gather stamina for the supreme effort of the last climb.

All winter long, from Sheep Camp to the summit, for four weary miles the endless line of men stretched up the slippery slope, a human garland hanging from the summit and draped across the expanse of the mountainside. From first light to last, the line was never broken as the men who formed it inched slowly upward, climbing in that odd rhythmic motion that came to be called the Chilkoot Lock-Step. As on the White Pass, all individuality seemed to end as each man became a link in the chain. Even separate sounds were

319

lost, merged in the single all-encompassing groan which rose from the slow-moving mass and echoed like a hum through the bowl of the mountains.

This was no Technicolor scene. The early photographs render it faithfully in black and white: the straining men in various shades of dun limned against the sunless slopes. For two months of perpetual twilight the Chilkoot was without tint or pigment.

To any alpinist, even an amateur one, the ascent of the pass would have seemed child's play, for it was in no sense a difficult or arduous climb. But the men of '98 were not mountaineers. Poorly attired in heavy furs and wools, rather than in the light hooded parkas which were far more practical, the novices sweated and froze alternately. Unable to disrobe or bathe, seldom free of the winds that were the terror of the trail, bent double under their packs by day and by the need to curl up for warmth at night, half nourished by cold beans and soggy flapjacks, plagued by the resultant dysentery and stomach cramps — filthy, stinking, red-eyed, and bone-weary, they still forced themselves upward. The delays were interminable. Blizzards and gales made the slopes impassable for days on end. Mishaps on the trail caused the line to move by fits and starts. A single trip from Dyea to Lake Bennett was no great hardship, but the goldseekers had to suffer it over and over again. It took the average man three months or more to shuttle his ton of goods across the pass, and by that time the word "stampede," which connotes a thundering herd running untrammelled across an open plain, seemed a cruel misnomer.

As the winter progressed, the more enterprising men began to hack steps out of the ice wall above the Scales. The first stairs were chopped out of the last one hundred and fifty feet of climb, where the going was so steep that one stampeder compared it "to scaling the walls of a house." Two partners cut the steps out with axes in a single night and collected more than eighty dollars a day in tolls, and then, after six weeks, took the money, went on a tear, and blew it all. But others came after them to cut more steps and to charge more tolls until there were fifteen hundred steps cut in the mountainside, with a rope balustrade alongside and little shelves where men could step out of line and rest their packs. Yet few stepped out, because a man might have to wait all day before slipping back into place. Each paid his toll in the morning to climb the "Golden Stairs," as the stampeders called them, and for this set fee could use these stairs as many times as necessary until nightfall. Most used them only once a day, for it took them six hours to climb a thousand feet encumbered by a fifty-pound pack, and fifty pounds was as much as the average man could handle.

Up the golden stairs they went, the men from the farms and the offices, climbing into the heavens, struggling to maintain the balance of the weight upon their shoulders, occasionally sinking to their hands and knees but always rising up again, sometimes breaking down in near-collapse, sometimes weeping in rage and frustration, yet always striving higher and higher, their faces black with strain, their breath hissing between their gritted teeth, unable to curse for want of wind yet unwilling to pause for respite, clambering upward from step to step, hour after hour, as if the mountain peaks themselves were made of solid gold.

The packers took the ascent more casually. Most of them carried one hundred pounds, and one or two performed memorable feats of physical stamina. An Indian packer managed to reach the summit with a three-hundred-and-fifty-pound barrel on his back. A Swede crawled up on his hands and knees with three huge six-by-four timbers strapped to him. An Iowa

321

farm boy on a wager carried a hundred-and-twenty-five-pound plough up the final slope. A Swede named Anderson and a Siwash Indian called Jumbo each made one trip from the Scales to the summit on a bet with a staggering three hundred pounds. They returned in a dead heat, whereupon the Swede immediately hoisted a second three hundred pounds on his shoulders. The Indian stared at him in dismay and retired from the contest.

The new arrivals quickly learned that their ton of supplies had to be packed in such a way that it could be divided into fifty- or hundred-pound portions. Fresh eggs survived the haul in special canvas-covered cases. Flour was poured into light sacks which, in turn, were placed in heavy canvas sacks sewed so tightly that water could soak into only one quarter-inch of flour, turning it into a protective crust. The two prize cargoes were whiskey and silk, one for the Klondike dance halls, the other for the dance-hall girls. The silk was soldered into waterproof tin boxes and packed in stout wooden crates, but the whiskey presented a more difficult problem, since every packer was intent on smuggling it past the Canadian customs officials. Scores of ingenious devices were designed by San Francisco wholesalers to move liquor across the border. They built special kerosene tins whose spigots produced coal oil but whose interior content was a tin of whiskey. They invented egg crates with false bottoms and white-lead kegs that contained no white lead. In bales of hay they concealed small barrels of liquor, which the customs officials finally detected by means of specially made steel needles attached to long rods. Sometimes the Frisco merchants played it safer, sending a duplicate bill to the Canadian customs men so that the whiskey would be confiscated and the customer would have to order a second shipment.

322

Whiskey and silk, steamboats and pianos, live chickens and stuffed turkeys, timber and glassware, bacon and beans, all went over on men's backs. If a man was too poor to hire a packer, he climbed the pass forty times before he got his outfit across.

A representative list of groceries required for one man, to be lugged over the mountains, suggests the magnitude of the task:

400	lbs. flour
50	lbs. cornmeal
50	lbs. oatmeal
35	lbs. rice
100	lbs. beans
40	lbs. candles
100	lbs. granulated sugar
8	lbs. baking powder
200	lbs. bacon
2	lbs. soda
36	yeast cakes
15	lbs. salt
1	lb. pepper
½	lb. mustard
¼	lb. ginger
25	lbs. evaporated apples
25	lbs. evaporated peaches
25	lbs. evaporated apricots
25	lbs. fish
10	lbs. pitted plums
50	lbs. evaporated onions
50	lbs. evaporated potatoes
24	lbs. coffee
5	lbs. tea
4	doz. tins condensed milk
5	bars laundry soap
60	boxes matches

323

15 lbs. soup vegetables
25 cans butter

But this was not all. There were a steel stove, a gold-pan, three nests of granite buckets, a cup, plate, knife, fork, two spoons, two frying-pans, coffeepot, pick, hand saw, whipsaw, whetstone, hatchet, two shovels, three files, draw-knife, axe, three chisels, twenty pounds of nails, butcher knife, hammer, compass, jack-plane, square, Yukon sled, two hundred feet of rope, fifteen pounds of pitch, ten pounds of oakum, and a canvas tent.

And there were clothes: three suits of heavy underwear, a mackinaw coat, two pairs of mackinaw trousers, a heavy rubber-lined coat, a dozen pairs of wool socks, half a dozen pairs of mittens, two overshirts, two pairs of snag-proof rubber boots, two pairs of shoes, two pairs of blankets, four towels, two pairs of overalls, a suit of oilskin clothing, and five yards of mosquito netting.

When he had dumped his day's load on the summit and marked it with a pole, each man turned back down again, for there was no shelter at the top. The return trip was swift and precipitous; the stampeders simply tucked their boots beneath them and tobogganed down the slope on their rumps, gouging deep chutes in the snow, and hitting the bottom in a matter of minutes.

Inevitably, human ingenuity won over nature. By December, 1897, the first crude tramway — an endless rope wound around an upright wheel and turned by a horse moving in a circle — had been opened by Archie Burns, a sourdough from Fortymile and Circle City. Burns's tramway set the pattern for later and more ambitious devices. By May there were at least five of them operating over the pass. One consisted of a heavy cable, powered by a steam engine, which carried two buckets each capable of holding five hundred pounds.

Travelling some three hundred feet above the ground, the buckets made the round trip from the Scales to the summit in about fifteen minutes. Another, operated by the Dyea and Klondike Transportation Company, consisted of an endless chain of buckets — hundreds of them — each carrying a hundred pounds. These soared a mere fifty feet over the line of struggling men. A fourth, worked by a gasoline engine and a rope wound around a drum, dragged sled loads of equipment up the ice of the pass directly beside the climbers. By far the most ambitious device was the one built by the Chilkoot Railroad and Transportation Company, whose president, Hugh C. Wallace, later became United States Ambassador to France.

Wallace's tramway did not open until the spring of 1898, but it made it possible for a man's goods to be transported aerially all the way from Canyon City to the summit of the pass. Its copper steel cable, supported by towering tripods anchored in concrete, was originally dragged up, a coil at a time, on the backs of mules and men. There were fourteen miles of it, with only one splice. At the time the tramway was built, it had the longest single span in the world, twenty-two hundred feet from one support to the next. Steam engines at each end supplied the power, and men struggling along the trail could gaze up and see carloads of goods hurtling through the snow-filled air eighteen hundred feet above them. The cars, each loaded with three hundred pounds, were dispatched at the rate of one a minute, day and night, so that by spring freight was being dumped on the summit of the pass at the rate of nine tons an hour.

3: *One of everybody*

On top of the pass a silent city took shape. The "buildings" were towering piles of freight; the "streets" the spaces left between. The blizzard that rarely ceased covered the goods soon after they were dropped, making it necessary for the owners to leave poles or long-handled shovels marking their property. Even these were ineffectual, for almost seventy feet of snow fell on the summit of the Chilkoot that winter, and before spring two "cities" of goods had been buried and could not be retrieved until the thaw.

The pass at this point was a trench one hundred yards wide, through which a spray of snow whirled. On either side the mountains rose for another five hundred feet, their tops masked by clouds and blowing snow. Occasionally the weather cleared, and then, for a few brief moments, a watcher on the summit could look back towards Dyea, thirty-five hundred feet below, or forward towards Lake Lindemann, twelve hundred feet below, and see the unending line of men merging with the horizons. Then the storm would close in again and nothing would be visible for more than ten feet.

The piles of freight provided the only shelter on the summit. Firewood was priced at a dollar a pound to cover the cost of hauling it seven miles by sled from the timberline on the Canadian side. Those who could afford to paid two dollars and fifty cents for a stale doughnut and a cup of weak coffee (five times the price of a three-course meal in Seattle), gulped it down, and were away, for no one wished to tarry. Only the North West Mounted Police held fast to their post. The presence of these men in their huge buffalo coats with the brass buttons of the Force marked the summit as the international border. The first Canadian post had been established farther inland at Tagish Lake, but when the

United States failed to take possession of the headwater lakes, the Canadian government placed the Mounties on the mountaintops. It was this summary action that, in the end, established the much contested border at this spot. The sight of a tattered Union Jack fluttering in the storm, and the blurred outlines of a sentry with a Maxim gun, always on duty, was the first indication the stampeders had that they had reached Canadian territory.

Here, every man was required to pay duty on the outfit he had hauled across from the Alaskan side. The prices ranged from three-quarters of a cent on a pound of corn syrup to sixty cents for a barrel of flour. Many an American resented having to pay such prices. One man, whose total duty came to four dollars and ninety cents, paid up with a five-dollar bill and demanded change. The policeman in charge had none.

"Well," came the reply, "you'd better cough it up; you can't rob me more than the law allows."

The Mountie went to some trouble to borrow the necessary ten-cent piece but then walked outside and asked to inspect the traveller's outfit.

"As you were so particular about that ten cents, suppose you open it up," he said. "It's just possible you may have been overcharged. There may possibly be another ten cents due to you and, combining that with a nickel, you can buy a cup of coffee on the trail."

In the end the luckless stampeder paid more than twenty additional dollars for goods he had not declared. He had no choice: when he tried to protest he was told that if he did not pay, his goods would be confiscated and he himself would be sent back into American territory.

In spite of the Mounties' general reputation for honesty, a few stampeders insisted there was graft at the customs house. One writer, P. Bernard, told the Dyea

327

Trail that after he had paid duty of $20.40 he was asked for an additional five dollars "for sinkerage." As he handed over the money he asked what sinkerage was.

"For this," said the customs collector, dropping the bill into his pocket.

Others were high in their praise of the good sense of the police at the summit. Captain Jack Crawford, the noted "poet scout" of the western plains, moved two tons of goods over the pass under difficult conditions. He hired packers to take his outfit to the summit while he followed on horseback. He managed to ride as far as the Scales, at which point his horse broke through the snow and rolled over on him, causing some injuries. It was so cold by this time that everyone had fled from the area of the pass for shelter; even the tramways had stopped operating because of the severity of the storm. But Crawford was so worried about his supplies, on which no duty had been paid, that he hoisted his bedding on his back and made the climb through the whirling snow, in spite of the protests of his comrades. When he reached the customs house he discovered that it was empty; the storm was so fierce that all business had ceased and the broker's office was covered by twelve feet of snow. The Mounted Police invited him in for a roast beef dinner and told him that because he was so well known they had let his goods go through with the packers on credit. Crawford was elated. He exclaimed: "I would not have missed seeing the Chilkoot summit and climbing it, and sliding down again to its base, for a thousand dollars." He told the press that "the Canadian officials are neither strict or offensive and not one party in five hundred had their outfits closely examined. If a man has common sense he need have no trouble with the customs officers."

At night, when the summit was silent and empty, when the climbers had retreated to Sheep Camp on the

328

south or moved on down to Crater Lake on the north, the police held their ground in a tiny hovel perched in the shadow of the overpowering mountains on the rim of the precipice. So thickly did the snow come down on cabin and tents (six feet in a single night, sometimes) that Inspector Bobby Belcher, the officer in charge, had to post a sentry to shovel it away as it fell, to prevent the sleeping men from smothering to death. One storm raged for two months, stopping almost all movement on the trail, but still the police clung to their post, their hut dripping like a shower bath as the snow was melted by its warmth, while the supplies, the blankets, the documents, and the records were slowly coated with a creeping fur of mildew.

On one occasion the detachment was driven from its post by the shrieking gale. The Mounties retreated into the lee of the mountains, pitching their tents on the ice of Crater Lake, a cupful of frozen water in an old volcanic hollow just below the peak of the pass. Here in a below-zero blizzard they crouched while the water rose six inches above the ice, soaking their bedding. Unable to move their tents in the storm, they pulled their sleds inside and slept on top of them. Then, when the wind abated, they returned to their perch on the mountain.

The police checked twenty-two thousand men across the pass that winter — Scots and Canadians, Yanks and Greeks, Swedes and Australians, Japanese and Kanakas. And there were women, too: stocky soubrettes heading for the dance halls of Dawson, their charms concealed beneath their heavy clothing . . . lithe Indian girls who carried seventy-five pounds on their backs and scaled peaks more nimbly than some of the cheechakos . . . an old German woman, almost seventy, in a full dress and a lace apron . . . and, on the lower slopes, a middle-aged woman, all alone, who tugged a hand sled onto which a glowing stove was fastened, so

329

that whenever she stopped she was able to warm her hands and enjoy a hot meal. Jack Crawford, trudging back to the summit from Lake Lindemann, met "a handsome girl, straight as an arrow, blue eyes, curly blonde hair, dressed in boy's clothes — blue shirt, no coat, with a belt with a .44 Colt pistol strapped around her waist." Her brother walked ahead of her, carrying a guitar.

Mixed in among the real gold-seekers were fake stampeders sent up from Skagway by Soapy Smith to fleece the argonauts. These confidence men mingled with the endless line of plodding figures, tugging sleds behind them or carrying authentic-looking packs that seemed to be bulging with Klondike gear. Actually the packs were stuffed with feathers, hay, or shavings, while the sleds were specially built dummies designed for fast travelling and a quick getaway. The canvas lashed down over them concealed a hollow shell from which protruded the occasional axe-handle, at the proper angle, to preserve a bona fide effect.

It was difficult for many of the weary climbers to resist the blandishments of Smith's gang along the trail. The con men built fires for them to warm themselves by, and put up tents to keep out the piercing winds, and constructed seats or ledges for the tired packers to rest on, with shelves at the back so that a gold-seeker could ease the weight of his pack from his shoulders. To a physically demoralized man toiling up the straight and narrow path of the Chilkoot, such temptations could not but appear inviting. On a single mile of trail one observer counted four shell games in operation, each surrounded by an eager knot of players.

As each man, with his ragged beard and sunken eyes, looked as sinister as the next, the devil himself could have moved among them without remark; and if his minions had any distinguishment, it was that — being well fed and unburdened — they appeared slightly less villainous than the shaggy, red-eyed men upon whom they preyed. Old Man Tripp, the saintly looking sinner, was here in his element, working with a younger colleague, Frank Brown, nicknamed "Blue Jay." One would carry a cane which unfolded into a three-legged support, and the other a book which opened into a counter twelve by eighteen inches across. Thus equipped with the traditional con man's "tripe and keister," Tripp ran the game while Blue Jay acted as shill. Tripp could slip a rubber pea out from under the shells so deftly that no one could tell it was gone. As it was impossible for anybody but Blue Jay to win at the game, the two men made daily clean-ups equal in size to those of some of the Eldorado kings. One Skagway pioneer wrote that, as Soapy's men never lifted a shell for less than twenty dollars, it was not uncommon for the gang to realize two thousand dollars in the space of a day.

Every variety of the human species had a representative on the pass that year. On one hand there was an English nobleman, fastidiously dressed in tweeds, with a valet who, in the late fall, fed him morsels of food while he reclined beneath a net to protect his skin from insects. On the other, there was Wilson Mizner, wit, *bon vivant*, and gambler, who was later to become famous as a Broadway playwright and as the owner of Hollywood's Brown Derby restaurant. Mizner, scarcely old enough to vote, was the son of an aristocratic Californian family, a towering figure of a man who had already, by his own account, been a pimp and an opium-smoker, as well as a crooner in the bar-rooms of the Barbary Coast. Mizner's ton of goods on the Chilkoot included certain luxuries; his main item of baggage was a dance-hall girl from San Francisco named Rena Fargo.

331

Like Soapy Smith and his men, Mizner was not so much interested in finding a gold mine as he was in finding a man who had already found a gold mine. Many of those who crossed the pass with him had the same idea, although their methods were more legitimate. A newsboy struggled up the slopes with a sackful of old newspapers which he hoped to sell at high prices to miners starved for information. Another managed to lug a grindstone over the summit; it had occurred to him that by spring most of the picks in the Klondike would need sharpening. Frank Cushing of Buffalo took ten thousand bottles of mosquito lotion across the slopes. He had bought them for twenty cents each and hoped to sell them in Dawson for ten dollars to the insect-maddened prospectors.

Some showed a profit long before they reached the gold-fields. One woman brought a banjo over the pass and paid her way by giving impromptu concerts as she went along. She wore a man's tweed coat and heavy pants, but made one small concession to her femininity by carrying, under one arm, a fancy mirror.

Arizona Charlie Meadows planned to arrive in the Klondike with a fortune. He carried a portable bar with him which he set up on every possible occasion, raising the price of the drinks in direct ratio to the height of the trail. At Canyon City, for instance, Arizona Charlie served whiskey for twenty-five cents a shot, but at Sheep Camp the price was doubled, and by the time the Scales were reached every drink cost seventy-five cents. The price, no doubt, would have risen to a dollar at the summit, but a sudden flood was the finish of Charlie's outfit. This did not deter him, for he was an old western scout and sharpshooter inured to vicissitudes, whose family had been wiped out by Apaches and who had himself fought hand to hand with Geronimo. A veteran of both the Buffalo Bill and the Pawnee Bill wild-west

332

shows, he picked up loose change whenever he needed it by shooting the spots off a playing-card at thirty feet.

The singleness of purpose with which these men and women flung themselves at the mountain, time and time again, would have astonished a dispassionate observer. It was as if each was pulled by invisible strings from whose insistent tug he could not free himself. The worst hardships, the most racking personal tragedies often failed to dampen the fanaticism which impelled each one. A man lay on the trail for all of one day, in agony from a broken leg, while hundreds passed him by, unseeing, their eyes fixed firmly on the road ahead, almost as if each was wearing blinkers. At last a professional packer, Tom Linville, who had carried heavier loads and walked farther than any of them that day, happened by, and picked up the sufferer and trudged uncomplaining all the way to Dyea with his hundred-and-eighty-pound burden.

The harsh story of the trials of an English couple named Rowley who attacked the Chilkoot that winter illustrates the intensity of the common desire to reach the Klondike.

The Rowleys' first misfortune occurred when the S.S. *Corona,* on which they were Dyea-bound, was shipwrecked. The couple lost their entire outfit, but, rather than turn back, they attempted to earn enough to keep going by freighting goods across the pass. The effort was too much for Rowley, who took sick at Sheep Camp, but this only caused Mrs. Rowley to redouble her efforts as a packer. She managed to move thirteen hundred pounds of goods as far as the Scales, often working twenty hours at a stretch and seldom leaving the trail before two in the morning. The strain was too great, and before her husband was fully recovered, she herself was worn out from fatigue. Rowley resolved to send her back to San Francisco. Her brother wrote that he had sent her one hundred dollars to the Dyea post office, but she did not receive the money. This was too much to endure. Distraught and enraged at the supposed theft, Mrs. Rowley bought a gun and tried to shoot the postmaster. She was shipped to Sitka, the Alaskan capital, on a charge of attempted murder. En route she leaped from the steamer, but her husband pulled her from the water, and she was shortly released from jail on grounds of insanity. While all this was going on, the Rowleys' entire second outfit, purchased with money earned from freighting, was stolen at Lake Lindemann. Did this deter them? Not in the least. As the Reverend J. A. Sinclair of Skagway wrote to his wife: "You can imagine the intensity with which the gold fever possesses these men when I tell you that Rowley still intends to go on to Dawson."

4: *Death beneath the snows*

The greatest crime on the Dyea Trail that winter, as on all the trails, was not murder but theft. On the American side of the border any man caught stealing from his fellows faced the swift verdict of a miners' meeting.

The most macabre of these summary trials was held within a tent saloon at Sheep Camp on February 15, 1898. Here, in the capricious flicker of smoking oil lamps and candles, three men, Wellington, Dean, and Hansen by name, went on trial for their lives, accused of theft. The circumstances of their apprehension were as freakish as the environment of their inquisition. Their capture had been effected through an odd quirk of the weather: a thin coating of ice on the side of their stolen sled had acted like a varnish on a painting to reveal the half-obliterated name of the rightful owner.

Into the tent, with its leaping shadows — the scene was worthy of a Goya — each prisoner was conducted separately. The first, Dean, was swiftly freed, since it was obvious that he had but recently joined the other two. But Wellington's and Hansen's stories conflicted so seriously that both were found guilty. The verdict was scarcely rendered when Wellington broke from his captors, whipped out a hidden pistol, tore a hole in the tent wall with a knife end, and, firing over his shoulder at the pursuing pack, flew off down the trail. It was a futile gesture. As the leading man reached him, Wellington turned the gun on himself, blowing most of his face off and falling into the arms of Wilson Mizner's brother Addison, an architect who was to become the most flamboyant figure in the Florida real estate boom of the 1920s. The two men plowed into a near-by tent, one dead, the other drenched with blood.

Three Mizner brothers were all witnesses to this incident. Edgar, the Alaska Commercial Company's manager at St. Michael (who was known as the Pope of Alaska because of his arrogant manner), had persuaded Wilson, Addison, and a third brother, William, to join him in Dawson. It was the start of two eccentric careers which have been chronicled several times in the folk-history of the continent.

The meeting, on reconvening, sentenced Hansen to fifty lashes rather than death, and a small wiry man with dark beady eyes volunteered to carry out the punishment. Outside the blood-spattered tent, a great circle was formed as the thief, stripped to the waist, was tied to a post; men climbed up on cabin roofs to take photographs, while one woman squeezed into the front row and asked the prisoner to look at her as she snapped him with her Kodak. Then a hush fell over the buzzing crowd as the man with the whip stepped up.

"I do not do this because I like it," he announced, "but because I like honesty and feel that it must be preserved in this community to save lives."

His actions belied his protestations, for he seized the knotted thong and swung it with his full weight across the miscreant's naked back so that two purple stripes, showing every twist of the rope, followed each blow. The miserable Hansen writhed and leaped in the air as the whip descended, but this only seemed to increase the passion of the executioner, who shrieked and howled crazily as the vigour of his blows increased. By this time the crowd, too, was caught up in a frenzy, some shouting "More!" while others cried "Enough!" until the Mizners moved forward at the fifteenth stroke and freed the prisoner. Apparently unconcerned about his ordeal, Hansen consumed a monstrous meal and was then marched down the trail, smoking his pipe and wearing a large placard on which had been scrawled the word THIEF.

Wellington was buried at once, and an itinerant minister preached a solemn two-minute sermon ending with the words: "He that maketh haste to be rich shall not be unpunished." It was not a particularly propitious text, as Addison Mizner was quick to discern. "I thought this odd," he wrote dryly, "as everybody on the trail, including myself, was on a gold rush."

The remarkable thing about this affair was that it was the exception rather than the rule. There were hardships on the trail, certainly, but comparatively few deaths and, considering the circumstances, little major crime. Soapy Smith's nnen did take some money from the stampeders; there were a few suicides and some murders on the American side; there were a few score deaths from meningitis, influenza, and pneumonia; a large number of men turned back rather than face the final moments of the climb; but a great multitude, leaderless and unorganized, passed over the summit of the divide like an army on the march.

336

It is equally remarkable that only two natural disasters marred the course of the winter's progress across the Chilkoot, although both were spectacular in the extreme.

The first occurred in September, 1897. For years, travellers had been fascinated by a prodigious glacier that hung like a brooding monster over the pass. Harry de Windt, a British explorer who crossed the Chilkoot in the mid-nineties, saw it suspended insecurely between two granite peaks, looking "as though a child's touch would send it crashing into the valley below." The face was three hundred feet high, "indescribably beautiful" because of the shifting light effects — turquoise and sapphire on dull days, dazzling diamond-white in the sunlight, delicate mauve, pink, and green in the twilight hours. From this scintillating mass there issued occasional reports like the distant rumble of cannon, sometimes faint, and sometimes so deafening that the watchers below expected the entire ice sheet to tumble into the valley below. In the end, that is what happened.

During the summer the warm weather and heavy rains had caused a lake to form within the heart of the glacier. Then the autumn winds, whistling through the mountains, tore half an acre of ice from the edge of the mass. With a noise like a thousand cannon, a wall of water descended upon the pass. The reverberations woke the twenty-five campers who had pitched their tents on the dry ground of an old gorge, and these raced for the hills as a wave twenty feet high tore down upon them. The roaring waters picked up the Stone House as if it were a pebble and moved it a quarter of a mile down the valley, smashing to pieces about forty tents and outfits, including the entire gambling casino and liquor supply of Arizona Charlie Meadows. But there were only three deaths.

The second tragedy on the Chilkoot occurred on April 3, 1898, and it was far crueller. For two months an intermittent storm had been raging, making travel impossible on most days. For the previous two weeks the snow had fallen without respite. On Saturday, April 2, the blizzard increased in intensity, and six feet of wet snow was deposited, so that the peaks and glaciers were topheavy with it. The pass was now at its most treacherous, and those few who dared to climb it did so only in the cool of the evening. The Indians and experienced packers refused to go up at all.

In spite of their warnings, large numbers who had been fidgeting for weeks unable to scale the mountains, took advantage of a lull in the storm to make for the summit. The first hint of impending tragedy came early on Sunday. A bent old man, groaning and waving his arms, hammered on the door of a restaurant owned by two partners, Joppe and Mueller, at the Scales, woke them from their Sabbath rest, and cried out that several people had been buried alive by a snowslide up the trail. The two men roused a dozen others, and these dug frantically through ten feet of snow and succeeded in rescuing all but three. Now every person was thoroughly alarmed, and a headlong race began for Sheep Camp, two miles below.

Higher still in the mountains, the guttural rumble of avalanches could be heard. A group of tramway workers had made their way in at mid-morning to report that enormous mounds of snow, piled high along the peaks, were starting to slip down the smooth glaciers. This lent wings to the retreat. Downward the fleeing men and women scrambled, staying close together in single file while clinging to a rope that had been strung along the way. They did not follow the main trail which led down "Long Hill" from the Scales to the Stone House, but went by way of a natural ravine which had long been considered treacherous by knowledgeable guides.

At noon it happened. One of the survivors, a man from Maine named J. A. Rines, described his own feelings: "All of a sudden I heard a loud report and instantly began to feel myself moving swiftly down the hill and, looking round, saw many others suddenly fall down, some with their feet in the air, their heads buried out of sight in the snow." Rines braced himself as best he could, kept to his feet, and let himself be carried along. He was caught by the snow and buried instantly thirty feet deep.

Others had similar experiences. Some grasped the rope that was used to haul freight to the summit. Some, feeling themselves buried hip-deep by the weight of loose snow which struck them first, struggled with it only to be smothered by the main force of the avalanche which followed. Mueller, the café-owner from the Scales, felt himself held as fast as if he were in a cast.

The avalanche had tumbled from a peak twenty-five hundred feet above the trail, just above the Stone House. It covered ten acres to a depth of thirty feet. Within twenty minutes a thousand men from Sheep Camp were on the spot digging parallel trenches in an effort to locate the victims. The scene was a weird and terrible one. Small air holes sometimes appeared in the snow to mark the spot where a man or woman had been buried, and somewhere beneath them the searchers could hear the muffled cries of the victims. Those who still lived beneath the snow (and only a few had been killed by the slide) could hear one another talking, and conversations were carried on between them. Relatives above called out their last good-byes to those entombed below. One old man could be heard alternately praying and cursing until his voice was stilled. But even the

339

strongest could not move a muscle, for the snow was packed around them as tightly as cement.

As the hours wore on, those who were not rescued at once slowly became anesthetized by the carbon dioxide given off by their own breathing; they began to feel drowsy, and drifted off into a dreamless sleep from which few awoke. Their corpes were lifted out in the days that followed, many of them still in a running position, as if forever fleeing from the onrushing avalanche.

More than sixty perished. A handful were rescued alive, some of whom had been three hours under the snow. Four of them died later, but others, including Mueller and his partner, Joppe, made extraordinary recoveries. Joppe's was Lazarus-like in its drama. When he was lifted from his frozen tomb, apparently dead, his sweetheart, Vernie Woodward, was beside herself. She was a resilient young woman who had been packing on the pass since the previous summer, first carrying freight on her back like a man and later working with horses. Now all her surface masculinity was shucked off as she flung herself hysterically upon Joppe's limp figure, begging him to return to her, manipulating his arms and legs, rubbing his back, breathing warm air into his lungs, and crying and praying by turns. For three hours she continued in this manner while those around tried to drag her away. Then, to the stupefaction of all, Joppe suddenly opened his eyes and spoke her name, and it was as if a dead man had miraculously come alive again.

There were other strange rescues: a woman hauled from the snow where she had been buried head-down, hysterical but living; and Marc Hanna, the ox, found after two days contentedly chewing his cud in the natural stable of a snow cave, which he had tramped out himself when the avalanche buried him. But for days

340

after the tragedy, sled after sled loaded with corpses moved down the trail to the mass morgue. Here Soapy Smith's predators were awaiting them. Smith, indeed, had himself appointed coroner. Near the site of the tragedy he set up a tent to which the corpses were brought for identification, and here each frozen cadaver was expertly stripped of rings, jewellery, cash, and other valuables.

The businessmen of Skagway, locked in a mercantile war with Dyea, lost no time in pointing to the disaster as a solemn warning to anybody using the rival town as a port of entry into the Yukon. This drove the *Trail,* one of Dyea's two papers, to a bitter tirade:

"The Skagwayans have no shame. Their ambition seems to be to heap misery upon others. They glory in publishing false statements; they are ghoulish enough to wish there had been five thousand if it only happened on the Chilkoot trail. . . . They show no respect for the dead; but apparently take hellish delight in magnifying the awful fiction and in the hour of death take advantage of the sad calamity by advertising their fever-stricken hole of Hell."

One other person enjoyed the dubious benefits of the Sheep Camp slide, besides the merchants of Skagway. An enterprising newspaperman named Bert Collyer, who had a working arrangement with the Hearst press, gathered a full account of the tragedy and chartered the steamer *Ning Chow* for Victoria. A wild race ensued, for a rival news bulletin had been placed aboard the *Al-ki,* eleven hours earlier. The *Ning Chow* caught and passed her rival in Wrangell Narrows only to discover that a copy of the bulletin had been transferred to the swifter *Amur.* With volunteers breaking coal for the *Ning Chow's* stokers and the *Amur* belching flame six feet high from her stack, the race continued until Seymour Narrows was reached. Here Collyer won the day. His

341

ship passed the *Amur*, and he landed at Victoria ahead of his rivals only to discover the wires were down. Immediately he chartered a launch for Port Angeles on the U.S. mainland, and in this way scored a notable scoop in the San Francisco *Examiner*. He returned north at once and continued his newspaper career in the Klondike. Later in life he ran *Collyer's Weekly,* a sporting journal, and made his reputation as a champion handicapper.

Some of the bodies of the victims of the slide were buried in a little hollow in the mountains not far from the scene of the disaster, and even as the services were held, the long line of men resumed its inexorable grind across the mountains. The sun increased its arc as the days lengthened, the snow grew softer and started to slide in lacy cataracts from the high peaks, the wild flowers soon spattered the mountainside, while the sedges and the grasses began slowly to creep over the debris of the previous winter's rush. The hollow where the bodies rested became a lake, and when summer arrived the last stragglers following in the wake of the main wave of stampeders came upon the grisly spectacle of dozens of bloated corpses floating about on the surface of the water. Thus was the epitaph to the story of the Chilkoot written. The following winter a railway was pushed through the neighbouring White Pass, and the mountains that had resounded to the groans and the shouts of thousands were as silent as the graves of those who had perished beneath the snows.

Chapter Nine

1
Rage in the sawpits

2
The Lion of the Yukon

3
The outlandish armada

4
Split-Up City

1: *Rage in the sawpits*

All winter the twin lines of humanity flowed through the two gaps in the Coast Mountains until by the spring of 1898 the shores of the slender mountain lakes feeding the Yukon's headwaters were clotted with people. The two trails from Dyea and Skagway, running almost parallel, ended at adjoining lakes: the Dyea Trail at Lake Lindemann and the Skagway Trail at larger Lake Bennett, a few miles below. A boulder-filled canyon connected the two, and those who portaged past it could not fail to read a lesson from the grave of John A. Matthews, a twenty-six-year-old Idaho farmer who had come this way the previous June. Twice Matthews had attempted to navigate the canyon, and twice he had foundered with his entire outfit. "My God," he cried out in despair after the second mishap, "what will become of Jane and the babies?" And he pulled a pistol from his pocket and put a bullet through his brains.

On reaching Lindemann from the Chilkoot, thousands came to a halt and proceeded at once to build their boats along its shores. Thousands more, fearful of making the spring boat trip through these rapids that had driven a fellow man to despair, kept moving over the ice until they reached Lake Bennett. And still more, eager to be in the very forefront of the flotilla that was to sweep down these lakes and out into the Yukon, pushed ever farther on, until by spring more than thirty thousand men were strung out for sixty miles, from Lindemann to Tagish, hard at work building a fleet of more than seven thousand boats.

On Bennett's snow-covered shores the greatest tent city in the world was springing up. They encircled the lake in a white cloud: the bell tents and the pup tents, the square tents and the round tents, the dog tents and the Army tents, the tiny canvas lean-tos and the huge circus marquees, some of them brand-new, and some

344

soiled, patched, and tattered by the winter storms. There were tents for hot baths and tents for haircuts, tents for mining agents and tents for real estate men; there were tent hotels, tent saloons, tent cafés, tent bakeries, tent post offices, tent casinos, and tent chapels. In between the tents was heaped the familiar paraphernalia of the stampede: sleds stacked vertically against mounds of supplies; crates of food and tinned goods; furniture, sheet-iron stoves, mining equipment, and tethered animals — oxen, pigs, goats, and chickens. And everywhere, occupying every flat place along the beach, sandwiched between the tents and the shacks and the supplies, were half-built boats and mounting piles of logs and lumber. Indeed, from the hills above, the lakeshore had the appearance of a vast lumberyard. Planks were stacked like cordwood in towering heaps, or up-ended in wigwam shapes, or strewn haphazardly like toothpicks among the rocks and stumps. Boats by the thousands, of every size, shape, and description, lay bottom-up in various stages of construction, most of them still in skeletal form with their gaunt ribs visible.

A few years earlier this sinuous lake, one of the most beautiful in all of the north, had been as silent as the tomb, but now the frosted mountains that enclosed it looked down upon a fevered and incredible spectacle. As spring crept closer, the rumble of avalanches mingled with the screech of the new sawmills, the crash of toppling timber, the rasp of saw and plane, the pounding of mallets, the incessant tap-tapping of a thousand hammers, the shrill altercations of embittered partners, the neighing of horses, the bleating of goats, and the howling of malemutes. Down the long mountain corridor through which the lake wound, the echoes of this dissonance resounded, rising in intensity as the days grew longer and as new hordes descended from the mountains to join the sweating multitude

345

along the shoreline. The very surface of the lake seemed to vibrate as sleds propelled by great square sails swept by in the teeth of the alpine gales, and dog-teams darted hither and thither across the slushy surface.

And now a stranger, plucked from familiar surroundings and dropped here without warning, might easily imagine himself in another world among a race of inhuman and half-savage creatures, for the boat-builders on the shores of Lake Bennett bore little resemblance to the clean-cut youths who had set off so lightly with their brand-new outfits the previous autumn. These were the men who had conquered the mountains; each had learned something from the ordeal. They had grown tattered beards to protect their faces from the elements, and they had smeared their skin with charcoal to prevent blistering sunburn, and they had fashioned slitted masks of wood to protect their eyes from snow-glare. The stiff new mining costumes in which they had been proudly, if awkwardly, photographed clung to them like a second skin, worn and faded, and patched neatly in a dozen places by unaccustomed hands. Almost all had lost weight; gaunt and paunchless now, with their coal-black, whiskered faces and their primitive eye-shields, they presented a weird and fearsome sight.

Their ordeal was not yet over. Facing each one was the supreme test of the stampede — the whipsawing of green logs into dressed lumber. Next to tracking up-stream, whipsawing was the cruellest toil of all, because its effects were mental as well as physical. All along the lakeshore the raised platforms known as "sawpits" became crucibles in which tempers boiled, sputtered, and exploded. Friendships that had withstood the strain of the terrible climb over the mountains snapped under the psychological tension of the jag-toothed whipsaw.

To produce the rough-dressed planks, the peeled logs were laid on top of scaffoldings (called sawpits) and a line was chalked down the sides. One man stood upon the platform and held the six-foot saw vertically against the end of the log while his partner beneath grasped the lower handle. Together they were supposed to guide it along the line for the full length of the log, but it demanded a superhuman faith for each to believe the other was doing his full share of the work.

The cutting was done on the downward stroke only. The man above guided the saw and pulled it up; and then the man below, watching the chalk line on the log, hauled it down again, letting its great hooked teeth bite into the green lumber. As he did this, he received a shower of sawdust in his eyes, and while he swore in his rage at the man above, he himself received a bitter tongue-lashing for hanging on too tightly.

This back-breaking work played out the strongest after a few hours and caused the end of hundreds of comradeships. No story of broken friendship is more heart-breaking than that of two bank clerks who came over the Chilkoot Pass that winter. They had been friends from childhood, had gone to school together and worked side by side in the same bank as youths. They became so inseparable that, rather than be parted from each other, they married sisters. Yet the whipsawing turned them into enemies so insensate that when they decided to divide their outfits, they insisted on cutting everything exactly in half. So bitter and obdurate was their enmity that, rather than divide twenty sacks of flour into two piles of ten sacks each, they persisted in sawing every sack in two. Then each set off with his twenty broken halves, the flour spilling away from the torn and useless containers.

2: *The Lion of the Yukon*

Down from his eyrie in the mountains to control the feverish throng on the lakes came Samuel Benfield Steele, the Mounted Police superintendent who was slowly gaining his reputation as "the Lion of the Yukon." Steele's entire career as well as his family heritage had fitted him perfectly for the job of controlling the swelling rabble preparing to assault the Klondike. His kinsmen for three generations had served king and country and helped make history in the trouble spots of Empire. One had been with Wolfe at the capture of Quebec. One had been with Nelson at Trafalgar. A third had died of wounds and exhaustion after Waterloo. Another had been the tallest soldier in the British army of occupation in Paris following Napoleon's final overthrow. Steele's father had been the midshipman who, from the decks of the British ship *Leopard,* fired the broadside that touched off the famous *Chesapeake* affair of 1807. Steele himself had been a militiaman since the age of fifteen, when he had done his part in repulsing the raids of the Fenians across the Upper Canadian border. As one of the original North West Mounted Policemen he had helped negotiate with Sitting Bull after the Custer massacre, policed the construction of the Canadian Pacific Railway, and led the pursuit of Big Bear during the Saskatchewan Rebellion. If ever a man was the prototype of the legendary Hollywood Mountie, it was he. His very name had a ring to it that was to make "Steele of the Mounted" a catchphrase. James Oliver Curwood borrowed it as a book title; and Steele's own character, thinly disguised, appears in various novels about the gold rush.

He was a big man of magnificent physique, tall, powerful, deep-chested, and massive-shouldered, "erect as a pine tree and limber as a cat," as a colleague once described him. He ran the stampede like a military manoeuvre, and it was due largely to his efforts, and those of his men, that there were so few tragedies along those routes the Mounties policed.

Because of Steele's iron rule, the knavery practised in Skagway was unknown on the Canadian side of the mountains, and it was said, truthfully, that a miner could lay a sack of nuggets on the trail and return in two weeks to find it untouched. One day a man sent up to manage one of the Dawson banks confided to Steele that he was afraid for the safety of the bank-notes entrusted to his care, whereupon the policeman took the package and shoved it carelessly under his own bunk, where, he assured the uneasy banker, it would be quite safe.

On rare occasions one or another of Soapy Smith's Skagway gang tried without success to cross the border and operate in Canadian territory. A member of the gang walked into the police post on the White Pass summit in the early spring and asked what was needed to enter the Canadian Yukon. The constable on duty replied that a year's outfit was required.

"Well, supposing I don't want to comply with your regulations," the con man said. "Suppose I decide to shoot my way into the country — what then?"

The constable opened a drawer in his desk, pulled out a pistol, and laid it down.

"There's a gun," he said. "Go ahead and start shooting. That's the easiest way to find out what will happen."

The visitor retreated to Skagway.

One evening in May, Steele himself was sitting in his headquarters cabin on Lake Bennett when he heard two shots ring out.

"Sergeant," Steele snapped, "go out and see what that was and report."

The sergeant returned to say that an American claimed to have been cleaning his gun when it went off accidentally. He added that he thought it was one of Soapy Smith's men.

"Arrest him, lock him up, and go through his things," Steele ordered.

The police quickly found a complete thimblerig outfit and some marked monte cards. One of the detachment identified him as a member of the Smith gang.

The culprit was very indignant. "I'm an American citizen," he told Steele. "I'll have you know you can't lock up a United States citizen and get away with it. My God, sir! The Secretary of State himself shall hear about it!"

"Well," said Steele, "seeing you're an American citizen, I'll be very lenient. I'll confiscate everything you have and give you half an hour to leave town."

The man's jaw dropped, but before he could say a word the sergeant rapped out a "Right wheel" and he was marched from the room and straight up the trail twenty-two miles to the summit with a redcoat at his heels all the way telling him to "step lively."

It was Steele who enforced the order that no man could cross the border without a year's supply of food. Undoubtedly this helped save the country from the kind of famine that had threatened Dawson the previous fall. At the lakes he instituted another rule: every boat must carry a serial number painted on the bow. Steele's men went from boat to boat recording the numbers, the names of the occupants, and the addresses of their next of kin. These lists were sent to police posts strung out along the river; if a boat failed to check in at each post within a reasonable time, the Mounties went searching for it. As a result of this foresight an undisciplined armada of more than seven thousand boats was safely convoyed through some five hundred miles of unknown water.

As the boat-builders worked away on the shores of the mountain lakes, Steele's men moved among them, advising on methods of construction and urging the amateur carpenters to "build strong — don't start out in a floating coffin." They settled disputes, helped recalcitrant partners divide their outfits, acted as general administrators and settled the estates of those who died, selling those effects which were not worth shipping home and dispatching the funds to the next of kin. And when real estate speculators tried to seize the land around the lakes and charge the stampeders a fee for its use, the police sent them packing.

They were all gallant young men, these constables with the neat, aquiline profiles and soft accents that hinted at their background. The large majority were Englishmen, younger sons of well-to-do families, seeking adventure and service in the outposts of Empire. They seldom raised their voices, almost never drew a gun, and rarely had to give an order twice. Their chivalry is attested to by the incident of a honeymoon couple crossing the White Pass that spring in search of gold. Their outfits had been taken ahead by pack train, and they were carrying only a small valise with no change of clothing when they suddenly crashed through the melting shore-ice of the lake. A Mountie NCO appeared at once and placed his tent and wardrobe at the disposal of the drenched and shivering bride, who rode into Bennett dressed in scarlet jacket and yellow-striped breeches.

By late spring the Mounted Police had collected one hundred and fifty thousand dollars in customs duties and Steele was faced with the problem of transporting this sum through the lawless American territory under the noses of the Soapy Smith gang. Inspector Zachary

Taylor Wood, a grandson of a former U.S. president, was chosen for the job. To allay suspicion Steele spread the story that Wood was being transferred back to the prairies and was taking only baggage and boatmen. Actually the policeman's kit bags were stuffed with gold and bank-notes and were so heavy that it took several men to lug each one. Steele dared not risk sending Wood down the White Pass and through the town of Skagway; instead, he dispatched him on a more circuitous route — over the Chilkoot to Dyea and thence by boat to Skagway, where the steamer *Tartar* was waiting to take him to Victoria.

Halfway across the bay between the two ports, Wood's boat was attacked by another loaded with thugs who tried to ram him. Wood held them off at gunpoint until he reached the dock. At the wharfside he could see a dapper group of men and at their head a slender figure with a neat black beard. It was Smith himself.

The scene was a tense one. Ringed around the gangway was a group of sailors brandishing loaded rifles, placed on guard by the captain of the *Tartar*, who had steam up and was ready to push off. Only a few feet away stood Smith and his men with pistols under their coats. Then, as Wood's embattled craft touched the dock, Smith broke the tension. He sauntered easily across to Wood, with a smile of greeting.

"Why not hang around and visit Skagway for a while?" he invited.

The policeman gave him a wry smile in return and politely declined. A few minutes later he was safely on his way to Victoria, and Smith returned to easier pickings along the boardwalks of his little kingdom.

352

3: *The outlandish armada*

Spring had come, but the ice on the lakes still held. The purple pasqueflower poked its hairy stem above the snow, and the snow melted around it. Water gurgled beneath the mosses, ran in torrents between the rocks, and tumbled in lacy cascades from the peaks above. The sun shone on the glistening hills on the carpets of wild flowers that sprang up: on the little mountain forget-me-nots, the pink snakeweed, the Dutchman's breeches, and the delicate blue harebells, on the wild bleeding-hearts, the white alpine geranium, the twin-flowers, and the mauve shooting-stars. The sparrows were back and so were the robins, and in the sky the geese were honking north. Bears, hungry from their winter's fast, lumbered along the snowline, and occasionally a bull moose plunged through the thickets. Suddenly the world was warm again and drenched with sunlight and vibrant with colour, from the reds of the rust-stained mountains to the pure greens of the water that showed through the melting ice.

On the rotting surface of the lake a furry layer of slush grew thickly, and as water formed along the bank a hedgerow of boats and scows, four or five deep, encircled the shores of Bennett. On its margin the boat-builders sat, and smoked their pipes, and waited.

On May 29, with a creak and a rumble, the ice began to move in the lower lakes and the great boat-race was on. During that first day eight hundred craft set sail for the Klondike, with every man bending to the oars in an attempt to maintain a lead on those behind. One or two who looked back espied a solitary figure standing on a small hill behind the police post. It was Sam Steele, watching his brood depart, like a mother hen. The policeman's brow was creased with worry, for he knew

353

that the boatmen had no more experience with river navigation than they had in boat-building.

Within forty-eight hours all the lakes were clear of ice and the whole freakish flotilla of 7,124 boats loaded with thirty million pounds of solid food was in motion. Out onto the mint-green water the ungainly armada lazily drifted. Then as a slender breeze rippled down the mountain passageway and caught the sails, a tremor of excitement could be felt in each man's heart as it quickened with the speed of his craft. Off they sailed like miniature galleons, seeking the treasure that lay beyond the horizon's rim, the most bizarre fleet ever to navigate fresh water. Here were twenty-ton scows crammed with oxen, horses, and dogs, one-man rafts made of three logs hastily bound together, light Peterborough canoes packed over the passes on men's shoulders, and strange oblong vessels that looked like — and sometimes were — floating packing-boxes. Here were slim bateaux brought in sections from the Outside and canoes made from hollow logs with sticks for oarlocks and paddles hand-whittled from tree trunks. Here were skiffs and cockleshells, outriggers and junks, catamarans and kayaks, arks and catboats and wherries. Here were boats with wedge bottoms, and boats with flat bottoms, and boats with curved bottoms; boats shaped like triangles and boats shaped like circles; boats that looked like coffins, and boats that were coffins. Here were enormous rafts with hay and horses aboard, propelled by mighty sweeps; and here were others built from a single log with only a mackinaw coat for a sail. Here was a craft modelled after a Mississippi side-wheeler with two side-wheels operated by hand cranks, twisting and turning awkwardly in a zigzag movement down the lake. And here was a boat with two women who had sewn their undergarments together and suspended them between a pair of oars to make a sail.

354

From each mast fluttered a makeshift flag, usually a bandanna or a towel, and on each bow was daubed the name of a wife, a sweetheart, a home town, a good-luck slogan, or a memory — *Yellow Garter, Seven-Come-Eleven, San Francisco, Golden Horseshoe.*

The setting of this odyssey was Olympian. The mountains, their tops still frosted, turned to an azure blue in the summer's haze and were perfectly reflected in the shimmering glacial waters. As the bright sub-Arctic evening fell, the breeze dropped, the sails went limp, and every boat drifted to a stop. The sun was still high in the skies and, softened by the haze, seemed to bathe the water in a golden mist. Now a feeling of strange contentment spread across the argonauts as each man settled back in the stern of his vessel and, often for the first time, contemplated the scene around him. This was a sight that no man had seen before: thousands of boats becalmed on the blue-green waters of a mountain lake. No man would ever see it again. For a moment the race for the gold-fields was lulled as each contestant, thinking back to the toil on the passes and the strain in the sawpits, to the furies that had possessed him on the trail and the despairs that had seized him on the slopes — thinking back to all the wild fancies and snares and sophistries to which he had fallen prey — realized that the worst was behind him at last. Few made any attempt to move on that first night. One or two broke into song and were joined by others until, in the larger boats and scows, quartets could be heard carolling in harmony. The Klondike was still five hundred miles distant, but, as all could see, it was a boat-ride all the way.

But the following morning the race was renewed; the flotilla lost its bunched-up character, and within a few days the entire lake-and-river system from Bennett to Dawson was alive with boats. Soon the passage was

355

marked with those small human dramas that had become a feature of the stampede and which, in retrospect, have the ring of a dime novel about them. On Lake Bennett a sudden squall sprang up and drove a heavily laden scow onto a rock. There were three people aboard: Mrs. Mabel Long of California, her new husband, and a young man named Rossburg whom the couple had picked up the week before. Mrs. Long was eighteen years old and had been married six months earlier, much against her will but on her parents' insistence, to a man twenty years her senior. As the vessel struck the rock, she was flung into the water while her husband stood panic-stricken in the boat, wringing his hands and calling for help. Rossburg jumped overboard at once, swam to the drowning woman, and dragged her onto a sand-bar. When the scow drifted over, Mrs. Long announced that she was leaving her spouse forever. In the confusion she and Rossburg escaped and fled downstream with the estranged husband in hot but vain pursuit. Eventually she obtained a divorce and married her young rescuer, who, in the best tradition of nineteenth-century fiction, turned out to be the heir to a Boston fortune.

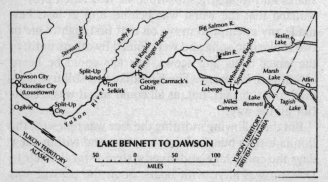

LAKE BENNETT TO DAWSON

4: *Split-Up City*

On leaving the mountain lakes, each boat had to run the gantlet of Miles Canyon and the rapids beyond it before the river proper could be reached. All had heard of this canyon, but few knew exactly where it was until, at a turn in the river, they saw a piece of red calico and then a board upon whose rough surface the single word "CANNON" had been scrawled. Suddenly, dinning into their ears, came the roar of tumbling waters beyond.

And there before them lay the gorge, a narrow cleft in a wall of black basalt with an unholy whirlpool at its centre. Beyond this dark fissure lurked two sets of rapids: the Squaw Rapids, where the river raced over a series of jutting rocks; and the White Horse Rapids, so called because the foam upon them resembled white steeds leaping and dancing in the sunlight.

As the river descended into the canyon it narrowed to one third of its size, so that the water was forced to a crest four feet high. From this funnel of foam, small geysers erupted, and the boats sweeping between the rock walls were forced to teeter precariously upon it, as on a tightrope, while the helmsmen tried to veer around the obstacles that blocked the way — the huge intertwining drifts of timber, the jagged reefs of boulders and sand-bars, the twisted roots of trees, and the sharp little rock teeth that tore the bottoms from the scows and barges.

Schwatka, the military explorer of the Yukon, who had passed this way fifteen years before, called it "a diminutive Fingal's Cave . . . resembling a deep black thoroughfare paved with the whitest of marble." The walls rose a sheer hundred feet from the foaming crest, and the whirlpool in the centre was so swift and fierce that in the spring of 1895 two Swedes, carried into the

357

canyon by accident, were spun for six hours in a dizzying circle before escaping from the trap. But this was by no means the end of the hazard, for, after broadening out to form the whirlpool, the canyon narrowed again to a mere thirty feet, so that the water spurted from it into the Squaw Rapids as though it were gushing from a hydrant.

Into the gloomy gorge the first stampeders plunged, almost without stopping, for they were at the head of the fleet and eager to maintain their positions. Most had never handled a boat before, but this did not deter them. Indeed, one lonely and melancholy Englishman made the entire five-mile journey without realizing he was in danger. But others, in spite of their bravado, were less fortunate and shared the fate of the Norwegian who went through aboard a great bateau, calmly playing on a music box, only to be swamped by a wave. In the first few days one hundred and fifty boats like his were wrecked and five men drowned, so that those behind hesitated to chance the surly waters and hung back until several thousand craft were crowded together at the bottleneck of the canyon in a bewildering traffic jam. At this point Sam Steele appeared upon the scene.

When the Mountie arrived, the banks along the canyon and the rapids presented a picture of indescribable chaos. At the head of the gorge was a disordered throng of men, some erecting tents, others sitting glumly on the bank staring at the frothing waters, and all trying to decide whether to attempt the canyon or whether once more to shoulder their packs and shuttle their ton of goods around it. Five miles away at the far end was another dishevelled and demoralized mass of people. Many had lost their entire outfits, others had lost portions; large numbers were crying and wringing their hands in despair while their goods and chattels,

358

stretched across the shattered bottoms of their upturned boats, lay drying in the summer sun. Thomas Lippy of Eldorado was one of these; his scow had been shattered in the rapids, which were no respecters of wealth.

Through the mob the policeman's giant and strangely comforting figure made its way. They gathered about him like errant children, and when he had their attention Steele spoke:

"There are many of your countrymen who have said that the Mounted Police make the laws as they go along, and I am going to do so now, for your own good. Therefore the directions that I give shall be carried out strictly, and they are these: Corporal Dixon, who thoroughly understands this work, will be in charge here and be responsible to me for the proper management of the passage of the canyon and the rapids. No women or children will be taken in the boats; if they are strong enough to come to the Klondike, they can walk the five miles of grassy bank to the foot of the White Horse, and there is no danger for them here. No boat will be permitted to go through the canyon until the corporal is satisfied that it has sufficient freeboard to enable it to ride the waves in safety. No boat will be allowed to pass with human beings in it unless it is steered by competent men, and of that the corporal will be judge. . . ."

Steele announced a fine of one hundred dollars for anyone who broke these rules, and as a result of his strict measures the wrecks in the canyon virtually ceased. Meanwhile, an enterprising young man named Norman Macaulay was building a tramway with wooden rails and horse-drawn cars around the rapids. When it was completed, he made a small fortune charging twenty-five dollars to take a boat and outfit beyond the fast water. The Yukon River had become as safe as a millpond. In all that vast army of thirty thousand that floated down to Dawson that year, only twenty-three were drowned, thanks to the ministrations of the Mounties who shepherded the stampeders from checkpoint to checkpoint all along the way.

By mid-June small steamers were being convoyed through the gorge. Captain Goddard, having assembled one of the little steamboats that he and his wife brought across the mountains, determined to take it through under its own power. His passengers included two singing sisters named Polly and Lottie Oatley, who were later to make their names in Dawson, and Coatless Curly Munro, Harry Ash's partner, who had been sent out the previous fall to bring in a bevy of beauties for the Northern Saloon. Goddard ordered his passengers ashore and then sent the snub-nosed steamer into the teeth of the combers. In the heart of the canyon, soaking wet from the waves that crashed into the pilothouse, the wiry little captain looked back over his shoulder and saw to his astonishment that Munro, who was as curious as he was coatless, had sneaked back on board, lashed himself to the ship with a three-inch line, and was boldly riding out the passage.

The swift journey down the Yukon to Dawson now took on all the elements of a race. Two large boats contained the personnel, equipment, and hard cash of two leading Canadian banks — the Bank of Commerce and the Bank of British North America — and each was eager to be the first to obtain the bulk of the mining business. Two more contained the printing-presses and staffs of two would-be Klondike newspapers, one of them to be named the *Klondike Nugget,* the other the *Midnight Sun.* The *Sun* published along the way under various names; the *Nugget*'s bright-eyed proprietor, a bundle of nervous energy named Gene Allen, had left his own boat and press far in the rear, racing on over the ice by dog-team in an effort to be in town, even without

360

equipment, before his rivals. A variety of other boats contained perishables and luxuries which the owners hoped to sell at sky-high prices to the starving and isolated camp. Thirty or forty were loaded with eggs; several more with recent newspapers; one contained fifteen hundred pairs of boots, another was stocked with tinned milk, and a third carried a case of live chickens which the owner had managed to pack intact across the Chilkoot. One man had a scow-load of cats and kittens, a cargo that puzzled most of the stampeders. Signor R. J. Gandolfo, an Italian fruit merchant, had sixteen thousand pounds of candy, oranges, lemons, bananas, and cucumbers. H. L. Miller had a milking cow aboard a barge and was determined that it should be the first in Dawson. Mike Bartlett, a famous packer on the Chilkoot, moved his entire outfit downriver aboard a series of scows fifty feet long, each laden with twenty tons of grain and provisions.

E. A. Hegg, the Swedish-born photographer from Bellingham Bay, Washington, who had moved his portable darkroom across the passes on a goat-drawn sled, was now in the forefront of the race. Hegg travelled in a poling boat which bore the legend VIEWS OF THE KLONDIKE ROUTE. He had photographed the weary climb up the Chilkoot and the tent town of Bennett. He had photographed the flotilla as it set off across the lake. He had photographed the scenes at the canyon and the rapids. Now, as the river broadened and the armada began to come apart, he continued to record the sweep and grandeur of the stampede: a raft crammed with men and animals moored in an eddy, a flag dropping from its mast; a stern-wheeler being guided through Five Finger Rapids by a scow; and the serene face of the river, still shining brightly at midnight when the sun had dipped briefly below the placid hills. Such photographs would make Hegg immortal, but in July of

1898, his floating darkroom was just another dot on the muddy surface of the Yukon.

Below the rapids, for hundreds of miles, the swift-flowing waters were speckled with boats. There were half a dozen to be seen around every bend, from Bennett to Dawson City. In the broad, terraced valley of the Yukon, once so silent, empty, and unknown, a man was never free of the sight of his fellows. All along the banks were camped the Stick Indians, dirty, ragged, and sick-looking, smoking salmon and offering to buy or sell everything and anything from those who floated by. They traded like Arabs, and the cry "How muchee? How muchee?" rang through the low blue hills.

The early spring flowers had given way in June to bluebells and lupins, which ran in violet drifts across the high tableland. The perfume of brier rose was carried across the valleys by the hot summer breezes. Among the rocks and mosses the wild fruit was ripening — clusters of currants, scarlet and glossy black, acres of raspberries and cranberries, and, in the open headland, the creeping vines of blueberries. But by midsummer much of this lotus land lay under a pall of yellow smoke, for the stampeders had left their campfires smouldering, and these touched off raging blazes in the tinder-dry woods until it seemed as if the entire countryside was aflame.

The boats, on leaving the rapids, whisked down that section of the Yukon river system which is called the Lewes, and then, after checking in at the Lake Laberge police post, hoisted their sails once more to let the wind sweep them down thirty miles of ice-choked water. The lake, in its turn, led into the twisting Thirtymile, a swift, clear stream of beautiful blue, but so treacherous that it was lined with wrecks for all of its brief length; on July 8 the remains of nineteen boats were counted on a single rock in the main channel.

There were no further obstacles of importance. Five Finger Rapids looked formidable, but few found them really troublesome. Here the river took the shape of an outstretched hand, pointing towards the gold-fields, the five fingers of water frothing between four knuckles of conglomerate rock. The Mounties, who were on the spot as usual to counsel and to caution, warned each boat to follow the right-hand channel, where a swift whirlpool appeared to dash the craft against the rock but at the last moment spun each one about and into the clear. There were few who had time to notice the small cabin perched on the left bank of the river, but some of those who tarried could still discern the name G. W. Carmack on the door.

As the main fleet slipped down the river it was joined, or preceded, by smaller flotillas. Men frozen in for the winter along the upper Yukon were on the move, and, indeed, in the very vanguard of the race. Some had made boats out of their sleds, and one youth was seen sitting on his Yukon sled with his dogs around him, having lashed two logs to the sides to serve as floats. A contingent of about one hundred and fifty boats moved directly behind the crumbling ice, long before the upper lakes gave way. These included the government party under the new Commissioner of the Yukon, J. M. Walsh, the fifty-four-year-old ex-Mountie who had been frozen in at Big Salmon all winter and who was now heading for Dawson post-haste to take over his duties as virtual dictator of the Klondike district.

Other boats poured down from the Teslin River loaded with men who had successfully negotiated the Stikine and Ashcroft trails, while some others slipped down the Pelly and the Stewart, bringing a remnant of the stampeders who had come overland from British Columbia and Edmonton. Like the rivers that fed the

Yukon, these small human tributaries nourished the main stream of the stampede.

Twilight and darkness had been banished by the sun, which dropped below the horizon shortly before midnight, to rise again around two o'clock each morning. At the peak of the day the temperature rose to the nineties, and the merciless light beat harshly on the blistered faces of the boatmen. In the steaming forests, mosquitoes, gnats, and blackflies buzzed and hummed in clouds as thick as wood smoke, driving the newcomers to a state of near-dementia. Without the protective covering of a fine-meshed net, sleep was impossible. The mosquitoes were so fat that they seemed more like blowflies, and if a man as much as opened his mouth, he sucked in a horde of insects.

Now the tensions which had subsided momentarily on the calm lakes sprang up again, and bitter feuds arose once more between comrades who had survived previous estrangements. It was as if, with the goal in sight at last, each man was intent on casting off his friends and seeking his fortune in splendid isolation. George T. Moir, a young telegrapher from Stratford, Ontario, who passed down the river with the main flotilla, summed up the situation when he wrote that "brother fought brother and father fought son, and the spirit of forbearance and forgiveness was not known on the trail of land and water into Dawson."

A man sitting in a boat and watching the banks roll past him like a moving scrollwork could watch in fascination the little human scenes which, like brief tableaux, illuminated and punctuated this final chapter in the movement north:

— Two men caught on the rocks in the middle of the Thirtymile River and, oblivious of their surroundings, fighting with their fists in white-hot anger;

— Two more, on a lonely beach not far from the mouth of the Teslin, solemnly sawing their boat down the middle;

— Ten men at Big Salmon dividing everything up ten ways onto ten blankets, including an enormous scow, which was torn up to build ten smaller scows so that each could go his separate way in peace.

Once again the Mounties were called in to arbitrate these disputes. Two men tried to divide up a single skillet and, this being impossible, were at each other's throats until a policeman arrived and solved the situation by tossing the implement into the river, to the satisfaction of both. Sometimes, however, arbitration was out of the question. Inspector Cortlandt Starnes listened for an entire day while six ministers of the gospel, who had formed themselves into a mining company, tried to unform themselves again. The policeman finally threw up his hands in despair and reported that each of the reverend gentlemen had accused all the other reverend gentlemen of telling un-Christian falsehoods.

The names along the river attested to the bitterness which was engendered in these last few miles before the gold-fields. There were a Split-Up Island and a Split-Up City on the Yukon that summer. The former was at the mouth of the Pelly, and here boat after boat put ashore to allow partners to divide up their goods and find new partners. There were so many men on this island that they picked a "mayor," a man from Worcester, Massachusetts. He wore a red oilcloth heart sewed into the seat of his pants as a mark of good will, so that he could be identified as adjudicator when he stepped between two angry associates tearing up a tent or cleaving a stove in two.

Split-Up City lay at the mouth of the Stewart River, where the Yukon splays out into a confusing tangle of

365

channels and islands and where a boat can be lost for hours or even days. The selection of the wrong channel led to endless recriminations, and the halves of boats lying all along this section of the river were mute evidence of a common disenchantment.

From this point it was only a few hours' run to the Klondike. Eagerly the stampeders pushed on, travelling without sleep during nights as bright as the days, the tension rising as the miles ticked by until every man was taut as a watch-spring. Each boat kept close to the right bank in case, by error, it should be swept right past the city, for no one knew quite where the city was.

Then at last each in turn swung around a rocky bluff and saw spread before him a sight he would remember all his life. Roaring into the Yukon from the right was the Klondike River, of which he had heard so much. Beyond the river rose a tapering mountain with the great scar of a slide slashed across its face. And at its feet, spilling into the surrounding hills and along the swampy flats and between the trees and across the junction of the two rivers, were thousands of tents, shacks, cabins, caches, warehouses, half-erected hotels, false-faced saloons, screeching sawmills, markets, shops, and houses of pleasure. Here, in the midst of the encroaching wilderness, a thousand miles from nowhere, was a burgeoning metropolis. It seemed a little unreal, shimmering in the June heat, bathed in a halo of sunlight, blurred slightly at the edges by the mists that steamed from the marshes. The stampeders caught their breath, half expecting the whole phantom community to vanish as in a dream. This was the goal they had set themselves; this was the finish of the long trail north; this was where the rainbow had its end. They turned their boats towards the shore — a shore already thickly hedged by scores of other craft — and they

366

debarked, still in a daze, yet inwardly exultant at having, after long vicissitude and much remorse and no little disillusion, set foot upon the threshold of the golden city.

Chapter Ten

1
"Cheechako!"

2
Carnival summer

3
Champagne for breakfast

4
Remember the Sabbath . . .

5
Graft and the Nugget

1 *"Cheechako!"*

Dawson was waiting — for what it did not quite know.

From those few dog-drivers who had pierced the winter wall of isolation, the townspeople had heard tantalizing tales of an army of gold-seekers camped on the upper lakes. Everyone sensed that the stampede was reaching some sort of climax; none realized the dimensions of the human torrent.

The spring was unseasonably hot. The sun shone eighteen hours out of the twenty-four, and in the afternoons the temperature rose to one hundred and ten degrees. The snow vanished from the mountains at an alarming rate, and a dense sub-tropical growth sprang up along the hillsides. Through the leafy woods the sound of gurgling water came rippling. Frothing little streams bubbled where no streams had been visible before; small cataracts tumbled from the clifftops; and far back in the mountains the tributary creeks broke their fetters and ran black between ragged lines of shore ice. On Bonanza and Eldorado, sweating men dammed the unleashed waters and guided them into flumes and sluiceboxes, and began to shovel the paydirt from the winter's dump into the foaming current. As the water did its work and the dross gravel and mud was swept off down the valley, the greenish glitter of fine gold could be seen caught in the cross-riffles at the bottom of the long, slender boxes.

By May, nature was at work filling up the great Yukon River as if with a thousand pumps. Dark spots appeared on its still frozen surface. And then, on May 6, the great ice mass was gradually forced upward at the centre by hydraulic pressure until it resembled the crown of a road. The water drained off the middle of the slushy surface to the shorelines, where it flowed in channels above the ice. Now the Indians recalled that these flats had been flooded one spring twenty years before, and that they had paddled their canoes across the very spot where the new dance halls were being erected. Everyone saw by this time that Dawson had been built in the wrong place; yet how could it have been built elsewhere? After all, it was built where the gold was.

Constantine came up from Fortymile and walked the riverbank all night, watching the ice rising stealthily, his brow creased with worry. Just as Steele felt himself the protector of the stampeders, so Constantine, in an inexplicable way, felt himself the guardian of the gold camp. Already a wave of panic was sweeping over the community; a bad flood could sweep the city from its precarious position and send horses, tents, dogs, and men hurtling down the ice-choked river.

The water rose to within two feet of the top of the bank, so that Constantine could dip the toe of his polished boot into it. Then, on May 8 at four a.m., there came a crackling roar; the ice, weakened by the shore connection, was forced into motion at the centre by the current beneath. It split asunder, and slowly and smoothly the entire mass started on its long journey towards the Bering Sea. Faster and faster the ice seemed to move until jagged lines like glacial crevasses appeared in the surface. The swift current, catching the ice masses, whirled them about so that they ground into each other; and the black water boiled up from below, spurting in dark fountains between the heaving blocks.

The river was a hissing mass of ice. In the narrow curves the grime-encrusted cakes were squeezed out of the channel and flung high onto the shore. Scenes of natural carnage followed as the banks along Front Street were piled high with mounds of broken ice and snow, covered in muck and gravel, some of the individual pieces higher than a man. As the townspeople

371

watched in horror and fascination, the river crept upward towards the bank.

There was no time for panic, for even as the water started to spill into the city the cry *"Cheechako!"* went ringing through the hills. The first boat had already arrived, amid the ice blocks still running in the river. With the water lapping at their boots, several hundreds trotted along the bank, following the craft for about a mile before it could be beached. There were five men with dogs and sleds aboard; but, as it turned out, they were from the Stewart River coun-try a scant hundred miles away, and had no news at all. Disappointed, the crowd melted away.

A second cry went up. In between the ice cakes slid a green Peterborough canoe, and again the whole town rallied to the waterfront. The new arrivals were also old-timers, but they had actually been at Bennett earlier that winter. They had dragged their canoe on sleds down the frozen Yukon until the ice broke, then floated down with it, and now for the expectant throng on the riverbank they painted a verbal picture of thousands of men camped as close to Dawson as Lake Laberge, waiting for the ice to break and hoping to steal a march on the main body of stampeders.

A few more boats arrived, and then a lull followed. The ice had jammed at the mouth of the Pelly, stopping all movement.

All during the month of May, while the water rose slowly upon the town, boats in twos and threes slipped in from various wintering-points between Bennett and Dawson. But, as everybody knew, the main onrush was yet to come. Arriving from his camp on the upper Yukon, the new Commissioner of the Yukon, J. M. Walsh, told the excited town that the police at Tagish had already checked three thousand boats, and more were pouring through every hour.

372

A few hardy souls bent on winning the race to the Klondike had sledded their outfits down the river before the break-up. Few of these intended to stake claims; they brought eggs, which were worth as much as gold. A Seattle entrepreneur who reached Dawson City with two hundred dozen eggs disposed of them all in less than an hour for thirty-six hundred dollars. He had neglected to include a newspaper, which would have increased his profits, but he consented to give verbal news: war had been declared on Spain, he said, and the cruiser *New York* had reduced the fortifications of Havana to rubble within three hours. A second arrival, who also offered eggs, denied this story flatly: he insisted the Spaniards were winning the war. He, too, sold his eggs, but the price had already dropped to fourteen dollars a dozen. Within a week so many boats had tied up loaded with eggs that the price was reduced to three dollars. But when one man drifted in with an ancient newspaper soaked in bacon grease he was able to sell it for fifteen.

More boats trickled in. The man with the boots arrived and sold all fifteen hundred pairs at fifteen dollars a pair, which was twice what he paid for them in Montreal. The man with the load of tinned milk was paid a dollar a tin for it. Another made a clear profit of five thousand dollars on women's hats and dresses. The man who had struggled over the Chilkoot with a crate of live chickens set them up in a box at the police barracks, and a crowd gathered to watch the first egg laid that year in Dawson. It sold for five dollars before the hen had finished cackling. The man who dragged a grindstone over the pass set to work sharpening miners' picks for an ounce of gold per pick. The newsboy who lugged a pack of papers across the mountains was able to return home, his passage paid and two hundred and fifty dollars in his wallet. The man who brought in the scow-load of kittens confounded the scoffers by getting an ounce of gold per kitten from lonely miners craving the companionship of a pet. But Frank Cushing of Buffalo, who had planned to sell cheap mosquito lotion at ten dollars a bottle, arrived empty-handed. He had tested a sample on himself while floating down the Yukon; it had certainly discouraged the mosquitoes, but had raised such painful skin blisters that he had thrown the entire consignment of ten thousand bottles into the boiling river.

Gene Allen, the gimlet-eyed newspaper editor, arrived in town over the ice, stubbornly determined to produce his paper ahead of his rivals. Having no printing-press, he launched it as a bulletin. The *Klondike Nugget* appeared on May 27, typed on a machine borrowed from the correspondent of *The New York Times*. Thus, though the *Midnight Sun* was to be the first to get its printing-press into operation, Allen was always able to say that he had launched the first newspaper in the Klondike. Not far away, in a log shack with a canvas roof, E. A. Hegg opened a studio and continued his remarkable photographic record of the stampede.

The day after the *Nugget* was published, most of Dawson's business section found itself under five feet of water, with the cabins near the river already afloat and the townspeople fleeing into the hills. It was impossible to move about except by boat, and passengers were being rowed along Front Street at fifty cents a head, the main point of attraction being the *Nugget*'s bulletin board, now in the centre of a muddy, swirling channel. The town, however, did not float away. The water subsided on June 5, leaving behind an ocean of mud so deep that horses could not move in the main street.

A calm of expectancy hung over the community as Dawson waited for the human flood to engulf it. A day passed; two days, and no sign yet of the great flotilla from Lake Bennett.

Then, suddenly, on June 8, the river came alive with boats. They poured in day and night like a parade, without a break, the men tumbling from them as soon as they touched shore and spraying out into the mud-filled streets. Soon there was no space along the shoreline, and newer arrivals had to tie their boats to other boats and leap from craft to craft to reach the bank, until the boats were six deep for nearly two miles, and Dawson's waterfront resembled a Cantonese seaport.

On the same day that the first wave of small boats struck Dawson, the first steamboat arrived from the opposite direction. She had been spotted from the hill-tops, a flyspeck on the grey water. Across the town, at four in the morning, rang the long-awaited cry: "Steeeeamboat!" and thousands, roused from their beds, raced to the waterfront in the early sunshine to greet the vessel. Bets were laid as to whether she would turn out to be the *Bella* or the *Weare,* the last boats out of town the previous fall. To the surprise of all, she was the diminutive *May West.*

By the time the little boat puffed into the bank, there were five thousand men and women crowded together to welcome her with cheers and rifle-fire.

"Has she whiskey aboard?" came the cry. She had indeed: sixteen barrels. It went on sale at once in the bars at a dollar a drink.

Five days later the first steamboat to navigate the upper Yukon chugged in: the tiny little *Bellingham,* scarcely big enough to bear the title, only eight feet wide and thirty-five feet long, packed piecemeal over the mountains. Captain Goddard's larger steamer was ten days behind her. His trip was so successful, establishing as it did a steamboat link between the gold-fields and the Pacific coast, that the merchants of Skagway tendered him a civic banquet on his return and carried him through the streets on their shoulders.

Meanwhile, a late edition of the Seattle *Post-Intelligencer* had been brought in, and a struggle ensued for its ownership. The two local papers bid for it, but a miner from Hunker Creek secured it for fifty dollars. He paid "Judge" John F. Miller, a lawyer who later became mayor of Seattle and a U.S. congressman, to read it aloud in the Pioneers' Hall. A crowd followed Miller down the street as he tantalized them with snatches from the headlines. To hear the news of Dewey's victory at Manila and the annihilation of the Spanish fleet, hundreds cheerfully paid a dollar each; the affair was so profitable that it was repeated the following day.

And still the boats kept coming. H. L. Miller floated into town with his cow on June 29 and achieved his ambition to be the first man to sell fresh milk in the Klondike at thirty dollars a gallon. Forever afterward he bore the nickname of "Cow" Miller. Tom Chisholm, the expansive and florid owner of the Aurora Saloon, managed to get some of the milk to sell over his bar at five dollars a mugful, just five times the price of whiskey.

Day after day for more than a month the international parade of boats continued. They brought hay and horses, goats and cattle, kittens and mastiffs, roosters and oxen. They brought sundowners, shantymen, sodbusters and shellbacks, buckaroos and bluenoses, *vaqueros* and *maquereaus,* creoles and métis, Gaels, Kanakas, Afrikaners, and Suvanese. They brought wife-beaters, lady-killers, cuckolded husbands, disbarred lawyers, dance-hall beauties, escaped convicts, remittance men, card-sharps *Hausfraus,* Salvation Army lasses, ex-buffalo-hunters, scullions, surgeons, ecclesiastics, gunfighters, sob sisters, soldiers of fortune, and Oxford dons. They brought men seeking gold and men seeking adventure and men seeking power. But more than anything they brought men seeking escape — escape from a nagging wife, or an overpowering mother-in-law, or a bill-collector, or a deflowered virgin, or, perhaps, simple escape from the drabness of the un-gay nineties.

Each man, whoever he was, brought along his tent, long since worn ragged by the elements, and these sprouted everywhere, crowding along the black muck of the waterfront, overflowing across the swamp, spilling into Lousetown on the south side of the Klondike or onto the shoreline opposite Dawson on the west side of the Yukon. They blossomed out on the slopes and hilltops and benches that overlooked the town, and they straggled by the hundreds along the trails that led to the gold creeks. From the top of the Midnight Dome, Dawson that spring seemed to be a field of billowing white, like a vast orchard in bloom.

Half a dozen canvas cities — Bennett, Lindemann, Sheep Camp, Dyea, Tagish, and Teslin — had simply been packed up and transferred to Dawson, and the same feverish scenes which had marked each one were here re-enacted on a grander scale. Sawmills screeched incessantly; hammers and saws pounded and rasped through the bright night; planks, rough timber, ladders, and sawhorses encumbered the thoroughfares; mountains of logs and piles of freshly sawed lumber grew everywhere. Dawson was a city of sawdust and stumps and the skeletons of fast-rising buildings, its main street a river of mud through which horses, whipped on by clamouring men, floundered and kicked. In between these threshing beasts moved a sluggish stream of humanity. They trudged up to their calves in the slime, or they negotiated the duck-boards that were thrown across the black morass, or they shambled in a steady flow along the high boardwalk that was mounted on one side of the street.

This wretched, swampy land was prohibitively expensive. Building-lots were fetching as much as forty thousand dollars. The cheapest single room on the far edge of town rented for a hundred a month, while log cabins in good locations were bringing up to four hundred. Along the waterfront, the government was leasing property for twelve dollars per front foot per month. Signor Gandolfo, the Italian merchant, managed to secure for his fruit stand a slender space just five feet square for which he was happy to pay a monthly one hundred and twenty dollars. A four-room apartment in New York City could have been leased for two years for exactly the same amount, but then the value of money in the two cities was hardly comparable. In New York two baskets of tomatoes could be had for a nickel. At Gandolfo's they sold for five dollars a pound.

Dawson's character and shape changed from day to day. Tents, cabins, and men were being shifted constantly, and, as there were no street addresses, it was difficult for new arrivals to find their friends. Those who had spent months in each other's company lost track of one another. Most had been known on the trail by their first names or by their nicknames; now, dumped from their boats, they were lost in the swirling crowd that moved restlessly back and forth along Front Street. Dwelling-places, in lieu of addresses, acquired nicknames of their own, such as "the cabin with the screen door," or "the big tent with two stovepipes," or "the slabhouse facing the river." The only way to find an acquaintance was to post a notice on the bulletin board at the A.C. store.

378

Lost

June 24, 1898 about 11 at night a gold sack
containing all a poor woman had: between
Old Man Buck (Choquette) cabin and small
board House selling Lemonade upon bank
on the Troandike River any person finding
same will confer a very great favor a poor
woman who is sick and must go out. she
made Her Dust by washing and mending a
Liberal reward will be paid by Enquiring at
Ferry Beer Saloon at Lousetown Bridge.

An Oxford don, Arthur Christian Newton
Treadgold, who had dropped his classical career to join
the stampede, described for the *Manchester Guardian*
the scene on Front Street in July: "The main street is
nearly always crowded with men trying to find one
another for ... it is a hard matter to find a man in
Dawson and much time is wasted thereby. When you
find your man the two of you sit on the edge of the
sidewalk (raised a foot above the road for cleanliness)
and talk. This is a picturesque sight, for men are of all
nations in all kinds of quaint garments, standing or
sitting in business on the main street."

Some men died and their friends did not hear the
news for weeks. Others suffering from typhoid and
scurvy were spirited off to hospital and given up by
their comrades, who could not find them. If a man so
much as moved his tent he was often lost to his friends.
There is one ghoulish tale of a new arrival who spent
weeks searching for a missing partner until one day he
was asked to act as pallbearer at the funeral of a typhoid
victim. He accepted and shouldered his burden, but
before the last rites were read he looked casually at the
corpse in its pine box. To his horror, he found himself
gazing down upon the dead face of the friend he sought.

379

2: *Carnival summer*

By July 1, Dawson City had two banks, two newspapers, five churches, and a telephone service. The Yukon Telegraph Company strung its first wire and shouted its first "hello" from the Dominion Hotel to its main office in Lousetown; its best-known stockholder was Big Alex McDonald. The two papers were locked in a circulation duel, each with its own cartoonist, its own press, and its own engraving-plant. The copies were snapped up quickly at fifty cents, and the newsboys who peddled them could expect in addition substantial tips from the Eldorado kings, hungry for news and willing to pay for it. Charley Anderson, the Lucky Swede, gave one boy fifty-nine dollars in gold for a single paper.

Others made small fortunes importing papers from the Outside. An enterprising Polish gambler named Harry Pinkert arranged to have the San Francisco papers send to the Klondike surplus copies of their Sunday editions which he agreed to distribute as free advertising. He made a killing selling these at fifty cents each. So great was the hunger for Outside news that the bundles were tossed from the upper decks of the steamboats before they docked, and the newsboys were able to sell as many as four hundred by the time the boats were tied up.

In addition to Father Judge's Roman Catholic church, four other faiths were establishing themselves in Dawson: the Church of England, the Methodist Church, the Presbyterian Church, and the Salvation Army. Hall Young, one of Alaska's best-known Protestant ministers, had arrived in 1897 and opened a Presbyterian church in a cabin rented from a saloon-keeper, using blocks of wood and rough planks for pews, a miner's copper blower as a collection plate, and a whiskey bottle for a candelabrum. He was replaced the following summer by a Canadian, Dr. Andrew S. Grant, a surgeon who had studied under Osler and then taken to the cloth. Young's makeshift church had burned to the ground, and Grant held services in the Pioneers' Hall until the building was submerged in the spring floods. Nothing daunted, the minister gathered up his flock and marched them to St. Paul's Anglican Church, walking in through the doors just as the congregation commenced to sing the second stanza of a grand old hymn:

> *See the mighty host advancing,*
> *Satan leading on.*

But temples to Mammon were rising as swiftly as those to God. The Bank of British North America won its race with the Bank of Commerce and opened for business in a tent with an unplaned board for a counter and an old open trunk as a safe. Here, in careless piles, lay thousands of dollars in currency to be traded for gold dust at sixteen dollars an ounce. David Doig, the manager, a shrewd Scot, lived in appropriate style. He enjoyed whiskey, cigars, and women, dined on *pâté*, oysters, and caviar, wore a soft slouch hat and grey flannels in the English style, smoked a small wooden pipe with a white horn mouthpiece, played the harmonium, made a habit of drinking a pint of champagne for breakfast, and brought a general air of sophistication to the community.

The Canadian Bank of Commerce was not far behind. Its foresight in bringing an assay plant over the pass enabled it to buy gold dust the moment it opened and to make outward shipments ahead of its rival. Within two weeks it sent three quarters of a million dollars out aboard the *Weare*.

The bank immediately issued one million dollars' worth of the paper money brought in over the trail, with

381

the words "DAWSON" or "YUKON" surprinted on each bill in heavy type, a precautionary measure taken in case the entire issue should be lost en route to the Klondike. Miners discounted their gold in order to obtain the less awkward bank-notes, and before long paper currency from almost every country was circulating in Dawson, including Confederate notes and bills on the Ezra Meeker Bank, which had gone out of business a quarter-century before. Everything from gold dust to scraps of paper was used as legal tender, and the Bank of Commerce on one occasion cleared a three-dollar cheque made from a six-inch square of spruce plank with a nail driven through it for the convenience of the filing clerk.

In spite of the new notes, the great medium of exchange continued to be gold dust, and because of its uncertain quality a continual tug-of-war was maintained between merchant and customer. Most men used the so-called "commercial dust," heavily laced with black sand, to pay their bills. As the bank valued this commercial dust at only eleven dollars an ounce, a customer using it to buy groceries or whiskey could reckon that he was saving five dollars an ounce, since the normal price of clean Klondike gold ran around sixteen dollars — and the tradesmen tacitly accepted all dust at this price. This profit was increased by some who judiciously salted their pokes with fine brass filings. On the other hand, the bartenders and commercial businessmen weighed the dust carelessly, so that a poke worth one hundred dollars was usually empty after seventy dollars' worth of purchases were made. Thus, as was often the case in the Klondike, the gain was largely ephemeral.

The Bank of Commerce occupied a small building that had once been used for storing fish, and it kept its money in two big wooden chests. One of its first customers was a plump and heavily rouged dance-hall girl who walked up to an astonished clerk with the words: "Have you got my tights and slippers? I'm Caprice." The manager was hastily summoned, as the only official equipped to deal with such an unorthodox request. Caprice repeated the query, adding that "Joe Brooks told me he'd send them here." After a hasty search, the bank discovered that ever since Skagway it had been carrying with its bank-notes a parcel containing Caprice's brief but effective costume.

Another early customer was Big Alex McDonald, and the bank's official history describes his first verbal statement of his business affairs as "a classic." It took the combined staff several hours to extract all the necessary information from the slow-spoken King of the Klondike. Each time he was about to sign a deposition listing his assets he would drop the pen, rub his chin, and exclaim that he had just remembered another claim he owned. The list, when it was at last completed, showed fifty mining properties. McDonald at once borrowed an enormous sum from the bank to buy another, and before the summer was over had recovered the purchase price, paid off the loan, and realized an equal amount in gold dust as profit.

By this time Dawson was crawling with men. In one month it had become the largest Canadian city west of Winnipeg — and Winnipeg itself was not much larger. In size of population, Dawson was only slightly smaller than the Pacific-northwest cities of Seattle, Tacoma, and Portland, and it dwarfed both Vancouver and Victoria. A rough census by the Mounted Police in mid-summer put its population at about eighteen thousand, with another five thousand or more working and prospecting on the creeks. But with men continually arriving and leaving, changing their addresses, moving into the hills and back into town, pouring off the steamboats and back aboard again, it was really impossible to estimate the true population at any given moment. The police calculated that more than twenty-eight thousand men had passed the Tagish post, but that five thousand of these had stopped to prospect on the tributaries of the Yukon before reaching Dawson in 1898. Another five thousand or more, however, arrived from various other points, largely via St. Michael, on board one of the sixty steamboats that made the trip up the river that summer. The *Klondike Nugget* reckoned that sixty thousand persons would reach the gold-fields before freeze-up, which would have made Dawson the largest city north of San Francisco and west of Toronto. This was probably an exaggeration, but undoubtedly well over half that number did touch at the Klondike for a few hours or a few days or a few months to form part of the jostling throng that plodded up and down, "curious, listless, dazed, dragging its slow lagging step along the main street."

The strange lassitude of the crowd tramping slowly back and forth through the mud was one of the singular features of Dawson in the summer of 1898. It was as if the vitality that had carried these men across the passes and down the rivers, shouting, singing, bickering, and slaving, had been sapped after ten months of struggle. For the best part of a year each had had his eyes fixed squarely upon a goal and had put everything into attaining that goal: but now that the goal was reached, all seemed to lose their bearings, and eddied about in an aimless fashion like a rushing stream that has suddenly been blocked. Some took out miners' licences and went through the motions of searching for gold. Paul T. Mizony, a seventeen-year-old from San Diego, wrote that "hundreds . . . expected all they would have to do was to pick the nuggets above the ground and some even thought they grew on bushes." But there were large numbers who spent only a few days in Dawson and did not even bother to visit the hypnotic creeks that had tugged at them all winter long. They turned their faces home again, their adventure over; and by August the *Nugget* reported that a third of them had departed. It was as if they had, without quite knowing it, completed the job they set out to do and had come to understand that it was not the gold they were seeking after all.

All of them realized at last that none had won the great race to the Klondike; the best ground had long been staked out by men who were on the spot before the name became a byword. Yet none had lost either. There was a strange satisfaction in the simple fact that they had made it. Suddenly they uncoiled, like springs that have been wound too tightly, and hundreds began to seek out, sheepishly, the former friends with whom they had quarrelled in the tense months on the trail, until the sweet laughter of reunion rippled across the canvas city.

All summer long, thousands of aimless men shuffled up and down Front Street, still dressed in the faded mackinaws, patched trousers, and high-laced boots of the trail. Their faces, like their clothes, seemed to be the colour of dust, seasoned in the crucible of the mountains; they wore their fur hats, many of them, as a kind of badge, with their snow-glasses still perched above them, and many retained their unkempt beards as if in memory of the winter of their travail.

They were like a crowd on a holiday, sightseers at the carnival of the Klondike. They jostled each other and they pointed as the Eldorado kings went by — at the Berrys and the Stanleys, at Big Alex, the Lucky Swede, Dick Lowe, and Antone Stander. These men, who a few years before had been cheechakos themselves, were now the star attractions of the Front Street midway as they played to the grandstand from their boxes in the

Combination dance hall, where each door was marked with the name of a famous creek and where every pint of champagne was worth two ounces of gold.

Down the boardwalk the newcomers trudged, and through the sticky ruts of the roadway, bent slightly forward as if the memory of their packs was hanging heavy on them — the same men who had once formed the liquid line over the Chilkoot. Behind them, like a hastily built theatrical backdrop, were the false-fronted dance halls and gambling-houses, some of them only half finished: the Pioneer and the Dominion, the Opera House and the Monte Carlo, the Bank Saloon and the Aurora, the Combination, Pavilion, and Mascot. A hodge-podge of banners, pennants, signs, and placards, suspended from door and window, tacked onto log walls and slung on poles across the street, advertised the presence of a dozen mining exchanges, transport companies, outfitters, information booths, gold-dust buyers, dentists, doctors, lawyers, and merchants.

"Gold! Gold! Gold!" the signs read. "Gold dust bought and sold . . . Jewelry . . . Fine diamond work . . . Watches . . . Tintypes . . . Cigars . . . Souvenirs and fine native gold."

At eight in the evening the crowd thickened about the dance halls as the callers, megaphone to mouth, stepped outside and for ten minutes barked out the merits of their wares to the accompaniment of tinkling pianos, scraping fiddles, and blaring horns. On the inside, silk-clad women danced, liquor flowed over mahogany counters, chips clicked on green felt tables, vaude-villeans cracked stale jokes, stock companies staged earnest if awkward dramas, while Projectoscopes and Animatagraphs, the mechanical wonders of the decade, flashed pictures that actually moved on bed-sheet screens, showing U.S. soldiers en route to Manila, or

Gentleman Jim Corbett trying to regain his heavy-weight title.

Outside on the crowded street, in the light dusk of midnight, an enormous magic lantern projected advertising messages on the side of a frame building. Dogs dashed madly up and down through the mud, harassing Gerry the Bum, Belinda Mulroney's drunken donkey, who staggered about poking his nose into the saloons and cadging drinks from the patrons until the barkeeps threw him out. Racing spryly along the duck-boards, "Uncle Andy" Young, the town's crack newsboy, sixty-five years old, cried over and over again: "The *Nugget!* The *Nugget!* The dear little *Nugget!*" with such vigour that he sold a thousand papers of an evening. And from the wharves could be heard the hoarse whistles of steamboats disgorging new arrivals, or departing with a load of disillusioned argonauts.

Just off the main street, from a niggerhead swamp behind Silent Sam Bonnifield's Bank Saloon, came the wheezing sound of a portable organ and the light tap of dancing feet. The crowd flowed towards it nightly, for here the Oatley Sisters, two pretty, petite girls, danced and entertained on a rough platform while a big pompadoured German made music for them. After twenty dances with the customers at a dollar a dance, the sisters stopped for breath and sang sentimental songs; and as their clear, bell-like voices piped in two-part harmony in the bright evening air, a hush fell over the throng clustered about the little stand. They sang "Break the News to Mother," and they sang "A Bird in a Gilded Cage," and they sang "I Love Her, Yes I Love Her Just the Same." And as they sang, each man fell silent, alone with his thoughts. Most of them were two thousand miles from home; some ten thousand; and the sound of the organ and the words of the familiar songs brought tears to many eyes.

"A lot of those songs are graven on the walls of my memory," Bert Parker wrote fifty years later. "I stood there with my mouth open, listening to the Oatley Sisters sing those sad ballads. I never knew them personally and didn't have enough money in those days to get near enough to really get a good look at them. But they sure helped me to put many a lonesome night behind me and gave me something to think about when I crawled into my bunk at night and parked my weary head on a pillow made of my two high boots."

The little organ groaned on. The girls finished their song. The canvas above their stand rippled in the breeze. Then the spell was broken as the organ struck up a bright two-step and the dance began again. Up onto the little stand the men climbed and paid their dollar for three rounds with one of the sisters or with one of the other girls who worked with them. All night long, with the sun still bright on the horizon, up and down the length of Front Street, the dance whirled on. Only at six or eight a.m. did the revelry cease as the men by the thousands drifted off to their tents and the exhausted girls were free to collapse into insensibility.

If by night Dawson was a great carnival, by day it was an enormous bazaar. Thousands who had thrown themselves body and soul into the task of dragging their ton of goods over the mountains and down the rivers were now intent on selling everything in order to realize enough money to go home. The wet sand-bar in front of the city was quickly laid out into two principal thoroughfares, Wall Street and Broadway Avenue, and these were lined with goods selling, for the most part, at half the prices they had fetched in the Pacific coast ports.

You could buy almost anything under the sun during that climactic summer in Dawson City. You could buy clothes and furs, moccasins and plug hats, shoes and

388

jewellery, fresh grapes, opera glasses, safety pins, and ice cream. You could buy peanuts and pink lemonade, patent-leather shoes, yellow-jacketed novels, cribbage boards, ostrich feathers, and oxen on the hoof. You could, if you were so inclined, buy for one hundred dollars the tusk of a prehistoric mammoth, dredged out of the frozen ground by prospectors — or, for twenty-five cents, a slicker coat with a bad cigar thrown in as premium. You could have your palm read, your picture taken, your back massaged, or your teeth filled with nuggets. You could buy Bibles and sets of Shakespeare and pairs of gold-scales by the hundreds, for these had been standard equipment with almost every man. You could buy rifles by the gross at one dollar each; they were worthless in a town where nobody was allowed to pack a gun. Many men stripped off the barrels to use as pipes for transmitting steam into the frozen ground and thawing the soil at the mines, and others bought them by the score and shipped them back Outside at a profit.

Down to the market place the crowd swarmed. Signs flapped in the breeze above tents that had been turned into emporiums by men who were trying to scrape together enough money to leave the Klondike forever.

DRUGS DRUGS
Rubber boots shoes Etc.
bacon, flour, rolled oats, rice, sugar,
onions, tea and coffee, fruits,
cornmeal German sausage,
Dogs Dogs

Vegetable and fruit stands, like booths at a county fair, crowded against tents selling dry goods or hardware. Women hawked ice cream made from condensed milk, while others stood perspiring at open bake-ovens redolent with the odour of steaming bread. Piles of

389

clothing and piles of provisions lay in heaps in the open, unprotected from the summer rains, while inquisitive men picked at them and bargained, Arab-fashion, with their owners.

Some piles contained musty flour and clothes that had been washed and rewashed, mended and re-mended, and provisions that had obviously been soaked, dried in the sun, and soaked again. These were leftovers from the Edmonton trails and the portages over the Liard, the Gravel, the Rat, and the Wind rivers.

Just two years before, this flat had been silent and empty, the domain of Carmack and his Indians, the province of the moose and the migrating caribou, the croaking ravens and the spawning salmon. Now for two miles along the river it throbbed and quivered like the aspens on the hillsides.

Once again the law of supply and demand was at work. Few had thought to bring in brooms over the trail: these were now so scarce that they sold for seven-teen dollars. The building boom was gobbling up twelve million feet of lumber as fast as the twelve sawmills could disgorge it, and nails were selling at almost eight dollars a pound. It cost five dollars to cash a cheque in Dawson and seventeen to call a doctor. Gold-dust weighers were paid twenty dollars a day, and teamsters one hundred. Lawyers made as much as five thousand a month. (In the rest of North America workingmen that year were receiving an average dollar-twenty-five a day; union carpenters, about one dollar and a half.)

The carnival was building to a climax, and on July 4 the climax came. For days, tension had been building in the community because of rumours that no American holiday could be celebrated on British soil, but the Mounted Police tactfully decreed that both Dominion Day and Independence Day would be marked by com-

390

mon festivities. At one minute past midnight a rifle shot rang across town, and within a few moments hundreds of others exploded. But this was not enough. Men scurried about procuring anvils, on which mounds of blasting-powder were placed, and upon these other anvils were piled, so that a piece of red-hot iron run between the two touched off a sound like a cannon's roar.

Across the bowl in the hills the explosions reverberated. It was as if each man had been waiting for this moment to celebrate his conquest of the mountains and the rivers. By five a.m. the din was so ear-splitting that four hundred dogs, driven to near-panic, fled through the madding crowds, leaped into the river, and swam across it in one long animal streak. Most of them came back after the festivities had subsided, but about one hundred preferred to remain wild in the forest, where they ran like wolves, never to return to the crazy community on the banks of the Klondike.

3: *Champagne for breakfast*

Pat Galvin of Bonanza Creek summed up the spirit of '98 in a few pithy sentences of advice given to his nephew, who had arrived from the Outside that summer and, observing Galvin's free-handed methods, muttered a few cautionary words about expense.

"Expense! Expense!" cried Galvin. "I am disgusted with you. Don't show your ignorance by using that cheap Outside word. We don't use it here. Never repeat it in my presence again. You must learn the ways of Alaska. That word is not understood in the north. If you have money, spend it; that's what it's for, and that's the way we do business."

This might easily have stood as the Klondike's creed in the year of the stampede. The gold which had lain hidden for so long in the frozen gravels now moved as swiftly as those nuggets which Pat Galvin gave away like souvenirs to any passing stranger who would listen to the story of his life. The kings of Bonanza and Eldorado, who had been common labourers two years before, saw themselves as captains of industry and determined to invest their money in an assortment of schemes and enterprises. Some built hotels and fitted them out with Persian carpets and mahogany furniture. Others financed restaurants that served everything from oysters to sherbet. Dozens were sucked into mining companies, syndicates, trading firms, and transportation companies.

By the end of the summer, thirty more trading and transportation companies had joined the two pioneer firms, the A.C. and N.A.T. companies, in traffic on the river. They operated sixty steamboats, eight tugboats, and twenty enormous barges. One Seattle shipyard knocked together twelve stern-wheelers for the Yukon trade that year and moved ten of them safely to their destination; they were "built by the mile and cut apart in proper lengths," as one of their officers put it. There seemed, sometimes, to be a boat around every bend in the river, and there could be as many as a dozen tied to the bank along the Dawson waterfront. Ship after ship puffed into town, many of them loaded with champagne and brightly plumaged dancing-girls, pennants, flags, and bunting fluttering gaily from their masts, clouds of white smoke bursting from their yellow stacks, a Niagara of spray churning back from their orange paddle-wheels.

Many of these new vessels were floating palaces in every sense of the word. The Alaska Commercial Company, which was a Jewish-owned firm, launched the three biggest of all that summer, the *Susie, Sarah,* and *Hannah,* naming them, as was its gallant habit, after the wives and daughters of its directors rather than after the

392

directors themselves, as the crustier N.A.T. Company did. They were built in Louisville, Kentucky, these monoliths, and designed after Mississippi packets, with palatial dining-rooms of mahogany, and staterooms equipped with two or three berths, and upper decks that ran the length of each vessel. Directly behind the big twin stacks the company's bold red pennant fluttered, and on each boat the specially made silver service, dishes, bed linen, and blankets all bore the firm's monogram. It was a far cry from the crude days of the *New Racket* or the airless cells of the little *Bella.*

Up the river at top speed that summer came the dashing John Irving aboard his trim steamboat, the *Yukoner,* on the fastest trip ever recorded from St. Michael to Dawson. A great gold eagle was fastened in front of his pilothouse as a talisman, and a huge picture of a bulldog hung, at his whim, in the dining-salon, while an enormous Negro bodyservant stayed constantly at his side during the journey. Irving was as skilled in navigation as he was eccentric in personality, an old-time river man who had waged many an epic steamboat war on the Fraser River decades before against his fierce rival — the same William Moore who founded Skagway.

He was a man who did everything with flair, and this record trip from St. Michael to Dawson aboard the *Yukoner* was unlike any other voyage made on the river. Irving launched his ship with pomp and ceremony: a stunning blonde, en route to a dance-hall engagement, was recruited to smash a bottle of vintage champagne across the stern — an appropriate beginning since the cargo consisted almost entirely of wines and spirits, while the passenger list was composed largely of theatrical people, dance-hall entertainers, and gamblers. An orchestra contributed to the general air of festivity and bonhomie.

Like all the steamboats on the run, Irving's *Yukoner* was a wood-burner, and thus regular stops had to be made to take on cordwood, which was stacked at depots on the riverbank along the way. Most pilots nudged their craft gingerly into the shore, loaded the wood at top speed, and pushed off as quickly as possible, but Irving made an adventure and a ceremony out of this prosaic task. On spying a cordwood depot it was his practice to aim the bow of his boat directly at the bank, pull the whistle cord wide open, order the engines full speed ahead, and charge. At the very last instant he would order full speed astern, calculating the distance so nicely that the boat would come to a shuddering halt a few inches from the bank. The scene that followed was always flamboyant. The captain, leaping from his ship, would invite the delighted woodcutters aboard for a round of champagne, while the band, assembled on the deck, played furiously and the girls, in their finest satins and laces, danced wildly to the music.

Irving handled his steamer as if she were a spirited mare and he an accomplished rider. Nothing appeared to give him greater pleasure than a charge through the waters at some object. On the return trip from Dawson he nosed his boat out of the delta and into the Bering Sea, where he spotted the ocean steamer *Danube,* the ship which was to pick up his passengers and cargo. Irving promptly charged the *Danube,* but miscalculated his speed by a fraction with lamentable results. Unabashed, he puffed on to St. Michael, where, to keep his hand in, he charged the dock, almost reducing it to matchwood. This was the climax of his voyage. He quickly unloaded the *Yukoner,* for forty-five thousand dollars, to Pat Galvin, the man who bought steamboats the way others buy a suit of clothes.

Galvin was a one-time town marshal from Helena, Montana, who had run a hardware and tinsmith shop at

Circle before the Klondike strike. Enriched by his Bonanza claim, he sought, like so many of his fellows, to form a corporation and become a financial titan — not so much for wealth as for fame. His new firm bore the proud title of "North British American Trading and Transportation Company, Pat Galvin president." Galvin insisted that his name, and his alone, stand above the doors of all the trading posts and appear on all merchandise and canned goods which he proposed to import into the Yukon and sell at various points along the river.

Galvin's reputation for free-handed spending had preceded him, and the crew of the *Yukoner* awaited their new employer with pleasure and anticipation. It was said that he was good for two thousand dollars a night in Dawson, and on entering a bar it was his custom to treat everybody in the house.

"Come on, boys," Galvin would shout, "open up the best you have, the drinks are on me!" and, in case he might have overlooked anybody in the street, he would send the bartender outside to drag in any passers-by. He was a commanding figure, dressed entirely in black, slender and wiry, with eyes that gleamed from a pale Irish face. A crowd usually followed him, for his generosity was legend; on a whim, on occasion, he distributed as much as a thousand dollars' worth of nuggets at a time.

He did not disappoint the *Yukoner's* crew. As soon as he bought the steamer he lined them all up on deck and gave each man a twenty-dollar goldpiece. This was all the cash he had, but he set out blithely upriver towards Dawson without further funds to purchase fuel or hire hands. The boat had steamed only a few miles when the boiler exploded, almost wrecking a large crate of plate glass which Galvin had planned to install, at exorbitant expense, in the show windows of his establishment in

Dawson. Long before the journey was completed, the ship froze in, and did not reach Dawson until 1899. By this time matters had deteriorated to the point where she became the scene of the only mutiny on the Yukon River, but Galvin himself had long since departed for Dawson by dog-team. At the peak of the stampede he was offered seven million dollars for his holding. He turned it down. In another year he was bankrupt.

Other Eldorado kings were following Galvin's example and becoming, if only briefly, shipping magnates. Big Alex McDonald bought the *W. K. Merwyn,* the same stern-wheeler which had been part of the *Eliza Anderson's* strange entourage. He also acquired the *W. S. Stratton,* named for the eccentric Black Hills mining millionaire who had had ambitions to invest some of his rapidly diminishing wealth in the Klondike. Nels Peterson, who had grown rich from one of the early bench claims, formed the "Flyer" line with two spanking new steamboats, the *Eldorado* and the *Bonanza King.* The original name of the *Eldorado* was *Philip B. Low,* but she sank so many times that the wags were referring to her as the *"Fill Up Below"* and so the name was changed. Peterson offered a free ticket from Dawson to Seattle to the first person to spot either boat when the two arrived on their maiden voyage from St. Michael in the fall of '98. Hundreds who had no other way of quitting the country climbed the Midnight Dome above the town, straining for a sight of steamboat smoke. One ingenious pair won handily by arranging a system of wig-wag signals from the mountaintop to the main street. Dozens risked breaking their necks in a pell-mell race down the hillsides when the *Bonanza King* at last appeared, only to find they had been outwitted. But Peterson's showmanship was better than his financial acumen: he sank ninety thousand dollars in the two ships, which in the end helped to ruin him.

396

By the end of August, fifty-six steamboats had dumped seventy-four hundred tons of freight — everything from fancy porcelain chamber pots to flagons of Napoleon brandy — on the new docks. Dawson's isolation was at an end; it was no longer a beans-and-bacon town. Indeed, as early as July 1 the imported San Francisco chef who presided at the Regina Café had produced the following Dominion Day menu:

> Consommé à la jardinière
> Rock Point oysters
> Piccalilli
> Lobster Newburg
> Chicken salad en mayonnaise
> Broiled moose chops aux champignons
> Cold tongue
> Roast beef
> Boiled ham
> Bengal Club chutney
> Saratoga chips
> Cakes and jellies
> Pears and peaches
> Cheese
> Coffee

The Regina Hotel, which was under construction all summer and fall, was slated, in the words of the *Klondike Nugget,* to "more than rival more pretentious caravanserais in much more metropolitan cities," for its floors were covered with Brussels carpets and its woodwork with gold-leaf trimming, and it rose four stories, the tallest building in Dawson.

Its chief rival was the equally elegant Fairview, which Belinda Mulroney was constructing on Front Street. She intended it to be the finest and best-appointed hostelry in town: it was to have twenty-two steam-heated rooms, a side entrance for ladies, electric lights (with power supplied by a yacht anchored in the river), and Turkish baths. The tables were spread with linen, sterling silver, and bone china. In the lobby an orchestra played chamber music. And the bar was staffed by young American doctors and dentists who, unable to get a licence to practise on British soil, quickly learned to mix drinks instead of medicines.

Although it opened in July, more than a year was required to put the finishing touches on the Fairview. All of its furnishings — from cut-glass chandeliers to brass bedsteads — were packed in over the White Pass, and the efficient Belinda, who left very little to others, went personally to Skagway to supervise the operation. She arrived in the nick of time: Joe Brooks, the packer, had moved her outfit only two miles up the trail and then dumped it when he received a better offer to transport a cargo of whiskey for Bill McPhee. In a black rage, Belinda headed for the Skagway wharves and recruited a gang of destitute men. She incited them to fight among themselves until they found out who was the toughest, and he was elected foreman. This done, she accompanied the gang up the trail to take over from Brooks. Her men beat up Brooks's foreman, imprisoned him in a tent, set a guard on it, dumped McPhee's whiskey onto the side of the trail, loaded Belinda's hotel equipment on Brooks's mules, and started over the pass with Belinda herself, mounted on Brooks's own pinto pony, triumphantly riding at their head. In this manner Belinda convoyed the entire shipment safely over the mountains and down the Yukon on fifteen scows, and the Fairview stood complete, a sumptuous hostelry with only one real flaw: the interior walls were made of canvas over which wallpaper had been pasted, so that the slightest whisper anywhere in the building could be heard by every guest.

398

The Fairview made money. In its first twenty-four hours of operation the bar took in six thousand dollars. The dining-room was equally lucrative. Thomas Cunningham, purser of the *Yukoner,* once invited Belinda to have breakfast with him at the hotel. She accepted demurely, and the bill, when it was totted up, came to sixty dollars. This staggered Cunningham a little.

"Think of a woman ordering champagne for breakfast!" he exclaimed later. "It is not done."

Over the trails and up the river the cargo poured into Dawson. Jack Smith paced the riverbank that June, impatiently awaiting the ten-foot mirrors, the velvet carpets, the oil paintings, and the ten thousand dollars' worth of fixtures which his partner, Swiftwater Bill Gates, was supposed to be bringing into town along with a bevy of dance-hall beauties. He had cause for concern: disquieting rumours of Swiftwater Bill's exploits in San Francisco had already reached his ears.

When Swiftwater arrived in San Francisco he rented a suite of rooms in the Baldwin Hotel, and in the Klondike manner began distributing gold dust to one and all. He tipped the bellboys to walk about the lobby and point him out to other hotel guests as "The King of the Klondike," and when the newspaper notices showed signs of diminishing he paid an itinerant journalist one hundred dollars to publish a lurid account of his own drowning. In his new Prince Albert coat, with diamond cuff-links and diamond stickpin, he presented a glittering façade to the world, but his diminutive five-and-a-half-foot figure and his scraggly moustache subtracted from the dignity borrowed from his clothes. Gussie Lamore had preceded him to the coast with a promise of marriage, as a result of the famous incident with the eggs, but in San Francisco she refused to go through with the bargain, possibly because she was already married and had a three-year-old child. Swift-

399

water, undismayed, married her sister Grace, bought her a fifteen-thousand-dollar house in Oakland, and, while it was being renovated to suit her tastes, installed her in the bridal chamber of the Baldwin. Alas for Swiftwater Bill, the honeymoon was short-lived. After three weeks Grace threw him over, and he emerged from their new home carrying seven thousand dollars' worth of wedding presents wrapped in a blanket. It was, however, almost impossible to discourage him. A few days later he was earnestly wooing the youngest Lamore sister, Nellie.

Swiftwater by this time was running perilously short of funds and had as yet made no purchases for the Monte Carlo. This did not worry him particularly, since — while lacking many qualities, including horse sense — he was never wanting in the ability to dig up finances at short notice. He was a born prospector who for all of his long life was always able to spot a likely piece of ground — and, when no ground was available, to spot a likely-looking sucker. In the course of time his eye fell on a Dr. Wolf who had twenty thousand dollars to invest. Swiftwater talked so swiftly and glibly that he was able to pre-empt all of it. In return he gave the gullible Wolf a ninety-day note promising to pay the astonishing interest rate of one hundred per cent.

Wolf's imagination was so fired by Swiftwater's tale of fortunes to be gleaned from Klondike stampeders that he decided to become a stampeder himself, forgetting perhaps that Swiftwater had already gleaned his fortune. The two laid plans to organize a trading and transportation company and set off at once for Seattle, where the doctor plunged into the business end of the matter while Swiftwater paraded up and down the streets with the girls whom he had hired for the Monte Carlo. He lived sumptuously at the Rainier-Grand, one of the city's leading hotels, ordering gallon upon gallon of champagne, not to drink (for he was a teetotaller) but to bathe in. He splashed about in the effervescent tub for the benefit of the press, announcing that a bath was a rare thing in the Yukon. When he took his leave, the bill for damages alone came to fifteen hundred dollars.

None of these shenanigans was calculated to soothe the rapidly fraying nerves of Dr. Wolf. Slowly it began to dawn upon him that his new partner was not the solid businessman he had thought. By the time the expedition arrived at Lake Bennett, he was thoroughly alarmed and, abandoning Swiftwater to his own sybaritic devices, sped on ahead by dog-sled, travelling light in order to reach Dawson and investigate his partner's background before the main rush. The enthusiastic accounts he received of Swiftwater's escapades glowed with local colour but only served to confirm the doctor's worst fears. He was waiting impatiently on the riverbank beside Jack Smith when Swiftwater arrived at last in a Peterborough canoe with two scowloads of girls and whiskey in its wake. Swiftwater himself sat in the prow of the canoe, a silk topper cocked on his head, his prince Albert coat draped across his shoulders, his arms extended in welcome to the crowd that stood on the banks to greet him. Directly behind him a girl was perched on a case of whiskey, and on the scows other girls waved prettily and shouted saucy greetings to the onlookers. Swiftwater stepped ashore in triumph and into the arms of his enraged partner.

"You've got just exactly three hours to pay back the twenty thousand," Wolf told him. "To hell with the interest!"

"I'll have it," Swiftwater gasped.

"Get started!" Wolf rapped back.

Swiftwater raised the money, and Wolf took the next boat Outside, declaring he had had all he wanted of the Klondike. Jack Smith lost no time in attaching twelve

401

thousand dollars of Swiftwater's mining profit at the bank and Swiftwater's share of the dance hall to boot. With scarcely an instant's hesitation, Swiftwater plunged into a new scheme. He announced the formation of the British North American Trading and Exploration Company and left directly for London to raise the capital for it. He was not a man whose spirits were easily dampened.

All these proceedings were watched curiously and with a certain genteel detachment by two wealthy ladies who appeared briefly upon the scene in July. These were the first two bona fide tourists to reach Dawson, and with their advent the community might be said to have arrived. One was Mrs. Mary E. Hitchcock, the widow of a U.S. admiral; her companion was Miss Edith Van Buren, the niece of the former U.S. President. It was the habit of this pair to visit various watering-places and points of interest each summer, and this particular summer, rather than Paris, Bath, or Shanghai, they had chosen Dawson City, for it seemed the most interesting place to go. Of all the thousands who poured into the Klondike that season it is probable that these two were the only ones who came merely as sightseers.

They had brought with them what a fellow traveller described as "the strangest agglomeration of cargo that ever women and wit devised." It included two Great Danes, an ice-cream freezer, a parrot and several canaries, two cages full of live pigeons, a gramophone, a hundred-pound Criterion music box, a coal-oil stove, a zither, a portable bowling-alley, a primitive motion-picture projector, a mandolin, several air mattresses and hammocks, and box after box of rare foods: *pâté* and truffles, stuffed olives and oysters. This vast cargo was transported some five thousand miles by water to the accompaniment of the tart tongue and hot temper of

402

Mrs. Hitchcock, the buxom matron who was in charge of the expedition and who complained incessantly about the freight charges on the steamboat that brought them from St. Michael. She had not been used to this when crossing the Atlantic.

The most singular item was an enormous marquee tent which covered twenty-eight hundred square feet and was the largest ever brought into the Yukon Territory. There was no space for it in the main town, so the ladies had it raised on the bank on the far side of the Yukon River, where it dominated the landscape. It was so cavernous that they soon found it expedient to pitch another, smaller tent in one corner in order to keep warm at night.

Soon this extraordinary couple was to be seen walking the duckboards of Dawson in their tailored suits, their starched collars, their boater hats, and their silk ties. Occasionally they affected a more picturesque garb — large sombreros, blue serge knickers, rubber boots, striped jersey sweaters, and heavy cartridge belts to which were strapped impossibly big revolvers.

In their gargantuan marquee the two ladies held court. They searched about the town for the right people and quickly sensed that the leader of Dawson's four hundred was Big Alex McDonald. He became guest of honour at intimate little dinners within the great tent. The menu included anchovies, mock-turtle soup, roast moose, escalloped tomatoes, asparagus salad with French dressing, peach ice cream, chocolate cake, and French drip coffee. Indeed, the bounty of the ladies' board made the Regina Café seem like a one-arm joint. Both women were large of girth and, having heard tales of the Klondike's starvation winter, had no intention of going hungry. Their memoirs, while somewhat vague on the specifics of the gold rush, are enlivened with

403

detailed accounts of what they consumed daily, down to the last crisp potato ball.

Here on this frozen strip of riverbank they observed the niceties of Philadelphia and Washington. One English physician who had known Miss Van Buren's father in Yokohama expressed a desire to call, but sent his card saying that he would be unable to do since he could not procure a starched shirt. She graciously accepted his excuse, waived all formality, and received him anyway in his serge suit.

The Salvation Army, meanwhile, had dispatched a troupe to Dawson, and these bonneted servants of the Lord, covetously eyeing the marquee, summoned up courage to ask the ladies if they might use it for their Sunday service. The ladies were happy to oblige. The following Sabbath, as the voices were raised in prayer, it was noticed that the pigeons had escaped from their cages and were fluttering above the heads of the uneasy congregation. One of them finally perched on the music box, which mechanically responded with "Nearer My God to Thee" and the entire assemblage rose and repeated the grand old hymn, which they had already sung.

Mrs. Hitchcock and Miss Van Buren stayed out the summer and then booked passage upriver on the tiny little steamer *Flora*. They were shocked by the primitive stateroom to which they were assigned. There was only a one-foot space to turn around in between the double bunks and the wall and it was quite impracticable to undress save for the removal of an overcoat or so. Nor were there any washing facilities except for a bucket with a rope attached to it which one had to lower over the side and into the muddy river. As the boat departed the two outraged women could be heard complaining shrilly about these arrangements. It was not at all what they had been used to, really.

4: *Remember the Sabbath . . .*

Dawson has occasionally been depicted in song and story as a lawless and gun-happy town. Indeed, a U.S. marshal, Frank M. Canton, sent up to Circle City by his government at a late date to keep the peace, described Dawson in his memoirs as a "wild, picturesque, lawless mining camp. The like had never been known, never would be seen again. It was a picture of blood and glittering gold-dust, starvation and death. . . . If a man could not get the woman he wanted, the man who did get her had to fight for her life."

Canton knew lawlessness when he saw it, for he was a former western sheriff, a one-time range detective, and one of the leading figures in the Johnson County War of 1892, when Wyoming cattlemen mounted an army against the encroaching homesteaders. But his assessment of Dawson is sheer fiction — the embellishment, no doubt, of his ghost writer, Edward Everett Dale. The truth is that, thanks to the presence of the Mounted Police, not a single murder took place in Dawson City in 1898, and very little major theft. It was possible to leave one's cabin or tent wide open, go off on a six-week trip, and return to find all possessions intact. James Dalziel, a New Zealander, used to go away for a month at a time and leave his cabin unlocked with his best suit hanging on the wall for all to see. In the vest pocket was a solid-gold watch in a solid-gold case with a massive gold chain whose every link was stamped *18k*. It was never touched.

The nearest thing to mayhem occurred when Coatless Curly Munro had a quarrel with his wife. Both reached for revolvers which they kept under their pillows, then took one look at each other and fled the premises by different doors. (Coatless Curly was a man who believed in such melodramatic gestures. It was his habit never to wear an outer jacket, but to go about in vest and shirt-sleeves even in the coldest weather. It was generally conceded, however, that he wore three suits of heavy underwear beneath his outer clothing.)

Side arms were forbidden in Dawson. No man could carry a revolver on the streets without a licence, and few licences were issued. There is the story of the one-time Western badman from Dodge City who was ejected from a saloon by a Mountie constable for talking too loudly. He left like a lamb. The Mountie discovered that he was carrying a gun and asked him to hand it over. "No man yet has taken a gun away from me," the badman snarled in the best tradition. "Well, I'm taking it," the policeman said mildly, and did so without a murmur from his opponent.

As one resident wrote, "You can call the toughest gambler in town anything you wish, or slap him on the wrist and all he can do is sue you for slander or have you arrested for assault. But he will do nothing for himself. If you get into trouble call a policeman. ... The old American stall of self-defense just doesn't go."

If there had been a Dan McGrew in Dawson, and a Malemute Saloon, as Service's fictional verse suggests, there could never have been a shooting because a Mountie would have been on the spot to confiscate the guns before the duel began. So many revolvers were confiscated in Dawson in 1898 that they were auctioned off by the police for as little as a dollar and purchased as souvenirs to keep on the mantelpiece. The chief crimes that season included such heinous offences as nonpayment of wages, dog-stealing, operating unsanitary premises, fraud, unlawfully practising medicine, disturbing the peace, deserting employment, and that vicious crime "using vile language." Most of the six hundred and fifty arrests made in the Yukon in 1898 were for misdemeanours of that order. One hundred

406

and fifty were for more serious offences, but of these, more than half were concerned with prostitution. No other community on such a remote frontier could boast a similar record.

By fall, Sam Steele was in command not only of Dawson but also of all of the Yukon and British Columbia. Constantine relinquished his post on June 24 and proceeded Outside to a new assignment. When he left town the old-timers presented him with a silver plate containing two thousand dollars' worth of selected nuggets. This was all the gold he took from the Klondike, but he left with the lasting respect of the community.

To newcomers and old-timers alike, the police often seemed superhuman. There was something miraculous about the ability of Inspector W. H. Scarth, Constantine's deputy in charge of the Dawson barracks, to work cheerfully in below-zero weather without ever wearing gloves or mitts — and without ever seeming to freeze a finger. Scarth had been the hero of a disconcerting mishap on the steamer that brought him north in 1897, and all of Dawson knew the story. A rope against which the policeman was leaning gave way, and, toppling head-first into the hold of the *City of Topeka,* he landed upside-down in a barrel. In spite of this, he emerged smiling, his forage cap still in place and his ever-present monocle screwed as firmly as ever into his eye-socket.

When Steele arrived on the heels of the main rush, his reputation had come ahead of him, and he proceeded to rule Dawson with the firm hand he had displayed on mountains, lakes, and river. Fines were stiff, sentences stiffer. For all crimes Steele imposed one of two main punishments. A culprit was either given a "blue ticket" to leave town, or he was sentenced to hard labour on the government woodpile. The blue ticket was considered a serious penalty by gamblers and saloon-keepers, since it meant they could no longer ply a lucrative trade on Front Street. The woodpile kept more than fifty prisoners busy at all times, for the police and government offices alone used enough fuel to make a pile two miles long and four feet square, and all of it had to be sawed into stove lengths by prisoners who worked from morning until night, winter and summer. In July, for instance, a man convicted of cheating at cards was sentenced to three months on the woodpile; in October a man who had been given a blue ticket and had not left town fast enough was sentenced to six months. It was back-breaking work; nobody wanted it.

One American gambler, so the story goes, who came up before Steele was contemptuous when the policeman fined him fifty dollars.

"Fifty dollars — is that all? I've got that in my vest pocket," he said.

Whereupon the superintendent added: ". . . and sixty days on the woodpile. Have you got that in your vest pocket?"

Steele allowed the saloons and the gambling-halls, the dance pavilions and the prostitutes' cribs on Paradise Alley behind Front Street to run wide open; but he would not countenance disorderly conduct, obscenity, or cheating. Shortly after his arrival he called a meeting of saloon-keepers and told them that if he received any complaints of unfair gambling he would close them up. As a result, disgruntled players were always paid off without argument, ejected promptly from the premises, and not allowed to return.

He did not interfere with the liquor traffic — one hundred and twenty thousand gallons were imported into Dawson during the '98 season — but he would not allow spirits to be sold to minors, nor would he countenance the employment of children in the saloons. If a man made a remark that he judged to be either obscene

408

or disloyal during a theatrical performance, the theatre was fined, and if such remarks continued, the theatre faced closure. When Freda Maloof, a Greek girl billed as "The Turkish Whirlwind Danseuse," tried to repeat the hootchie-kootchie dance with which Little Egypt had startled the patrons of the Columbian Exposition, Steele had it stopped at once. There is evidence, however, that he used these corrective measures sparingly in order to keep matters from going too far. Years after the incident two old-timers, Bert Parker and a lawyer named De Journel, met on a Yukon riverboat and recalled old times. Parker described the belly dance that was too hot for Dawson. De Journel stared out into the river, his eyes glazing.

"Do you remember it?" Parker prodded.

"No," said De Journel softly, "I don't. But I certainly would have liked to see that dance. It must have been some dance if they wouldn't let her do it in those days." He paused for a moment, then turned to his companion: "I myself saw Captain Harper of the North West Mounted Police bet a hundred dollars that he could strip off naked, stand on his head on the stage of the Monte Carlo Theater, and eat a pound of raw beefsteak off the floor, and he won the bet." De Journel resumed his inspection of the Yukon River and was silent again. "Yes," he said thoughtfully, "it must have been some dance if they wouldn't let her do it in Dawson!"

Even more remarkable to the free-wheeling Americans who formed the majority of the population was the Dawson Sunday. On the Sabbath the town was dead. "On Sundays there is quiet," one man wrote home, "and the old familiar strains of ancient hymns steal through the clear northern air."

Saloons and dance halls, theatres and business houses were shut tight one minute before midnight on Saturday. At two minutes before twelve the lookout at the faro table would take his watch from his pocket and call out: "The last turn, boys!" A rush would follow as the players placed one last bet. At the next table the roulette ball gave a final click; in the saloon the bartender was already stacking the chairs. Without a word the crowd silently moved out into the street, bidding the lone Mountie a quiet good-night. The lights, at Steele's insistence, stayed burning so that the policeman on the beat could make sure the premises were empty until two a.m. on Monday, when they were allowed to reopen.

There were many ingenious attempts to circumnavigate these blue laws. Some of the theatre-owners instituted what they called "sacred concerts," at which a silver collection was taken. The *pièce de résistance* was a series of "living pictures" of various religious scenes, chosen with the eye of a De Mille for their voluptuous quality. The climax of these tableaux was reached on a certain Sabbath eve when the curtains parted to reveal Caprice, the dance-hall queen, plump and blonde, attired only in pink tights and slippers and clinging suggestively to an enormous cross.

Another device, during the summer months, was the Sunday excursion. As the American border was less than fifty miles away, a boatload of holidayers could easily be transported beyond the reach of the Mounted Police to a Promised Land where wine flowed like water and joy reigned supreme. On one memorable occasion some three hundred and sixty-eight people, largely gamblers, dance-hall girls, and theatrical men, clambered aboard the *Bonanza King* while another hundred embarked on the *Tyrrell.* One boat ran out of fuel and the other developed engine trouble, so that the two pleasure ships drifted helplessly downstream into the heart of Alaska until the liquor was consumed and the novelty of the occasion began to pall. Monday had come and gone meanwhile, but Dawson remained a dead town, the liveliest members of its population taken from it, and the theatres, dance halls, saloons, and gambling-houses closed for lack of staff.

When the steamers finally limped back upstream and hove into sight, the town rushed *en masse* to the wharf to welcome the prodigals. One old-timer, years later, likened the scene to Lindbergh's reception in New York. With the steamers' whistles blowing wide open and every dog in town howling in chorus and several thousand people cheering, the girls in their rumpled dresses walked unsteadily down the gangplank and the community once more returned to normal.

But the Sunday laws were never relaxed. No work of any kind was allowed on the Lord's Day. One man was arrested for fishing on the Sabbath, another for sawing his own wood, and in August, 1898, the *Nugget* noted that two men were each fined two dollars and three dollars costs simply for examining their fishing-nets on a Sunday. One Lord's Day event had a touch of high comedy to it: a race was arranged between two famous dog-teams and was organized for a Sunday so that the sporting fraternity could attend. The scene along the Klondike valley road was a gaudy one: in the glittering spring sunlight scores of dance-hall girls and actresses, their hair piled high in the pompadour style of the day, and dressed in their finest beribboned silks with enormous leg-of-mutton sleeves, lined the course arm in arm with saloon-keepers and gamblers in hard hats, stiff collars, and diamond studs. Cheers rang out as the two teams came bolting down the hard-packed road — and then raced neck and neck into the arms of the waiting police, who arrested all and sundry on a charge of desecrating the Sabbath.

411

5: *Graft and the* Nugget

The honesty and finesse of the Mounted Police stood out sharply against a background of governmental ineptitude and petty graft. On the one hand there is a picture of four Mountie constables, each earning one dollar and twenty-five cents a day, escorting five tons of gold ingots safely out of the country. On the other, there are the scenes in the mining recorder's office where bribery, inefficiency, and small corruptions were the order of the day. Here, changes on recorded claims could be made by running a pen through a name and date, or by scratching or erasing names, or — even more brazenly — by cutting them out and pasting in fresh slips of paper with new signatures. Here palms often had to be crossed before records could be inspected, and crowds waiting to record or transfer a piece of ground might wait in line for as long as three days unless they were admitted through what was known as "the five-dollar door" at the side, where speedy service was secured by a bribe.

Women were given the right of way into the recorder's office, an apparent chivalry that led to many instances of collusion, especially through the agency of prostitutes or dance-hall girls. Many a man who staked a claim would arrive at the office only to be told that the ground was closed by government order, and then to discover that it had been given, later, to friends or accomplices of the recorder.

In the winter of 1898-99 the government refused to record any further fractional claims, reserving these for the Crown, but, nevertheless, favoured individuals and clerks in the offices seemed able to stake these fractions. Sometimes when a man successfully staked a claim he was informed that he could not officially record it until he had it surveyed for a fee of one hundred dollars.

412

While the survey was in progress he might find that others, with obvious knowledge, had jumped the claim and recorded it themselves. As Lord Minto, the Governor General of Canada, who visited the Klondike after the turn of the century, wrote, "It has been said with some truth that to settle the boundaries and titles of a good claim requires two or three surveys and as many lawsuits."

The natural discontent with the government arising from these outrages was magnified by the fact that the great majority of Klondikers were U.S. citizens living reluctantly under the British flag. Here was a unique situation: Dawson, one of Canada's largest cities, was four-fifths American. The foreigners' feelings were reflected in the editorial pages of the *Klondike Nugget,* an American-owned newspaper devoted to the interests of the U.S. section of the population. The *Nugget*'s editorials and news stories were scathing, and for more than a year the paper regularly attacked Canadian officialdom. It did not spare its own highly placed fellow citizens when the situation warranted, however, and in one celebrated instance incurred a libel suit from the U.S. consul himself.

The action sprang from a news report in the *Nugget*'s uninhibited pages which detailed the actions of the consul, a plump and fun-loving official named James McCook, at the hour of 3.30 on a certain April morning. McCook, the *Nugget* informed its readers, had entered Pete McDonald's Phoenix dance hall with Diamond-Tooth Gertie, one of the reigning dance-hall queens, on his arm. He was bursting with patriotic fervour and announced that he would buy drinks for any true American. A large number of girls immediately identified themselves as true Americans and stepped up to the bar, but one prospector refused the offer, saying that *he* was a true Canadian. McCook

413

roared that he would rectify the error and make the man an American, whereupon a brief and inconclusive fracas occurred. The consul turned from this interruption to the pleasanter task of distributing all his wealth. He dispensed money and nuggets to the girls at the bar, gave one of them his heavy gold watch, and then, in a burst of enthusiasm, turned his pockets inside out, crying: "Take the whole works!" Several scuffles followed, in which the consul was seen rolling about on the floor. He recovered himself, produced a small Stars and Stripes, pinned it to the seat of his pants, placed his hands on the bar, and, leaning over, requested Pete McDonald to give him a good square kick.

When McCook read this account of his actions in the *Nugget*, he sued the paper for five thousand dollars and Gene Allen and his brother George, the proprietors, for twenty thousand. The newsmen lined up such a phalanx of witnesses that the case was dismissed and the consul shortly afterward relieved of his post.

A more scurrilous paper than the *Nugget* was the short-lived *Gleaner*. Bert Parker, who sold it on the streets, described it as "one of the hottest sheets that was ever published in Canada, and I don't except the Calgary *Eye-Opener*." The paper was published twice a week, and, more in the interests of circulation than public spirit, roasted the government unmercifully. "They blamed the government for everything, not excepting the weather," Parker recalled. The *Gleaner* was finally closed down because of obscenity and its publisher given a blue ticket to leave town. But the hatred of Canadian policy did not die away. In one extreme case a lady physician named Luella Day, from New York City, became so incensed at the government that she actually came to believe that the local officials were trying to poison her under direct orders from Clifford Sifton, the Canadian Minister of the Interior. She held to this conviction to her dying day, wrote and published a book repeating the charge, and found an audience for it.

A good deal of the discontent sprang less from public graft than from public mismanagement. The gold office was staffed by men who had little experience of a stampede and who could not handle the enormous demands made upon them. Pandemonium reigned in the government offices, which in the summer of '98 were snowed under by one hundred thousand official documents. There was not a duplicate copy of any of these, for paper had been so short that some records had to be kept on pieces of wood. The government staff lived in dread of a fire, which would have produced utter chaos, as every record of every mining transaction would have been irretrievably lost. All that season the queues of people trying to record claims, or purchase miner's licences, or simply get information, stretched for blocks. Thomas Fawcett, the gold commissioner, was followed by a swarm of petitioners whenever he appeared on the streets. So great was the press of the crowd about him that at twelve noon sharp he would burst from his office and head for his boarding-house for lunch at a dead run, his petitioners in hot pursuit. Fawcett was one of the chief targets of the *Nugget,* which eventually helped to secure his removal; but there is no evidence that he was dishonest — only harassed. Some of his staff, however, were certainly culpable.

Scenes similar to those in front of the gold office took place at the post office. No one had foreseen the blizzard of mail that would descend upon the Klondike; no one had made arrangements to handle it. All the previous winter, deliveries had been sporadic and uncertain. In December, 1897, Captain Ray, the U.S. infantry officer at Fort Yukon, had accidentally found a

415

second-class-mail sack lying in the snow and on opening it had discovered, to his astonishment and frustration, several hundred letters that should have been delivered to Dawson. It transpired that one hundred such sacks, all intended for the Klondike, had by an error been put ashore at Fort Yukon, on U.S. soil.

All winter long, United States citizens in Dawson had been fuming over a piece of bureaucracy that did not take into account the enormous distances in the northwest. All letters mailed from the U.S. and addressed to Dawson were placed in the Circle City sack at Juneau on the coast. They were then brought through Dawson and on to Circle before being returned for distribution. This involved a delay of two or three months, and as a result some men did not hear from their families for months or even years. One man, awaiting a letter at the Dawson post office and not receiving it, sobbed out that he had been eighteen months in the country without word from home. Letters were subjected to so much handling that some were stripped of their envelopes by the time they reached their destination. In the fall of 1897, before a proper post office was established, three boxes of mail were placed at the A.C. store, the N.A.T. store, and Jimmy Kerry's saloon, all filled with coverless letters, many entirely unidentifiable. One, dated June 1894, opened with the words "My darling boy" and closed with "Your anxious but everloving mother." Letter after letter of this kind was read and pawed over by hundreds of men trying to find their own mail.

The hard-pressed Mounted Police, who had become jacks of every trade in the Yukon, took over the handling of mail in October, 1897, and were still in charge when the main rush reached Dawson. It was a task for which they were neither trained nor prepared. William Ogilvie reported to the Minister of the Interior that the

Dawson post office entailed as much work as that of a city of one hundred and fifty thousand because there was no delivery. One arriving steamboat brought fifty-seven hundred letters in a single batch. Every resident had to collect his own mail. Some waited vainly in line three days, until the price for a place in the queue rose to five dollars. Women made wages holding places for wealthy prospectors who could not afford the time to wait for their letters. The supply of stamps was so inadequate that the police were forced to dole them out two to a customer. No matter what the denomination, the price was always twenty-five cents because there was no small change in the community.

Against this background the cauldron of Dawson boiled and steamed. There was even talk of revolution, but none dared to flout the iron rule of Sam Steele. The *Nugget* continued to rail at the government, while the two other papers, the *Midnight Sun* and the *Miner*, took the opposite side. Canadian mining regulations were considered harsh by the Americans, who tended to forget that on the other side of the border no foreigner could stake or own a claim at all. Because most of the Klondike claims were held by foreigners who were intent on taking the gold out of the country, the government imposed a royalty of ten per cent on everything that was mined. This almost unheard-of regulation, which came into force on September 11, 1897, stuck in the craw of Canadians and Americans alike, especially as it was increased to twenty per cent if the output of any mine exceeded five hundred dollars a week. As a result, every kind of deception was used to falsify the amounts being mined, so that today no true record exists of the real value of gold taken from the Klondike, and all figures showing output during the peak years can be considered low. Major Nevill Armstrong, who operated rich claims on Bonanza Creek and on Cheechako

Hill, wrote: "I do not believe more than one-tenth part of the correct tax was ever recovered from individual miners."

The royalty underwent many changes. On June 1, 1898, Commissioner Walsh reduced it to a straight ten per cent on output, with an annual exemption of five thousand dollars. This still did not satisfy the miners, who held bitter meetings of protest and dispatched delegations to Ottawa. The *Nugget* called Fawcett and Walsh grafters, and when the former was finally relieved of his post in November it ran a sardonic headline: "Goodbye Fawcett!" The harried gold commissioner must have been happy to depart. Thrust into the maelstrom of the Klondike from a quiet sinecure in a British Columbia backwater, he had never been equal to the task. He much preferred the quiet of a Dawson Sunday, when he led the choir of the Presbyterian church and forgot the hurly-burly of the weekday.

Of the two government figures, Fawcett, the gold commissioner, and Walsh, the commissioner (or governor) of the Yukon, it is Walsh, the ex-Mountie, who in retrospect seems the more tragic, for his truly great career was blemished by his Klondike experience.

When he arrived in the Klondike, charged with governing the Yukon, Walsh still bore himself with the military vigour that matched his background. His iron-grey hair was brushed back from his broad and weather-beaten forehead. His moustache and short beard bristled. He still stood straight as a rapier, a broad-shouldered, square-jawed, athletic-looking man of fifty-four. Although he had been retired from the police for fifteen years and had become a coal dealer in Winnipeg, the aura of a legend still surrounded him. This was the same commanding figure who, a quarter-century before, immaculate in pillbox hat and polished boots, had been the first uniformed man to ride into the armed camp of

418

Sitting Bull and his warriors, from whose saddle horns the scalps of Custer's men still joggled. This was the man who had literally kicked the famous medicine man in the pants, and who had humiliated White Dog, the fierce Assiniboine, in the presence of hundreds of armed Indians. This was the conqueror of Little Child, the horse-stealing chief of the Salteaux.

But Walsh lasted only two months in the Klondike. In August he was recalled and the post of commissioner of the Yukon given to William Ogilvie. It was Ogilvie who presided in midwinter at a royal commission investigating charges of government graft brought by the *Nugget* and by others. He was hampered by the fact that the commission's terms of reference did not extend past August 25; by the time of the hearings most of the witnesses had left the country. For this reason, and no doubt for political ones, its results were inconclusive, but it did throw a long shadow over the hitherto unsullied character of Walsh. The ex-commissioner's cook, Louis Carbeno, testified under oath that he had got his job only by signing a document giving three-quarters interest in any claim he staked to either Walsh or Walsh's brother Philip. This was particularly damning because Carbeno was one of the men who had successfully staked claims on Dominion Creek during the infamous stampede of July 1898, and Walsh of course had inside knowledge of Dominion.

The Dominion Creek stampede provides the best evidence of the chaos and chicanery that existed in the government offices in Dawson that summer. The thirty-mile-long creek flows down from King Solomon's Dome, directly opposite Hunker, and into the Indian River. So rich was it that half a century after the stampede two dredges were still taking large quantities of gold from it. Within a few months of being staked (June, 1897) some of its claims were selling for as much as forty thousand dollars. But it was staked so haphazardly, especially along the benches, that a large section had to be closed until a proper survey could untangle the endless disputes that sprang up about overlapping claims. It was announced that no new claims after November 15, 1897, would be recognized, and that the creek would not be reopened for staking until July 11, 1898. It was further announced that nobody could prospect on Dominion without a permit; these permits would be given out at ten a.m. on July 11. This meant that — on the face of it, at least — all comers would be given an equal start from Dawson, which lay forty miles from the head of the creek.

In spite of these arrangements, a large number of stampeders, including Walsh's man Carbeno, headed for Dominion Creek three days before the deadline, without bothering to wait for permits. Carbeno did so with Walsh's permission. The morning after he left — July 9 — a notice appeared, dated July 8, announcing that no permits were needed after all, and all claims were open. Thousands headed for Dominion, forcing their horses through forty miles of brush and muskeg, but the government favourites were already on the site, staking out the best ground. Carbeno turned over his claim and that of two Indian helpers to the commissioner's brother Philip, who, he swore, had provided him with the inside information. The barefaced audacity of the Dominion Creek muddle brought tempers to boiling-point and resulted in the royal commission hearings. But because of the lack of conclusions, there were no indictments. Little was published about Walsh's part in the affair, except in the fine print of the commission's report, which was relegated to a dusty shelf in Ottawa.

The Mounted Police kept out of this cesspool, did their duty, and asked no questions. But their relations

420

with the veteran ex-Mountie must have undergone considerable strain, for Walsh still felt himself in charge of the force. It was his occasional habit, as commissioner of the Yukon, to place parties of police under his own civilian staff to perform tasks that were not properly part of their duty. Constables found themselves being ordered about like servants, chopping wood for civilians, until the habit of having a Mountie do one's chores spread to other government officials. This irksome and touchy situation came to an end when Walsh departed, but to the incorruptible Steele it must have been maddening. If so, he betrayed no hint of it. He was working twenty hours a day, seldom retiring before two in the morning and always rising at six. He was out of doors by seven, and in the next hour walked briskly for five miles over the Klondike hills. All day until midnight he officiated on boards and committees, squeezing his routine work in between, but always making a point of seeing every one of his fifty prisoners daily. And he was not too busy to perform small gallantries. One day Faith Fenton, the Toronto *Globe*'s woman reporter in the Klondike, came to him in tears. Three Indians had been scheduled to hang for the murder of two stampeders in the Tagish area the previous spring, and she had arranged to scoop her competitors by writing the story in advance and shipping it out by fast dog-team. Now a postponement had come because the execution had been unwittingly scheduled for All Saints Day, a religious holiday. Steele instantly dispatched a dog-team on a fifty-mile run to recapture and destroy Miss Fenton's premature report.

He ruled his men with the same good sense with which he ruled the town. One night his sergeant-major rapped on his door to report that some of the constables had been breaking barracks and were not at their beds

421

when night roll-call came. Steele waved the complaint aside.

"They're young," he said, "and they'll never see a mining camp like this again. So long as they do their duty, it won't hurt them to go a bit large."

For Sam Steele understood, far better than most men in the Klondike, that he was presiding at a bizarre and unforgettable moment in history.

Chapter Eleven

1
Soapy Smith takes over

2
Alias Robin Hood

3
The Committee of 101

4
Dictator of Skagway

5
Shoot-out at the Juneau dock

6
No escape

1: *Soapy Smith takes over*

Skagway . . . the Fourth of July, 1898. . . . Independence Day in a town that has known little real independence. The streets are gay with miles of bunting and acres of flags and rockets, with firecrackers and popping six-guns, with exploding dynamite and blaring bands and marching men.

Down Broadway Avenue the procession advances, and at its head, mounted upon a handsome dapple-grey, is a pale-faced man with the eyes of a poet and the beard of a Mephisto, who waves his spotless white sombrero in greeting to the crowd. And the crowd waves back and cheers as Jefferson Randolph Smith, the marshal of the parade and the dictator of Skagway, goes riding past.

Little children are munching Jeff Smith's free candy and peanuts; the male adults have had their bellies warmed by his whiskey. Behind the dance-hall band that follows his lead down Broadway come the Skagway Guards, Jeff Smith's personal military unit, armed and uniformed and marching in step to the music. And threaded in among the mob, at every street corner and intersection, are the members of the carefully organized spy system through which he controls the town.

On the procession moves towards the flag-draped platform where Jeff Smith, once known as "Soapy," will be joined by the Governor of Alaska himself for the official Independence Day ceremonies. It is Smith's supreme moment: he has come a long way since he began his career in Leadville a quarter-century ago. Now that career has reached its climax; let him savour it; in just four days he will be dead, and there will be none to mourn his passing. . . .

The means which Soapy Smith employed in his subjugation of a town of ten thousand were tried and tested in the school of experience. He knew exactly what he was doing because he had done it all before; Skagway was the crowning-point in a long and rich career of knavery.

He had been born in Georgia and liked to give the impression that he was the son of a prominent Southern family, although this fact has ever been in dispute. But the Dixie background had contributed a soft accent and a courtly manner that remained with him and were of immeasurable value in convincing the unwary that he was a man of honour and upbringing. He had, indeed, studied for the Baptist ministry as a youth, and often boasted that he could "straighten out Greek hexameters with the best of them." He had a wife and six children in St. Louis, and a brother on the editorial staff of the Washington *Star,* and he maintained a vast and often rewarding correspondence with congressmen, Senators, civic officials, and prominent citizens throughout the western hemisphere.

It was in Leadville, the stamping-ground of Calamity Jane and Wild Bill Hickok, that his career had its chequered start. He had arrived from Texas driving longhorn steers up the old Chisholm Trail; it was the last time he soiled his hands in common toil. He learned the soap game from its inventor, a man named Taylor, and prospered so mightily that he earned the nickname which clung to him long after his death. He became a master of the shell game, the standby of all bunko men. And he could make a pack of cards do anything he wanted.

In the con man's pantheon Smith occupies an honoured place, for his contributions to the craft were considerable. The phrase "sure-thing game," with its companion phrase "sure-thing men," came into the language as the result of a retort made by Smith to the Clerical Association of Denver, which fought him vainly.

425

"I'm no ordinary gambler," Smith declared. "The ordinary gambler hazards his own money in an attempt to win another's. When I stake money, it's a sure thing that I win."

One of Smith's cohorts, Doc Baggs, was the inventor of the famous gold-brick game. In Denver, one of the most corrupt towns on the continent, Smith, as king of the underworld, operated almost every known bunko game. He even had the barbers working for him: they would nick the necks of wealthy customers as a signal that they were ripe for fleecing.

Smith had come to Denver from Leadville. In 1892 he moved on to the mushrooming silver camp of Creede. This roaring community, entirely without government or police, served as a sort of training-ground for Smith's later conquest of Skagway. His gang simply moved in like an invading army and took over the town, their only serious rival being Bob Ford, that "dirty little coward" who, ten years before, had laid Jesse James in his grave. Smith easily brought Ford into line and went on to rig the election, name the police chief, select the executive council, and appoint every civic official from justice of the peace to coroner. He controlled the town until the silver boom petered out, and then returned to Denver, which remained his operating base until 1897.

He was a man of considerable imagination and dry humour. Once, when haled before the fire-and-police commission on a charge of bilking two visitors out of fifteen hundred dollars, he produced such an ingenious and farfetched defence that it won his acquittal. He argued that his gaming-house was really an educational institution, similar to the famous Keeley Institute, affording its patients release from the curse of gambling. Smith went on to nail down his arguments by explaining that in his establishment gamblers had no chance of

426

winning — and were told as much by a sign displayed prominently at the head of the stairs: "LET THE BUYER BEWARE." (To give the place a suitably high tone, the words had been rendered in Greek.) Smith ended his harangue by exclaiming that as a result of his ministrations the two victims would never gamble again:

"In fact, gentlemen, I should be recognized as a public benefactor! Praise, instead of censure, should be our portion."

Occasionally, circumstances were such that Smith found it prudent to leave Denver temporarily, but when this occurred he merely transferred his operations elsewhere. There was the time that the dictator of Mexico, Don José de la Cruz Porfirio Díaz, suddenly found a "Colonel Smith" on his doorstep, a slender, grey-eyed gentleman, sallow of face and smooth of tongue, who claimed to be a military organizer and martial genius. Before Díaz quite knew what was happening, he found himself persuaded to set up a Mexican foreign legion under Colonel Smith's command. There was only one catch: the bearded colonel wanted eighty thousand pesos to do the job. The canny Díaz countered with an offer of four thousand, which Smith accepted. Back in Denver he actually opened a recruiting office, but Díaz, who was no easy mark, sent out spies to find out who Smith was and the scheme collapsed.

Smith was one of a generation that had grown up on the success stories of Horatio Alger, and he was in the habit of keeping the door ajar to anticipate the knock of opportunity. When the news of the Klondike strike flashed through Denver, he sensed that his hour had come and that he must move swiftly, as he had at Creede, before the new boom towns were properly organized. He made his decision at once to go north. By August he and his men were running shell games on the Skagway Trail.

427

He took five men with him as a nucleus for a new organization. His closest henchman was the "Reverend" Charles Bowers, who had been with him since Leadville days, a notorious bunko man whose saintly appearance, gentle voice, and benevolent mien made it possible for him to masquerade as a man of the cloth. Bowers's whole being exuded sanctimony, but he was as hard as sheet steel beneath the velvet exterior. There is a story that he once shot a peace officer, whom he recognized only when he had rolled him over. "Looks like I shot the sheriff," Bowers drawled, placing his foot on the corpse. "Ain't that too bad." Because of his personality Bowers was a first-class "steerer": he guided suckers to the various fake business establishments where other members of the gang lay in wait to fleece them. He was also known as a "grip man," for he had mastered the secret handshakes, signals, and distress signs that embellish most fraternal orders. Once Bowers had disarmed his victims with the fraternal signal, they were putty in his hands.

Two other long-time confreres of Smith went along to the North — Syd Dixon and George Wilder. Wilder, who acted as advance man for the gang, gave the impression of being a prosperous businessman, his personality suggesting such financial well-being that he was useful in playing the role of a stockbroker letting a new-found friend in on a sure thing. Actually he was a shrewd and thrifty man, and the only one in Smith's entourage who had a bank account and drew interest on it. Without his available funds, the sextet would never have been able to quit Denver. Syd Dixon came from a wealthy family and looked the part; a playboy and a globe-trotter, he had been driven to the gutter by an opium addiction and had taken to fraud only to raise money to buy more drugs. His dress, his manner, and his obvious gentility made him a valuable member of

428

the gang. These men and two newer members, Slim Jim Foster and Red Gibbs, formed the hard core of the organization that was to dominate Skagway.

On arrival, Smith went about his plan with care and dispatch, charting the ground as meticulously as any military commander bent upon conquest. Before settling definitely on Skagway as a seat of operations he moved up and down the Panhandle, examining both Wrangell and Juneau, each of them swollen by the flotsam and jetsam of the stampede. Juneau he discarded at once as a community too well established to lend itself easily to the kind of thralldom he had in mind. Wrangell, at the Stikine's mouth, lawless, mercurial, and utterly disorganized, was made to order, but Smith dismissed it, rightly, as a dead end. He quickly saw that Skagway would retain its position as the main floodgate through which the human torrent would surge in and out of the Yukon Valley. It commanded all American territory from the source streams of the Yukon to the salt water of the Lynn Canal, and the only law in all this region was a single U.S. marshal and his deputy. It was on Skagway that he pounced, with his walnut shells and his marked decks and his sure-thing games and his bogus establishments. Success was instantaneous; by October he was so well established that he was able to inveigle a missionary from a leading U.S. church into a shell game on the White Pass trail and separate him from all of his money.

2: *Alias Robin Hood*

One of the keys to Smith's success was that he never appeared to be what he was. His willowy physique, his broad-brimmed hat, his dark, conservative clothing embellished by a heavy gold watch-chain, his pleasant baritone and soft, grammatical speech all gave him the appearance of a Southern planter. He cultivated jour-

429

nalists, clergymen, and small children. Whenever an opportunity presented itself, he contrived to appear on the side of law and order, and his career is peppered with examples of his continuing resolve to maintain an aura of respectability. It had been his habit in Denver to send new twenty-dollar bills to needy men and widowed women at Christmas, to make donations and raise funds among his followers for churches, and even, on one occasion, to address a men's Bible class — ingeniously using himself as a bad example of what could happen to a man who eschewed a Christian life.

When a slim, sharp-nosed, and mysterious cowpoke named Ed O'Kelly shot down Bob Ford on the main street of Creede, it was Smith, playing the role of a man who respects the law, who saved him from a lynch mob. "Stand back! Let this man alone! Justice is going to be done!" Smith cried piously, and the mob obeyed him, for he was a man who always commanded authority.

On one of his early voyages up the Alaskan coast, when he was casing the various gold-rush towns, Smith again placed himself on the side of constituted authority and earned the everlasting gratitude of Dynamite Johnny O'Brien, the two-fisted skipper of the steamer *Utopia*. O'Brien, perhaps the most colourful sea captain on the Pacific coast, had a history so garish that it tended to read like one of the more florid sea novels popular at the time. He had narrowly missed being eaten by cannibals; had fought off Chinese pirates with cannon fire; had supped with the royal family of Hawaii; had made love to a Tahitian princess; had been offered a partnership by King O'Keefe, the famous white emperor of the island of Yap; and had shipped with the hairy and villainous Robert O'Malley, prototype for Jack London's *Sea Wolf*. But when Smith encountered him, Dynamite Johnny had reached the low point of his career. He had managed to survive an

430

operation for a burst tumour which had been performed in a hut on the shores of Cook Inlet, Alaska, by a pseudo-doctor whose makeshift instruments were a knife and a pair of scissors honed to razor sharpness. He was lying in his bunk in Seattle harbour, burning with fever and without enough ready cash to buy fuel for his ship, when Smith appeared with a bankroll and two heavy-framed revolvers, the two items that O'Brien needed most. The bankroll purchased enough cheap coal to raise steam and head for Juneau with Smith aboard; the revolvers helped stem a mutiny which sprang up because of the wretched quality of the fuel. When the crew stopped the ship, eight hours out of Seattle, Smith, a revolver in each hand, guided the ailing captain to the deck, where the two men browbeat all hands into continuing the voyage. From that moment on, Smith's men travelled aboard O'Brien's ships en route to Alaska, striking up acquaintanceships with wealthy stampeders, who were marked for subsequent plucking.

It was aboard the *City of Seattle*, in January, 1898, that another made-to-order incident occurred which allowed Smith to pose on the side of constituted authority. He had taken advantage of the midwinter lull in the stampede to return to St. Louis and Washington, D.C., partly to visit his family, partly to recruit more men in anticipation of the second wave of the gold rush. One of the passengers aboard ship had been swinging in the halyards and in doing so loosened a heavy lamp, which plummeted down, striking him neatly on the head and killing him outright. This was all that was needed to provoke a dangerous situation on the overcrowded vessel, where, as on every ship that plied Alaskan water that winter, the passengers nursed a burning hatred for the ship's officials. In a high state of agitation, they called a mass meeting and prepared to launch a fifty-

431

thousand-dollar damage suit against the company. Smith seized the occasion to present himself as a man who believes in order and fair play. He went through the corpse's pockets and produced a packet which he claimed the victim had stolen from him.

"Now, you scum," he cried, brandishing this evidence, "if you want to stand up for a man who is a stowaway, a cheat, and a bum, I'm off with you." The meeting broke up, and a few days later the champion of law and order was hard at work in Skagway cheating his fellow passengers.

He was back in Skagway only three days before a double shooting occurred that served to demonstrate the unseen power that he wielded. The affair started when Andy McGrath, a worker on the Brackett toll road across the White Pass, put a bill down for a drink in a saloon and was refused change — a standard practice in Skagway that winter. When McGrath protested, the saloon-keeper, John Edward Fay, threw him out. McGrath, a stubborn man, sought out the deputy marshal, a man named Rowan, who at that moment was seeking a doctor to deliver his wife of a child. As the marshal was away and there was no other law officer available, Rowan postponed his quest long enough to accompany McGrath to the saloon, and in doing so sealed his fate. As the two men burst through the doors, Fay shot them both. McGrath fell dead, and Rowan was mortally wounded. To add to the confusion, a night watchman named Jones, on hearing the shots, drew his gun and shouted: "If there's shooting to be done, I'm in it!" whereupon he fired at random into the street, hitting a saloon habitué in the knee.

Within an hour the town was in an uproar. Rowan lay dying in the office of Dr. J. J. Moore, who had just delivered his wife of a child. Fay had escaped during the confusion and was being concealed by his gambler

432

friends, all of them in loose association with Smith. A mob was combing the alleyways for the saloon-keeper and howling for his blood.

Smith threatened a general slaughter if Fay were lynched. "We muster upwards of two hundred men with their guns, and if anyone tries to put a rope over Ed Fay's neck he'll get a bullet in his own head mighty quick," he announced. Then he laid plans secretly to control the lynch mob and at the same time curry general favour with the populace.

Fay surrendered the following day, and a mass meeting was called that evening in the Union Church to bring him to justice. Smith did not attend, but he dominated the affair. A committee was appointed to guard Fay and another to investigate the murder and empanel twelve jurors to try the culprit. The names of these committeemen were suggested to the chairman of the meeting by the editor of the Skagway *Alaskan*, who, unbeknown to the townspeople, was in Smith's pay. As a result Fay escaped the town's vengeance and was spirited off to Sitka, where he stood trial and received a light sentence.

While all this was going on, Smith was raising a purse for Rowan's widow, with his own name at the head of the list of subscribers. Thus, in a single stroke, he was able to pose as an enemy of mob rule, a friend of destitute widows, a contributor to charity, and — by virtue of saving Fay's neck — a refuge for criminals.

These matters astonished the Reverend J. A. Sinclair, a Presbyterian minister who arrived shortly after the event to spread the gospel in Skagway. "A lynching bee held in a church!" he wrote his wife. "And the Robin Hood of the town controlling that meeting's proceedings and practically nominating the committee; and the desperado at the same time protecting the murderer and taking up a public subscription for the relief of the widow of his victim." In such a community, Sinclair realized, a minister's work would be cut out for him.

3: *The Committee of 101*

In the six weeks that followed, a seesaw battle was waged between the gamblers, saloon-keepers, and confidence men of Skagway, on the one side, and the more law-abiding citizenry on the other. For although the stampede had attracted the grifters and the sharpers, the camp-followers and the hoodlums, it had also acted as a magnet for a quite different type of man. This was the restless wanderer, the frontiersman and Indian-fighter, who moved just ahead of the tide of civilization, settling for a few months or a few years at one place, accepting a sheriff's badge occasionally, and then pushing on as the frontier advanced. Every mass movement since the California rush had benefited from this breed: they shot straight, feared nobody, were generally incorruptible, and had the interests of the community at heart. Such a man was Frank Reid, the city engineer of Skagway, and it was around this granite-faced and cool-eyed wanderer that the opposition to Smith rallied.

Reid was in his mid-fifties, but he had been one of the first men on the beach when Skagway was founded. Indeed, it was he who laid out the townsite over the protests of Captain William Moore. Born in Illinois, he had been working his way west and north for most of his life. He had gone to the University of Michigan, moved across the plains, fought the Indians in Oregon during the Bannock-Piute wars, settled as a school-teacher among the pioneer families of the Willamette Valley, and stampeded north at the first news of the Klondike strike. He was a good surveyor and construction en-

434

gineer as well as a fine outdoorsman and a crack shot. He feared nobody, and it was said that he was the only man of whom Soapy Smith was ever wary.

Reid and his two close friends, Major J. M. "Si" Tanner and Captain J. L. Sperry, both former police officers and Indian-fighters, were at the core of the vigilante movement which sprang up in Skagway, as it had in every U.S. mining camp since the days of California. On January 31, one week after the Fay incident, a group of aroused citizens petitioned Washington for federal troops and asked that the town be placed under martial law. The infantrymen were dispatched on February 8, and the newly formed vigilantes, emboldened by the federal support, decided to drive the underworld element from the town. Suddenly most of the confidence men and gamblers seemed to melt away, and the committee felt that its brief efforts had been more than successful.

Incredibly, Smith himself was not asked to leave. Some of the committeemen thought him harmless. "Jeff's a good fellow, generous and public-spirited," one of them said. "When his gang is gone he can do no harm." Others were undoubtedly afraid to put the finger on him. At one mass meeting he had suddenly appeared with a drawn gun and single-handedly dispersed the cowed assemblage.

The gang had not fled; Smith had merely sent them out onto the trails, where they preyed upon the stampeders. By now the lawless element in the community, realizing that there was more profit and less risk in being part of a single organization, had accepted Smith as their leader and protector. By late February he was able to write to a friend in Seattle that "we have got them licked and mean to rule absolutely." At the same time the following news dispatch appeared in the nation's press:

435

"Seattle, Feb. 25 — Officers of the steamer *Noyo* from Skagway today reported conditions of lawlessness at Skagway beyond description. Soapy Smith and his gang are in full control. Law-abiding people do not dare say a word against them. Holdups, robberies and shootings are part of the routine. Eight dead bodies were picked up on the White Pass on February 15."

On March 6 a man was sandbagged outside his home on Broadway, Skagway's main street, and the following morning there were twelve robberies and a murder on the White Pass trail, the victim shot at such close range that there were powder burns on his face. Again the vigilantes called a mass meeting, and the militia, which had been reluctant to interfere in Skagway's civic affairs, was called in. On March 15 infantry officers posted notices closing the gaming-rooms, and at one p.m. two companies of soldiers arrived from Dyea to enforce the order.

Emboldened, the vigilantes held a second mass meeting and, the following day, posted this notice:

> ### WARNING
> A Word to the Wise should be sufficient.
> All con men, bunco and sure-thing men and
> all other objectionable characters are noti-
> fied to leave Skagway and the White Pass
> Road immediately and remain away.
> Failure to comply with this warning will be
> followed by prompt action.
> *(Signed)* The Committee of 101

Smith now moved to confuse the issue so completely that no one would know who represented law and order in Skagway. His strategy was to form his own vigilante committee, which he titled "The Committee of Law and Order." (Significantly, the name was the same as that taken by the corrupt element which defied the vigilante movement in San Francisco in 1856.) Although Reid, for one, had been in Skagway from the very first, Smith shrewdly manoeuvred himself into the position of protecting the "business interests" of the town against "newcomers," the business interests being the barrooms and gaming-houses. There were no less than seventy saloons in operation in Skagway, all of them outside the laws of Alaska, which forbade the sale of alcohol.

Within a few hours of the posting of the vigilantes' warning, Smith placarded the town with posters of his own:

> The business interests of Skagway propose to put a stop to the lawless acts of many newcomers. We hereby summon all good citizens to a meeting at which these matters will be discussed. Come one, come all! Immediate action will be taken for relief. Let this be a warning to those cheechakos who are disgracing our city. The Meeting will be held at Sylvester Hall at 8 p.m. sharp.
>
> *(Signed)* Jefferson R. Smith, Chairman

Smith addressed the meeting himself, his cool grey eyes, which seemed to bore right through a man, rubbering swiftly over each member of the audience.

"Fellow citizens!" he cried, while his cohorts, placed strategically about the hall, stomped and cheered. "We are here to form a real committee, not a half-baked, irresponsible committee such as we have been hearing about. We have the support of the business element of Skagway. We deplore present conditions, which are caused not by our own people but by riffraff from all parts of the world. We will protect ourselves, even at the cost of our lives."

437

Having offered to sacrifice himself, if necessary, for the good of the town, Smith issued the following proclamation:

PUBLIC WARNING

The body of men styling themselves the Committee of 101 are hereby notified that any overt act committed by them will promptly be met by the law-abiding citizens of Skagway and each member and his property will be held responsible for any unlawful act on their part, and the Law and Order Society, consisting of 317 citizens, will see that justice is dealt out to its fullest extent as no blackmailers or vigilantes will be tolerated.

(Signed) The Committee

The situation was now utterly confused. Half the people of Skagway saw Smith as the devil incarnate. Half saw him as a good fellow and public-spirited townsman trying to bring order out of chaos. Smith's own men, under the guise of ordinary citizens, infiltrated the vigilantes' meetings and produced further confusion and vacillation. The anti-Smith movement ground to a stop, the soldiers returned to their base at Dyea, and within a month Smith was being referred to as "the Uncrowned King of Skagway."

4: *Dictator of Skagway*

By April, Smith's organization numbered somewhere between two and three hundred confidence men, harlots and pimps, thugs, gamblers and cardsharps, most of them operating under colourful nicknames such as the Moonfaced Kid, the Lamb, the Doctor, the

438

Queen, the Blackjack, Fatty Green, Yank Fewclothes, and Kid Jimmy Fresh.

Each of these men acted out a role — like Bowers, the pseudo man of the cloth, and Old Man Tripp, the fake stampeder — but the greatest actor was Smith himself, who continued, for the rest of his days, to play the part of a respectable, public-spirited, and openhanded citizen. There is little doubt that towards the end of his reign the role took over from the real man, and that Smith sincerely believed himself to be the protector and benefactor of Skagway.

To all intents and purposes, he was the proprietor of an oyster parlour which served the best food in town. He had opened it in partnership with two of Skagway's most prominent saloon-keepers, Frank and John Clancy, and it stood in the geographical centre of the business district, just off Broadway, with the number "317," emblematic of the Law and Order Committee, emblazoned on its white false front. It looked innocent enough, with its polished mahogany bar, its fretwork screens, and its artificial palm trees, but into Jeff Smith's Parlour the suckers were lured like so many flies by the spider web of his expanding organization. Behind the main restaurant and bar was a "'pretty back parlour, as cozy as a lady's boudoir," in the words of the Skagway *Alaskan*, and it was here that the unwary were cheated or robbed of their money. Behind this was a small yard enclosed by a high board fence especially constructed with a secret exit through which Smith's men could disappear with their loot. The enraged victim, rushing after his vanishing bankroll, would burst out the back door only to be baffled by an empty yard and a blank, unbroken wall.

Smith never involved himself with these affairs and at no time became entangled with the law. He sought, instead, to maintain the impression that his only inter-

439

est in the law-breakers was to preserve such influence with them as would enable him to get them at times to make restitution to needy victims. But all the plunder snatched from well-heeled suckers was taken straight to his safe, where it lay until the furore was over. Smith took a fifty-per-cent commission, much of which he used to bribe law officers, conduct legal defences, or make a partial restoration to the victims to prevent them from complaining too loudly. The more direct methods of silencing a man were left to his bouncers — to the villainous Yeah Mow Hopkins, whose name meant wildcat in Chinese and who had once been a bodyguard for wealthy Orientals in the San Francisco tong wars, or to Big Ed Burns, who had been with him since Denver days and who made a habit of chewing cigars whole.

Smith was philosophical about the beatings that Burns or Hopkins administered to the swindled clerks and bookkeepers who came to his parlour and protested too loudly. "The greatest kindness one can do such people is to force them to get out of Skagway and to take the first boat home," he once remarked.

This was Smith's great propaganda argument on the street corners of Skagway and in the various places of business where his smooth tongue was seldom still: the sure-thing men were a public benefit to the town, he argued, for they not only kept business brisk by putting into circulation money that would otherwise leave the city, but also they performed an act of charity in keeping the innocent from going deeper into the Arctic wilderness.

"Infinitely better," Smith would argue, "that any man who is such an infant as to try to beat a man at his own game should lose money here at the seaport, than he should get into the inhospitable Arctic, where such an idiot would lose it anyway or be a burden on the community."

And then he would go on to discuss the universal corruptibility of character and to praise the public-spirited attitude of the saloon men and gamblers, while his flunkies applauded and the hangers-on nodded their heads sagely and said, yes, there was something to that, all right.

In some ways Smith was a generation ahead of his time, for, although he operated on a small stage, the tactics he used in Skagway were remarkably similar to those employed by various European dictators in the years that followed. All the basic elements were present: the hard and disciplined core of ruthless men who swiftly went to work under cover; the leader who presented himself as a champion of the people; the spy system and the secret police; the relentless propaganda machine; and, most important, the careful cultivation of the basic elements in the community — business, labour, church, and press.

The business community tolerated him and, in some cases, applauded him because he seemed to bring order out of chaos; as is so often the case, men preferred order to liberty, which they confused with anarchy. One of Smith's first moves, on consolidating his power, was to make it a rule never to fleece or molest a permanent citizen of Skagway, but only transients. When some of his men sheared the youthful chief of the local fire department, he was aghast and returned the victim's money, at the same time giving his followers a tongue-lashing. Moreover, he managed to exude an aura of law and order by halting minor misdemeanours and performing such incidental acts of justice as returning runaway daughters to frantic fathers.

When another group of outlaws tried to take possession of the toll road that George Brackett of Minneapolis was attempting to open up along the White Pass trail, Smith came to the rescue. He told the trespassers they ought to be ashamed of themselves: "The opening of that highway was being done at great expense and ... without it none of them could have any money or get through the country." When the gang refused to move, Smith told them that he would give them so many hours to get off the road "or I will come up with my Indians and throw your whole gang into the Skagway river." He did not need to make good his threat; the outlaws had vanished by the following morning.

He made himself popular with the workingmen by taking the side of the stevedores in a strike that swept the waterfront. He distributed twenty-dollar goldpieces among them "just to see the fun," as he put it, and the speech he made to the strikers was in the best tradition of labour agitation:

"Your cause is just — make 'em come through! These owners are clearing fortunes by the sweat of your brows. They're making slaves of you. Stick for better wages, and if they won't pay, let their ships lie at the wharves. ... They're raking in barrels of dough."

With that he appointed himself strikers' representative in negotiations with the dock-owners and continued to back the stevedores until they won the dispute.

He continued his policy, established in Denver, of outward support of the church, and there are two recorded instances of charity drives backed by Smith in the Skagway area, although there is some evidence that, at least in one case, all the money was stolen back within twelve hours.

He had very little difficulty in suborning the press. It was generally agreed that the editor of the *Alaskan* was in his pay. And when a prominent newspaperman, Billy Saportas of the New York *World,* lost his money at one

442

of Smith's gaming-tables and found himself stranded in Skagway, the dictator installed him on the staff of the paper at a salary of three hundred dollars a month. Saportas became his willing tool, describing him in print as "the most gracious, kind hearted man I've ever met" and adding that "to know him is to like him." When Edward F. Cahill was sent to Skagway by the San Francisco *Examiner* to investigate reports of lawlessness, Smith handled him with delicacy and dispatch. He took Cahill under his personal wing and showed him the town. Cahill was charmed by Smith's attention. "Soapy Smith is not a dangerous man," he told the outside world. "He is not a desperado. He is not a scoundrel. He is not a criminal. . . ." Cahill exhausted his stock of superlatives in describing the dictator. He called him cool, fearless, generous, and honourable, and wrote that "he bitterly resents the imputation that he is a thief and a vagrant." Before Smith was through with Cahill, the newspaperman had turned to poetry to eulogize him and had soon produced a flowery ode which extolled Smith's patriotism and Americanism.

All this time Smith kept in touch with the world outside, and especially with the underworld, through a remarkable correspondence which ranged far and wide, from the Pacific northwest to Central America. He got letters from politicians, lawyers, professional men, journalists, and crooks. He got letters from El Paso, Texas, and from Guatemala, from confederates who had "bought" towns and civic governments. He got letters from Cy Warman of *McClure's* magazine, which wanted to publish an article about him. He got a letter from a congressman in St. Louis enclosing two pairs of brass knuckles, and another from a political fixer named Mulgrew who wrote: "I can get police indulgence if anybody can." He got letters from chance acquaintances asking for money, which often enough he sent as insurance against the future, and he got letters from old accomplices warning him of enemies in Skagway or advising him of suckers en route north.

"It seems you will be the next chief [of police]," one correspondent wrote from San Francisco on February 28, "and, if so, I am glad of it so that you can regulate some of the wolves that's in our line of calling. They must have some man of judgement to regulate them or they will break up any place they try to go. There is one in particular who is strictly out for himself and I hear he is in your town. . . . I tell you, Jeff, he would put you and everyone else in jail to have the graft himself."

Smith's staff of correspondents formed an endless chain, a sort of continental spy-network, and he carefully pasted every letter into a huge scrapbook, which he kept up to date and concealed in a drawer of his old-fashioned roll-top desk along with the badges and emblems of the Masons, Oddfellows, and other fraternal organizations which, from time to time, were of value to him.

On the local scene Smith operated an equally efficient spy system. "You never knew who was who in Skagway, in Smith's day," J. E. C. Beatty, a worker on the White Pass Railway, once recalled."Your next-door neighbor, or the man at the next table in a restaurant, might be in his pay." Smith's methods of recruitment were straightforward enough. Harry L. Suydam, who served as city assessor, wrote that "while 'Soapy' Smith was not implicated in all the black deeds of the trail, he never failed to take the side of the guilty party, and often fought hard to have him go unpunished, no doubt anticipating that the rescued villain would not fail to do anything for him when called upon." Both the Land Commissioner and the Deputy Marshal, whose office was in the same building as Suydam's, "willingly stood in with 'Soapy' in his atrocious deals, for a con-

444

sideration." Suydam personally helped arrest several men on the White Pass trail who were caught stealing from caches; in every case, after they were turned over to the marshal, they were allowed to escape.

If Smith understood the principles of espionage, he was also well aware of the value of good public relations. Stray dogs and helpless widows have long been recognized as proper subjects for front-page stories, and Smith fully understood the necessity of cultivating human-interest items about himself. By the spring of '98, Skagway was ridden with abandoned dogs of every size, shape, and pedigree. They had all been purchased at astronomical prices in Seattle by greenhorns, who brought them north under the mistaken impression that they could be trained to pull a sled. When the stark truth was discovered and the cheechakos realized that the dogs were eating them into early bankruptcy, the canines were abandoned to roam the streets in packs. Smith launched an "Adopt-A-Dog" campaign and set a good example by taking on six strays himself.

At the same time he publicly began to provide for women whose husbands had met death on the trail and for luckless stampeders who had lost their money before reaching the gold-fields. As many of the unfortunate ladies had been brought to widowhood by Smith's own men, and most of the penniless Klondikers had been deprived of their funds in Smith's own establishments, they were thus being supported with their own coin. An astonished Denver merchant, on arriving in Skagway, wrote to a friend that their former townsman had accounts at merchants' stores for provisions and fuel for needy people that amounted to "several hundred dollars a week" and that "he pays for the funerals of friendless persons, and I can assure you that is no small item."

Now an odd thing happened: Soapy Smith's character began to undergo a subtle change. He had been playing Santa Claus in Skagway for coldly practical reasons, but as time went on he began to relish the applause that his small philanthropies brought him. There had always been a streak of vanity and of prodigality in his nature; years before when William De Vere, the "tramp poet," wrote a ballad in his honour, Smith was so pleased he gave him a thousand dollars. Now wealth and power were no longer enough for him; he wanted homage. Like everybody else, he had gone north seeking a fortune, but in the weeks that remained money ceased to have meaning to him and he gave the entire fortune away. He liked to see his name in the papers; he liked to be known as a good fellow; he liked to be seen patting children on the head and tipping lavishly. For him, the fealty of his followers had become insufficient; he craved the devotion of the entire community. And when, at the end, the community turned against him he acted quite humanly, with pain, astonishment, hurt, resentment, and finally unreasoning rage.

The outbreak of the Spanish-American War on April 24 gave Smith a further opportunity to entrench himself in Skagway. Within three days of war's declaration he had appointed himself captain of Company A, 1st Regiment, National Guard of Alaska, and, in a burst of old-fashioned patriotism, had opened a military office in a tent and begun recruiting soldiers for service in the Philippines. This move gave him an excuse to arm and drill his followers, so that he had a disciplined force under his command. It also provided his cronies with a perfect base of operations for an ingenious confidence game. The wave of patriotism that swept the nation following the sinking of the *Maine* rapidly made itself felt on the trails to the Klondike, and many stampeders

446

decided to forsake the gold-fields for the service of their country. Pouring back through Skagway, these would-be soldiers were attracted to a sign on a tent reading "United States Army Recruiting Station." Inside, a brisk, military-looking man, flanked by armed guards, swiftly signed each man up for service, congratulated him on his patriotism, and waved him into the rear for the necessary medical examination. While a fake doctor examined the recruits, others swiftly went through the pockets of their discarded clothing for valuables; if the patriots protested they were thrown out into the street in their underwear.

Captain Smith's military staff were all close cronies. His lieutenant was a three card monte man known as "the Senator." The bouncer at Clancy's Music Hall was named sergeant. The bartender at the Klondike Saloon became chaplain to the Guards, while Stroller White of the Skagway *News* was placed in charge of publicity — an item that Smith never ignored. The Captain bought up all the ribbon in town to make badges for his men, and when the supply ran out he made do with butcher paper. In a few days scores of his followers were decked out in bright badges bearing the words "Smith's Alaska Guards."

On Sunday, May 1, Smith arranged the greatest demonstration that Skagway had yet seen, in honour of his newly formed military unit. He marched at the head of a procession that stretched for two blocks, while two thousand people cheered on the sidelines, hundreds of them wearing badges of gold, white, and blue which read: "Freedom for Cuba! Remember the *Maine!* Compliments of Skagway Military Company, Jeff R. Smith, Captain."

The parade, which was accompanied by a brass band hastily organized by Jake Rice of the People's Theatre, suffered only one major interruption. When it passed the so-called Princess Hotel, a group of scantily-clad young women, headed by one Babe Davenport, demanded that Smith stop proceedings long enough to organize a women's auxiliary. "Your turn will come later," Smith is said to have replied, somewhat cryptically, and the parade got under way again.

At the meeting that followed, the crowd howled for Smith to make a speech, and the self-appointed captain mounted the rostrum, and in a ringing voice offered the services of himself and his men for president and country. As the crowd applauded Smith cried:

"There is one man who, in this terrible strife, has transcended the bounds of fair war. He has murdered the helpless and the weak, debauched women, butchered and starved little children. Mr. Chairman, this man we have with us today. I have him here, and we will proceed to hang and butcher Weyler!"

At a pre-arranged signal, an effigy of the Spanish general in Cuba was swung in the breeze and a bonfire kindled beneath. According to Stroller White, who was present, Smith then cried: "You are fine and brave men, each and every one of you, and I am sure you will unhesitatingly follow me anywhere and at any time." With that he turned on his heel and marched into his saloon, where seven extra bartenders had been retained "aproned and waiting to start, as they put it 'shovin' de booze over de wood.'" The Stroller claimed that Smith took in twenty-five hundred dollars that night.

Smith continued to mix patriotism with profit. Shortly afterwards he announced that a benefit would be staged for the widows and orphans of his troops, though he did not explain (nor did anyone dare ask in that emotion-charged period) why such an event was necessary. Smith was able to sell fourteen hundred and fifty tickets at a dollar apiece for the affair whose treasurer, a long-time crony, subsequently vanished with all

448

but seventy-five dollars of the proceeds. Few there were by this time who doubted that Soapy Smith was the benefactor of Skagway, its guiding light, the symbol of its honour and its pride, the emblem of its future prosperity. And when a few days later a personal letter came to Smith from the Secretary of War, thanking him for his patriotism (but politely declining his offer to serve in foreign climes), it seemed to set the seal on the affair. Smith treasured the document. He had it framed and hung in a prominent place on a wall in his oyster parlour. It told the world that Jefferson Randolph Smith was something more than just another tinhorn gambler.

5: *Shoot-out at the Juneau dock*

Independence Day in Skagway ... The sharp white peaks look down upon a sea of waving flags. The wind, whistling incessantly through the long shaft of the White Pass, rustles the gay bunting with which Jeff Smith has bedecked the main streets. The air is blue with gunsmoke and the scent of burning powder, and the mountain walls resound with the shouts of the holiday crowd and the blare of martial trumpets.

On a flag-draped rostrum the Governor of Alaska is speaking, and beside him, cross-legged and smiling, sits the dictator of Skagway. This is his moment of triumph. The world is his oyster. And yet, almost at this very instant, his nemesis is trudging down the White Pass trail towards the town. ...

J. D. Stewart, the prospector, did not look at all like an instrument of fate. There is a picture of him extant, and if ever a man looks like a sucker, it is he. There he stands, in front of a Skagway shack, clutching his poke of gold fiercely in his right hand, his cloth cap, a little too small for him, perched squarely across his bullet head. It is ironic that this square-faced, sombre-eyed man, with his thickly knotted tie, his heavy boots, and his shapeless, high-waisted trousers, should have been the unwitting instrument that brought the sudden downfall of the suave and elegant con man.

Stewart was in the advance guard of a human exodus from Dawson, and Skagway stood to be enriched by it. With the river open again after the long winter, the successful miners were clamouring to reach civilization and spend their gold. They could go downriver via St. Michael, or upriver and across the pass via Skagway. The former route was the easier, but the upriver route was the shorter, and Skagway was waiting in anticipation for hundreds of wealthy men to descend upon the town.

Stewart had twenty-eight hundred dollars in gold dust when he arrived in Skagway on July 7, en route to his home at Nanaimo, British Columbia. Friends in town warned him about Smith's gang and urged him to lock his gold in a safe at a hotel and leave it there until he booked passage south. It says something for the gang's powers of persuasion that they were able to talk Stewart out of it. On the morning of July 8 the sanctimonious Tripp and the saintly Bowers, posing as gold-buyers for a fake assaying company, convinced the prospector that he could get a better price for his dust if he brought his poke over to Jeff Smith's Parlor.

Stewart was taken into the notorious back room, and here, while the supposed price was being negotiated, a member of the gang, dressed like a fellow Klondiker and laughing to give the appearance of a joke, seized the bag and made for the door. The thief was almost out of sight before Stewart, in a daze, took after him. At this the others in the gang, pretending to misunderstand the situation, seized him and treated him as if he were drunk. Before Stewart knew it, he had been eased out into the street, the crowd had melted away, and all his gold was gone.*

This was too much. He went straight to the U.S. deputy marshal, a man named Taylor; but the officer, who was in Smith's pay, retorted that he could do nothing, as Stewart was unable to identify the man who had stolen the gold. He had only one suggestion: why didn't Stewart head back for the Klondike and dig out another twenty-eight hundred dollars? Having said this, he returned to the task at hand — supervising the carpentry work on a handsome new home for himself.

This infuriating attitude got Stewart's dander up, and he began to spread the story of his loss about the town. He told Calvin Barkdull, a horse packer who had brought his duffel bag over the pass the previous day, and Barkdull told his boss, Charles DeWitt, who owned one of the large packing outfits. DeWitt was shocked — not so much, apparently, by the moral aspect of the robbery as by its economic significance.

"My God," he exclaimed, "this won't do! If word gets down the river that the first man coming out by way

* This account, taken largely from the special edition of the Skagway *News* of July 8, 1898, agrees with that of several witnesses who were in Skagway at the time including the Rev. J. A. Sinclair, whose papers contain a personal account of Stewart's trouble. A somewhat different version of the affair was published in the *Alaska Sportsman* of March, 1958, by Stewart's daughter, Hazel Stewart Clark, who wrote that two of Smith's gang persuaded her father to put his poke of gold in the vault of a local hotel for safekeeping. When Stewart went to the hotel the following day to get his poke, he was told that nothing of his was in the vault and that no one at the hotel had ever seen him before. I find it difficult to believe that Stewart would not have asked for a receipt for a poke of gold worth close to three thousand dollars. In addition, the eyewitness accounts set down at the time describe an incident more in keeping with the gang's known method of operation.

of Skagway was robbed, no one else will come this way."

The three men walked a block to Sperry's sheet-iron warehouse, where Frank Reid's friend and cohort, Captain Sperry, operated a storage place for miners who wanted to leave their valuables behind before risking the pass. By noon of Friday, July 8, Reid and Sperry, together with Major Tanner, had reorganized the vigilantes, and the story of Stewart's loss was being discussed all over town. Tension began to rise as knots of people gathered in the street. The news went round that the U.S. commissioner at Dyea, C. A. Sehlbrede, had been sent for. Men began to mutter that all of Dawson's wealthiest prospectors were leaving the country by way of St. Michael because they were afraid to use the Skagway trail. As suddenly as the wind shifts in the mountains, the whole town started to turn against Soapy Smith.

Smith himself did not remain oblivious of this change of temperament. He had runners all over town bringing him news of the excitement. One arrived with the intelligence that M. K. Kalem, a Yukon outfitter, was haranguing a throng in front of his store a block or two up Broadway. As the crowd discussed ways and means of getting Stewart's poke back, Smith suddenly arrived in their midst. He was wearing a mackinaw coat and he kept both his hands in his pockets, but the square lines of a revolver showed in each. He shouldered his way through the throng and faced it, as he had faced so many others in his lifetime.

"You're a lot of cowardly rope-pulling sons of bitches!" he cried. "Now come on! I can lick the whole crowd of you."

Silently the crowd melted away, as it had melted away so often before in the face of Smith's guns.

Meanwhile, Judge Sehlbrede, a distinguished figure with his aquiline features and white mutton-chop whiskers, had arrived from Dyea. Together with some of the re-formed vigilantes, he called upon Smith and asked him to order his men to return the missing poke. Smith retorted that Stewart had lost his money in a fair game of chance and then went on to boast that he was backed by one hundred men "who would stand behind him and see that they were protected." The judge told Smith that he could not afford to stand up for a bunch of thieves, whereupon the con man, pounding on the table, cried out: "Well, Judge, declare me in with the thieves. I'll stay with them."

Some of Smith's own gang now started to lose their nerve. Even Old Man Tripp sounded a note of caution. "People are making such a stink about the job it would be wise to give the stuff up," he told Smith.

This advice had a strange effect on the con man. With the entire town opposing him, with his own men wavering and calling for surrender, Soapy Smith turned stubborn. If he backed down now, he would lose his dignity, and this he could not countenance.

"I'll cut the ears off the first man who makes a move to give it back," he said.

The same morning he had a street-corner encounter with Reid and tried to provoke him to combat. Reid, who was unarmed, went directly to his cabin, got his gun, then strode into Smith's oyster parlour and asked John Clancy to produce the dictator. But Smith did not appear.

By four o'clock — the deadline for the return of Stewart's gold — an air of foreboding hung heavy over Skagway and a sullen crowd filled the street outside the parlour.

"There'll be trouble unless the gold is returned," a reporter for the Skagway *News* told Smith.

"By God, trouble is what I'm looking for!" Smith retorted.

As the bedlam increased, he strode to the door, rifle in hand, and announced in surly tones that he had five hundred men behind him, ready to do his bidding. The crowd fell silent at this warning, but for the first time in Smith's experience it did not disperse. And so they faced each other for a few moments, the sallow-faced con man, burning now with an inner fury, and his fellow townsmen, who, just four days before, had cheered him to the skies. Then Smith turned on his heel, went back into his parlour, and swallowed some whiskey. It was the first sign of tension on his part, for he was a man who rarely drank.

By now the town was preparing for trouble, and a sinister hush fell over much of the business section as offices, shops, and saloons closed their doors. Some of the fainter-hearted members of Smith's gang slipped quietly out of town, seeking refuge on the mountain trails and in the forests. From the dock area came an angry buzzing as from a nest of wasps. Citizens who had never uttered a peep against Smith since his arrival suddenly became brave and flocked to Sperry's warehouse, where they made spirited speeches about (*a*) the evils of crime and (*b*) the money they were going to lose if travellers avoided their town.

The changed temper of the town impressed itself on Samuel H. Graves of the White Pass Railway, who was about to pay an Italian bootblack a quarter to shine his shoes that afternoon. A friend tapped him on the shoulder. "It's hardly wise just now," he warned and went on to explain that public feeling was running so high that a man with polished boots might easily be subjected to violence as one who earned his living by questionable methods.

454

Smith himself still insisted that he could bluff out the gathering storm, but the cocksureness and the calm that had been his stock in trade for so long were beginning to drain from him. He was drinking steadily now, and between drinks he was stalking up and down Broadway, rifle in hand, hurling challenges at the occasional passer-by. It was an ominous spectacle — the dictator of Skagway, defiant and alone, prowling the silent street like a caged and thwarted beast.

The gathering at Sperry's warehouse, meanwhile, had lapsed into confusion, for it had been infiltrated by Smith's own men, who had succeeded in bringing all business to a standstill. The meeting was adjourned and set again for early evening in Sylvester Hall.

By nine p.m. the hall was so crowded that the vigilantes were again forced to adjourn the meeting, this time to the end of the Juneau dock, where eavesdroppers could not overhear the proceedings. Four men, including Frank Reid, stood guard at the end of the ramp leading to the dock, while a chain across the entranceway effectively stopped each newcomer until he could be challenged and identified.

As the crowd gathered on the dock, Smith, in his parlour, edgy, irritable, and half drunk, decided at last to act. "I am about due to kill a man and I have lived long enough myself anyway," he told a crony. A note arrived from Billy Saportas, the newspaperman who had been "covering" the meeting: "The crowd is angry. If you want to do anything do it quick."

"I'll drive the bastards into the bay," said Smith.

He slipped a derringer into his sleeve, thrust a .45 Colt revolver into his pocket, and slung a Winchester .30/30 onto his shoulder. He moved west along Holly Street to State, which runs parallel to Broadway, and then turned south towards the waterfront, muttering that he would "teach these damned sons of bitches a lesson."

Behind him, at a respectful distance, a knot of curious people followed. Smith swung his rifle off his shoulder and brandished it like a fly-swatter.

"Chase yourselves home to bed!" he shouted.

The crowd hung back, but did not disperse. About a dozen of Smith's men swung in behind him, at a distance of twenty-five feet. The others had already fled to the hills.

John Clancy, Smith's erstwhile partner, his wife, and his six-year-old son were out for a walk when Smith passed them by. Clancy tried to dissuade him from going to the wharf, but Smith was in no mood for chatter. He pulled the revolver from his pocket and pressed it against Clancy's side.

"Johnny," he said, "you'd better leave me alone."

"All right," said Clancy in disgust. "If you want to get killed, go ahead." As the trio stepped aside to let Smith by, Mrs. Clancy began to cry.

The dock lay dead ahead. It was built like a causeway, set up on pilings over Skagway's tidal flats and stretching like a long finger into the mountain-ringed bay. At the far end, in the bright evening sunlight, Smith could see the gesticulating throng of vigilantes. In the foreground, the four guards barred the way to the ramp.

Smith ignored them all but Reid, who was standing about one hundred feet from the dock.

"You can't go down there, Smith," Reid said.

Smith unslung the Winchester from his shoulder.

"Damn you, Reid," he said, "you're at the bottom of all my troubles. I should have got rid of you three months ago."

The two men were now almost nose to nose, and as Smith levelled the Winchester at Reid's head, Reid seized the muzzle with his left hand, pulling it downward, while he reached for his six-gun with his right.

"Don't shoot!" Smith cried, in sudden panic. "For God's sake, don't shoot!"

It was over in an instant.

Reid squeezed the trigger of his six-gun, but the hammer fell on a faulty cartridge, and an instant later a bullet from Smith's Winchester struck him in the groin, shattering his pelvic bone. Now both men fired again. Smith dropped to the dock, a bullet in his heart. Reid, wounded now in the leg, crumpled with him but fired again, striking the dying dictator above the left knee.

The two men lay on the ramp in a widening pool of blood, the one gasping out the last seconds of his life, the other in mortal agony.

A scream cut the still air, from the lips of Mrs. Harriet Pullen, the hard-working widow who was out looking for one of her small sons and had passed the dock at the moment of the tragedy. One of the guards, a tough little Irish blacksmith named Jesse Murphy, ran up, seized Smith's Winchester, and warded off his bodyguard of men, who had drawn their guns. They stood for a moment at bay and then, seeing the onrushing mob on the dock, fired a few aimless shots into the air and took to the hills. Sinclair, the Union Church pastor, who had been up the street when the shooting occurred, was one of the first to reach the fallen men. He looked at the corpse of the outlaw and muttered a simple "Thank God."

Meanwhile, the vigilantes were running up the wharf at a full gallop, falling automatically into step as they did so, causing the entire structure to sway crazily.

Reid saw them and raised himself on one arm. "I'm badly hurt, boys," he muttered, "but I got him first."

The crowd threw their hats in the air and gave three cheers while four or five men raced off to a nearby cabin

457

and commandeered a cot to serve as stretcher. They placed Reid on it and headed up the street for the Bishop Rowe hospital. In spite of his pain, Reid was in a state of high elation. He raised himself on an elbow and addressed the crowd that moved along with him.

"I got the sonofabitch," Reid kept saying. "He may have got me, boys, but by God I got him first."

A block past the wharf, the stretcher-bearers passed Reid's cabin-office.

"Let me down, boys," Reid said. "I want to take one last look at my cabin."

Dr. F. B. Whiting, the surgeon on the staff of the White Pass Railway, whose construction had commenced only a few days before, was sent for. He arrived on a dead run, tore open Reid's clothing, and exposed a hideous wound from which the blood gushed in great spurts.

"Rub my leg, Doc," Reid was gasping. "It cramps! It's killing me."

The doctor rubbed as Reid urged him on.

"Rub harder! If you can't rub it, get a big railroader to rub it — somebody that can rub!"

And thus Reid continued in his agony, crying out that if his gun hadn't missed fire he would never be in such shape, while down at the wharfside the body of the fallen dictator still lay where it had crumpled. It lay there far into the night, unguarded and unclaimed, as the midsummer sun dipped briefly behind the mountains and the long shadows of the peaks crept across the tidal flats of Skagway Bay.

6: *No escape*

Within a few minutes of the shooting, Skagway was in an uproar. Si Tanner, sworn in by Judge Sehlbrede as deputy marshal, ran up Broadway calling his townsmen to arms:

458

"I advise all good citizens to go home and get their Winchesters."

Tanner himself borrowed a rifle from Captain William Moore and proceeded to deputize a posse of twenty-five vigilantes under Sperry to guard the docks and search the trails for Smith's followers. He gave orders that every boat in port was to be tied up and prevented from sailing until the gang was corralled. The streets were soon alive with men armed with revolvers and rifles and some with coils of rope calling for a lynching.

Now Smith's fleeing men came face to face with a frightening truth: there was no escape from Skagway. In previous encounters with the law, with posses and with vigilantes in the American West, they had been able to ride off across the bald prairie in almost any direction. But Skagway was a cul-de-sac, and they had not foreseen it. On the one side were the mountains, guarded by the Canadian Mounted Police; on the other was the cold sea. By midnight more than twenty of them had been captured and lodged in the log building that did duty as a town hall, and more were being brought in hourly. The following day, Saturday, with every saloon closed, Skagway was like a morgue. So great was the change in the temper of the town that lawyers who had worked steadily for various gang members now refused to visit them in jail.

Meanwhile, a squad of vigilantes went to the cabin of Deputy Marshal Taylor to arrest him for his obvious complicity with the Smith gang. The marshal, a barrel-chested, pot-bellied man, was hiding under the bed. His sobbing wife and two little girls, aged five and seven, pleaded with the men not to take Taylor away, but he went along without fuss and was lodged with the others in the town hall.

459

The "Reverend" Bowers, Old Man Tripp, and Slim Jim Foster had fled towards the White Pass immediately after the death of their leader and were holed up in the forest. They spent all of Saturday concealed in the thickets, living on berries and roots and sleeping on the damp ground while posses nosed through the woods seeking them.

On Sunday morning Tripp announced that he had had enough. "They're going to hang us," Bowers warned him.

"We should have been hung twenty years ago," the old man said contemptuously. "You're young and maybe can do it, but I can't. I'm going to get something to eat. I'd rather be hung on a full stomach than die of starvation in these goddam mountains."

Tripp moved down the trail into town, walked into a restaurant, and ordered a meal. It was here that one of the vigilantes spotted him.

"I've ordered a good dinner and I need it," Tripp told him calmly. "May I have it?"

The vigilante assented, but a threatening crowd soon gathered outside.

"They don't look good to me," Tripp said. "Will I be protected?"

The vigilante assured him that he would.

"Well," Tripp said, "I'll chance it," and calmly proceeded with his meal.

That afternoon a woman spotted Bowers and Slim Jim dodging through the trees of the graveyard at the start of the White Pass trail. She called the trail guard who had been posted by Tanner, and the two were swiftly apprehended.

By Sunday night the news was spreading that Reid was under opiates and his condition growing worse. Sentiment was rapidly increasing, and a mob of about one thousand people gathered outside the makeshift jail crying for a lynching.

"Hang them! Hang the whole gang!" the crowd screamed. "Bring out Tripp. This is just right for his neck," and men waved ropes already tied into hangman's knots.

Tanner arrived and climbed upon a wagon to plead for order.

"Don't hang the evidence," he shouted. "Let law and order rule and we'll get Stewart his money back. We have a lot of men inside who had nothing to do with the robbery. If you want to hang someone, hang me!"

This quieted the crowd momentarily. By now the town hall was overflowing with captured men, and Tanner decided to move some of the key prisoners, including both Tripp and Slim Jim, to the second floor of Burkhard's hardware store across the street. He did this so swiftly and boldly that there was no interference from the people in the jammed thoroughfare, who quietly gave way and let him pass.

Tripp, who was one of the toughest nuts in the gang, showed no emotion at all, but Slim Jim Foster was terrified by the mob, and the devilish Tripp amused himself by baiting him and adding to his fright.

Finally Foster could stand it no longer. Tripp got him into such a panic that he flung himself through an upper-storey window, bounced on a shed roof, and landed in French Alley. Someone at the back of the building took a shot at him, but missed. The noise brought the main body of the crowd around from the street at a dead run. The leaders had ropes in their hands and were intent on stringing him up.

"For the sake of my poor widowed mother, boys!" Foster cried in terror, as one man slipped the noose round his neck.

461

Two of Tanner's men tore it off again, and a seesaw battle for the panic-stricken con man ensued in which the rope was several times tightened around the outlaw's neck and several times removed. By now, however, the soldiers from Dyea had arrived. Down the street they moved on the double, with fixed bayonets, the crowd scattering before them. Martial law was proclaimed, and Foster was hustled back to prison, where he collapsed from fright.

That night Stewart's poke of gold — about five hundred dollars of it missing — was found in Soapy Smith's trunk. The following morning the captured members of his gang were shipped out of town. Eleven of the gang, including Marshal Taylor, Tripp, Foster, George Wilder, and Bowers, were sent to Sitka to face the Alaskan Grand Jury, charged with a variety of offences ranging from extortion and grand larceny to the possession of firearms. They received prison sentences ranging from one to ten years. Nine more, including Saportas and the editor of the *Daily Alaskan,* were bundled aboard the *Tartar* bound for Seattle. A large crowd on the dock watched them ascend the gangplank, one by one, and admit grudgingly to the commissioner that they were leaving "of their own free will." The police met them at Seattle and arrested several on various charges that had been pending against them.

Both the Baptist and the Methodist ministers refused to bury Soapy Smith, so Sinclair, the Presbyterian, did it alone, taking along a vigilante as protection. In the dreary morgue he preached a brief sermon, using as a text "The way of the transgressor is hard," while the con man's former mistress and sole mourner stood framed in the doorway. Then, with John Clancy, the executor of Smith's estate, Sinclair took the body out to the little cemetery along the White Pass trail, where, to the monotonous roar of the mountain streams and the occasional rattle of a passing freight wagon, it was committed. The worldly assets of the ex-dictator amounted to no more than five hundred dollars cash. He had squandered the rest or given it away.

Reid was operated on at five a.m. on Tuesday.

"If that bullet hasn't punctured my insides and if blood-poisoning doesn't set in and if you damned doctors don't butcher me, I'll have some chance for life yet," he remarked as, coolly smoking a cigar, he watched the surgical table being prepared.

But his wound was mortal. He lingered on for a few days and then died, and his funeral was the largest in Skagway's history. A handsome monument was erected over his grave a few feet from Smith's final resting-place. In the years that followed, thousands of tourists beat a path to the little graveyard under the hill to view these twin symbols of Skagway's shame and Skagway's honour.

But it was to Smith's tomb that the curious turned. In death he continued to exert a strange fascination. An unknown admirer sent fifty dollars annually to Mrs. Harriet Pullen for the upkeep of his grave. Some of the money had to be spent for wire mesh to protect the gravestone from souvenir-hunters who chipped away at it.

No such precautions were needed for Frank Reid's marble slab. It is almost seventy-five years since it was erected, but it stands today, like his memory, half forgotten but unblemished. On its face is a simple inscription: "He gave his life for the honor of Skagway."

Chapter Twelve

1
Gold, restless gold

2
The San Francisco of the North

3
The false fronts of Front Street

4
Queens of dance-hall row

5
Fortune's wheels

6
The last stampede

7
Tales of conspicuous wealth

8
Money to burn

1: *Gold, restless gold*

In Dawson the gold was changing hands.

On the creeks, men by the thousands tore at frozen ground, in a frenzy to reach the pay-streak, and then, in another kind of frenzy, rushed into town to squander the results.

The winding, wooded valleys through which Carmack and Henderson had made their way were unrecognizable by the spring of 1899. The hills, once thick with timber, were denuded even of moss, their flanks gouged into a cliff-land by the swift human erosion. Their tops looked like extinct volcanoes, stained as they were with newly washed gravel which ran down the sides in streaks as white as lava. On the rims of the hills cabins sprouted in clusters, and along the benchland more cabins ran in ragged tiers, each tier separated from the next by a bleak rubble of rock and clay.

The valley floors, which had once been choked by a jungle undergrowth of matted foliage, were stripped clean of verdure, except for the occasional dying spruce rising gauntly from the stark landscape; and the little streams, dammed, cribbed, diverted and bridged, ran naked through a desert of bleached gravel.

From the hills above, the creeks presented scenes of utter disorder. Cabins, sheds, tents, caches, and privies lay scattered in every direction as if a superhuman hand had tossed them casually into the valleys. Logs were piled so thickly that from a distance they resembled stacks of straw. Roadways, trails, narrow-gauge rail lines, trestles, flumes, ditches, and the long skeletal fingers of sluiceboxes criss-crossed the terrain between the conical mountains of gravel and dirt. All the impedimenta of the placer process — rockers and boilers, steam engines and pumps, hoses and winches — littered the landscape.

As spring crept onward and the snows melted, the valleys began to ooze with mud and men. The miners emerged from their smoky shafts like insects seeking the sun, until there were thousands of them at work, trundling wheelbarrows, hammering away at trestles, ripping into hillsides, standing in long lines at the sluiceboxes to shovel tirelessly from dawn until dusk, or winding away at the creaking winches as if they were turning fortune's wheel.

Thus the gravels yielded up the gold, and the gold slipped from hand to hand, as though it were red-hot. It poured into Dawson in an endless, shining stream, in greasy pokes of moose-hide or in hundred-pound sacks strapped to the backs of plodding mules. It was sprayed onto the bars of the Front Street saloons, shovelled into the slender purses of the dance-hall girls, or flung carelessly on the gaming-tables.

The very air glittered with it. Some of the bartenders developed long fingernails so that when they weighed out a pokeful of dust a little of it was left behind; they panned their own fingernails at night and enjoyed a neat profit. Every gold-scale rested on a thick velvet cloth into which the gold filtered while the bands played and the kings of Eldorado danced the night away. At dawn the velvet cloths themselves were panned, and they in turn yielded up their treasure. The waiters kept their hands damp with beer or wine so that some of the gold stuck to their fingers and was transferred to secret pockets in chamois vests. These, too, were panned nightly, as though they were part of the dump from Paradise Hill.

The gold moved swiftly from pocket to pocket and poke to poke, as if carried by the wind. Some of it rested momentarily in the safe of Silent Sam Bonnifield, the gambling king, and some of it found its way into the flashing nugget belt of Cad Wilson, the dance-hall queen. Some of it was carried from crib to crib along the length of Paradise Alley, where fat Belgian girls in shapeless outer garments leaned from doorways and plied their trade for the profit of the sleek little pimps or *maques* who had brought them across the Chilkoot Pass or up the river like so much freight. Some of it, eventually, reached the bank, where it was melted into bricks or bars and transported Outside to start its whirl again. Some of it was lost for years or forever in the muck of Front Street or in the dusty corners of the frame saloons. The Kansas City Kid, who slept in the sawdust under the crap tables at the Monte Carlo, was actually permeated with gold dust — or at least his clothes were. Once, when he took ill and was sent to the hospital, the laundry that handled his washing returned $39.75 to him, that being the amount that had collected in the bottom of the tub when his clothes were washed.

So much gold was caught in the sawdust of the Monte Carlo's floor that two children who panned the area beneath the front bar made twenty dollars a day from it. Forty years later, when some of the old dance halls were torn down in Dawson, thousands of dollars' worth of this fine gold was recovered. Indeed, the town's streets could be said to be paved with gold, for during the depression of the thirties dozens of destitute men made wages by panning the ground beneath the wooden sidewalks. In the early forties, when the Bank of Commerce was being repaired, two carpenters secured the panning rights and realized fifteen hundred dollars from the foundations. About the same time the proprietor of the Orpheum Theatre decided to have his floor repaired, and in the half-day available to him while the planks were torn up he was able to pan one thousand dollars' worth of gold that had been hidden there for almost half a century.

468

The Klondike ran on gold, and so did its people. Because of it, they faced typhoid, malaria, frostbite, and scurvy. And, though they often treated it as offhandedly as if it were so much sand, they were always ready to look for more. The slightest whisper of a new find could send hundreds stampeding up and down the river or across the hills in the bitterest weather. In the end, this constant quest was the undoing of Dawson City, as it had been the undoing of Fortymile and Circle before it.

2: *The San Francisco of the North*

Dawson existed as a metropolis exactly twelve months: from July, 1898, to July, 1899. Before this period it had been nothing more than an overgrown frontier community of shacks and tents. Afterward it subsided slowly but inevitably into a ghost town. But for one glorious twelvemonth it was the "San Francisco of the North," enjoying almost every amenity available to civilized cities the world over.

Although it lay in the shadow of the Arctic Circle, more than four thousand miles from civilization, and although it was the only settlement of any size in a wilderness area that occupied hundreds of thousands of square miles, Dawson was livelier, richer, and better equipped than many larger Canadian and American communities. It had a telephone service, running water, steam heat, and electricity. It had dozens of hotels, many of them better appointed than those on the Pacific coast. It had motion-picture theatres operating at a time when the projected motion-picture was just three years old. It had restaurants where string orchestras played the *Largo* from *Cavalleria Rusticana* for men in tailcoats who ate *pâté de foie gras* and drank vintage wines. It had fashions from Paris. It had dramatic societies, church choirs, glee clubs, and vaudeville companies. It had three hospitals, seventy physicians,

469

and uncounted platoons of lawyers. Above all, it had people.

None of its citizens were ordinary, for almost every one of them knew how to build his own boat or his own cabin out of green lumber, how to handle a dog-team on a narrow trail, how to treat scurvy with spruce-bark tea, how to carry a pack on a tumpline, and how to navigate fast water. Some had more individual accomplishments: there were gamblers ready to bet fifty thousand dollars on the turn of a card, and dance-hall girls willing to be purchased for their weight in gold.

They came from all over the world and from every background and creed. Arthur Treadgold, a direct descendant of Sir Isaac Newton, was in the gold rush; so were the nephew of H. Rider Haggard, the novelist, and the nephew of Jay Gould, the Wall Street financier, and the son of William Lever, the soap king. Frank Slavin, the heavyweight champion of the British Empire, was part of the throng that surged into Dawson, and so was W. J. "Sailor Bill" Partridge, who had become so rich from Queensland gold that he never wore the same suit twice, even though he changed clothes several times a day. There were scores of newspaper correspondents in Dawson, many of them women — ranging all the way from Nelly Bly, the New York world-girdler, to Flora Shaw, the aristocratic colonial expert of *The Times* of London, who crossed the White Pass dressed as a perfect English gentlewoman, her skirts of ladylike length, her hair neatly coiled, and her neckpiece carefully fastened.

The town was crowded with men who made their names and their fortunes after leaving the Klondike: Augustus Mack, from Brooklyn, the inventor of the Mack automobile and the Mack truck; Sid Grauman, whose name was later immortalized on Hollywood's famous Chinese Theatre, where movie stars left
470

footprints in the wet cement; Tex Rickard, who became the manager of Madison Square Garden; Jack Marchbank, the one-legged gambler who was to run the great Tanforan race track in San Francisco; Key Pittman, who became a controversial and ebullient senator from Nevada and chairman of the U.S. Foreign Relations Committee; Alexander Pantages, the little Greek immigrant who laid the foundations for his chain of motion-picture theatres in Dawson; and, of course, the Mizner brothers, about whose exploits three books and countless magazine articles were to be written.

But to another group, whose careers were ending, Dawson City was the last stop. Joseph Juneau ran a restaurant in Dawson; his discovery of gold on the Alaska Panhandle had enshrined his name on the territory's new capital city, but he himself was without funds. Buck Choquette was in Dawson, too: he had made and lost a fortune in the early days of the Cariboo gold rush. Buckskin Frank Leslie, a famous gunman from Arizona, joined the gold rush and faded into obscurity, as did Calamity Jane, the camp-follower from Deadwood, a pale reminder of the era of Wild Bill Hickok. Irish Nellie Cashman, "the miners' angel," ran a boarding house in the Klondike, just as she once had on Tough Nut Street in Tombstone, where she sheltered the homeless and relieved the afflicted.

For such people there was nowhere else in the world to go but Dawson. All their lives had been spent on the frontier, on the plains of the American West or in the untamed little towns of legend and story with names like Deadwood and Tucson and Cheyenne — or in some other out-of-the-way corner of the world. But the West was no longer wild, and the frontier had moved away three thousand miles. And so they walked the streets of the golden city, many still clinging to their fringed gauntlets and their hide vests and their broad-brimmed hats. Here, in this familiar garb, they felt at home.

Tom Horey, a half-breed famous as one of three scouts who had captured Louis Riel, the leader of the Saskatchewan Rebellion, was in town; because of his exploits, the Mounties let him get roaring drunk without arresting him. F. R. Burnham, a noted African scout and one of two survivors of an expedition which had been massacred in Matabeleland in 1893, arrived at the height of the stampede. He later returned to the Dark Continent and became a Boer War hero. Captain Jack Crawford, the "poet-scout" of the West, turned up, with his white goatee, buckskin shirt, long silken hair, and scout's hat. He had fought the Indians in the border wars, hobnobbed with Buffalo Bill Cody and Wild Bill Hickok, and served a stint as U.S. marshal. Now from a hovel dubbed The Wigwam he sold everything from hay to ice cream, and doubled as a popular entertainer because of his ability to compose a poem about anything or anybody on the spot.

Jack Dalton, another frontiersman and a veteran of the Yukon and Alaska, was a respected figure in Dawson. He had constructed his own personal trail into the country, from Pyramid Harbor on the Lynn Canal to Fort Selkirk on the Upper Yukon River, charging two hundred and fifty dollars toll to anybody who wanted to use it. Other men had tried to establish toll roads and toll bridges on the various trails of '98, but Dalton was the only man who made a toll stick. One party announced they would drive a herd of beef cattle over this trail without payment. As they were about to set out, Dalton appeared with rifle and six-gun and told the leaders he would shoot the first man or beast who set foot on it. Then, as the party floundered through the bushes and scrub timber alongside the trail, Dalton

472

kept guard in splendid isolation on the right of way for three hundred miles to show he meant business. He was a tough man to tangle with — short, thick-set, and uncompromising. He beat one man to a pulp for trying to establish a saloon on his property, and he shot another dead (and was acquitted) for trying to turn the Indians against him. His trail turned out to be a boon to Dawson. In the summer of 1898 two thousand beef cattle successfully traversed it.

One towering figure on the streets seemed to have stepped straight out of a wild-west show. This was Arizona Charlie Meadows, the old Indian-fighter and rodeo king whose portable saloon had been swept away in the Chilkoot flood. He suffered a series of mishaps, including a devastating boat wreck on Tagish Lake, but within four months of his arrival in town he had made a small fortune. He conceived the idea of producing a souvenir newspaper which would glorify the Klondike kings, and swiftly raised fifty thousand dollars for it. Charlie rightly regarded Front Street as better mining property than any to be found on the Klondike watershed, and by the winter of 1898-99 was hard at work planning the Palace Grand dance hall and theatre, which, he promised, would be the most lavish establishment of its kind in the North.

Dawson in its climactic year remained a town of nicknames. Half the community, it seemed, went under such pseudonyms as Limejuice Lil, Spanish Dolores, Deep-Hole Johnson, Billy the Horse, Cassiar Jim, and Two-Step Louie. There were Spare-rib Jimmy Mackinson, so thin that his landlady was said to have refused him sheets for fear he might tear them with his bones; and Waterfront Brown, the debt-collector, who haunted the riverbank in order to capture fleeing defaulters; and Phantom Archibald, who spent twenty-five thousand dollars in gold on a colossal binge and

473

thought himself pursued by a long black python; and Doc Stearnes, the "Gambler Ghost," a wisp of a surgeon turned faro-player; and Hamgrease Jimmy, the dance-hall caller; and last, as well as least, that curious little creature known as the Evaporated Kid because he was so small that he "looked like a bottle with hips."

At first glance, this mélange of humanity seemed to be an odd and insoluble mixture of nationalities, races, and pursuits, yet it was really remarkably cohesive. Although the men and women who reached the Klondike came from every corner of the globe, and although their backgrounds were entirely dissimilar, they had one thing in common: they were there. Others, with weaker wills and weaker constitutions, had given up the struggle and retreated, but each of these disparate citizens had succeeded in what he had set out to do. They were like war veterans who, having served their time in action, now found themselves bound together in a camaraderie born of fortitude. They were all part of a proud élite who, in spite of every vicissitude, had managed to reach their goal.

3: *The false fronts of Front Street*

Although Dawson covered several square miles, spilled across two rivers, and was squeezed up the sides of the surrounding hills, its pulse beat swiftest in those three or four short blocks of Front Street where the saloons, dance halls, and gaming-houses were crowded together. This was the most unstable as well as the liveliest section of the town. The buildings here were continually burning down and being rebuilt, changing ownership and managership, being lost and won in gambling-games, and sometimes changing both name and locale, so that the street was seldom the same from one month to the next. And yet, in another sense, it never changed, for any man who walked inside one building might be said to have walked inside them all. The outer façade of the street was a deceptive one. The carved scrollwork, the ornate bay windows and balconies with their intricately wrought balustrades, the elaborate cornices and pillars presented a rococo elegance which was as false as the square fronts which hid the dingy, gabled log building behind. Hollywood films have presented the Klondike dance halls with Parisian splendour, but the real edifices were cheaper and shabbier than their dreamworld counterparts. So were the girls who danced within them, especially in the early days. Like the furniture and the trimmings, they had to be brought in over the mountains, and thus they were plain, sturdy, serviceable, and without embellishment. Most of them ran to weight; only the huskiest, after all, were able to withstand the rigours of the journey.

The interiors of the dance halls were of a piece — and a description of the Monte Carlo serves for them all. It was a hastily erected two-story building with large plate-glass windows, on which its name was inscribed, facing the street. Upon entering it, the newcomer found himself in a small, rather dark room dominated by a sheet-iron stove, with a long polished bar to his left, behind which the bartenders in starched shirts and aprons, with white waistcoats and diamond stickpins, stood reflected in the long mirrors at their backs.

Beyond the saloon was a smaller room, where faro, poker, dice, and roulette were played continually, day and night, and behind this room was the theatre, consisting of a ground floor (with movable benches), a balcony (three rows and six boxes), and a small curtained stage. The remainder of the establishment's upper storey was given over to about a dozen bedrooms, which could be rented by the night or by the week for any purpose, even including slumber.

This layout differed only in detail up and down the street. One dance hall sported elaborate murals ("Midnight on the Yukon"); another was lighted by acetylene lamps instead of the usual oil. (Electricity did not come until later in the season.) But each contained the same divisions of gallery, boxes, and common dance floor.

A sign on the balcony of the Opera House reminded customers that "gentlemen in private boxes are expected to order refreshments," and these instructions were rarely ignored, for it was a mark of affluence for a man to be seen in an upper box, encircled by a bevy of soubrettes, drinking champagne at sixty dollars a quart. The men of the Klondike craved such outward signs of success more than they craved the actual champagne or the favours of the women; their presence in the balcony surrounded them with a kind of aura which proclaimed to all who watched that they had won a hand in the hard game of life. The private box in the Dawson dance hall thus became a sort of symbol; suspended above the turbulent and sweaty masses on the floor below, a miner flush with gold could feel that he had indeed risen in the world. In a single night in the Monte Carlo one such celebrant had seventeen hundred dollars' worth of champagne brought to his box.

To some, the dance hall itself became the supreme emblem of achievement and nothing would do but that they own one outright. Many a Klondike king invested his gold in a palace of pleasure, although not always with crowning success. Charlie Kimball, who built the Pavilion with one hundred thousand dollars which he received for his mining property, took in twelve thousand on opening night in June, 1898. He was so delighted by this new way of mining gold that he began to celebrate. The bender lasted three months, and during this period Kimball made — and spent — three hundred thousand dollars. When he eventually sobered up

476

he had lost his dance hall and was penniless. But for one brief whirl he had been Somebody.

In the larger establishments the bar, gaming-room, dance hall, and stage entertainment were operated as separate concessions. The bar ran twenty-four hours a day, except Sundays, and so did the gambling. The dance hall came alive about eight in the evening and ran until six or seven the following morning, but actual dancing did not really begin until after midnight, being preceded by lengthy entertainments: a drama first, and then a series of vaudeville turns on the tiny stage.

The most versatile of the entrepreneurs was John Mulligan, who with his wife, Carrie, had been staging vaudeville and burlesque in the various Pacific coast towns before coming north. Mulligan wrote the entire show himself, a series of bawdy and satirical commentaries on the times made up from suggestions he received from gamblers, miners, dance-hall girls, and bartenders. His best-remembered drama was *The Adventures of Stillwater Willie,* a satire on the exploits of Swiftwater Bill which Mulligan produced first in the Combination — or Tivoli, as it was renamed — and later repeated by popular request in the Monte Carlo. With a fine sense of casting, Mulligan starred Nellie Lamore, the youngest of the three Lamore sisters, in the play. Swiftwater Bill would occupy the finest box in the theatre and applaud the caricature cheerfully — while the audience laughed. Swiftwater did not mind the laughter: he was being noticed, and that was what mattered. Nellie, thus emboldened, appeared at a masquerade ball in October, 1898, wearing a Prince Albert coat, a silk hat, and a placard inscribed: "Stillwater Willie, the Mayor of Lousetown." She won first prize.

Gussie Lamore was back in town, her reputation enhanced by the legend of the eggs, and she, too, was a

477

popular favourite. From the stage of the Monte Carlo she would sing directly to Swiftwater in his box:

> Give me a pen, I'll make my will,
> I'll will it all to Swiftwater Bill.
> I loved him once and I always will,
> For he was certainly good to me.

All eyes would turn upward to the little man with the Prince Albert coat, the diamond stickpin, and the comical moustache, applauding furiously; and the cheechakos in the pit would nudge each other and remember, years later, that they had once seen the legendary Swiftwater.

Another occasional stage entertainer was Wilson Mizner. He had a clear tenor voice, much in demand for the charity affairs and church socials at which, with a fine sense of impartiality, he also entertained. According to Mizner's biographer, Alva Johnston, one of these dance-hall appearances saved Mizner from a jail term. His girl friend was Nellie Lamore, who was also known as Nellie the Pig, perhaps because of her attractive retroussé nose, or possibly because once, in a heated moment, she bit off the ear of a bartender who she felt had insulted her. Nellie was making a handsome profit by selling tiny pieces of chocolate at a dollar a morsel, and Mizner, no doubt spurred on by the example of Swiftwater Bill and the eggs, decided to lay an enormous amount of chocolate at her feet. He held up a restaurant which sold the delicacy, but discovered to his chagrin that, although gold was to be had by reaching for it, the more valuable candy was kept locked in a safe. To confuse the issue he took the cash register with him, tossed it aside, ripped off his mask, ran to a saloon where he was known to entertain, and appeared, somewhat breathless but otherwise in good voice, singing

478

"Sweet Alice, Ben Bolt," thus establishing an iron-clad alibi.

Mizner fancied himself as a singer and as a piano-player during his year in Dawson. The most famous pianist in town was the Rag Time Kid at the Dominion Saloon, said to be the model for Service's subsequent Jag Time Kid in the famous poem about Dan McGrew. The Kid's mother was a Chicago music teacher, and it was his boast that he could play anything that was requested. Mizner, who came from a good family, was sceptical of the Kid's musical knowledge and rashly bet that he could play something the Kid could not copy. The Kid accepted, whereupon Mizner sat down and played "The Holy City." "Move over," said the Kid contemptuously, and before Mizner had finished the final notes he was rendering the grand old song in ragtime.

The incidental entertainments in the dance halls were usually supplemented by more serious dramas. Most of the plays of the day, from *East Lynne* to *Camille,* found their way to the Dawson stages, although a certain amount of invention was sometimes necessary in the properties department. In *Pygmalion and Galatea,* for instance, a Dawson stock company, vainly searching around for a faun, had to make do with a stuffed and mounted malemute. In *Uncle Tom's Cabin* the bloodhounds were represented by a single howling malemute puppy drawn across the stage by invisible wires, while newspapers were used to simulate ice floes. The critics, however, praised the realistic performance of the actress who portrayed Eliza; it was obvious that she had really seen people making their way across floating ice.

The *pièce de résistance* at Arizona Charlie's Palace Grand was a full-blown production of *Camille.* The ambitiousness of the production suited the theatre. To build the Palace, Charlie Meadows had bought and wrecked two steamboats, and to open it he had held a banquet for forty persons and laid a hundred-dollar banknote upon each plate. The stage production, alas, was not entirely successful, owing to a monumental piece of miscasting. The restless audience swiftly noted a distinct lack of ardour between Armand Duval and his consumptive lady. It appeared that George Hillier, the actor playing Duval, was the divorced husband of Babette Pyne, the dance-hall girl playing Camille. Babette hated him so much that she could not bear to speak with him in the wings, and at the end of each performance was in a state of nervous prostration from being forced to make love to him on the stage. This was only one of several flaws in the *Camille* production. The girls on stage also worked as box hustlers during the dancing that followed, as well as during the intermissions, and this double duty brought its own impasses. One night Babette Pyne, in her role as Camille, called over and over again for Prudence, her neighbour, but no Prudence appeared, and the action came to a dead stop. In the end, after repeated entreaties, the actress, Nellie Lewis, her hair tousled and her face flushed, poked her head from between the curtains of a wine box in the gallery and in a high-pitched and nearly incoherent voice called out: "Madame Prudence isn't here! Call all you like, but Madame Prudence ain't a-comin' tonight. Don't you think she's a-comin'." And although she was carried from the box by force, neither cajolery nor threats would force her to go onstage.

When such entertainments failed, Arizona Charlie could always rely on his shooting skill to pack the Palace Grand. Dressed in his familiar fringed buckskin, with his black locks hanging to his shoulders, the old scout presented a commanding figure. From his position at the far end of the stage he would shoot glass balls

480

from between the thumb and forefinger of his pretty blonde wife. One night he missed and nicked her thumb, and from then on the shooting exhibitions ceased.

Crude as they were, the stage shows in the Dawson theatres brought enthusiastic crowds to Front Street six nights a week, for the town was starved for entertainment. Indeed, the whole community was indulging in a gigantic year-long binge: those who had struck it rich were celebrating their good fortune, and the remainder were celebrating anyway after the long months on the trail.

Young Monte Snow and his sister once picked up one hundred and forty-two dollars thrown at them as they danced and sang on the stage, while little Margie Newman, "The Princess of the Klondike," sometimes stood heel-deep in nuggets after she rendered a sentimental song. The sight of this nine-year-old girl and the sound of her piping voice brought tears to the eyes of men far from their wives and families. They showered her with gold, and one even wrote a poem to her:

> *God Bless you, Little Margie, for you made*
> *   us better men*
> *God Bless you, Little Margie, for you take us*
> *   home again.*

When at last she left town, Frank Conrad of *Eleven* Eldorado tore off his solid-gold watch and nugget chain and tossed them to her as she stood on the steamer's deck. She smiled, and he pulled out a fifty-dollar bill, wrapped it around a silver dollar, and threw that. She smiled again, and he produced a hundred-dollar bill, wrapped it around another silver dollar, and threw that too.

A different form of entertainment consisted of prize fights, which also took place on the dance-hall stages.

Although the main object of all the stage shows was to pack the house with customers in order to keep the bar going, the fight-promoters were able to get as much as twenty-five dollars a seat for the better matches. Frank Slavin of Australia, the Empire's heavyweight champion, known as the Sydney Cornstalk because of his tall, agile figure and long, loose arms, figured prominently in the most memorable of Dawson's matches. Although Slavin was past his fighting prime and embittered by his failure to meet either John L. Sullivan or Jim Corbett for the heavyweight championship of the world, he was still more than a match for most of the men put up against him. He fought one Australian named Perkins for fourteen rounds and gave him such a beating that Perkins died eighteen months later from internal injuries. One night a rowdy named Biff Hoffman knocked Slavin to the floor in the Monte Carlo saloon when both men were drunk. The fighter took his measure and said: "You can knock me about when I'm drunk, but I'll show you what I can do in the ring when I'm sober." Wilson Mizner, who was weighing gold in the Monte Carlo at the time, heard these words and saw the incident as a heaven-sent opportunity for a grudge match. The fight was profitable but disappointing. Slavin did not even bother to don the regulation trunks, but climbed into the ring immaculate in white turtle neck sweater and white flannel trousers. He swung a right, knocked Hoffman cold, and collected one thousand dollars from Mizner. Another fight between Slavin and a wrestler named Frank Gotch (who later became world's champion) was less decisive. Gotch was faring badly until he clamped a half-nelson on Slavin and threw him out of the ring. Each fighter insisted loudly and threateningly that he was the winner until the terrified referee called "No contest."

482

Although the promoters tried to bill every fight as a grudge match, most were mere exhibitions between men who knew each other well. Slavin had come into Dawson in the company of Joe Boyle, his Canadian sparring-partner, with whom he had barnstormed around America. Boyle later became one of the great figures of the Klondike, securing an enormous concession on the main river, building the largest dredges in the world, and ending his years as "the Uncrowned King of Rumania," where he was popularly believed to be the lover of Queen Marie; but in 1898 he did duty as a bouncer in the Monte Carlo. Tex Rickard, who went from penury to fortune and back to bankruptcy again in Dawson, gained some early experience in fight-promoting by matching the two friends against each other and making the crowd believe they were enemies. He billed Boyle as a man who had defied Soapy Smith in Skagway, and he referred to Slavin as "the Sydney Slasher." He talked both men into acting infuriated whenever they saw each other, and, to whip up interest in the match, placed Slavin in a prominent position in a Front Street saloon where the crowd could see him. Rickard was disgusted to discover one day that Slavin's chief drinking-companion, in full view of the entire town, was Paddy Flynn, who was also billed as the referee. Rickard hustled Flynn out of town until the night of the fight and then extracted twenty-five dollars from every customer, including those who crowded in for standing room only. Boyle, when he grew wealthy from his mining concessions, did not forget his old sparring-partner. He put Slavin on his payroll in an imaginary job at a good salary. As for Rickard, he headed off to Rampart and thence on to Nome, Alaska, without a cent to his name. Within a year he had one hundred thousand dollars.

483

4: *Queens of dance-hall row*

Dawson's entertainments, although they brought thousands into the dance halls, were only a means to an end, and that end was to extract as much gold as possible from the audience when the entertainment was done. When the curtain finally fell about one a.m. the girls descended from the stage to mingle with the customers, whereupon the real business of the evening began. The floor was cleared and the orchestra, usually consisting of piano, violin, trombone, and cornet, struck up, while a caller or "spieler," standing on the stage, cried out to the high-booted crowd to "take your partners for that long, dreamy, juicy waltz." The miners paid their dollar for a dance ticket, grasped a girl, and tried to complete a single lap around the floor before the orchestra stopped, somewhat after the fashion of musical chairs. Like so much else in the Klondike, the long, dreamy, juicy waltz was not quite as advertised; it had lasted less than a minute, and the spieler was already shouting: "Belly up to the bar, you Rocky Mountain sportsmen!" The girls seized their partners, propelled them to the bar or to a curtained box, and ordered whatever the traffic would bear. For every dollar spent, each girl received a circular disk representing her percentage of the profits, and this she secreted in her stocking to cash the following day until her legs were lumpy with ivory vouchers. All night long the dances roared on — waltzes, polkas, schottisches, square dances, and lancers — while the horns blew and the violins sawed away and the callers kept the crowd in an unremitting state of excitement. All night long the wealth of the creeks was transferred bit by bit to the nugget belts and pouches of the dance-hall girls. As Diamond-Tooth Gertie remarked, not without a certain compassion, "The poor ginks have just gotta spend it, they're that scared they'll die before they have it all out of the ground."

To more than one man who struck it rich, dancing seemed more important than the gold they had struggled so hard to find. Casey Moran, an itinerant newspaperman who owned a claim on Sulphur Creek, was one of these. One night in the Monte Carlo, Humboldt Gates called him off the floor in order to offer him twenty thousand dollars for his property. Moran quickly accepted the offer, which was a generous one, but he demurred when Gates insisted on sealing the bargain then and there with a down payment of two thousand dollars, weighed out in gold dust by the head cashier. Moran declared that no man could dance properly with ten pounds of gold in his pockets. He rejected the offer and the dance went on.

Moran was, of course, an eccentric. He later startled the town by scooping the press of the world with a news story about the discovery of Noah's Ark on the top of a mountain in the Koyukuk country of Alaska. Yet he was no more eccentric than many of his fellow prospectors, especially the wealthier ones, who preferred immediate pleasure to long-term profit.

There was one man that winter who actually danced his fortune away — a short, thick-set Irishman, with a pointed moustache, named Roddy Conners. Such was his mania for dancing that he sold his claim on Bonanza Creek for fifty thousand dollars and spent the entire amount capering to the tunes of the Front Street bands. He began to dance the moment the orchestra started to play and he continued to dance until it stopped, and he never missed a dance. When he was too weary to dance any longer in time to the music, he paid his dollar anyway, put his arm around the girl's waist, and walked her around the hall. No one woman had the stamina to keep up with him, but two sisters, working in shifts, succeeded in cleaning him out. Their show names were Jacqueline and Rosalinde, but they were popularly known as Vaseline and Glycerine. Vaseline would fasten upon the exhausted Conners, steer him to the bar and force a drink down his throat, then hand him over to Glycerine to take out to the dance floor again. Conners spent between five hundred and two thousand dollars a night and ended his years in a home for indigents.

Most of the dance-hall girls disguised their true identity, dancing under such nicknames as Sweet Marie, Ping Pong, or Caprice, or under pseudonyms like that of Blanche Lamonte, a seductive nineteen-year-old from the Barbary Coast who took her name from that of the young victim in San Francisco's notorious belfry murder. Most of them had some distinguishing mark about them. Daisy D'Avara wore a belt of seventeen twenty-dollar goldpieces, a Christmas present from a wealthy miner. Gertie Lovejoy had a diamond fastened between her two front teeth and, despite the amour inherent in her original name, was known in Dawson as Diamond-Tooth Gertie. Flossie de Atley was always referred to as "the Girl with the Baby Stare" and was a favourite subject of the *Nugget*'s cartoonist, who delighted in showing her with a finger in her mouth and her Mona Lisa eyes staring innocently into space, though she was anything but innocent. "It was generally conceded by those in the know that Flossie could take a man to the cleaners a little bit faster and a good deal more completely than any other girl in town," one Klondiker recalled, and added: "That's saying a whole lot, for there were some very capable girls in the art of trimming a sucker." Flossie's story was always the same: she had a sick brother in a sanatarium Outside and she was trying to scrape up enough money to leave

486

the country and care for him. And in the end she did leave, with enough for a dozen sick brothers.

The Grizzly Bear, a gargantuan woman who weighed one hundred and seventy pounds, had an eye missing: it had been torn from her head, so it was whispered, in a fight with another dance-hall girl. The most printable explanation for the Oregon Mare's nickname was that she whistled and squealed like a horse when she was dancing, but it was said that she had other equine talents as well. She was one of the best-known girls in town — a big, handsome woman who made men get off the sidewalk when she walked by. Seldom short of funds, she would, when in an expansive mood, stand up at the bar and cry: "Here, boys — there's my poke. Have a drink with me, all of you." Jeremiah Lynch, an ex-senator from California, saw her spend one thousand dollars in a single hour at roulette. Like so many others, she wore a heavy nugget chain, the gift of an admirer, and was reputed to have hidden away fifty thousand dollars with which she helped pay off the mortgage on her mother's ranch near Sacramento.

The Oatley Sisters were, in the words of one newspaper correspondent, "the queens of the gold-fields." The Dyea *Trail*'s Dawson correspondent reported in the summer of 1898 that "their capacity for drink, if nothing else, should attract a good patronage out of mere curiosity to see two girls who are put to bed drunk every night and who yet retain the bloom of youth, bright eyes, good voice and lively heels. They are the wonders of their kind."

The most successful and celebrated of all the Dawson dance-hall queens was a diminutive redhead with large brown eyes named Cad Wilson, who was brought to Dawson at the highest salary ever paid to an entertainer on the Pacific coast. She was no beauty and she could not sing very well, nor did she have a good figure, but her personality was such that men vied with each other to throw nuggets and gold watches and pieces of jewellery onto the stage when she appeared. She would run about, laughing her famous laugh, picking up the baubles, and holding her dress out, apron-like, to display her legs. The audience stood on the benches in the Tivoli and the Orpheum when she sang and danced, and cheered for encore after encore.

She made no secret of the fact that she was in town to separate miners from their pokes. Eddie Dolan, the stage-manager at the Tivoli, used to introduce Cad when she first appeared on the stage. Dolan would pretend that he had seen a letter from the actress's mother telling her "to be sure and be a good girl and pick nice clean friends." Then he would turn to the audience, wave Cad on with a flourish, and cry: "I leave it to you, fellers, if she don't pick 'em clean!"

Soon Cad was sporting the largest and most famous nugget belt in the Klondike. It was presented to her one Fourth of July by a group of Eldorado claim-owners who had been arguing for months as to who had found the biggest nugget. Each man put his choicest nugget into Cad's belt, which was so large that it went around her waist one and a half times, and made such a glittering display that a Klondike jewellery store asked and received permission to exhibit it in the window.

Cad Wilson's theme song, "Such a Nice Girl, Too," became a byword in Dawson. One man was so enamoured of her that he paid a waiter to fill a bathtub full of wine, purchased at twenty dollars a bottle, for her to bathe in. She did not so much as allow him the privilege of scrubbing her back or watching her splash about in the tub, and there was a good deal of speculation as to whether she took the bath at all. Bert Parker wrote that he was sure of one thing: "The wine would be salvaged, re-bottled and go into circulation again."

488

All of these women were a cut above the common prostitutes who inhabited Paradise Alley and who were later moved to a section of swampland well back from the business section and known as "Hell's Half Acre." The girls in the dance halls enjoyed freedom to come and go as they pleased and to pick and choose among the men who lavished attention upon them, but the prostitutes were white slaves in the proper sense of the word. Paradise Alley ran conveniently behind dance-hall row, and here, from a double line of identical frame shacks, each with a single window facing the two board sidewalks that ran down the narrow street, the girls plied their trade. There were at least seventy of these "cribs," with a girl's name painted on every door.

In the early days these women had been spread all about town, identified by a red lampshade or a special colour of curtains or a certain shape of cap. In the spring and summer of 1898 they lived in open tents all along the street like "a small-town annual fair for breeding animals," as one reporter put it. The most notorious of all, Big Sal, pitched her own tent in the middle of a roadway with her name painted on the front in large letters. But Sam Steele made them move to one section of the town, and from then on they were barred from the streets until four in the afternoon. They lived a wretched life, for most of them were in bondage for their passage money to the pimps who had brought them to the Klondike.

It is doubtful if the girls who laughed and sang so easily in the dance halls were really much happier. Most of them were involved in tempestuous love affairs, not with the miners who coveted them so much, but with the gamblers and saloon-keepers and dance-hall operators. In the winter of 1898-99 the *Nugget* periodically reported the suicides or attempted suicides of half a dozen of them: of Stella Hill, a nineteen-year-old from

Oregon who swallowed strychnine four days before Christmas when she learned that her boy friend, the bartender at the Pioneer, had taken up with another woman; of Libby White, whose lover, a one-time Welsh miner, shot her to death in the Monte Carlo in a fit of jealousy and then took his own life; of Helen Holden, who tried to kill herself with chloroform because she was insanely jealous of a saloon proprietor.

The most pathetic tale of all was the tragedy of Myrtle Brocee, one of two sisters who danced and sang at the Tivoli. She shot herself to death in a room over Sam Bonnifield's gambling-house in a fit of despondency. The coroner's inquest into her death was marked by an odd gallantry: half a dozen men took the stand to testify that they had been sleeping with Miss Brocee, but each blandly swore under oath that, though he had shared her bed, she remained virtuous to the end. She had been living with Harry Woolrich, one of the most famous of the Klondike gamblers, and it was, indeed, in his room that she took her life, but Woolrich testified with a straight face that his bed companion was a virgin. The remarkable instance of mass chivalry on the part of the leaders of the demi-monde inspired the entire community, and when Myrtle Brocee, her honour preserved, went to her rest, it was in a coffin with silver-plated handles and a silken interior of blue and white, and with half of Dawson weeping quietly at the graveside.

5: *Fortune's wheels*

In the gaming-rooms, which ran twenty-four hours a day, the gold never stopped circulating.

The entire stampede, from the first moment when Carmack met Henderson, had been an enormous and continual gamble, and when the rush reached its height men were ready to make any kind of wager for any kind

490

of reason. Two old-timers bet ten thousand dollars on the accuracy with which they could spit at a crack in the wall. Swiftwater Bill and John J. Healy lost five thousand dollars between them in a single side bet on a stud-poker game in which they were merely kibitzers. Thomas Wiedemann stood in the gaming-room of the Northern one night in the fall of '98 and watched a neatly dressed man with clean-cut features thoughtfully saunter over to the roulette wheel and lay a thousand-dollar bill on the red. The black came up. He laid a second on the red, and again the black came up, and so he laid a third and lost again. Ten times he laid a thousand dollars down upon the green baize table, and ten times he lost. He showed no emotion, but strolled over to the bar and nonchalantly asked for a drink. "I went broke," he told the bartender, and with that gulped his whiskey, turned about, thrust a single fleeting glance at the wheel, walked into the street, and shot himself.

Edgar Mizner, on the other hand, lost his job as manager of the Alaska Commercial Company in Dawson through similar circumstances. Mizner invited a group of his fellow merchants to have a drink with him in the saloon of the Opera House. The bill came to four dollars, and Mizner remarked with a chuckle that he would get it back on the roulette wheel. He lost on the first spin, and so, with his friends laughing beside him, took a second whirl and lost again. He began to double his bets in order to recoup, but still could not win. Soon he was plunging, and as the word went across town that he was playing for enormous stakes, a large and gener-ally unfriendly crowd gathered to watch him bet; he had remained an unpopular man. By dawn he was down fifteen thousand dollars. In desperation he made four long-shot bets at one thousand dollars each — and lost each one. It was the end for Edgar Mizner.

Scores were destroyed for almost identical reasons. Silent Sam Bonnifield, a famous gambling-house operator in Dawson, used to say that the house made its money because, once a man had won what he set out to get — a dinner, perhaps, or a round of drinks — he quit and went home; but if he lost, he played on to the bitter end. It was true of the operators themselves as well as their customers. Often enough when the faro-dealer and his lookout had finished their stint behind the tables they would take their pay from the pot, sit right down, and lose it.

Because it was fast and offered the players the closest thing to an even break, faro remained the most popular game of chance. In principle it was somewhat similar to roulette: every card from ace to king was painted on the faro table, and the players laid their money on these painted squares. A metal box containing a deck of cards was attached to the table, and the dealer slipped off the top card, exposing the one beneath. If the card that a player was betting on came up first, he lost; if it came up second, he won; if neither, he bet again. Above the dealer was a rack with thirty or forty compartments which held the players' pokes. Into the rack with each poke went a slip of paper charging the owner for the chips he bought. At the end of the play, chips were balanced against slips and the poke was diminished or increased depending on whether the player had lost or won.

Each gambler had his own set methods of playing. For instance, the Oregon Jew, a meticulously dressed man who wore spats and carried a gold-headed cane, would walk into one or another of the houses every afternoon about four and buy a stack of chips and sit down to try his luck. If he lost, he quit. If he started to win, he played long enough to find out how lucky he was. If he felt he was really lucky, he would begin to bet

492

the limit. But he rarely played in the evening unless luck was coming his way, for he was a family man who cloaked his identity, as so many others did, behind a nickname.

The best-known gambler in Dawson was Sam Bonnifield, known as Silent Sam" because of his taciturn nature and sometimes as "Square Sam" because he always ran an honest game. His Bank Saloon and Gambling House at the corner of Front and King, across from the Alaska Commercial store, was the most celebrated establishment of its kind in the Klondike. He was a handsome man in his early thirties, tall and slender, with eyes of a peculiar unfading blue, who never cracked a smile or uttered a word as he pulled in bets of five hundred dollars at the roulette or faro tables. He came originally from West Virginia but had worked through Kansas and Montana and California before coming north through Juneau and Circle City. Tex Rickard's biographer, Charles Samuels, credits Bonnifield with having given the fight-promoter his start in life as a gambler by equipping him with an entire outfit and a shack to operate in at Circle City. Rickard lost the layout in two weeks, but for the rest of his life "gambled as though Sam Bonnifield were looking over his shoulder."

Rickard once watched Bonnifield lose seventy-two thousand dollars in a poker game — and his gambling-establishment into the bargain. At the eleventh hour a crony arrived and loaned the gambler enough to keep going on, and within six hours Bonnifield had won it all back again and cleaned out the customer.

Bonnifield came north with another bold and persistent gambler named Louis Golden, better known in the North as Goldie. The two ran rival establishments in Juneau, Circle City, and Dawson, but it was their practice to close up once a week and play at the other's table until one of them went broke. Goldie made sixty thousand dollars in 1897 and lost it all the following year — twenty-five thousand of it in a single night.

He and Bonnifield took part in the biggest poker game ever recorded in the Klondike. There was fifty thousand dollars in the pot when Goldie raised it by twenty-five thousand. Bonnifield called him and raised again, bringing the pot to one hundred and fifty thousand. Goldie triumphantly laid down four queens. Bonnifield, without a word or a change of expression, turned his hand over to show four kings and raked in a fortune.

Bonnifield made it a habit never to turn down a bet. When Al Mitchell of Missoula, Montana, tackled him on one occasion and challenged him to a game, Bonnifield sat down immediately. Mitchell tried to unnerve him with a huge raise. Without the flicker of an eyelash Bonnifield casually turned around and asked the porter to stoke the fire. Then he turned back and called the bet. He was a past master at this form of gamesmanship, and when they got up, two and a half hours later, Mitchell had lost fifty-seven hundred dollars, which was all he had. Bonnifield tossed him a twenty-dollar goldpiece for breakfast and left the room without a word.

He not only played everybody, but he also played as long as anybody else was playing. One memorable game began at seven one evening and went on steadily until seven the following night. The players were Bonnifield, the Montana Kid, and Harry Woolrich; their meals were brought to the table, and they ate without dropping a hand.

Woolrich, who was from Montana, reached Dawson in November, 1898, after having achieved the distinction of winning and losing fifty thousand dollars in a game in Butte. Once he started playing, he often played for days, taking his meals at the table, a quiet, sallow man of about fifty-five, smoking a perpetual cigar, his expression never changing. Rubbernecks and kibitzers would stand five or six deep behind him, but this did not perturb him. Often enough he was playing with other men's money. More timid plungers, believing that Woolrich had a magic touch with cards, would stake him; thus, if he lost, he lost nothing, while if he won, he took half the profit. As a result, he was able to take big chances with no risk to himself.

Woolrich ended up in Dawson running the gambling concession at the Monte Carlo. One night he cleaned up sixty thousand dollars and determined to renounce gambling forever and leave the Klondike to settle down. Ticket in hand, he boarded a departing steamer to the cheers of a large crowd of well-wishers who came down to the docks to see him off. Alas for Harry Woolrich, the boat was delayed. Back he went to the gaming-tables and with a magnificent gesture pulled a half-dollar from his pocket, flung it on the counter, and cried: "Here's my farewell to gambling, boys; I'm through!" He lost the half-dollar and so matched it with another half. He lost again. Twenty-four hours later he was still in the same spot, the boat long since gone. When his money ran out, he pulled out the steamer ticket and flung it on the table. And he lost that, too.

The Monte Carlo was forever changing hands over games of chance. One evening Kid Kelly sauntered into the gaming-room and initiated a casual game with Ed Holden, the owner. It looked innocent enough, for each man was playing with one yellow chip at a time. Only a few of the spectators realized that each chip was worth an enormous sum and that every bet was the limit. The two men laughed and joshed each other as they played, and then, just as casually, Holden rose from his chair and walked out while Kelly took his place at the faro table as the new proprietor. This change in ownership wreaked havoc in the Monte Carlo dance hall. John Mulligan, who ran the stage show, had once refused to hire Kelly's girl, Caprice, as an actress. Kelly installed the plump blonde as stage-manager, and her first act was to fire Mulligan. He and Holden left town shortly afterward.

All during the winter of '98-'99, gambling provided the town with its chief amusement. When a big game was under way, hundreds and sometimes thousands would pour down to Front Street to watch the excitement; it was good entertainment, and it was free. More than that, if a player had a streak of luck, others could make minor fortunes by laying bets on the same cards. On the memorable evening when One-Eyed Riley contracted a winning streak, hundreds followed at his heels as he moved up and down the street from table to table and saloon to saloon. Riley was a night watchman for a navigation company and was known as a faro-bank fiend who spent all his wages on the game. His lunch hour was at midnight because of his job, but, rather than eat, he would go straight to the tables and play everything he had. He always lost; he was always broke.

And then one night in Bonnifield's Riley started to win. Soon he was playing the limit. He forgot about his job and stayed at the tables until, by morning, his winnings were in the thousands. He left Bonnifield's to get something to eat and then began to move from saloon to saloon with the crowds following him. Wherever he went he asked: "What are you going to set as the limit?" and whatever the limit was, Riley played it and won, and moved on. His last stop was the Monte Carlo. It was well into morning now, but Riley's luck still held. Dealer after dealer was thrown in against him to try to buck his winning streak, without success. A mystic aura seemed to surround him, and scores profited by following his bets with money of their own. In a last-ditch attempt to stop him, the management recruited a card wizard named Shepherd to deal to him, and Riley finally called it a day. By now he had piled up twenty-eight thousand dollars, and he was determined to quit the Klondike as quickly as possible before he lost it all again. So great was his haste that he did not even bother to collect his wages, but, as it was midwinter, paid a dog-driver one thousand dollars to rush him out over the winter trail.

In Skagway somebody inveigled him into a dice game. Riley, flushed with success, lost his fortune in three straight passes.

6: *The last stampede*

Far from the carnival of Front Street, in his makeshift hospital under the hill at the north end of Dawson, Father William Judge, the frail and cadaverous priest, quietly toiled away. All the previous summer, the steaming undrained swamp on which the town was built, rank with undisposed sewage, had spread typhoid, malaria, and dysentery among the unwitting stampeders. These, together with the scurvy cases, jammed every available cot in the hospital, filling the very hallways and crowding Father Judge himself out of his own spartan bedroom.

The overworked priest had one quality in common with all the others who descended upon the Klondike: he was a believer in miracles. For him, if not always for others, the miracles seemed to come true. It was his practice, for instance, never to turn a patient away, but one afternoon he accepted twenty more than he had bedding for. Then the miracle came: at nightfall three bales of blankets arrived mysteriously on an unidentified sleigh and were dumped at the door. Again, early in the fall, he had so many patients pouring into the

497

hospital that he was forced to put some of them in the upper rooms which were not yet finished, for the roof of his hospital had not been completed. As if in answer to his prayers, the storms relented and there was clear weather for three weeks until the last board was in place. During the winter he found that he could not hire workmen to dig a grave in the frozen ground of the cemetery for one of his dead patients, and so struggled himself with pick and shovel until he was about to give up in despair. Suddenly, out of the gloom, two husky miners appeared; they told him they had heard that they were wanted at the hospital and proceeded at once to complete the grave and to cover the coffin.

In a sense, Judge was the conscience of Dawson. Men watched him at his work and felt a little better that they belonged to the human race; it was as if his own example cleansed them of their sins. His little office, which contained nothing more than a board lounge, two blue blankets, and a rough wooden drawer in which his worldly possessions were kept, had long since been given over to the sick. The priest, when he slept at all, curled up in the hallways, or in a corner by the stairs, or in any cranny he could find. When his nurses pleaded with him to take more rest, he replied only that when his work was finished he would have plenty of time for sleep. It was his habit to rise at five a.m. to hear Mass, to eat a spare breakfast — frequently sharing his food with another — and to work until eleven at night. He always insisted that he be awakened if any patient asked to see him, and all through the dark hours he could be seen moving quietly, like a guardian shade, through the wards.

He rarely smiled, and yet his face was forever radiant, beaming with what one man called "an indescribable delight." Despite his frailty, he moved with catlike speed; he did not walk upstairs, but always ran.

It would have horrified him to know that his hospital was a hotbed of graft and chicanery; that many of the male nurses were little better than thugs who waited, like ghouls, for a man to expire; that they borrowed money from the dying, knowing they would not need to pay it back, or sent the invalids' watches to be repaired, hoping to claim them for themselves if the owners died. It was customary to prescribe stimulants for a patient recovering from typhoid — a bottle of brandy or whiskey — but the attendants drank most of this liquor, pouring out drinks for their charges and then pretending that the hour had not arrived for the dose.

All that fall the priest remained on the town's conscience, and in December of '98 the feeling grew that something tangible should be done for him. In spite of some heavy donations from Big Alex McDonald and Pat Galvin, the hospital was still in debt, and so the people of Dawson proposed to pay it off as a Christmas present. A benefit show was planned, and, although December 25 was the best-paying night of the year, Joe Cooper offered his Tivoli theatre free for the affair.

As Judge's only outer garment in all his months in Dawson had been a tattered black cassock, patched and worn, it was decided that he must have a new suit of clothes for Christmas. A tailor was dispatched to get the priest's measure, but Judge politely refused. The tailor was told to make the suit anyway, together with a sealskin coat, cap, and gloves (for Judge dressed lightly, with shocking disregard for the severity of the Yukon winter). A presentation was made a few days before the show; but Judge, although moved, explained that as a Jesuit he could neither own chattels nor accept gifts. The presentation committee urged the clothing upon him, pointing out that most of the donors were Protestants, and in the end the priest relented. He was reluctant to attend the minstrel show in his honour, but was

499

prevailed upon to do so. When George Noble, the inter-locutor, rose to make a little speech, referring to him as "the grand old man of Dawson," the audience went wild. Judge was taken up on the stage, much against his wishes, and the cheering continued for five minutes. But this was the only time he appeared in his new clothes; the following day he was seen again in his threadbare robes.

His time was running out, and the whole town knew it. Although he was but forty-five years old, he looked closer to seventy. Overwork had lowered his resistance, and two weeks after Christmas the word sped across the community that he was ill with pneumonia and would probably not recover. A pall settled over Dawson. As if to accentuate the mood, the temperature dropped to fifty below, and the snow turned dry as sand, squeaking eerily beneath men's feet, while the smoke from the buildings pillared vertically into the still air to hang across the river valley in a pale shroud. The whole community, it seemed, was slowing to a dead stop. It was so cold that horses could not be worked, and after a few days there was scarcely any life in the streets. Moving slowly, like ungainly animals, to protect their lungs, and bundled in furs to the very ears, men made brief forays into the cold and then retreated again into the steaming interiors. Windows frosted solid, while cabins even a few yards distant were blurred by the fog that encompassed the community. In the hospital on the hill the death watch began.

Then, suddenly, tantalizing rumours began to seep through the saloons, and a bizarre charade, half comic, half tragic, broke the spell and shook the town from its lethargy. Gold, it was whispered, had been discovered on an unknown creek down the river. . . . Nobody knew exactly where the gold was, but Nigger Jim Daugherty had the secret. . . . He was planning an expedition in the
500

dead of night to stake out a fortune. Like a hive prodded by a stick, the community began to buzz as hundreds laid in stocks of provisions, mended the harness on their dog-teams, and did repair work on their sleds.

No one was quite sure how the Nigger Jim Stampede originated. Some there were who swore that a mysterious prospector had sold Jim a map for a thousand dollars and produced a poke of gold dust as evidence of his good faith. Others claimed that Jim had started the stampede on a wager, to prove that nobody could keep a secret in Dawson. Whatever its beginnings, the stampede itself was the most frenzied that the town had seen since the rush to Dominion Creek.

Nigger Jim was a member of the Klondike aristocracy, a blond giant of a man who had quit his job as logger on the Pacific coast to go north to Circle City in 1894. His claim on Upper Bonanza netted him three hundred and sixty thousand dollars, enough to purchase two dance halls for the singing Oatley Sisters, one of whom he was eventually to marry. He was called Nigger Jim, not because of his colour, but because of his soft Missouri accent and because he liked to sing spirituals and accompany himself on the banjo. He was seldom seen without a cigar in his mouth, or a sombrero on his head, or a heavy diamond ring on his finger, or a glittering stickpin in his tie. Like Curly Munro, he wore no coat, but his fine silk shirts and vests were specially tailored for him in London. He preferred to drink champagne, and to impress Lottie Oatley he would stand at the bar until dawn treating every comer to the best vintages. In Skagway the previous spring he drank up all the champagne in town, then chartered a steamer to go to Juneau, one hundred miles down the coast, for a new supply. His generosity was a byword. Two months before the stampede he had been robbed of twenty thousand dollars. A friend captured the thief, and as a reward Jim bought him a saloon. The free lunch at the bar in his own New Pavilion was so Lucullan that one man is said to have lived for a year in Dawson without eating elsewhere. Stroller White recalled that "for two years after he opened the New Pavilion, Nigger Jim could neither spend nor give away the money as fast as it came his way, although he did the best he could along both lines."

At eleven p.m. on January 10, Jim stood in the Aurora Saloon with some of the Klondike élite to whom he had disclosed his secret: Charley Anderson, the Lucky Swede; Skiff Mitchell of *One* Eldorado; Sam Stanley, Billy Chappell, and Ramps Peterson. Outside, all along Front Street, newly harnessed dog-teams lay waiting in the snow, while ghostly figures glided about town passing the word that the moment had almost come. Jim swallowed his eighth whiskey-and-soda and walked out of the door with his friends, and the rush was on. By two that morning there were fifty sleds dashing down the frozen river in the wake of the leaders, and behind these, plodding on foot, came stragglers, one or two of them with queer devices for carrying their outfits. Among these could be discerned the tall muffled figure of Arizona Charlie, leading a loaded ox.

Here was an odd pantomime; it was as if this small knot of men, forcing their way along the whitened river in the dark of the cold night, were bent on acting out for themselves, once again, the full drama of '98. For the Nigger Jim Stampede, with its wild rumours, its sudden frenzy, its optimism and despair, its trials and its yearnings and its ultimate irony, was a scale model of the Klondike gold rush itself.

The temperature dropped to sixty below, and the journey became a horror for all but the anointed few who had had the foresight to prepare for it. Nigger Jim and his friends slept soundly each night; they had

502

brought tents and Yukon stoves and thick fur robes. The rest cowered in the lee of their sleds, which were arranged in a huge circle, around the central camp so that Jim, in the words of one, "was enclosed like a Roman general."

Back in Dawson, in the hospital under the hill, Father Judge clung precariously to life.

By the second day the stampeders had left the main river to follow a tributary stream into the hills, wallowing in snow so deep that sleds and dogs had to be cast aside. Here some gave up the struggle and turned back in frustration, fatigue, and disgust, while others, like hounds on a scent, only grew more eager. On they floundered, up a miniature Chilkoot, the snow falling upon them as fast as their snowshoes packed it down, a vicious gale blowing into their frostbitten faces, their beards and moustaches stiff as boards.

On the far side of a razor ridge, in a valley of phantom white, Jim reached his goal and hammered in his stakes. The others followed suit; and then began the weary, anticlimactic trek back to Dawson some hundred miles away. By the time the town was reached, all were in a state of depression.

Some of these men bore the scars of the Nigger Jim Stampede all their lives. Several were maimed hideously, and one man lost both his feet. Few, if any, returned to the lonely valley to examine the ground that had been staked at such a cost. The word went around that it was quite worthless, and this was accepted as truth, just as the original tales had been.

On their return, the stampeders learned that Judge was sinking lower day by day. Hundreds of inquiries poured in asking how he was, while gifts arrived daily, including one case of champagne worth thirty dollars a pint.

Skiff Mitchell, just back from the stampede, made his way to Judge's bedside. He was an old friend of the priest, although Protestant, and when he saw the wasted figure on the couch the tears rolled down his cheeks.

"Why are you crying?" Judge asked him. "We have been old friends almost since I came into the country."

"We can't afford to lose old friends like you," Mitchell replied.

"You've got what you came for," the priest reminded him. "I too have been working for a reward. Would you keep me from it?"

He seemed anxious to die. When the nuns in the hospital said they would pray hard for him to stay alive, he answered quite cheerfully: "You may do what you please, but I am going to die."

The end came on January 16, and Dawson went into deep mourning. "If the whole town had slipped down into the river, it would not have been more of a shock," someone wrote later. Shops and dance halls closed their doors, and even the houses were draped in black.

It took two and half days to hack the dead priest's grave out of the hard-frozen soil, but there was no dearth of men for the task, and when the body was taken to its rest the grieving population followed. Nothing would do but that the casket cost one thousand dollars and be made of the finest material. It was a gesture in keeping with the general ostentation of the community, though the shrivelled figure within would have shuddered at the thought.

The following day the town returned to normal. At the Tivoli, where, less than a month before, Father Judge had received the homage of the camp, John Mulligan was winning applause with a topical new song:

504

> *Nigger Jim just wanted to know*
> *If a fresh cheechako could outrun a*
>   *sourdough.*

Jim himself sat in his box, with Lottie Oatley beside him, and laughed and applauded while the champagne ran as swiftly as the water in the sluiceboxes on Eldorado.

7: *Tales of conspicuous wealth*

The mining élite had become a distinct social class. They occupied royal boxes in the dance halls, stood shoulder to shoulder at the bars in Grand Forks, the town at the junction of Bonanza and Eldorado, and drove their fashionable dog-teams down the hard-packed snow of the Klondike Valley.

Indeed, the dog-team had become the chief symbol of conspicuous wealth in the Klondike. It was the Cadillac of its time. The more affluent saloon-keepers, gamblers, and mine-owners all kept expensive teams with expensive harness. Coatless Curly Munro, for instance, lavished, in a single season, 4,320 pounds of bacon, fish, and flour, at one dollar a pound, on his embryo team of six husky puppies. Nigger Jim's prize team of eight dogs was worth twenty-five hundred dollars, and his sled enjoyed the added refinement of a built-in bar. This was a specially made tin tank he kept filled with alcohol, which he poured out by the dipperful to mix with hot water and sugar so that he might treat his friends wherever he stopped.

If there was conspicuous wealth, there was also conspicuous waste. Dick Lowe, the ex-mule-skinner who had, on Ogilvie's suggestion, staked the famous fractional claim on Bonanza, could be seen of a Sunday driving a spanking team of trotting-horses out along the Klondike Valley with a dance-hall girl on the seat beside him, or, of an evening, flinging a fortune on the bars at Grand Forks to treat the crowd. On Dominion Creek two neighbouring miners each installed a butler in his log cabin. On Eldorado, Clarence Berry, the ex-fruit farmer from Fresno, enjoyed a peculiar luxury. Berry, who had been the first on the creek to hit bed-rock, now owned the only cow in the valley, a pure-bred Jersey who supplied fresh milk from her sawdust-padded stable and munched hay worth four hundred dollars a ton. His wife, who had come into the country strapped to a sled, now travelled in style, and when she complained that her stateroom on one of the steam-boats was too small, the owner immediately hacked down some partitions so she might have the space she needed. In front of Berry's cabin, along the Eldorado trail, stood a coal-oil can full of gold and a bottle of whiskey beside it. A sign between the two of them carried the blunt but inviting message: "Help Yourself."

The old-timers were dying. Ladue was dead, and so was Harper. Bill McPhee, the giant barkeep from Fortymile who now ran the Pioneer Saloon, lost both of his partners, Harry Spencer and Frank Densmore — each of them veterans of some fifteen years in the North. Typhoid, pneumonia, and tuberculosis had taken their toll, but the real killer was the Yukon climate, which, over the years, had wasted the constitutions of these early prospectors. Now those who survived began to spend their fortunes as if they, too, had death at their heels.

George Carmack arrived in Seattle and announced that he was building a yacht to sail to the Paris Exposition, the South Seas, the Mediterranean, and the Orient. His Indian wife, Kate, who had never been away from her native Yukon, was ensconced with him in Seattle's Butler Hotel — a situation which she found bewildering. To her the hallways and staircases were like a labyrinth, and in order to find her way back to the room she produced her little hatchet and blazed a trail, Indian style, on banister and doorway. With her brothers, Skookum Jim and Tagish Charley, she continued to make headlines. They loaded up with champagne and were arrested and fined for drunkenness. They caused a near-riot by throwing banknotes and gold nuggets from their hotel window until a scrambling crowd, fighting for the money, brought traffic to a stop. Meanwhile, Carmack himself was riding up and down the streets with an expensive cigar in his cheek and a sign emblazoned on his carriage identifying him as "George Carmack, Discoverer of Gold in the Klondike."

Clarence Berry's partner, the handsome Austrian Antone Stander, landed triumphantly at San Francisco with his new wife, Violet Raymond, the ex-dance-hall girl. He planned to take her on a honeymoon to China and he had one thousand pounds of gold, as pocket-money, in his stateroorn, which was the finest on the *Humboldt*. Violet wanted to go ashore, but Stander feared to leave his treasure. "It would be hard to tell which [he] guards more jealously — his bride or his gold," a reporter for the *Examiner* wrote. It was a hard choice; the only solution seemed to be to give the gold to Violet, and this Stander did, bit by bit, until it was all gone.

Charley Anderson, now known universally as the Lucky Swede because he had bought a million-dollar claim while drunk, was on his way to Europe accompanied by his wife, Edgar Mizner's former inamorata Grace Drummond, the toast of the Monte Carlo. Grace had promised to cast off Mizner and marry the Lucky Swede if he would pay fifty thousand dollars into her bank account, and the Lucky Swede was delighted to do just that. Off the happy couple went, arm in arm, to

507

Paris and London and New York and finally to San Francisco, on whose outskirts the Lucky Swede built a monument to his bride in the form of a turreted castle worth twenty thousand dollars.

Big Alex McDonald went to Paris, too, and thence to Rome, where he was granted an audience with the Pope and made a Knight of St. Gregory on the strength of his donation to Father Judge's hospital. Then he was off to London, a huge and awkward figure in his formal clothing, with his immense ham hands fairly bursting from his gloves. He spent a good deal of his time riding up and down in elevators, which he referred to as "heists," having never been in one until this time. Before he returned to Dawson, in April 1899, he married Margaret Chisholm, the twenty-year-old daughter of the superintendent of the Thames Water Police. The story went around that, on emerging from Alaska, Big Alex had seen his first pretty girl and asked her name; it had been Chisholm, and in his mind the word had been forever identified with desire.

There seemed no end to his wealth. In Dawson that spring his fifteen-mule pack train, laden with gold, was a familiar sight on the Klondike river road. On one of his claims a single man was able to shovel in twenty thousand dollars in a twelve-hour stretch. One payment made by McDonald to the Alaska Trading and Transportation Company amounted to one hundred and fifty thousand. He erected his own building, The McDonald, in Dawson and lived lavishly on its first floor. On his sideboard there rested a bowl containing forty-five pounds of large nuggets. When Alice Henderson, a newspaper correspondent, dropped in, McDonald waved airily at this treasure.

"Help yourself to some nuggets," he said casually, with the attitude of a man proffering a box of chocolates. "Take some of the bigger ones."

508

She hesitated, and McDonald made a gesture of impatience.

"Oh, they mean nothing to me," he said. "Take as many as you please. There are lots more."

His contempt for gold was quite genuine, for it was not nuggets McDonald desired. His mania for property was still unsatisfied. It was to him what champagne, dog-teams, and dancing-girls were to his fellow claim-owners. He could not stop buying, but roamed farther and farther from the Klondike, amassing more and more claims, turning down offers of millions for what he had, always accumulating land. As one newspaper wrote, his life "in point of riches promises to outrival that of the fabled Count of Monte Cristo." But, as events turned out, the newspaper was wrong.

While McDonald was in Rome and London, Swift-water Bill Gates, unabashed and unrepentant following his ill-fated venture with Jack Smith of the Monte Carlo, was cutting his own swath across North America and Europe. He and Joseph Whiteside Boyle, the sparring-partner of Frank Slavin, were off to London to raise money for a company which was to exploit the mining concession on Quartz Creek that Boyle had wangled from the Canadian government. How much of that money the company would ever see was problematical, since Swiftwater, now hailed in the press as "the Klondike Prince," was publicly offering to bet seven thousand dollars on the turn of a card with anybody who cared to challenge him.

In Seattle, where he arrived en route back to Dawson, Swiftwater became embroiled in another of those astonishing marital adventures that marked his life. He was occupying an elegant suite in the Butler Hotel when Mrs. Iola Beebe, a Seattle widow, visited him. She had been to St. Michael the previous fall and was now trying to secure backing to open a hotel in Dawson. Swiftwater received her in his black Prince Albert coat, his patent-leather shoes, and his boiled shirt from whose centre a fourteen-carat diamond glittered. In the hallways outside, a shouting mob was trying to gain admittance, but the Klondike Prince had eyes only for Mrs. Beebe — or, more accurately, for her two daughters, Bera, aged fifteen, and Blanche, nineteen, both just out of convent school.

Swiftwater wasted no time. Mrs. Beebe's back was scarcely turned before he had spirited both her daughters aboard the *Humboldt,* which was about to steam north. Their alarmed mother took up the scent, stormed aboard the ship, and discovered Swiftwater cowering under a lifeboat. She rescued the girls and took her leave, but her adventures were by no means over. Undeterred by this brush with a Klondike prince, she determined to go on to the north and seek her fortune. With her daughters she landed in Skagway some days later to find Swiftwater lying in wait, his ardour in no sense dampened. This time his blandishments were more successful. Mrs. Beebe awoke one morning to find that the fifteen-year-old Bera, a plump, pink-cheeked, and blue-eyed morsel, had decamped for Dawson with her Casanova. Before she could overtake the errant couple, they were man and wife. When the newlyweds reached Dawson, Swiftwater presented his bride with a characteristic gift: the town's only melon, price forty dollars. Mrs. Beebe's account of all this, which was privately printed some years later, leaves something to be desired. Her exasperation with Swiftwater is evident, and yet here and there a note of tenderness creeps into the narrative. No matter how badly Swiftwater behaved, Mrs. Beebe always forgave him, and the reader is left with the inescapable suspicion that Mrs. Beebe, like her two daughters, was enamoured of the little man in the Prince Albert coat. How else to

510

explain her subsequent mollification? Far from financing Mrs. Beebe in the hotel business, Swiftwater Bill managed to extract from her all the money she owned, thirty-five thousand dollars, which he sank into his Quartz Creek mining venture. Swiftwater's talent in raising money was always equalled by his ability to get rid of it. By the end of the year he was magnificently bankrupt and had run up bills that totalled one hundred thousand dollars. Off he went, down the river, with his child bride and his incurable optimism, leaving his wretched and now destitute mother-in-law to care for a four-week-old granddaughter.

There were other bankruptcies equally catastrophic. Pat Galvin, the free-spending Irishman who had sunk the profits from his Bonanza claim into a transportation company, was teetering on the edge of ruin by the spring of 1899, as were so many of the successful Klondike claim-owners who had ventured into the business world. Galvin's first steamboat, the *Mary Ellen Galvin,* which he had designed to be the finest vessel on the river, was a complete failure; although she had four decks and was advertised as "mosquito proof," she drew too much water to cross the Yukon flats and had to be abandoned. His second boat, Captain Irving's *Yukoner,* lay stranded in the ice fourteen hundred miles downstream, a mutiny brewing aboard her. Galvin had planned to have one of his boats in Dawson in time to steam upriver and pick up a load of cattle he had ordered brought in over the Dalton Trail at heavy expense. But with no transportation available the animals had to be slaughtered and the meat went bad, and his plans for a Yukon packing business melted away.

An even heavier millstone around Galvin's neck was his financial manager, James Beatty, whose silken moustache, iron-grey hair, courtly manner, and English polo-playing background had earned him the nickname of "Lord Jim." Lord Jim was even more indulgent than Galvin. Not only did he import the finest china and bed linen for Galvin's proposed chain of Yukon River hotels, but also he imported the best-looking girls to be had in San Francisco for himself. He did this out of frustration: he had been sending fifteen-dollar breakfasts to the bedroom of a Dawson soubrette for weeks on end as a gesture of his affection. The price was steep even in Klondike currency — the voracious young lady seemed to be eating enough for two. Lord Jim investigated and learned that this was only too true: his intended was in the habit of sharing both breakfast and bed with a faro-dealer. There was nothing to do but replace her with an import, and this was one of the reasons why the company's auditors found forty thousand dollars unaccounted for in Lord Jim's books. Lord Jim was arrested and charged with embezzlement, but Galvin had him released on bail and paid his way across the border. Once on Alaskan soil, Lord Jim promptly forged a cheque and lit out for South Africa with a troop of detectives behind him in what was billed as the longest manhunt on record. Galvin by now had lost everything, but he was not a man to whimper. When he learned of Lord Jim's defection, he merely shrugged.

"He was a good fellow," he observed.

8: *Money to burn*

More than one visitor to Dawson during the stampede remarked that the wealthier miners seemed to have money to burn. In this observation there was literal truth. Although there are no recorded instances of men lighting cigars with fifty-dollar bills, there are dozens of examples of others who put tens of thousands into a frame hotel, saloon, or dance hall and then watched it reduced to ashes.

Dawson's two worst fires occurred in its gaudiest year. The winter of '98-'99 began and ended with conflagrations that destroyed, in each case, the most expensive section of the town.

The first fire took place almost exactly one year after the Thanksgiving fire of 1897 and, by coincidence, was started by the same dance-hall girl. Half a million dollars' worth of real estate went up in smoke because Belle Mitchell set off for Lousetown leaving a candle burning in a block of wood. Three Eldorado fortunes were badly dented by the inferno that followed. Arkansas Jim Hall saw his Greentree Hotel burned to the ground. Charlie Worden saw his Worden Hotel follow. Big Alex McDonald watched his post-office building, which he rented to the government for a substantial sum, vanish in the flames. The fire roared up and down the street and back towards the hills, leaping from cabin to cabin and crib to crib along Paradise Alley, while two thousand men chopped up neighbouring structures to stop it from spreading.

In front of John Healy's N.A.T. store the town's newly purchased fire-fighting equipment lay in a state of disassembly; it could not be used because it had not been paid for. Building after building, in which scores of men had flung pound after pound of gold dust, toppled and crumbled because the community as a whole would not raise twelve thousand dollars for reels and hoses. Men had bet more on a single card at the faro tables.

The following day a finance company hurriedly signed a note, and a fire-fighting company of one hundred men went into operation. Dawson breathed more easily with this safeguard, but its sense of reassurance was premature. In April, when the newly trained firemen asked for better wages, the town council demurred. The firemen struck, and the fires in their boilers died. And then, at this crucial moment, late on the night of

513

April 26, 1899, a tongue of flame shot from the bedroom of a dance-hall girl on the second floor of the Bodega Saloon. Within minutes a holocaust far worse than the town had yet known began.

Scores dashed to the river in the glare of the flames and tried to break through the ice to reach the water supply. With the boilers cold, fires had to be set to melt the frozen surface so water could be pumped to the scene. In the meantime, half of Front Street was ablaze. The temperature stood at forty-five below — so cold that the heat had little effect even on those standing close to the spreading flames. Many discovered that their fur coats were scorched and charred, and yet they felt nothing. There was no breath of wind, and the tongues of flame leaped vertically into the air like flashes of lightning, causing clouds of steam to condense into an icy fog which soon encompassed most of the city. Within this white envelope the ghostly and frantic figures of the fire-fighters dashed about ineffectually against the background of the crackling fire. As the dance halls and saloons began to char and totter, hogsheads of liquor were overturned, and whiskey ran into the streets, where it instantly froze solid in the biting cold. Behind dance-hall row, Paradise Alley was aflame again, and the prostitutes poured, naked and screaming, from their smoking cribs into the arms of the fire-fighters, who ripped off their own coats to bundle up the terrified women.

The men on the river had meanwhile burned their way to the water supply; the pumps were started, and the hoses, long in disuse, slowly filled. But as the water was ice-cold and unwarmed by boiler heat, it froze solidly long before reaching the nozzles. Then there came a ripping, rending sound as the expanding ice tore open the hoses, followed by a moan of despair as the crowd realized the town was doomed.

514

"What's to be done?" cried Tim Chisholm, as the flames darted towards his Aurora Saloon.

Captain Cortlandt Starnes of the North West Mounted Police, plump and red-faced, his mustachios stiff with his frosted breath, supplied the answer: "Blow up the buildings in front of the fire!"

A dog-team went racing to the A.C. warehouse for fifty pounds of Giant blasting-powder so that Starnes and his police could demolish the Aurora and Alex McDonald's new building to leave a blank space in front of the moving wall of flame.

By this time the fire was occupying the energies of the entire town. Thousands struggled in and out of the condemned buildings carrying articles saved from the blaze until the marsh behind the business section was littered with chattels. Many were offering ten dollars an hour for help, and any two-horse team and driver could command one hundred dollars an hour. David Doig, the fastidious manager of the Bank of British North America, pledged one thousand dollars to anyone who could save the building, but the offer was made in vain.

The town shuddered with earthquake reverberations as the dynamite did its work in the face of the advancing flames. The firemen, unable to pump water, worked ahead of the explosion, soaking blankets in mud puddles to try to save the Fairview Hotel, which stood on the edge of the conflagration. In its adjoining stables were hogsheads of rum which Belinda Mulroney used to keep her horses warm and working during the chill winter days; she poured it by the dipperful down the grateful gullets of the fire-fighters.

At last the groaning multitude saw that further effort was useless. Half freezing, half roasting, they stood like lost souls on the edge of the Pit, their faces glowing redly in the reflected light of the vagrant flames. Before their

515

eyes, Front Street, with all its memories, was being consigned to the inferno.

Bill McPhee's Pioneer Saloon, one of Dawson's oldest log buildings, crumbled to ashes and was gone in a shower of sparks, the piles of gold and sacks of mail stacked behind the bar buried beneath the charred timbers.

"Gather up the money, the town is going to go!" Belinda Mulroney had called out as McPhee made a final dash into his building.

But this was not what he was after.

"To hell with the money!" he shouted. "I want to save my moosehead," and back he staggered with the prized trophy. It meant far more to him than fleeting gold, for it had hung above the bar since opening day — that day which seemed so long ago, when Dawson was young, and the cheechakos were in the minority, and his old, good friends Spencer and Densmore were alive, and the men from Circle City crowded around the glowing stove and made the Pioneer Saloon their home. Could it have been only two years past?

Harry Ash's Northern Saloon, whose sawdust floor had glittered with gold dust, went the way of the Pioneer; and across the street the Aurora was blown to bits to make a firebreak — the Aurora that had once been Jimmy Kerry's at the dawn of Dawson's brief history. And now the Tivoli was crumbling, the Tivoli once called the Combination, where John Mulligan had produced *Stillwater Willie* and Cad Wilson had danced and sung; and the Opera House, with its famous gallery of private boxes, where Edgar Mizner had gambled his career away; and the Dominion Saloon and Gambling House, where the stakes were so high that eight Mounties had sometimes to be posted to keep order.

Walter Washburn, a faro-dealer who had invested ten thousand dollars in the Opera House, watched with quiet resignation as it was devoured by the flames. "Well," he said, "that's the way I made it, and that's the way it's gone; so what the hell!"

As if to underline this statement, the vault within the tottering Bank of British North America burst wide open in the fierce heat and the contents spewed out into the debris — gold dust and nuggets scooped from the bowels of Bonanza by moiling men, heavy gold watches from the vests of gamblers and saloon-keepers left here for safekeeping, jewelled stickpins and bracelets and dance-hall girls' diamonds bought with favours and with wine and with music and now fused inseparably into the molten mass that oozed from the shattered strongbox to mingle with the steaming clay.

One hundred and seventeen buildings were destroyed that night, their loss totalling more than one million dollars. In the cold light of the ensuing day, the weary townspeople crept from their homes to view the havoc. The fire had died away, leaving a smoking ruin where the business section had been. On the north edge of this black scar was the Monte Carlo, scorched but still standing: on the south the Fairview Hotel, a grotesque sight completely sheathed in frozen mud. In its lobby, scores of exhausted and homeless men and women were sleeping in two-hour shifts. The river marked the western boundary of the fire, the littered swamp the eastern. In the heart of the city was an enormous gap, from the ashes of which a large number of shapeless sawdust-covered piles arose at scattered intervals. They revealed themselves as immense blocks of ice which had been cut from the river for summertime use and covered with sawdust as insulation. Of all things, they alone had survived the fearful heat.

At once the town began to rebuild. Less than twelve hours after his saloon was destroyed, Tom Chisholm had erected a big tent labelled "Aurora" and was doing

517

business again. Although nails sold for twenty-five cents each, the familiar ring of saw and hammer was quickly heard on Front Street.

But the town that rose from the ashes — a newer and sturdier metropolis — was not the same town; it would never be the same again. To walk down Front Street, Senator Jerry Lynch remarked, "was like walking for a block or two in the Strand." Sewers were installed, the roads macadamized, and new sidewalks built. The shops were full of fancy goods displayed behind plate-glass windows. Schools were going up. Scores of hand-some women sauntered up and down in fashions im-ported directly from Paris. And when the river broke, more and more steamboats lined the riverbank — as many as eleven at a time; already the trip from St. Michael had been cut from twenty-one to sixteen days.

Dawson was no longer a camp of tents and log cabins: dressed lumber and plate glass were replacing bark and canvas. The dog had had his day; horses now moved easily through the dry streets, drawing huge dray wag-ons. Houses had parlours, parlours had pianos, pianos stood on carpeted floors. Men began to wear white shirts, polish their boots, shave their beards, and trim their moustaches.

Although prices had been high that winter, with onions selling for a dollar and a half apiece and milk at four dollars a quart; although paper had been so short that the *Nugget* appeared for a month on butchers' wrapping-stock, yet Dawson was no longer the isolated community it had once been. In March one man actu-ally bicycled without mishap all the way to Skagway in a mere eight days. Already there was talk of a tunnel under the Chilkoot Pass, and a company was floated to drill one, but the scheme was abandoned because the White Pass Railway was swiftly becoming a reality. Thirty-five thousand men were at work on the grade

518

between Skagway and the Whitehorse Rapids, carving the right of way out of solid rock and blowing hundred-and-twenty-foot cliffs bodily away. Before the year was out, men would be riding in style where two seasons before horses had perished by the thousands. As for Skagway, it had become a respectable and law-abiding town of sixteen hundred people, with electric lights and a water supply.

And now the old-timers, who had witnessed the rise and fall of Fortymile, and who had seen Circle City turn from a frontier town of logs to a sophisticated community, began to get an uneasy sensation in their spines. It was as if the whole cycle of their experience was being repeated. This feeling was communicated to the cheechakos, who, by virtue of their year in the Klondike, were already thinking of themselves as sourdoughs. Some had spent the winter in hastily built cabins in distant valleys, sinking shafts on barren claims far from the golden axis of Bonanza and Eldorado; some had found work, as labourers in the goldfields (the glut of men had driven wages down from fifteen dollars a day to a mere hundred dollars a month), or as clerks in stores, or as bartenders or dockworkers; some had done nothing but sit in their cabins slowly consuming their thousand pounds of food, wondering what to do. Now a sense of anticlimax spread among all of them. Thousands walked the wooden sidewalks seeking work, but there was less and less work to be had, and a stale taste began to grow in the mouths of those same men who, a year before, had tumbled pell-mell from the boats with shouts of triumph and anticipation.

The *Nugget* reported that in the Outside world the word "Klondike," which had once inspired visions of fortune, had become an epithet of contempt and derision. The newest expression of disgust was the phrase:

519

"Ah — go to the Klondike!" In Seattle, gold-pans had been converted to dishpans and were selling at bargain rates, while costly hand axes, once destined for the gold-fields, were going at a fraction of their value. On July 1, five thousand dollars' worth of Klondike groceries, hardware, and clothing were thrown on the market at cost. The proud fleet of ships assembled for the Alaskan trade rode at anchor in San Francisco harbour, empty and neglected.

All through the spring vague rumours of something exciting on Norton Sound near the mouth of the Yukon River had been filtering into Dawson. It was the same kind of news that had once emptied Fortymile and Circle City. At first the news was sketchy, as it always was, and men refused to believe it, as they always did. But, sceptical or not, they began to trickle out of town and down the river in twos and threes, and then in dozens, and then in scores, searching not so much for new adventure or new wealth, perhaps, as simply for the love of the search.

One of the first boats to leave Dawson was the *W. K. Merwyn,* that same creaky little craft that had brought the *Eliza Anderson*'s party on her eventful trip up the river to the Klondike. The steamboat seemed fated to embark on the most harrowing journeys, and this was no exception. She was so crowded that Walter Russell Curtin, one of her two hundred passengers, wrote that they "had to stand like straphangers in a streetcar." The food supply was swiftly reduced to peanuts and corn-meal, and the passengers were forced to gather goose eggs along the shore to keep body and soul together. The following year the *Merwyn* sank in an ocean storm not far from the Yukon's mouth. Her timbers were washed ashore and, fittingly enough, burned by some of her ex-passengers who were by this time short of firewood.

By midsummer 1899 the news from the beaches of Alaska was confirmed. On the sands of Nome, just across the Bering Strait from Siberia, a fortune in fine gold dust had been discovered — a fortune that had been lying hidden all the time at the far end of the golden river on whose cold breast so many men had floated in a search for treasure.

The news roared across Alaska and across the Yukon Territory like a forest fire: a tent city was springing up on the beach at Nome . . . men were making fortunes and losing them just as quickly. . . buildings were going up, saloons opening, money changing hands . . . the beach was staked for thirteen miles . . . rocker and sluicebox were again in motion. . . . The experts were already predicting that Nome's beaches and near-by creeks would produce two million dollars in the first year alone — more than the Klondike had at the same point in its history.

The story was beginning again, like a continuous film show at a movie house. In Dawson, log cabins could be had for the taking as steamboat after steamboat, jammed from steerage to upper deck, puffed out of town en route to Nome. The saloon trade fell off; real estate dropped; dance halls lost their custom. Arizona Charlie Meadows announced that he would float his Palace Grand in one piece down the river to the new strike. Jacqueline, the dance-hall girl, complained that her week's percentage would hardly pay her laundry bill. In a single week in August eight thousand people left Dawson forever. The same week a few haggard and wild-eyed men with matted locks and shredded garments straggled in from the Rat River divide. These were the last of that eager contingent which had set off from Edmonton twenty-four months before to seek their fortune; there would be no more.

And so just three years, almost to the day, after Robert Henderson encountered George Carmack here on the swampland at the Klondike's mouth, the great stampede ended as quickly as it had begun.

Chapter Thirteen

1
Finale

2
The legacy of the gold rush

3
River of ghosts

1: *Finale*

I shall borrow from Epicurus: "The acquisition of riches has been for many men, not an end, but a change, of troubles." I do not wonder. For the fault is not in the wealth, but in the mind itself. That which had made poverty a burden to us, has made riches also a burden. Just as it matters little whether you lay a sick man on a wooden or on a golden bed, for whithersoever he be moved he will carry his malady with him; so one need not care whether the diseased mind is bestowed upon riches or upon poverty. His malady goes with the man.
— *Seneca ad Lucilium* Epistulæ Morales *XVII.*

The statistics regarding the Klondike stampede are diminishing ones. One hundred thousand persons, it is estimated, actually set out on the trail; some thirty or forty thousand reached Dawson. Only about one half of this number bothered to look for gold, and of these only four thousand found any. Of the four thousand, a few hundred found gold in quantities large enough to call themselves rich. And out of these fortunate men only the merest handful managed to keep their wealth.

The kings of Eldorado toppled from their thrones one by one. Antone Stander drank part of his fortune away; his wife deserted him and took the rest, including the Stander Hotel, which he had built in Seattle with profits from his claim. One cannot entirely blame her, for when Stander was drinking he was subject to crazy fits of jealousy; on one occasion he tried to cut her to pieces with a knife. Stander headed north again, seeking another Klondike, working his passage aboard ship by peeling potatoes in the galley, but got no farther than the Panhandle. He died in the Pioneers' Home at Sitka. His wife, who lived until 1944, left an estate worth fifty thousand dollars.

Win Oler died in the Pioneers' Home, too, plagued to the last by the knowledge that he had sold a million-dollar claim to the Lucky Swede for eight hundred. But Charley Anderson, the Lucky Swede, fared no better. His dance-hall-girl wife divorced him; the San Francisco earthquake laid waste to his wealth, since he had invested heavily in real estate. He remained, in spite of these setbacks, an incurable optimist, so convinced he would strike it rich again that he vowed never to shave off his little pointed beard until he recouped his fortunes. He was still wearing it in 1939 when he died, pushing a wheelbarrow in a sawmill near Sapperton, British Columbia, for three dollars and twenty-five cents a day. It had always annoyed him when people referred to him as a millionaire. "I never had a million dollars," the Lucky Swede used to say. "The most I ever had was nine hundred thousand."

Dick Lowe, the owner of the famous fraction on Bonanza, managed to get rid of more than half a million dollars. Part of it was stolen from his claim because he was too drunk to take notice of what was happening. Part of it was flung on the bars of saloons at Dawson and Grand Forks — as much as ten thousand at a time. He warned his friends against marrying a dance-hall girl, but in the end he married one himself. By the turn of the century Lowe was on the way down. He tried to recoup his fortunes in other gold rushes, without success. There is a pathetic picture of him pawning an eight-hundred-dollar monogrammed gold watch in Victoria, British Columbia. There is another of him peddling water by the bucket in Fairbanks, Alaska, in 1905. He died in San Francisco in 1907.

Others, with equally good prospects, met variations of the same fate. Sam Stanley of Eldorado married a dance-hall girl in Pete McDonald's saloon and died in poor circumstances. Nigger Jim Daugherty was broke

525

by 1902; he became a railroad worker and died poor in Fairbanks in 1924, divorced by Lottie Oatley who lived on in San Francisco until the early 1960s. Pat Galvin quit the Klondike in 1899, bankrupt — and died shortly afterward of cholera in the South Seas. Frank Phiscator killed himself in a San Francisco hotel. Oliver Millet, the discoverer of Cheechako Hill, died well-to-do, but his mind wandered in his later years. Nathan Kresge of Gold Hill sank all his funds in an abortive mine in Oregon and died while on relief in Seattle.

Even Tom Lippy, the God-fearing YMCA man who did not drink, whore, or gamble, ended his days bankrupt, though he took almost two million dollars from his Eldorado claim. After he sold out in 1903, Lippy and his wife made a trip around the world and built the proudest home in Seattle. The windows were of stained glass, the woodwork of intricately carved oak and mahogany. There were fifteen rooms, including an immense ballroom. Murals decorated the ceilings; a priceless collection of Oriental rugs covered the floor and hung from the walls like tapestries.

Some of Lippy's obscure relatives began to move to Seattle, and he took them all in and got them jobs. His philanthropies extended beyond this: he made extensive donations to the Methodist Church and the YMCA, gave twenty-five thousand dollars to the Anti-Saloon League, donated the land on which the Seattle General Hospital was built, and started the drive for Seattle's first swimming-pool.

Once, two Seattle reporters, on a stunt, dressed in old clothes, pretending to be down and out, and applied at the homes of the wealthy for a handout. They were turned away at every mansion but Lippy's. He gave them turkey sandwiches and coffee and sat down and ate with them.

526

He became a respected Seattle citizen. He was hospital president, YMCA president, Port Commissioner, and senior golf champion of the Pacific northwest, but he was no businessman. He sank almost half a million dollars in a mattress-and-upholstery company, a brick company, a trust-and-savings bank, and the Lippy Building. All went bankrupt, and Lippy was ruined. When he died in 1931, at the age of seventy-one, he had nothing to leave his wife. Fortunately for her, a chance clause inserted in the hospital land agreement by a cautious lawyer provided her with fifty dollars a month. She lived on this until she died in 1938. The Lippy home was eventually turned over to the followers of Father Divine.

Big Alex McDonald was ruined by the very thing that had made him wealthy — an obsession with property. For several years he continued, as a man of property, to be the leading light in Dawson, in spite of his awkwardness and lack of social presence. It was Big Alex the townspeople chose to preside at the farewell celebration when Sam Steele left the Yukon in 1899. As a special concession, the steamboat on which the policeman was leaving was brought up the river to the front of the barracks, and here Big Alex, who had been carefully rehearsed and drilled for several days, was supposed to make a graceful farewell speech and present Steele with a poke of gold. At the last moment the King of the Klondike lumbered forward sheepishly and thrust the poke into Steele's hand. The farewell speech went as follows:

"Here, Sam — here y'are. Poke for you. Good-by."

In spite of this lamentable performance, Big Alex was chosen again to make a presentation to Lady Minto, the wife of the Governor General of Canada, when the viceregal party visited Dawson in 1900. This time the gift was a golden bucket, filled to the brim with curi-

527

ously shaped nuggets, with a miniature golden windlass above it. Again Big Alex was carefully primed and rehearsed in a speech written especially for the occasion, but when the awful moment came, the King of the Klondike simply reached out his great ham hands towards Her Ladyship and said:

"Here. Tak' it. It's trash."

To McDonald, gold was always trash. He continued to use it to buy more land. When his claims on Bonanza and Eldorado were worked out he bought up new ones on more distant creeks. He had twenty claims on Henderson Creek alone, in the Stewart River country; none was worth a plugged nickel. In his last years he lived by himself in a little cabin on Clearwater Creek, still prospecting for gold, his fortunes long since diminished. One day a prospector happened upon his cabin and found McDonald's huge form lying prone in front of his chopping-block. He had died of a heart attack while splitting firewood. Because Belinda Mulroney had once persuaded him to take out a life-insurance policy, his widow was able to live on in some comfort.

It is pleasant, in the light of all this, to report that the two most industrious men on Bonanza and Eldorado enjoyed continued success and fortune for the rest of their lives. Louis Rhodes and Clarence Berry, who sank the first two shafts to bedrock in the Klondike while their fellows twiddled their thumbs, did not dissipate their riches, but, on the contrary, added to them.

Berry took a million and a half dollars from his claims on Eldorado. Then he and his brothers moved on to Fairbanks, where they struck it rich a second time on Esther Creek. They returned to California, secured oil property near Bakersfield, and made another enormous fortune. At various times they owned both the Los Angeles and the San Francisco baseball clubs.

528

Berry never forgot his original benefactor, Bill McPhee, the saloon-keeper. In 1906 McPhee's saloon at Fairbanks was destroyed by fire and the ageing barkeeper lost everything but the clothes he wore. Berry wired him from San Francisco to draw on him for all the money necessary to get back into business again. In his declining years McPhee lived on a pension from Berry, who died of appendicitis in San Francisco in 1930, worth several millions.

Louis Rhodes invested his Klondike fortune in mining property in Mexico and lost everything. Without a moment's hesitation he turned prospector again and headed for Alaska. With all the industry that he had shown in the early Bonanza days he began to explore the newly staked country near Fairbanks. He found gold-bearing quartz on a tiny outcropping of unstaked land and parlayed it into a mine which yielded him a profit of three hundred thousand dollars. He retired to California's Valley of the Moon and lived out the rest of his days in comfort.

As might be expected, the liveliest Klondike sequel is provided by Swiftwater Bill Gates. When Swiftwater reached Nome he repeated his Eldorado success in a mild way by taking a lay on a claim on Dexter Creek. He made four thousand dollars, but lost it just as quickly gambling. Broke again and back in civilization, still as irrepressible as he was irresponsible, Swiftwater left his young wife and ran off with a comely seventeen-year-old named Kitty Brandon. The affair was climaxed by the usual wild chase from city to city with an angry mother in hot pursuit, until finally in the town of Chehalis, Washington, Swiftwater collared a preacher and made an honest woman of the schoolgirl. The marriage was complicated by the facts that (a) Swiftwater was still married to Bera Beebe, and (b) Kitty Brandon was Swiftwater's stepniece.

529

He solved this problem by discrediting the unfortunate young woman a few months after the wedding, but he had scarcely made himself a free man again when, to his discomfiture, his first mother-in-law, the much abused Mrs. Beebe, banged on his hotel-room door with vengeance in her eye. It is a tribute to Swiftwater's way with women that he swiftly talked her into pawning her diamonds so that he could go north again to recoup his fortunes; and it is a tribute to his prospector's instincts that he did just that, on a lay on Number *Six*, Cleary Creek, Fairbanks.

Swiftwater took seventy-five thousand from this property, only to discover that he now faced the ire of two mothers-in-law — both of whom had followed him north. He gave Mrs. Brandon (who was also his sister) the slip; but Mrs. Beebe, who had had more practice by now, was not so easy to shake off. She pursued Swiftwater down the coast, and when the two reached Seattle she had him jailed for bigamy. In her memoirs Mrs. Beebe recounts that Swiftwater's answer to this was to call in lawyers, deputies, sheriff, judge, and reporters and present each of them with a twenty-dollar bill wrapped around a nugget. This eased matters considerably, especially as he had by now talked Mrs. Beebe into putting up bail. Somehow his marital difficulties were untangled, both girls were properly divorced, and Swiftwater announced he was ready for a new wife. At this point his story begins to get repetitious. There are more flights to Fairbanks; more enormous sums mined from Cleary Creek; more reconciliations; more betrayals. For thirty-odd years Swiftwater's name continued to turn up in the public prints here, there, and everywhere. None knew exactly where truth left off and myth began in his garbled but lively tale. He ended his days in Peru, where he was supposed to have wangled a twenty-million-acre silver-mining concession. He died there in 1935, and the *Alaska Weekly* dug up a photograph of him in his late years. It shows a wizened little man in a miner's hat, with sunken cheeks, an enormous white handle-bar moustache, and unrepentant glittering eyes — the perfect prototype of the traditional grizzled Hollywood prospector. But Hollywood has not filmed the story of Swiftwater Bill, perhaps because it is too farfetched to be credible.

The non-mining members of the Klondike élite met fates that differed only in detail from those who made their fortunes directly from the golden creeks. Harry Ash, who built one of Dawson's first saloons, went mad; his wife committed suicide. Tom Chisholm, who took seventy-five thousand dollars in profit from his Aurora saloon, ended his life as a caretaker in a small town in the Peace River country; he died in 1936 with scarcely a penny to his name. Sam Bonnifield, the gambler, moved to Fairbanks during the Tanana boom and opened the First National Bank, which shipped out three million dollars' worth of gold dust. In the depression that followed, the bank failed, and Bonnifield, who never worried about his own money but was vitally concerned with funds entrusted to him, suffered a nervous breakdown. One day passers-by saw him kneeling in the snow before his bank crying "O God! Please show me the way out." He was killed in Seattle in an automobile accident in 1943 at the age of seventy-seven. He had been living in a flophouse, and his body lay unclaimed for a week in the city morgue.

Bonnifield's partner Louis Golden lived the transitory life of a gambler after the stampede. One memorable winter's night in Nome he sat down at the faro table and played for seventy-two hours running until he had lost one hundred and eighty thousand dollars — everything he owned. He died at eighty-three in Reno, Nevada, still pursuing his uncertain profession. All the

531

Klondike gamblers seemed to attain a ripe old age. The one-legged Jack Marchbank was seventy-nine when he died in 1947. A one-time owner of the Tanforan race track, he left an estate of five million dollars to his secretary, whom he had married seven months before his death.

Gene Allen, the founder of the *Klondike Nugget*, was bankrupt before leaving Dawson City, the result of overextending his operations by launching an abortive express company. The *Nugget* itself folded in 1903. Allen remained a newspaperman for the rest of his life, working on small papers until his death in 1935. He helped found the Seattle Press Club. Stroller White, who worked on the Skagway *News*, Bennett *Sun*, *Klondike Nugget*, and Dawson *News*, continued as a northern journalist, later editing the Whitehorse *Star*. In 1920 he began publication of *Stroller's Weekly* in Juneau and continued it until his death in 1930. A mountain peak near the town bears his name. E. A. Hegg, the photographer, followed the golden trail to Nome and, after that boom subsided, visited and photographed other Alaskan communities until he drifted back to Bellingham to reopen his studio. He ran it until 1953. Two years later, aged eighty-eight, he died. His collection of photographs, now at the University of Washington, is the best-known pictorial record of the stampede.

John Healy of the N.A.T. Company died well-to-do, but Captain Hansen of the Alaska Commercial Company, his old rival during Dawson's starvation winter, took to drink and was fired in 1902. He never recovered from this blow; and one day a few years later, while working as a seaman on an Alaska-coast steamship, he jumped overboard. Of all the various trading firms that sprang up like mushrooms during the stampede, none survived. Only the A.C. Company, which had been in

532

Alaska from the beginning, stayed in business. It still operates under the name of Northern Commercial.

In the late twenties a murder trial in the United States briefly made headlines because of the curious name of one of the witnesses. He had been born aboard a Yukon River steamboat when the vessel stopped to take on wood, and was named Michael after his father, Edward after the reigning monarch, Seattle after the boat, Yukon after the river, and Woodpile after the circumstances. And thus Michael Edward Seattle Yukon Woodpile Bartlett testified at the trial of his father, the one-time packer Mike Bartlett, charged with murdering his wife, Mollie, whom he had met and wooed in the days when she was a pretty girl cooking meals at a station on the White Pass.

Other famous Klondikers turned up occasionally in the news, often enough in court cases. In 1905 Alexander Pantages, the theatre magnate who had got his start as a waiter in Dawson, found himself sued for breach of promise by Kate Rockwell, a one-time dancehall girl. When Pantages, a Greek immigrant, arrived in Dawson he could hardly speak the language, but before he left he was operating the Orpheum Theatre, the most successful in Dawson. In 1900 he became enamoured of Kitty Rockwell, a teen-aged dancer who wore a fifteen-hundred-dollar Parisian gown, a belt of twenty-dollar goldpieces, and a headdress of lighted candles, and who claimed to be the convent-educated daughter of a prominent jurist. In her court testimony Miss Rockwell swore that she bought seventy-five-cent cigars and fifteen-dollar silk shirts for Pantages, and that when they left Dawson together the following year she paid all the travelling expenses. She asked for twenty-five thousand dollars, but the theatre magnate settled out of court for less than five thousand. He went on to build his theatre chain into a fifteen-million-dollar asset, but he died a

533

broken man in 1936 after two lengthy bouts of litigation. He was found guilty of attempted rape, and, coincidentally, his wife was convicted of second-degree murder — the result of an auto accident. Both verdicts were ultimately reversed by higher courts, but the cases undoubtedly ruined Pantages. As for Kitty Rockwell, she took the name of "Klondike Kate," capitalized on her dance-hall career, and was a favourite of newspaper feature writers until her death in 1957.

One great figure of the Klondike lived on quietly in Seattle until the mid 1960s. Few of her neighbours knew the part played in the great stampede by a little grey-haired woman named Mrs. Charles Eugene Carbonneau. For this was Belinda Mulroney — the Queen of Grand Forks, the mistress of the famous Fairview, a figure in the novels of James Oliver Curwood, her dog immortalized by Jack London in *Call of the Wild*, hailed by *Scribner's* magazine as "the richest woman of the Klondike."

In spite of her prim ways and her plain Irish features, Belinda was undoubtedly the best catch in the Klondike for an enterprising bachelor. Such a man duly arrived on the scene. He sported a monocle, kid gloves, spats, a small, jet-black moustache, and a tall, bearded valet. From an elegant leather case he produced an engraved card:

M. Le Comte Carbonneau
Représentant
Messieurs Pierre Legasse, Frères et Cie
Bordeaux Paris New York

He was a champagne salesman, and he became enamoured of Belinda. Every day a bunch of red roses arrived at the Fairview from the Count, who was staying at the Regina. Belinda succumbed. In October of 1900 the coal-miner's daughter from Scranton became

534

a Countess. It did not matter to her that Tom Lippy's French-Canadian foreman, Joe Putraw, had positively identified her husband as a barber from Montreal's Rue St. Denis — and no count at all. Off the couple went to Paris, where they rode up and down the Champs-Elysées behind a handsome pair of snow-white horses, with gold-ornamented harness and an Egyptian footman, who unrolled a velvet carpet of brilliant crimson whenever they stepped out.

Belinda continued to prosper in the Yukon. She became, indeed, the only woman mining-manager in the territory — and of the largest mining company. The Gold Run Mining Company had got into financial difficulties largely because the owners were running a gaming-table and their employees were stealing gold from the property in order to gamble at it. The local bank-manager put Belinda in charge, and she pulled the company out of the hole in eighteen months. Her first move was to throw out the roulette wheel and replace it with a bridge table. Her second was to drive the female camp-followers from the property. As a foreman (or, more correctly, a forewoman) she was a holy terror. One old sourdough, C. W. Hamilton, retained vivid memories of working for her. The morally severe Belinda would allow no smoking on the job. Hamilton tried to break this edict, but before he had a match lit Belinda gave a low whistle, crooked her finger, and said sharply: "Get off this claim before nightfall." Hamilton obeyed.

Belinda and her husband went on to Fairbanks during the Tanana mining boom and left the north finally in 1910 to buy a ranch near Yakima, Washington, and, in the style of so many Klondikers, to build themselves a stone castle on the property. They commuted each winter to Europe, where Carbonneau became a bank director and a steamship magnate. They sank all their

535

money in the steamship company and were wiped out when World War I brought an end to merchant shipping. Carbonneau became a purchasing agent for the Allies and was killed by a German shell during an inspection tour of the Front. Belinda returned to her ranch at Yakima, which she later sold. She lived with her memories in Washington State until her death.

Most of the Mounted Police officers who served in the Klondike went on to promotion and glory. Two of them — Perry and Starnes — achieved the Force's highest rank, that of commissioner. A third, Zachary Taylor Wood, became an assistant commissioner, and his son, following in his footsteps, rose to commissioner. Sam Steele was chosen to recruit a cavalry battalion — the Lord Strathcona Horse — which fought with distinction in the South African war. Two of his old Klondike colleagues, Belcher and Jarvis, who had commanded the summits of the White and Chilkoot passes, fought with him. Steele went on during World War I to a knighthood and a generalship. He died in 1919.

Constantine suffered a different fate. This steadfast officer, the first Mounted Policeman to enter the Yukon Valley, was placed in charge of the Athabasca district after leaving the Klondike, and here he was handed a monumental task. The federal government, in 1905, decided to build a road along Moodie's old trail, seven hundred and fifty miles from the Peace River to Teslin Lake. A force of police, under Constantine, set about the job, bridging bogs and rivers, hacking through forests, and constructing rest stations every thirty miles. After three years and three hundred and fifty miles the government abandoned the project. By then the health of many of the men was wrecked; Constantine was among them. He died in San Francisco in 1912 as a result of his northern privations.

And what of the original discoverers of the Klondike — Carmack, Henderson, and the Indians?

Carmack abandoned his Indian wife, Kate, in 1900. She had been living rather unhappily in the civilized world, going to jail occasionally in the company of one of her Indian relatives after a drunken fight. She was staying with Carmack's sister when he wrote and gave instructions that she be sent back north. She returned to her home at Caribou Crossing on Lake Tagish and lived there on a government pension, wearing the cheap cotton clothing affected by northern Indian women, but always with a necklace of nuggets taken from the famous claim on Bonanza Creek that had started the gold rush. She died about 1917.

Carmack married again almost immediately. His wife was a pretty, dark woman named Marguerite Laimee, who had been on the fringe of three gold rushes — in South Africa, in Australia, and in the Yukon. She was pretty obviously a camp-follower, and in Dawson she ran what was known as a "cigar store," a phrase that was often a euphemism for bawdy house. Whether she dispensed cigars or something more exotic is not known, but business was so good that each morning, on panning the sawdust on the floor, she was able to realize about thirty dollars in gold dust.

She and Carmack lived happily until his death in Vancouver in 1922. He invested in Seattle real estate, built an apartment house and hotel which brought him an income of five hundred dollars a month, and operated a mine in California. He died a respected member of the Masonic Order and left a healthy estate. His wife, who died in California in 1949, inherited his money.

Tagish Charley sold his mining properties in 1901 and spent the rest of his years at Carcross, where he operated a hotel, entertained lavishly, and bought diamond earrings for his daughter. He was treated as a white man and so was allowed to drink heavily. One summer's day, during a drunken spree, he fell off a bridge and was drowned.

Skookum Jim was treated as a white man, too — but this was not enough. He wished to *be* a white man, and so, although his mining property was paying him royalties of ninety thousand dollars a year, he proceeded to live the hard life of a prospector, travelling ceaselessly across the North vainly seeking a quartz lode, often going for days without food, so fierce was his quest. In the end his magnificent physique was weakened. He died, worn out, in 1916.

Robert Henderson outlived them all. The Canadian government belatedly recognized him as co-discoverer of the Klondike and awarded him a stipend of two hundred dollars a month. For the rest of his life Henderson continued to look for gold. He sought it on Vancouver Island, on the Pelly River, and in northern British Columbia. In 1932 he joined two mining promoters in a pitchblende and placer discovery in the Upper Pelly country. A party was organized to fly into the area on a prospecting trip, but when the time came Henderson was not with them. He died of cancer in January 1933, still talking of the big strike he yet hoped to make.

But Henderson's descendants still live in Dawson City. His son Grant, a huge bear of a man, died shortly after World War II, frustrated in his life's ambition to find the mother lode from which he believed the gold of the Klondike came. Year after year Grant Henderson vainly drilled into the bowels of the great dome from which his father had first spied the radiating pattern of the tributary creeks. But no one has ever found the mother lode of the Klondike; there is little doubt that the veins were ground away long ago by glaciation and erosion.

538

Grant Henderson took various jobs in Dawson. The Yukon Consolidated Gold Corporation, which in the end came to control the lion's share of the creekbeds for dredging purposes, hired him occasionally. The company's president was a tiny white-haired Englishman named G. Goldthorpe Hay, who periodically visited his Yukon holdings, looking strangely out of place in his wing collar, director's suit, and gum boots. When the mud of the creeks got too deep, Grant Henderson was hired to carry the president about on his shoulders. It makes a curious tableau: the great bear-like prospector lumbering through the mosses of the creeks which his father had first happened upon, and the diminutive financier clinging to his broad back; but it is doubtful if the symbolism of the scene impressed itself on Henderson. He was an uncomplicated man, like his father before him, interested only in pursuing that kind of quest which has no ending.

2: *The legacy of the gold rush*

"I had thirty-five cents in my pocket when I set foot in Alaska, but I gave that to a mission church at Dutch Harbor. I did not have so much when I left the country more than two years later. . . . I made exactly nothing, but if I could turn time back I would do it over again for less than that."

So wrote Walter Russell Curtin thirty years after the gold rush, which he had witnessed as a youth aboard Pat Galvin's ill-fated steamboat the *Yukoner*. Curtin was frozen in for eight months on the river, a prisoner of winter on an icebound vessel. It grew so cold that mattresses had to be uncrated from the cargo to insulate the cabin walls. Curtin saw one man in a neighbouring camp go mad from the continual darkness and another die of scurvy. The tension drove the captain to such eccentricities that the crew mutinied and overthrew him. But when he recalled these scenes in his fading years, Curtin realized that the experience was the high point of his life.

Thousands like him looked back on the Klondike adventure for the rest of their days with insistent pangs of nostalgia. In all the written memoirs of the gold rush there is scarcely one note of regret, except the general regret that it ended so soon. Though few of the writers found any gold, it turned out in retrospect to have been a golden period for them. And the times that were remembered with zest and affection were not the easy times in the dance halls, but the hardest times: the chilling days on the passes, the thrilling moments in the rapids.

In this sense, as in so many others, the stampede resembled a great war. It was impossible to emerge from it unchanged, and those who survived it were never quite the same again. It brutalized some and ennobled others, but the majority neither sank to the depths nor rose to the heights; instead, their characters were tempered in the hot flame of an experience which was as much emotional as it was physical.

As is so often the case in war, they gave all the proper and conventional reasons for going, and set out for quite different ones. Because it was an age when a man must offer a practical motive for a foolhardy enterprise, they talked glibly of digging for gold and getting rich quick. To aspire to great fortune in the nineties was as respectable and as honourable an emotion as is patriotism in wartime; it excused and made sensible the wildest kind of goose-chase, and tens of thousands were ready for a fool's errand in the drab, adventureless days that followed the panic of '93. Like soldiers marching to the insistent beating of a drum, they set off with pounding hearts, mouthing pat slogans and often enough believing them, until months later when the

540

adventure was at an end they came to solve the personal riddle of why they had gone to the Klondike.

One forgets sometimes, on seeing the bearded faces in the old photographs, or on listening to the bent old sourdough recall the good old days, that the great majority of those who took part in the stampede were young men in their mid-twenties. It is this youth that helps explain the impetuosity of the gold rush. The argonauts were still young enough to want to search for something even though they did not exactly know what it was they were searching for. They were still young enough to be gullible, young enough to be foolhardy, young enough to be optimistic, young enough to be carefree. They were young enough to see a mountain and climb it, though they had never climbed a mountain before; to see a glacier and cross it without a second thought; to build a boat and attempt a rapid, though they had never wielded axe or paddle in their lives. The Klondike was their Everest; they sought to reach it because it was there.

Long before they attained their goal the subtle realization must have dawned upon them that there was no pot of gold at the end of their personal rainbow. The adverb "when" that distinguishes the early diary entries becomes an uncertain "if" as the journey progresses. "When I'm rich" is displaced by "if I should be lucky enough to strike gold"; then, as the journey grows harder, there is no further mention of gold at all.

Nevertheless, thousands continued to push northward, sometimes to their own apparent loss. Francis George Berton, of Saint John, New Brunswick, was one of these, a bearded young civil engineer fresh out of college. He had, on graduation, applied for a teaching job at Queen's University at Kingston, Ontario, a position he had long coveted; but before any reply came he was off to the Klondike with a train-load of his fellow

541

townsmen. He tried to drag his sled up the slushy surface of the Stikine River, but by the time he reached Glenora the whole land was a heaving swamp and he realized that attempting further passage by this route would be pointless. He turned back to the coast, then headed north to Dyea. At the foot of the Chilkoot Pass a letter caught up with him: the sinecure was his; he had only to return to civilization and a comfortable lifetime awaited him. He looked up at the pass, sheathed in its cold mantle of freezing cloud, with the ever-present human garland draped across it. Then he shouldered his pack and continued on, knowing that he was changing the current of his life. He was one of the breed recalled by Bert Parker in his memoirs of the White Pass trail "who finish anything they start, or die in the attempt." Parker himself was such a one. Fifty years after the rush, in which he took part as a teen-age boy, he was told that he was dying of cancer. Suddenly it occurred to him that he should write for his grandchildren the story of those golden days. And so, propped up at a typewriter, clinging to life as he had once clung to the mountain trails, refusing to quit until the goal was reached, he pecked out his memories. When the manuscript was finished, he died at peace.

To thousands of others the Klondike also became a sort of symbol. They strove to reach it as a matter of personal honour, and, like soldiers who fear to flinch more than they fear to fight, they stubbornly refused to retreat before the natural forces that threatened their passage. There is much about the Klondike story that is sordid and shameful and much more that is ludicrous. And yet there gleams through the whole tale this unifying thread of steadfastness.

This is the common characteristic that joins the thousands who poured up the coast and over the mountains like flocks of sheep; even more, it is the dis-

542

tinguishing mark of the shepherds who convoyed them. It can be seen in Tom Powers, the ebullient captain of the *Eliza Anderson,* roaring that he will sail his creaky vessel to St. Michael come hell or high water, and in Dixon, the bellicose master of the *Bella,* forcing his little steamboat through the grinding ice masses of the Yukon. It can be seen in the giant figure of Steele, bestriding the passes like a colossus, and in his colleague Moodie, hacking his way northward through the frozen jungles of the Peace River. It can be seen in Ogilvie, the incorruptible servant of the people, and in Judge, the inexhaustible servant of God, and in a dozen others of the calibre of Ray, Abercrombie, and Constantine. One other characteristic unites these men: not one of them showed any personal interest in digging for gold; in each case, duty was the main tenet of their personal creed. They are the great heroic figures of the gold rush.

Others, equally heroic, are all but forgotten. In the annals of the stampede there are two instances of men who followed no beaten pathway to the Klondike but hiked over country which no man, native or white, had traversed before and which no man traversed again.

One of these was Frank Neill, who was shipwrecked at Juneau with the eleven other technical school boys whose fathers had sent them around Cape Horn on a private schooner chartered from a smooth-talking Philadelphia promoter. All the others fled back to civilization, but Neill himself was determined to press on north. He bought himself a map of the Alaska coast and picked out the new gold-camp of Atlin, British Columbia, as his immediate goal. It did not occur to him to travel in any direction other than a straight line and it did not seem to matter that the straight line would take him directly across the dreaded Taku Glacier and then over the unexplored Llewellyn Glacier, one of the

543

largest ice-fields south of the Arctic. Miraculously, he arrived at his destination, went to work cutting logs, and then continued on to the Klondike to establish a profitable sawmill business.

The other expedition was even more astonishing. In the fall of 1897, Fred Fysh of London, Ontario, and his brother-in-law, Charles Williams, found themselves working a small creek flowing into the sea well to the north of the Seward Peninsula. They had travelled north from San Francisco on a small schooner to St. Michael. Then, hearing of a minor strike farther around the coast of Alaska, they had continued on north of the Arctic Circle. Their real destination, however, remained the Klondike. When freeze-up came, they realized that they had two choices only: to return at once to St. Michael by an overland route or to strike southeast to the Canadian Yukon. They unhesitatingly opted for the second plan and so, while thousands of others along the rich man's route holed up in cabins, waiting out the winter, Fysh and Williams pulled a hand-made toboggan across half of Alaska, crossing wind-swept tundra, snow-choked valleys, and ridge after ridge of unknown mountains until they reached Fort Yukon and the comparatively easy highway of the river. No man had ever come that way before, nor is there a record of any other stampeder who followed in their footsteps.

The days of '98 underline Elizabeth Barrett Browning's words, that "all actual heroes are essential men, and all men possible heroes"; for, in one sense, every man who reached the Klondike was a sort of hero — or would be considered so today. If, in 1972, anyone wishes to earn the plaudits of the popular press or to see his name enshrined as the central figure of a magazine article, he has only to repeat the achievements of the argonauts of sixty years ago: to haul a ton of goods on his back up the Dyea Trail and over the Chilkoot Pass in the dead of winter, to construct a serviceable boat of green lumber whipsawed by hand on the shores of Lake Bennett, to tempt the swift river and its rapids for more than five hundred miles, and, on arrival at the Klondike's mouth, to build a log cabin capable of withstanding temperatures of sixty below zero. It is doubtful if a single person has repeated this full exploit since the turn of the century, but seventy-five winters ago twenty thousand greenhorns did just that.*

They returned from the Klondike, as young men return from war, wise beyond their years. In the brief span of the gold rush they learned more about life, more about their fellows, and more about themselves than many mortals absorb in threescore years and ten. There was scarcely one of them who at some moment on the bitter road north had not descended into hell and risen again. They learned the hard way the same lesson that the early prospectors at Fortymile and Circle City had learned before them, until at last the slogan of the Yukon Order of Pioneers, "Do unto others as you

---

* In August 1971, at Lake Lindemann, I came upon a man who was trying to do just that. I suppose you could call him a hippy. He had lived for a time in the Haight-Ashbury district of San Francisco but had tired of that life. After reading *Klondike*, he decided that he would attempt to duplicate exactly the feats of '98. He went north to Juneau and work in the mines, accumulating enough cash for a grubstake. Then, wearing home-made clothing of homespun, he carried something like a thousand pounds of equipment over the Chilkoot Pass. When I encountered him he was building a boat, preparatory to heading down the river. He had never built a boat before, but there he was, whipsawing timbers and carving semicircular ribs out of the centres of large trees. He sent me a postcard in the fall, reporting that he had got safely through the rapids and had reached Whitehorse. He intended to winter at Dawson, then float all the way to Norton Sound.

would be done by," came to have a real meaning for each of them.

In some ways the great trek represents one of the weirdest and most useless mass movements in history. Something like fifty thousand men wasted something like one thousand dollars each on a fruitless errand. By 1901 the combined gold-fields of the Yukon Territory had scarcely produced that much money.

But the stampede also brought its benefits. It was the making of Alaska and, to a lesser degree, of the Canadian northwest. The great strikes that followed, at Nome and Fairbanks, at Keno Hill and Atlin, were spawned by the Klondike discovery. The North was flung wide open by the stampeders. Men clawing their way across the Valdez Glacier found copper and stayed to mine it. Men trudging through the wilderness of the Peace found land and stayed to farm it. The Klondikers were the first to see gold on Yellowknife Bay, cobalt bloom on the cliffs of Great Bear Lake, and lead-zinc ore at Pine Point — all sites of future mining development.

Half a dozen cities owe their growth to the gold rush. Tacoma, Portland, Victoria, and San Francisco all felt its impact. Vancouver's population almost doubled during the stampede period. Edmonton sprang from a hamlet of twelve hundred to a flourishing town of four thousand. The greatest effect was felt in Seattle; in 1899 alone, twelve hundred new houses mushroomed up in the city, and the merchants, who before the rush had sold goods worth an annual three hundred thousand, now found that their direct interest in outfitting amounted to ten million.

There were some subtler side-effects. In the United States the output of Klondike and later of Alaska gold from Nome produced the same results that Bryan had hoped for in his advocacy of free silver. It meant the end of the depression as much as it meant the eclipse of the Bryanites. North of the border, the transcontinental rail traffic that the Klondike inspired became an important factor in the great western Canadian boom that ran unfettered for more than a decade.

The real legacy of the stampede is less tangible, however, for it has to do with the shaping of human character. Sprinkled across the continent were thousands of men stamped indelibly with the Klondike experience. One such was Norman Lee, the thirty-six-year-old Chilcoten rancher who tried to drive two hundred head of cattle north to the Klondike along the Ashcroft Trail. Fighting mud, poisonous weed, and starvation, Lee and his wranglers somehow managed to get most of their beef to Teslin Lake. By then the animals were not much more than skin and bone, but Lee determined to push forward. He built two scows, butchered his meat, and sailed off down the long corridor of the lake, with a fresh breeze carrying him north. Three days later a storm came up, both scows were wrecked, the beef was lost, and Lee, who had operated a prosperous ranching business in British Columbia, was destitute. He sold everything he had, including his only overcoat, to raise enough money to buy provisions for the long journey back. And off he went, dragging his sleigh behind him — retracing the same dismal route through the ghost-towns of Glenora and Telegraph Creek and then down the slushy Stikine to Wrangell. By the time he reached Vancouver, after three months of hard travel, all he had left in the world was a dog, a blanket roll, and a dollar; but he did not seem particularly concerned with his plight. After the Klondike experience, there was very little that would faze Norman Lee. He started afresh again in the Chilcoten, and when he died at the age of seventy-nine — a prosperous rancher and merchant — he had become a legend in his own time.

It is not surprising that an extraordinary number of public figures in the last half-century have had a Klondike background. The Mayor of San Francisco during the earthquake was a Klondiker, and so, for seven terms, was the senior senator from Nevada. During the 1930s a Speaker of the Canadian House of Commons was a veteran of '98; so was the Premier of British Columbia. During the Great War, Joe Boyle, the sparring-partner of Frank Slavin, enriched by mining concessions, personally recruited and equipped a machine-gun battalion of Klondike pioneers. They became the most heavily decorated group of combatants in the Canadian Army; more than sixty per cent received medals for bravery.

The Klondike experience had taught all these men that they were capable of a kind of achievement they had never dreamed possible. It was this, perhaps more than anything else, that set them apart from their fellows. In the years that followed, they tended to run their lives as if they were scaling a perpetual Chilkoot, secure in the knowledge that any obstacle, real or imagined, can be conquered by a determined man. For each had come to realize that the great stampede, with all its searchings and its yearnings, with all its bitter surprises, its thorny impediments, and its unexpected fulfilments, was, in a way, a rough approximation to life itself.

3: *River of ghosts*

In Dawson City the weeds grow rankly along the rotting wooden sidewalks. The willows and the aspens, the currant bushes and the bearberries have encroached upon the town, blurring its edges and hiding the rusting

548

mining machinery that lies in heaps in some of the vacant lots. From the hills above, the checkerboard pattern of streets and avenues, laid out so neatly in the days of Ladue, can still be discerned; but there are great ragged gaps in the town now where buildings have been burned down, or been torn down, or simply fallen down.

There are about five hundred people living here today.

Lousetown has vanished and so has West Dawson, on the far side of the river; no vestige of them remains.

A few false-fronted buildings, empty now, still stand on Front Street. One or two of them go back as far as 1900. It is doubtful if a single one remains from the climactic days of 1898. There have been too many fires.

Around the corner, on King, only a few steps from the spot where the Oatley Sisters danced and Nigger Jim Daugherty ran the Pavilion, there stood until 1962 a reeling cadaver of a building whose former splendour could be seen dimly in the ornately carved pillars, the intricate cornices, and the rococo lines of its entranceway. It was propped up on one side by beams because the permafrost on which it rested had caused it to lean drunkenly to the east. A sign identified it as "The Nugget Dance Hall," but this was a modern title designed to attract the tourists who drove into Dawson from a spur of the Alaska Highway. This old and broken structure was really Arizona Charlie's famous Palace Grand, the only noteworthy landmark that had survived from the stampede days. In 1962, it was restored to its former splendour and it is today a major tourist attraction.

A road of pure white channel gravel winds out along the Klondike Valley towards Bonanza. But the Klondike and its tributary valleys would be unrecognizable to the men of '98; they are choked with mountains of

549

gravel tailings, churned up by the great dredges that for half a century have mined the creekbeds. These tailings run like miniature alps for miles; and the water, changed in its course by the dredging, finds its way between them in a thin trickle. The hills, still bare of trees, are marked by the hesitant lines of old ditches and broken flumes and the scars left by hydraulic nozzles.

Some of this ground has been worked three times — first by individual miners, next by early dredges, and later by more modern dredges. But there are no dredges left in the Klondike Valley. From Carmack's day until the end of the mining period it yielded more than three hundred million dollars in dust and nuggets. Now, only the tailing piles, blurred by willow and alder, remain.

Here and there, where no dredge has dug, the remnants of the great stampede can still be found: rusting picks and shovels lying among the alders; the crumbling boards of ancient sluiceboxes; old wheelbarrows; cabins with their roofs fallen in from the weight of winter snows; an occasional store of photographs, old newspapers, or letters from a bygone age; and sometimes an old man working slowly away at his claim, after the fashion of the early prospectors.

The Yukon River is no longer the great artery of the north. The planes that zoom off the tarmac at the great airports of Whitehorse, Fairbanks, and Anchorage; the cars, buses, and transport trucks that roar up the Alaska Highway and its tributary roads, have made the steamboat obsolete. In all the two thousand two hundred miles of the great river, from Whitehorse to Norton Sound, every foot of it navigable, there is not a single stern-wheeler today.

The bones and machinery of the floating palaces lie scattered along the length of the river. Captain Goddard's little boat can still be seen on a clear day beneath the waters of Lake Laberge. The little *May West* was

550

sunk in the same body of water. The famous *Yukoner* and the *Bonanza King* were used as warehouses for lumber storage at Whitehorse for decades. The *Weare* and the *Bella,* the *Healy* and the *Hamilton,* the *Susie* and the *Hannah,* and many of the other vessels operated by the N.A.T. and A.C. companies are rotting at St. Michael.

Skagway has become a quiet port of a few hundred people, living on its memories. Oddly, the town's greatest asset, from the point of view of the tourist trade, is the unseen presence of Soapy Smith. Trains rumble through the White Pass as William Moore once prophesied they would, and alongside the right of way an observant traveller can see a worn pathway which is the trail of '98. For half a century the Chilkoot remained as silent as it was in the days of George Holt, its first explorer. The towns it fed: the Scales, Sheep Camp, and Dyea, vanished. Then, in the early 1970s, with the trail freshly marked on both sides of the border and campgrounds established for hikers, a thin trickle of men and women once more began to cross the famous pass on a voyage of re-discovery.

Many of the old river towns along the Yukon — Selkirk, Stewart City, Big Salmon, Fortymile, Circle, and Rampart — have also disappeared from sight. A few moss-roofed cabins surrounded by a jungle undergrowth are all that is left of them; one or two are gone without a trace. And so a man in a poling-boat can drift downstream for mile after mile without seeing any sign of humankind, as in the distant days of Harper, McQuesten, Mayo, and Ladue. And were a visitor from those times dropped into the Yukon Valley today, he would find the great river unchanged by the passage of those delirious years, pursuing as always its quest for the ocean, moving like the stream of life out of its mountain cradle to its final rest in the Bering Sea —

551

hesitantly at first and then more strongly, faltering for a moment at the Circle's rim, then plunging confidently onward, surmounting obstacle and hindrance until its goal is reached.

Once again the land is silent, save for the sound of gurgling water. Down from the mountains the little streams tumble, plucking at the eroding rock and shale. Down through the forests the tributary creeks run, patiently fashioning the landscape. Down to the main river the water pours, bringing its tribute of rock and sand, gravel and silt. Men come and go, but the inevitable cycle of erosion continues as before, sand scouring sand, gravel grinding against gravel, boulder grating on boulder. High on the furrowed table land, deep in the clefts of the valleys, and on the headwaters of a thousand tentacle streams the inexorable process goes on. And perhaps somewhere in some untravelled corner of this wilderness, in an undiscovered nook or cranny, there is still gold.

Chronology

1896

Aug. 17   George Carmack and Indian relatives stake discovery claims on Rabbit (Bonanza) Creek.

Aug. 31   Antone Stander and party stake first claims on Eldorado.

Sept. 5   First steamboat, *Alice*, lands at Dawson.

Sept. 7   Robert Henderson gets first news of Carmack's strike.

Oct. 3   Louis Rhodes becomes first man to reach bed-rock on *Twenty-One Above* Bonanza.

1897

Jan. 21   William Ogilvie sends out news of Klondike's riches to Ottawa.

Mar. 19   Cariboo Billy Dietering records first bench claim on French Hill.

May 14   Ice goes out in Yukon River at Dawson.

June 5   Dog-driver Jack Carr leaves for Juneau with news of Klondike strike.

June 7   *Alice* and *Portus B. Weare* leave Dawson
(approx.)   with first Klondike gold.

June 12   Inspector W.H. Scarth and detachment of nineteen Mounted Police reach Fort Constantine.

July 14   *Excelsior* arrives at San Francisco. Stampede begins.

553

July 15	*Portland* arrives at Seattle with "a ton of gold."
July 19	*Al-ki* becomes first ship to leave for Alaska with stampeders aboard.
July 26	*Queen* becomes first ship to reach Skagway Bay.
Aug. 6	First detachment of Mounted Police reaches Skagway Bay.
Aug. 7	Miners' meeting takes over Moore townsite, names it Skagway.
Aug. 16	*Humboldt* party under ex-mayor Wood of Seattle leaves San Francisco for St. Michael.
Aug. 29	*Humboldt* reaches St. Michael.
Sept. 4	Inspector J. D. Moodie leaves Edmonton to explore a route to the Klondike.
Sept. 9	North West Territories government dispatches T. W. Chalmers to cut a trail to the Peace River via the Swan Hills.
Sept. 11	Ten per cent royalty established on all gold mined in the Yukon.
	Flood at Chilkoot Pass causes three deaths.
Sept. 20	Armed party holds up *Portus B. Weare* at Circle City.
Sept. 25	*Bella* held up.
	Hansen of A.C. Company arrives back in Dawson with news that no more supplies can get through.
Sept. 27	Exodus from Dawson begins.
Oct. 8	Major J. M. Walsh, Commissioner of the Yukon, arrives at Skagway.
Oct. 13	Yukon River freezes over, trapping boats.
Oct. 29	Captain P. H. Ray ambushed during miners' meeting at Fort Yukon.

554

Nov. 8	Work begins on Brackett wagon road over White Pass.
Nov. 19	N.A.T. store at Fort Yukon raided for food.
December	U.S. Congress appropriates $200,000 for Yukon relief.
	Archie Burns opens first ropeway over Chilkoot.

1898

Jan. 7	Inspector Robert Belcher and detachment of Mounted Police reach Skagway.
Jan. 31	Double killing of Andy McGrath of Deputy Marshal Rowan in Skagway.
Feb. 3	Governor Brady of Alaska petitions Washington to send troops to maintain order.
Feb. 25	First troops arrive at Skagway.
	Inspector Belcher begins to collect customs at Chilkoot summit.
Mar. 8	Vigilante "Committee of 101" formed at Skagway.
Mar. 15	Second detachment of troops arrives at Dyea.
	Infantrymen briefly close Skagway gaming-rooms.
April 3	Avalanche above Sheep Camp kills more than sixty stampeders.
April 22	Ice goes out in Athabasca River. Flotilla of stampeders sets off down Mackenzie water route towards Arctic.
April 24	Spanish-American War begins.
May 1	Soapy Smith's Skagway Military Company stages mammoth parade.

May 6	Judge C. A. Sehlbrede replaces John U. Smith as United States commissioner at Skagway.
May 8	Ice goes out in Yukon River at Dawson.
May 17	W. P. Taylor starts to blaze trail from Peace River Crossing to the Pelly.
May 27	First newspaper, the *Klondike Nugget*, begins publication at Dawson.
May 29	Ice goes out in Upper Yukon lakes. Flotilla of seven thousand boats sets off for the Klondike.
June 8	Vanguard of Lake Bennett flotilla reaches Dawson.
June 24	Sam Steele replaces Constantine as officer in charge of Dawson City detachment, NWMP.
July 4	Soapy Smith leads Independence Day parade at Skagway.
July 8	Soapy Smith shot to death by Frank Reid at Juneau dock, Skagway.
July 9	The stampede to Dominion Creek.
July 20	Frank Reid dies of wounds.
Sept. 22	Discovery claim staked at Anvil Creek (Nome), Alaska.
Oct. 24	Inspector Moodie finally reaches Fort Selkirk.

1899

Jan. 10	The Nigger Jim stampede.
Jan. 16	Father Judge dies at St. Mary's Hospital, Dawson.
Jan. 27	Remnants of relief expedition finally reach Dawson.
Feb. 16	First through train reaches White Pass summit.

556

Mar. 13	A. D. Stewart, ex-mayor of Hamilton, dies of scurvy on Peel River.
April 26	Fire destroys most of Dawson's business district.
July 6	White Pass railway completed to Lake Bennett.
July 27 (approx.)	Gold found on beach at Nome, Alaska.
July 29	Railway completed to Whitehorse.
August	Eight thousand leave Dawson for Nome.

A Note on the Revised Edition

When *Klondike* was completed in 1957, it did not immediately occur to me that the story of the gold rush was part of a larger saga. I intended to follow this book with another about the building of the CPR, for it seemed to me that the two stories had certain things in common: they were both sweeping tales of adventure involving the movements of large numbers of people through time and space. It was only after I had done considerable research into the railway odyssey that I began to glimpse the full dimensions of the over-all epic of the opening up of the North West. Between Confederation and World War I, an empty subcontinent, stretching from the Great Lakes to the Alaska border, was transformed into a populous domain, carved into sophisticated political units, intersected by road, rail, and wire, surveyed, mapped, settled, fenced, cultivated, and mined. Thus was created the Canada we know today—a transcontinental nation that was only dimly glimpsed by a handful of the men who sat down together in Charlottetown in 1864.

Klondike, then, forms a chapter in that story. The decision to reset the type and make the book uniform with those that cover the earlier chapters has allowed me to revise and expand the original edition. More than ten thousand words have been added to the main body of the text, based on material not available when the book was published in 1958. These occur in the form of inserts and revisions, more than fifty of them scattered throughout the text and ranging from a single sentence or paragraph to more than a dozen pages.

The new edition contains, for example, expanded sections on the early days of Dyea and Skagway and much new material on the Ashcroft Trail; there is more on the character and reign of Soapy Smith and his gang; I have also been able to flesh out my brief references to E. A. Hegg, the leading photographer of the stampede, and have introduced one or two new figures, such as Norman Lee, the Chilcoten rancher, whose diary was made public after *Klondike* was published, and Stroller White, the itinerant newspaperman, whose newspaper memoirs were recently anthologized. Here and there throughout the book, I have been able to add anecdotes which seem to me to further illuminate the period. There has also been one major revision: the two sections on the Edmonton trails have been completely overhauled and expanded, thanks in large part to the meticulous researches of J. G. MacGregor, whose book, *The Klondike Rush through Edmonton*, published in 1970, corrected or revised many conclusions (my own among them) that had previously been held concerning the back-door route to the Klondike.

The three maps in the original edition have been replaced by more detailed charts, prepared by Henry Mindak and placed at appropriate points in the text for quick reference. As in *The Great Railway* volumes, I have also thought it useful to include a cast of characters, a chronology, and, where possible, source notes. The point of view, of course, has not changed. *Klondike* remains the story of a quest. It is an allegory as well as a history and should be read as such.

The international character of the last great gold rush has made *Klondike* a popular work outside of Canada. The book has not only been published in England and the United States but it has also been translated into such unexpected tongues as Hungarian, Czech, Slovene, and German. Its influence, I am happy to report, has been considerable; indeed, of all my books this is the only one that seems to me to have had any influence at all. (*The Comfortable Pew*, by contrast, has caused scarcely a chip in the façade of the institution it criticized.)

It is now clear that the publication of *Klondike* touched off a process that helped to open the eyes of Canadians, and Americans as well, to the presence in the North of a vanishing historical resource. *Klondike* was the first book which attempted to tell the story of the stampede as a coherent whole and with a wealth of detail. It is difficult now to recall the indifference with which the Trail of '98 was viewed before its publication. Scarcely a soul, for instance, had been over the Chilkoot Pass for half a century. The tourist traffic to Dawson City, which had reached a peak in the twenties after Robert Service's literary success, was declining so badly that an attempt by Canadian Pacific Airlines to restore a riverboat to active service met with financial failure. While I was working on the research in the fifties, I can recall more than one colleague (and more than one Klondiker) saying to me: "Why would you want to write a book about the Klondike? Who will buy it?"

But in the first three months after its publication ten thousand Canadians bought it—a sale that astonished both author and publisher, since it was unprecedented at the time. One of those who bought the book was Tom Patterson, who had sparked the Stratford Shakespearean Festival. After reading *Klondike*, Patterson decided that an attempt ought to be made to restore and preserve some of Dawson's historical sites and that this could best be done by launching a Gold Rush Festival on the site, supported by federal funds. It was, admittedly, a bizarre idea, but it actually came to fruition in the summer of 1962. Because it "lost money" (what festival does not?), the press branded it a failure. In retrospect, it can be seen to have been an overwhelming success.

560

The Gold Rush Festival caused the immediate restoration of the only structure extant from stampede days—the Palace Grand Dance Hall—and of one of the historic river boats that were crumbling to dust on the ways along the Yukon. (The money was not allocated without a spirited debate in Parliament over the advisability of appropriating federal funds to recreate "a brothel.") In addition, the festival also reversed the declining tourist traffic, trebling it in the festival year. The reversal has continued. More important, it helped to change official attitudes towards the historical heritage of the Yukon. Since that time other buildings in Dawson have been restored, and that work is continuing. Carmack's Discovery Claim is one of several sites that have been marked with a suitable plaque. A second steamboat has been rebuilt in Whitehorse and is open to tourists. Most important of all, it now seems likely that the entire Trail of '98, from Skagway and Dyea to Lake Bennett and eventually to Dawson itself, will become part of an international gold rush park.

The initial impetus for such a park came from the Americans. Plans are already well advanced to restore sections of Skagway (in fact, by 1971 board sidewalks had replaced concrete on Broadway Avenue). The trail from Dyea to the Chilkoot's summit has been repaired and several camp grounds have been established en route. A historic research study of the area was completed late in 1970 for the National Park Service of the United States Department of the Interior. One of the major sources for this study was *Klondike*.

The Canadian government in 1971 commissioned a Vancouver firm to examine the area between the Chilkoot Pass and Lake Bennett and make specific recommendations for what is to be the first stage of the Canadian section of the park. I was appointed historic adviser to the group and in August, 1971, with a party of about forty persons, including both United States and Canadian park officials, I climbed the famous pass from Sheep Camp and walked over the old trail that leads down past Crater Lake, Long Lake, and Lindemann to the green waters of Bennett.

Here, again, the influence of the book was apparent. It has become, one of the Americans told me, the bible of the proposed park. Everyone seems to have a worn copy, as do many of the individual hikers who are now crossing the Chilkoot each summer in ever-increasing numbers (a Swiss couple, for instance, was carrying a German edition). Some there were on that trip who seemed to know the book better than I did myself and who were able to refer to passages that I had forgotten or to correct me on points on which I had become hazy.

And so, almost three-quarters of a century after my father climbed the Chilkoot, I followed in his footsteps, clambering on hands and knees over man-high boulders, slippery with fog, in the teeth of a sixty-mile wind that screamed through the notch of the pass. Some of the paraphernalia of the stampede days were still to be seen: old rubber boots, rusting food tins, the remnants of barrels, the bones of dogs and horses, the skeletons of boats and sleds, tangled cables, rope, glass insulators, and bits of tramway machinery—and, here and there, the rotting foundations of a cabin or a shack. These artifacts are also part of our heritage—the fading reminders of an incredible moment out of the past—and it is important that some of them be preserved before they are carted away by souvenir hunters, just as it is important that this hike through history be made accessible to those who wish to follow in the wake of the stampeders and re-live, in some fashion, the experiences of '98. For no man who crawls over the Chilkoot can help but think back on those who performed that feat not once, but thirty times or more, in the chill of winter, with a fifty-pound pack pressing down on their shoulders.

As I wrote in the 1958 edition, my whole life has been conditioned by the Klondike; it haunts my dreams and my memories, and although at the time I said I would never return, I find myself going back periodically to the ghost town that was, for so many childhood years, my home.

My father, having failed to reach the gold-fields by the abortive Stikine Trail in 1898, crossed the Chilkoot Pass and took a canoe down the Yukon River with the main stampede. He was a University of New Brunswick graduate, spoiling for adventure. In the summer of '98 he staked a claim on Quigley Gulch. It produced nothing but gravel, but, nonetheless, he lived for forty years in Dawson City, where he was variously miner, labourer, cook, Mountie, French professor, cabinet-maker, school principal, dentist, engineer, and civil servant.

My mother came to the Klondike as a kindergarten teacher in 1907. She married my father in 1912 when he was a labourer working on Bonanza Creek for the old Yukon Gold Company. They spent the first summer of their marriage in a tent on Sourdough Gulch. Her own story of that odd era can be read in her book, *I Married the Klondike*.

I was born in 1920 in Whitehorse but lived the first twelve years of my life in the shell of Dawson City, a town of about twelve hundred in those days. I suppose, really, that the research for this book began at that time, for my boyhood memories are tied up with the relics of the great stampede and its aftermath.

Our home was across the street from the cabin of Robert Service, who had known my parents but had departed the North before I was born; the cabin had

563

become a shrine which tourists visited each summer. I used to wade in the shallow waters of Bonanza Creek and, in the winter, drive my dog up the hard-packed snow of the Klondike Valley road. As children we played steamboat in the relics of some of the old stern-wheelers rotting in the boneyard across the river.

The names associated with that other era were always with us: there were a Harper and a Hansen Street in Dawson, and the name "Ladue" in cracked paint on a faded building, and a village called Carmacks up the Yukon River, and an Ogilvie Bridge, and a McQuesten Creek, and a town called Mayo, and two children named Henderson with whom I played at public school.

Around me were the relics of the early days, human and inanimate: old saloons, dance halls, and gambling-houses, creaky and vacant, crammed with Klondike bric-a-brac—old seltzer bottles and tarnished gold-scales; ancient calendars depicting the *Floradora* Sextette; stacks of gold-pans long disused and rusty; oil paintings, thick with dust, of voluptuous women; the occasional satin slipper, worm-eaten; creaky pianos long gone flat; chipped mahogany bars, glasses, beds, armchairs, hand organs, porcelain chamber pots, spittoons.

And once, digging into a dusty trunk in an abandoned dance hall which my father was using as a workshop in which to build a boat, I came upon a bundle of love letters tied with pink ribbon—from a miner on the creeks to a soubrette on Dawson's gay way.

On the streets, in the hotel lobbies, and, indeed, in my own home were the living reminders of that era: men and women whose lives had been wrenched into a new pattern by the experience of the stampede. They did not talk about it specifically, except at odd times, as men sometimes, as odd times, talk of war; but, like the

564

experience of war, the stampede was always an undercurrent in the adult conversation that swirled about me. Indeed, as a child, it never occurred to me that this was anything but normal; I did not realize I was living in a queer town (a ghost town, really), any more than I realized that there were people in the world who did not have this gold-rush background.

Yet, looking back on it today, I can see how remarkable and unusual it all was: the red-bearded man in tatters who sat in the public library gobbling up books on philosophy; the remittance men from England, with their impeccable public-school background, who were visitors in our home; the various cosmopolites not usually found in small towns; the little Japanese who read his way through the *Encyclopedia Britannica*; the Frenchwoman who sold Paris fashions from her frame store; the gaudily dressed, heavily rouged and veiled women who were the last relics of Dawson's dance-hall era.

Later, when I was in my late teens, I returned to the Klondike for three seasons and worked as a labourer on Dominion Creek, for the Yukon Consolidated Gold Corporation, in order to earn my university fees. Once again I was caught up, drowned almost, in the memories of the stampede. The valleys in those days were a thick mass of shovels, picks, wheelbarrows, machinery, cabins, dumps, old flumes, rotting sluiceboxes. Ancient newspapers from '98 littered the ground. Old roadhouses and tottering ghost towns from the old days were everywhere—and old miners, too. Here, really, my interest in the period began, but it was not until after the war, in 1946, that I started some hesitant research for a series of radio talks on the subject. This grew, eventually, into more serious research, and the present book is the final result.

Anyone who looks at the bibliography that appears in the hardcover edition of this book may well ask: why another book about the Klondike gold rush? The answer is simple; of more than one hundred volumes that deal directly with the phenomenon or some aspect of it, only two, in my opinion, make any attempt to describe the stampede *as a whole*. These are Tappan Adney's *The Klondike Stampede of 1897-98*, published in 1899, and Kathryn Winslow's *Big Pan-Out*, published in 1951. Both make excellent and lively reading, but neither is intended to be complete. Adney's work has one great advantage: he was there, as a correspondent for *Harper's Illustrated Weekly*; his book is written from first-hand observations and from interviews with people on the spot. This is also its weakness. Adney could not be everywhere, nor was the subsequent mountain of Klondike documentation available to him at the time he wrote. His book remains the single most valuable work on the subject, in my view. Miss Winslow's shorter work is also entertaining, but her terms of reference are narrower than my own. She deals in detail with the White and the Chilkoot passes, for instance, but makes only passing reference to the other routes to the Klondike.

One of the great problems in putting the story together was to separate fact from fiction. Fortunately, there is such a large body of evidence, published and unpublished, now available that it is possible, I believe, to do this. I have followed the rule of trusting more to contemporary first-hand witnesses than to later memoirs, and of cross-checking all dubious statements against others more reliable. In some cases where I have not been able to resolve conflicting versions of an incident (as in Carmack's encounter with Henderson or in the story of Swiftwater Bill and the eggs) I have so indicated in the body of the text.

It is undeniable that the Klondike odyssey has been subject in the past to some fantastic misstatements, errors, half-truths, garblings, over-romanticizations, and out-and-out fabrications. There are several reasons for this. One is that the tale is a very complicated one: the geography is difficult and the narrative sequence intricate. Writer after writer has put certain events in 1898 that actually occurred in 1897 or 1899 and vice versa, thus throwing the story out of kilter. I have tried to straighten this out by starting at the beginning and ending at the end. An added advantage has been my own knowledge of the ground. I have crossed the White Pass half a dozen times by rail and have been down the Yukon River by small boat, steamboat, and airplane. I have covered the whole of the Mackenzie route from Edmonton to the delta by boat and plane, and most of the Peace River and interior British Columbia routes as well. I have travelled the Alaska Highway for its full length by car and been up and down the Alaska Panhandle several times. I know the creeks of the Klondike and Indian River watersheds almost as well as my back yard.

A second problem in this field has been the tendency of so many writers to overdramatize the Klondike stories, to "build up" scenes that really need no further enrichment, to add to anecdotes which are complete and satisfactory in their original versions. During my researches I was to discover, time and again, that the stark facts, when tracked down and sorted out, were far livelier and often stranger than the gloss of fiction with which they had been overlaid. But old-timers in print and in person tend to stray from the truth; tales get changed in the retelling, memories fail. More than that, many Klondike stories are sifted through a third person, a ghost writer, whose own knowledge of the era is imperfect. These ghost-written books, though easy to spot, are a curse to the researcher.

A great Alaskan historian, Clarence Andrews, once wrote that if all the men who claimed to have seen the shooting of Soapy Smith were laid end to end "the line would extend to the Equator and back again." It is obvious that almost every man who wrote a personal account of his days in the Klondike wished to make it appear that he was in on the big events and knew all the colourful figures. Even such a respected writer and jurist as the Hon. James Wickersham writes (in *Old Yukon*) that, in the summer of 1900 in Skagway, "in one of the banks a gentlemanly clerk named Bob Service was introduced smilingly, as a writer of poetry." The fact is, of course, that Robert Service never worked in a Skagway bank and, indeed, did not reach the North or write any Yukon poetry until 1904. Writer after writer makes the same mistake. In *Far North Country*, Thames Williamson writes: "Service was in the Klondike during the fevered days of the gold rush," and Glenn Chesney Quiett falls into the same error in *Pay Dirt*. Actually, Service's most famous book of verse, *Songs of a Sourdough* (containing his three best-known poems, "The Law of the Yukon," "The Shooting of Dan McGrew," and "The Cremation of Sam McGee"), was written before he ever set foot in the Klondike. Stanley Scearce in *Northern Lights to Fields of Gold* says that he met Service in Dawson in 1898 (ten years before the poet actually arrived) and goes on to tell of his encounter with Soapy Smith in Skagway in the winter of 1899-1900, about eighteen months after Smith was killed. In *Gold, Men and Dogs*, A. A. "Scotty" Allan, a famous Alaskan dog-driver, also claims to have met Smith in Nome, although the outlaw was dead before Nome was properly established.

In spite of such errors, all the above-mentioned books can be useful, as long as the stories are taken with a grain of salt and the incidents cross-checked against other accounts. Some Klondike tales, however, seem to be made up entirely of whole cloth. Among the most preposterous are Frances Lloyd-Owen's *Gold Nugget Charlie* and E. C. Trelawney-Ansell's *I Followed Gold*. The latter persists in referring to Belinda Mulroney and the Oregon Mare as the same woman; it would be hard to imagine two more disparate characters.

Klondike legends die hard, and there will be many old-timers, no doubt, who will dispute some of the versions of the famous tales that appear in this book. I call their attention to a singular incident that took place at a Sourdough Convention on the Pacific coast some years ago, which featured Mike Mahoney, the hero of Merrill Denison's book *Klondike Mike*. For years Mahoney (who is popularly supposed to have carried a piano over the Chilkoot Pass) used to entertain at various gatherings by reciting Service's "The Shooting of Dan McGrew." The recital was enhanced by the fact that Mahoney claimed to have witnessed the incident and could, on request, give a glowing and detailed eyewitness account of it. When Mahoney's talents were finally pressed into service by the Sourdough association, one member, Monte Snow, decided that he had had enough. Snow (who, readers may recall, appears briefly in this book) had far more right to the name of "sourdough" than any others in the banquet hall that evening. His father, George Snow the entrepeneur, had taken him over the Chilkoot when Monte was still a boy. He had been brought up in Circle City before the Klondike strike and had reached Dawson early in 1897. He knew very well that there never had been a Dan McGrew in Dawson, or a Malamute Saloon, and he determined to expose Mahoney. Before "Klondike

Mike" could rise to speak, Snow was on his feet to announce in ringing tones that the featured guest of the evening was a charlatan making stories up out of whole cloth. But, to his dismay, the assemblage of old-timers shouted Snow down and then gave Mike Mahoney the greatest ovation of his career. They did not really want to hear the truth.

Nonetheless, the unvarnished story of the Klondike phenomenon is, in my opinion, the best story, and it is puzzling that anyone should feel the need to embellish it. It is really not necessary to invent any incidents because in every case somebody has been on the spot to record, somewhere, exactly what happened. Every Klondike historian must be grateful to William Ogilvie, for instance, for taking affidavits from Carmack and Henderson and the two Indians, Jim and Charley, so that we have a reliable account of the original discovery of gold. Ogilvie also cross-examined each of the participants in the drama and repeated his interviews some time later in order to discover whether any of the stories had changed over the intervening period. Here was a man with a sense of history, and his book *Early Days in the Yukon*, like Tappan Adney's, is invaluable. So is William Haskell's *Two Years in the Klondike and Alaska Goldfields*, on which I have drawn heavily in the early sections of this book. Several other books, notably Arthur Walden's *A Dog Puncher on the Yukon* (despite some obvious exaggerations), give a good picture of the early stages of the stampede.

My Chapter Four is drawn largely from the contemporary newspaper and magazine accounts as well as from the lengthy shelf of guidebooks to the gold-fields (many of them wildly inaccurate) published at the time.

There are several excellent personal accounts of the various routes to the Klondike. Some of the best include Mrs. George Black's *My Seventy Years* (the

570

Chilkoot Pass), Walter Russell Curtin's *Yukon Voyage* (the story of Pat Galvin and the steamer *Yukoner*), Arthur Arnold Dietz's *Mad Rush for Gold in Frozen North* (the Malaspina Glacier), Angus Graham's *The Golden Grindstone* (Edmonton to Wind River), Elizabeth Page's *Wild Horses and Gold* (Mackenzie and Peace River routes), Martha Ferguson McKeown's *The Trail Led North* (the White Pass), Thomas Wiedemann's *Cheechako into Sourdough* (the story of the *Eliza Anderson* expedition), Hamlin Garland's *Trail of the Goldseekers* (the Ashcroft and Teslin Trails), Walter Hamilton's *Yukon Story*, and, last but certainly not least, Colonel Sam Steele's own story, *Forty Years in Canada*.

The Alaskan Sportsman, in Ketchikan, has for almost half a century been publishing the personal memoirs of scores of Klondike old-timers, usually written without the dubious benefit of ghost writers. These eyewitness accounts have been invaluable as source material, and I place this magazine as the single most important periodical for anyone researching the Klondike story.

My chapter on Dawson's starvation winter (1897-98) comes from a variety of sources, but two, in particular, I found most useful: Captain P. H. Ray's reports to Washington of the events on the Yukon River and Sam C. Dunham's reports, made at the same time, to the U.S. Department of Labor.

My most valuable single source for the two chapters dealing with Dawson City in its heyday has been the *Klondike Nugget*. There is only one complete set of files in existence, that bequeathed by the editor, Gene Allen, to the University of Washington at Seattle. These have been microfilmed by the Public Archives of Canada since *Klondike* was first published. In addition, incomplete files of the other Klondike newspapers, in various libraries, were also valuable. As well as the books already mentioned I would rate Jeremiah Lynch's *Three Years in the Klondike* and Frederick Palmer's *In the Klondyke* as readable books about this later period.

My chapter on Soapy Smith comes from so many sources that it would be impractical to detail them all. I was fortunate in interviewing four men who had been present at the time of his death and in Skagway during the months leading up to it. In addition, through the kindness of his late widow, I was given access to the considerable store of letters and papers of the Reverend J. A. Sinclair, the Union Church minister in Skagway who also witnessed the shooting and presided at the fallen dictator's funeral. Soapy Smith's biographers, W. R. Collier and E. V. Westrate, give a detailed and lively account of his pre-Skagway history, but their narrative of his gold-rush period is, in my opinion, less satisfactory.

Most of the material in the last chapter of this book comes from personal interviews with Klondikers, all of whom have died since *Klondike* was first published. If I had waited a few more years to write the book, such personal memories would have been impossible; indeed, before I finished the text a good many of my informants had already gone. Yet without these personal conversations, the book would be much less effective: the facts that the old-timers provided were not as important as the feeling for the times that they communicated to me. The same is true, in large part, of the diaries and letters. A man sitting on a riverbank with a stub of a pencil and a tattered notebook after a hard day's travel has neither the time, space, nor inclination to write an essay. Klondike diary entries usually consist of simple statistics: miles covered, pounds carried, temperatures, and so on. Yet you cannot read these wavering pencilled entries without catching something of the spirit of those men and those days. And here and there, in the brief story of a bitter quarrel or a death or a sacrifice, the theme of the Klondike rush emerges.

Acknowledgements

Apart from forty or fifty personal interviews, the research for *Klondike* was done at the public and reference libraries in Seattle, San Francisco, New York, and Toronto; at the University of Washington library in Seattle; at the Pacific Northwest Library in Victoria; at the Public Archives of Canada, and, most especially, at the library of the University of Toronto.

I wish again to thank Helen Parker for permission to read and quote from the manuscript memoir of her husband, Bert Parker, "Kid on the Trail" (parts of it published in *Maclean's Magazine*), and also to record my gratitude to the late Mrs. J. A. Sinclair for her kindness in allowing me to use her husband's papers. I should also like to thank James Medill of Vancouver for making the papers of his father, Robert Medill, available to me for the Revised Edition, and Edward C. Bearss for lending me his microfilmed copies of the Dyea *Trail* and Dyea *Press*. Mr. Bearss's historic resource study for the United States section of the proposed Gold Rush Historic Park was also extremely useful to me in revising the text. The complicated business of providing source notes for a book that did not originally contain any was handled by Ennis Halliday Armstrong with great efficiency. Again I must record my gratitude to Mrs. Betty Johnstone for her very useful comments on two earlier drafts of the manuscript and to my wife, who was indefatigable and persistent over a period of five years in tracking down obscure books, periodicals, and people. Without her assistance I could not have completed my researches.

574

Index

580

581

582

583

585

587